the democratic surround

the democratic surround

Multimedia & American
Liberalism from World War II
to the Psychedelic Sixties

fred turner

The University of Chicago Press
Chicago and London

fred turner is associate professor of communication at Stanford University. He is the author of *Echoes of Combat: The Vietnam War in American Memory* and *From Counterculture to Cyberculture: Stewart Brand, the Whole Earth Network, and the Rise of Digital Utopianism*, also published by the University of Chicago Press.

The University of Chicago Press, Chicago 60637
The University of Chicago Press, Ltd., London
© 2013 by Fred Turner
All rights reserved. Published 2013.
Printed in the United States of America

23 22 21 20 19 18 17 16 15 14   1 2   4 5

ISBN-13: 978-0-226-81746-0 (cloth)
ISBN-13: 978-0-226-06414-7 (e-book)
DOI: 10.7208/9780226064147.001.0001

Library of Congress Cataloging-in-Publication Data

Turner, Fred, author.
   The democratic surround : multimedia and American liberalism from World War II to the psychedelic sixties / Fred Turner.
      pages cm
   Includes bibliograpical references and index.
   ISBN 978-0-226-81746-0 (cloth : alk. paper) — ISBN 978-0-226-06414-7 (e-book) 1. Mass media—Political aspects—United States—History—20th century. 2. Liberalism—United States. 3. Counterculture—United States—History—20th century. 4. Cold War. I. Title.
   P95.82.U6T87 2013
   302.23'0973—dc23

                                        2013022419

Were the world we dream of attained, members of that new world would be so different from ourselves that they would no longer value it in the same terms in which we now desire it. . . . We would no longer be at home in such a world. . . . We who have dreamed it could not live in it.

MARGARET MEAD, 1942

Contents

Introduction

"Media," intoned Marshall McLuhan in 1964, are "extensions of man."[1] Circling the globe in a benevolent electronic web, television, radio, film and the print press enabled men and women to stretch their senses, to reach out to one another, and to become equal citizens in a global village, he explained. Even as McLuhan spoke, the hipsters and artists of New York and San Francisco were building prototypes of the world he described: new multimedia environments in which they would soon conduct what amounted to tribal rites. Within little more than a year, colored lights, multiscreen slide shows, and walls of amplified sound surrounded dance floors and performance art spaces on both coasts and in more than a few Midwestern capitals as well. For McLuhan, as for much of the emerging American counterculture, to be ringed by media was to enter a state of ecstatic interconnection. At first to dance, and then later to gather at be-ins and rock concerts was to open oneself to a new way of being: personal, authentic, collective, and egalitarian.

But where did this vision come from? Only twenty-five years earlier, most American analysts had been convinced that mass media tended to produce authoritarian people and totalitarian societies. Accounts of just how they did this varied. Some argued that mediated images and sounds slipped into the psyche through the senses, stirred the newly discovered depths of the Freudian unconscious, and left audiences unable to reason. Others claimed that the one-to-many broadcasting structure that defined mass media required audiences to turn their collective attention toward a single source of communication and so to partake of authoritarian mass psychology. In the late 1930s, if anyone doubted the power of mass media to remake society, they only needed to turn to Germany. How could the mustachioed madman Adolf Hitler have taken control of one of the most culturally sophisticated nations in Europe, many wondered, if he hadn't hypnotized his audiences through the microphone and the silver screen?

In the months leading up to America's entry into World War II, Hitler's success haunted American intellectuals, artists, and government officials. Key figures in each of these communities hoped to help exhort their fellow citizens to come together and confront the growing fascist menace. But how could they do that, they wondered, if mass media tended to turn the psyches of their audiences in authoritarian directions? Was there a mode of communication that could produce more democratic individuals? A more democratic polity? And for that matter, what *was* a democratic person?

The answers to these questions ultimately produced the ecstatic multimedia utopianism of the 1960s and, through it, much of the multimedia culture we inhabit today. To see how, this book returns to the late 1930s and early 1940s and tracks the entwining of two distinct social worlds: one of American anthropologists, psychologists, and sociologists, and the other of refugee Bauhaus artists. At the start of World War II, members of the first community believed that the political stance of a nation reflected the psychological condition of its people. That is, fascist Germany represented the triumph not only of Hitler's party, but of what would later be called the "authoritarian personality."[2] In 1941, more than fifty of America's leading social scientists and journalists gathered in Manhattan to promulgate a democratic alternative to that personality as members of the newly formed Committee for National Morale. Though largely forgotten today, the committee was very influential in its time. Its members published widely in the popular press and advised numerous government officials, including President Roosevelt.

Across the 1930s, committee members such as anthropologists Margaret Mead and Gregory Bateson and psychologist Gordon Allport had worked to show how culture shaped the development of the psyche, particularly through the process of interpersonal communication. In the early years of the war, they turned those understandings into prescriptions for bolstering American morale. First, they defined the "democratic personality" as a highly individuated, rational, and empathetic mindset, committed to racial and religious diversity, and so able to collaborate with others while retaining its individuality. Second, they argued that the future of America's war effort depended on sustaining that form of character and the voluntary, non-authoritarian unity it made possible. In their view, both individual character and national culture came into being via the process of communication. Since mass media prevented precisely the sorts of encounters with multiple types of people and multiple points of view that made America and Americans strong, the shoring up of the democratic personality would require the development of new, democratic modes of communication.

For that reason, members and friends of the committee advocated a turn away from single-source mass media and toward multi-image, multi–sound-source media environments—systems that I will call *surrounds*. They couldn't build these systems themselves. With a few exceptions, they were writers, not media makers. But they knew people who could build surrounds: the refugee artists of the Bauhaus. Since the early 1930s, Bauhaus stalwarts such as architect Walter Gropius and multimedia artists László Moholy-Nagy and Herbert Bayer had fled Nazi Germany and settled in New York, Chicago, and other centers of American intellectual life. They brought with them highly developed theories of multiscreen display and immersive theater. They also brought the notion that media art should help integrate the senses, and so produce what they called a "New Man," a person whose psyche remained whole even under the potentially fracturing assault of everyday life in industrial society. As World War II got under way, they repurposed their environmental multimedia techniques for the production of a *new* "New Man"—the democratic American citizen. By 1942, Bayer was collaborating with American photographer Edward Steichen to create complex multi-image propaganda displays at the Museum of Modern Art in New York. And Moholy-Nagy was working with composer John Cage, alerting him to the environmental and industrial-therapeutic aims of Bauhaus art, and also to the ways such things might be used in wartime America.

The first half of this book then, recounts the coming together of American intellectuals and artists with their Bauhaus counterparts. Under the pressures of World War II, these twinned communities created the pro-democratic surround and the networks of ideas and people that would sustain it in the years ahead. The second half of the book follows the surround into the propaganda and art worlds of the 1950s and, through both, into the American counterculture.

As the chill of the Cold War began to creep across America and Europe, communism replaced fascism as the source of totalitarian threat. But the wartime consensus persisted: intellectuals, artists, and many policy makers continued to agree that political systems were manifestations, mirrors even, of the dominant psychological structures of individual citizens. The surrounds developed during World War II lived on as models—for new exhibitions, new works of art, new modes of environmental media, and, ultimately, new patterns of democratic practice. Through them, the ideals of democratic psychology and democratic polity articulated by wartime social scientists remained available, not only as words in texts, but as invitations to embodied action. Anthropologists and artists gathered at places like Black Mountain College, where they worked to train a new generation of American artists in the multidisciplinary, psychologically integrated techniques of the Bauhaus and, at the same time, the progressive political ideals that infused wartime campaigns for democratic morale. Likewise, at the Museum of Modern Art in New York, Steichen transformed Bayer's wartime exhibition design into what almost certainly remains the most widely viewed photography exhibition of all time, *The Family of Man*— a show designed to help Cold War Americans imagine themselves part of a racially and culturally diverse global society.

At the same time, however, officials of the United States Information Agency or USIA—the postwar governmental agency charged with overseas propaganda work—quickly began exporting both *The Family of Man* and the surround form more generally to countries on every continent. As they did, they sought to instill the psychological proclivities that they believed defined democratic Americans in the citizens of other nations. By the end of the 1950s, multiscreen arrays and multi-sound-source environments had become mandatory features of American exhibitions abroad, most famously in 1958 at the Brussels World's Fair and in 1959 at the American National Exhibition in Moscow, where Khrushchev and Nixon staged their "Kitchen Debate." In Brussels and Moscow the original industrial-therapeutic aims of Bauhaus artists and the pro-democratic ambitions of the Committee for National Morale came together once again on behalf of a new mission: taking personalities that might be drawn toward communism and turning their perceptions and desires in more democratic directions.

The states of mind that the USIA sought to create, however, were not quite the same as those that defined the democratic personality at the start of World War II, nor was the USIA's surround quite the same form. Both had been changed by the embrace of a mode of control that had been part of the surround from its inception, and also by the rise of postwar American consumerism. In the 1940s, social scientists agreed that the democratic person was a freestanding individual who could act independently among other individuals. Democratic polity, in turn, depended on the ability of such people to reason, to choose, and above all to recognize others as being human beings like themselves. For these reasons, wartime propaganda environments such as Steichen and Bayer's *Road to Victory* turned away from the one-to-many aesthetics of mass media and constructed situations in which viewers could move among images and sounds at their own individual paces. In theory, they would integrate the variety of what they saw and heard into their own, individuated experiences. This integration in turn would rehearse the political process of knitting oneself into a diverse and highly individuated society. Ideally, visitors would come to see themselves not simply as part of a national mass, but as individual human beings among others, united as Americans across their many differences.

The turn to the surround form in World War II thus represented a break away from the perceived constraints of mass media and fascist mass society. But it also opened the door to a new mode of social control. Visitors to *Road to Victory* may have been free to encounter a wide array of images, but the variety of those images was not limitless. Bayer and Steichen had designed the exhibition space and selected the pictures viewers would see. Likewise, at *The Family of Man*, visitors were free to move, but only within an environment that had been carefully shaped by Steichen and his collaborators. When analysts at the time compared the surround to the one-to-many dynamics of mass media and of fascism, many found it to be enormously liberating. Even so, from the distance of our own time, the surround clearly represented the rise of a managerial mode of a control: a mode in which people might be free to choose their experiences, but only from a menu written by experts.

In the late 1950s that managerial mode met an American state campaign to promote American-style consumerism abroad. Visitors to the American pavilion at the 1958 Brussels World's Fair and to the 1959 American National Exhibition in Moscow enjoyed the same mobility and choice that had been offered to visitors to *Road to Victory* almost twenty years earlier. But they also found themselves surrounded by a cornucopia of consumer goods. In the surrounds deployed in Brussels and Moscow, political choices and consumer choices became a single integrated system. The democratic personality of the 1940s, in turn, melted almost imperceptibly into the consumer of the 1950s. The World War II effort to challenge totalitarian mass psychology gave rise to a new kind of mass psychology, a mass individualism grounded in the democratic rhetoric of choice and individuality, but practiced in a polity that was already a marketplace as well.

Surprisingly perhaps, it also helped give rise to the American counterculture. In the same years that the USIA was presenting *The Family of Man* around the world, John Cage was bringing his Bauhaus-inflected mode of performance to international music festivals, the Brussels World's Fair, and the downtown New York art scene. And like the USIA, Cage was working to create surrounds in which audiences could experience semiotic democracy. In *The Family of Man*, Edward Steichen hoped to surround museum visitors with images and so free them to see a whole world of people who were simultaneously unlike and yet like themselves. At about the same time, Cage was promoting modes of performance in which each sound was as good as any other, in which every action could be meaningful or not—a space, in short, in which audience members found themselves compelled to integrate a diversity of experiences into their own individual psyches.

In the summer of 1952, Cage staged a performance at Black Mountain College that transformed his efforts to democratize sound into key elements of one of the defining performance modes of the 1960s, the Happening. No single authoritative account of the event exists, but witnesses agree that many things happened at the same time: Cage lectured from a ladder, Merce Cunningham danced, Charles Olson and M. C. Richards read poetry, and David Tudor played something on the piano. Together they staged a pattern of interpersonal relations much like the one both Cage and the members of the Committee for National Morale had called for a decade earlier: one in which every person acted individually and yet in concert with the group. Though it lacked the commercial orientation of the USIA exhibitions overseas, Cage's performance shared their psychological ambition. He, too, hoped to surround his audience with sights and sounds that might free them from allegiance to more authoritarian modes of communication—and, by implication, from authoritarian political systems too.

By 1957, Cage had brought these ambitions to the New School for Social Research in New York, where he taught composition. Young members of Cage's class such as Allan Kaprow and Dick Higgins soon built elaborate Happenings across lower Manhattan. And in the early 1960s, inspired by Cage and Marshall McLuhan as well as the early Happenings, poet Gerd Stern and a tribe of painters, poets, dancers and sound and light technicians who called themselves USCO (short for the Us Company) began to build a new kind of multi-image, multisound environment. Their constructions aimed to produce in their audiences a simultaneous sense of their own individuality and of their membership in a global human collective. USCO hoped to awaken its audiences' senses—first of sight and sound, but soon thereafter, of their personhood and of the possibility of belonging to an egalitarian society.

In the fall of 1966, a reporter for *Life* magazine called one of USCO's installations a "be-in." The phrase caught fire, and in January 1967 thousands of San Franciscans streamed toward Golden Gate Park for the first "Human Be-In." Allen Ginsberg and Timothy Leary spoke. The Jefferson Airplane and Big Brother and the Holding Company played psychedelic rock. Attendees later recalled that they reveled in one another's company, crossing race lines, crossing class lines, and enjoying a shared sense of membership in a broader human community. By that summer, the Human Be-In had become an early emblem of what appeared to be a new American generation, a counterculture devoted to overthrowing the social and psychological hierarchies of the 1950s and exploring a more organic, more personally fulfilling way of life.

Yet, as this book shows, the kinds of personality, community, and media that defined the counterculture represented not only a new beginning for Americans, but an end point to a story that began in the late 1930s, on the verge of World War II. The vision of "man" that animated the writings of Marshall McLuhan was born not in 1964 but somewhere closer to 1944. And the media forms we so often think of as having been created within the American counterculture—immersive, multi-mediated environments designed to expand individual consciousness and a sense of membership in the human collective—first came into being as part of the same urge to defeat the forces of totalitarianism that animated the most aggressive cold warriors.

By making this case, this book joins a growing chorus of works challenging the view that the 1960s represented a top-to-bottom revolution in American culture.[3] In popular memory, the 1960s rose up in a Technicolor wave and washed away several decades of bland, black-and-white American life. But nothing could be farther from the truth. In the early 1940s, the intellectuals of the Committee for National Morale offered a genuinely radical vision for America. Defining their ideals in opposition to those of fascism, they called for a world of racial integration, sexual and religious tolerance, and individual freedom. In the wake of the civil rights movement of the 1950s and 1960s, and of the feminist and gay rights movements of the 1970s and beyond, we have tended to think of our own as the first era in which diversity has been celebrated as the foundation of an ideal America. Since the McCarthyism of the 1950s, we have also tended to think of the state as the enemy of such a vision. But for the intellectuals and artists of this book, the ability to embrace diversity was precisely what distinguished America from Nazi Germany, Fascist Italy, and Imperial Japan. For them, and for their backers in the federal government during and after World War II, it was the job of the state to defend that diversity, at home and overseas. And it was the job of intellectuals and artists to develop modes of media and mediated interaction that could transform the integration of diversity into an experience that could be enjoyed by everyday citizens.

This is not to say that the social networks at the center of this book were especially diverse. They weren't. The social scientists, artists, and government officials I discuss here include virtually no African-Americans and very few women. Yet they were among the most vocal and most widely recognized critics of American racism, sexism, and religious intolerance in their day. There is no way to say for sure what drove their activism, but it might well have had to do with the fact that many were refugees. Some were Jews or modern artists who had fled the discrimination of fascist Europe. Virtually all had lived overseas at some point in their careers, often in countries where they belonged to racial or religious minorities. Others were unusual in other ways. Though they were among America's leading intellectuals, women such as Margaret Mead habitually found themselves at conference tables surrounded by men. A number of the people profiled here were widely known to have had homosexual partners—and this at a time when such partnerships could land a person in jail.

Whatever their individual motivations, the artists and intellectuals in this book collectively found a way to call for a society in which individual diversity might become the foundation of collective life. They also called for a new, multisource, environmental kind of media to help bring that world into being. By coining the term *democratic surround*, I am trying to make that new media genre visible across its many different incarnations. In part, I want to reclaim a little-known history and, with it, a new understanding of the origins of contemporary multimedia. But I also want to show how a media form that was never named by its makers enjoyed substantial influence in large part because it lived just below the surface of public awareness. The democratic surround was not only a way of organizing images and sounds; it was a way of thinking about organizing society. Across a wide variety of communities and multiple decades, the democratic surround provided a set of agreed-upon aesthetic and political principles that could serve as scaffolding for new artistic and social projects. It was a flexible prototype, a sort of not-quite-visible image of the way the world could work that came to life at various times in words, in performances, and in museum displays.

By tracking the democratic surround across those platforms, I want to extend a project I began in my last book, *From Counterculture to Cyber-*

culture. That book showed how the cybernetics of the Cold War research world and the countercultural ideals of the New Communalist movement came together to give us a utopian vision of the internet and the World Wide Web. This book tracks the entwining of American idealism and multimedia further back, to an era that predates ubiquitous computing, and one with which we habitually associate neither multimedia nor radical progressive idealism. My last book argued that the counterculture of the 1960s shaped the cyberculture of the 1990s. This book demonstrates that World War II–era visions of a socially diverse American polity and a semiotically diverse media environment helped give rise to that counterculture and the visions of media's political potential that informed it. In other words, this book is a prequel to my last.

It is also an attempt to show how media and politics were entangled during and after World War II, not only at the level of representation, but at the level of attention. In recent years, scholars have done a thorough job of showing how images on television and the movie screen shaped mid–twentieth century American beliefs and, through them, American politics.[4] And for decades now, cultural historians have analyzed what they've seen in films and television programs as windows on the historical moments in which they were produced. This book however, worries less about the pictures on the screen than the relationships between those pictures and their audiences. For the media-makers and theorists I study here, it was not only the power of stories or pictures conveyed by media to change beliefs that mattered; it was also the power of media to solicit particular modes of interaction. For these analysts, patterns of media reception aped and foreshadowed patterns of political interaction. To listen to the radio, watch a movie, or wander among a roomful of sounds and pictures was to rehearse the perceptual skills on which political life—fascist or democratic—depended.[5]

At the start of World War II, the democratic surround presented a powerful alternative to mass media and totalitarian society. But it also represented a turn toward the managerial mode of control that haunts our culture today. In many ways, the multimedia landscape we inhabit represents a fulfillment of the dreams of writers like Margaret Mead or designers like Herbert Bayer. Screens surround us. Sounds come toward us from every direction. As we log on to our computers and finger our cell phones, we each find our own way through a landscape of images and sounds, and we practice the modes of interaction on which the Committee for National Morale once suggested democracy depends. But we do so in terms that have been set for us by distant experts: programmers, media executives, government regulators. In the 1940s and 1950s, many welcomed such expert management for the ways it granted the individual freedoms that were prohibited by fascism. Today, many continue to welcome such management, albeit on behalf of new freedoms: the freedom to stay in touch with distant friends and family, to take work on the road, or to catch up with a favorite television series.

What has disappeared is the deeply democratic vision that animated the turn toward mediated environments in the first place, and that sustained it across the 1950s and into the 1960s. This book aims to recover that vision. The ideal of a radically liberal, diverse, and egalitarian society once lived where we might least have expected it to: in media, at the heart of America's leading intellectual, artistic, and political institutions. I've written this book in the hope that with a new generation's efforts, it might yet live there again.

part one

World War II and the Making of the Democratic Surround

part one

World War II and
the Making of the
Democratic Surround

1

Where Did All the Fascists Come From?

On December 3, 1933, a reporter for the *New York Times Magazine* named Shepard Stone tried to answer a question that had begun to puzzle many of his readers: How was it that in a single year, the nation that had brought the world Goethe and Bach, Hegel and Beethoven, had fallen so completely under the sway of a short, mustachioed dictator named Adolf Hitler? To some analysts, the answer was fundamentally social, as Stone acknowledged. Starvation, political chaos, violence in the streets—all had plagued the Weimar Republic that Hitler's fascist state replaced. But neither Stone nor his editors thought such privations were enough to explain Hitler's rise. Rather, wrote Stone, "something intangible was necessary to coordinate the resentments and hatreds which these forces engendered."[1]

That something was propaganda. Above an enormous photograph of a Nazi rally, with floodlit swastika banners towering two stories high and row upon row of helmeted soldiers leaning toward the lights, the article's headline told its story: "Hitler's Showmen Weave a Magic Spell: By a Vast Propaganda Aimed at Emotions, Germany's Trance is Maintained." For Stone and his editors, fascism was a fundamentally psychological condition. Its victims swayed in time, linked by fellow feeling, unable to reason. In part, they responded to Hitler's charisma. But they also responded to the power of mass media. Hitler famously "hypnotized" the crowds at mass rallies until they roared with applause. His voice then traveled out from those arenas in radio waves, reaching Germans across the nation and inspiring in them the same hypnotic allegiance. As Stone suggested,

Hitler's personal appeal alone could not have transformed the mindset of the entire populace. Only mass media could have turned a nation famous for its philosophers into a land of unthinking automata: "With coordinated newspaper headlines overpowering him, with radio voices beseeching him, with news reels and feature pictures arousing him, and with politicians and professors philosophizing for him, the individual German has been unable to salvage his identity and has been engulfed in a brown wave. Today few Germans can separate the chaff from the wheat. They are living in a Nazi dream and not in the reality of the world."[2]

During and after World War II, this belief would drive many intellectuals and artists to imagine pro-democratic alternatives to authoritarian psyches and societies, and to the mass-mediated propaganda that seemed to produce them. But before we can explore those alternatives, we need to revisit the anxieties that made them so important to their makers. In the years leading up to the war, the fear of mass media and mass psychology that animated Stone's account became ubiquitous among American intellectuals, politicians, and artists. When they gazed across the Atlantic to Hitler's Germany and, to a lesser extent, Stalin's Soviet Union and Mussolini's Italy, American journalists and social scientists saw their long-standing anxieties about the power of mass media harden into a specific fear that newspapers, radio, and film were engines of fascist socialization.[3]

Since the late nineteenth century, writers in Europe and the United States had dreaded the rise of mass industrial society. Such a society fractured the psyches of its members and rendered them vulnerable to collective fits of irrational violence, many feared. Now analysts worried that mass media drew individual citizens into protofascistic relationships with the centers of political and commercial power and with one another. In the one-to-many communication pattern of mass media they saw a model of political dictatorship. In mass media audiences, they saw the shadows of the German masses turning their collective eyes toward a single podium and a single leader. To enter into such a relationship with media, many worried, was to rehearse the psychology of fascism. The rise of National Socialism in Germany demonstrated that such rehearsals could transform one of the most cultured of nations—and perhaps even America itself—into a bastion of authoritarianism.

COULD IT HAPPEN HERE?

In the early 1930s, popular writers tended to see Hitler as an ordinary man who had somehow risen to extraordinary heights. Journalist Dorothy Thompson, who interviewed Hitler in 1931, characteristically described him as "formless, almost faceless, a man whose countenance is a caricature, a man whose framework seems cartilaginous, without bones. He is inconsequent and voluble, ill poised, insecure. He is the very prototype of the Little Man."[4] How was it that such a man should have acquired such power? she wondered.

As Shepard Stone had pointed out, part of the answer was surely political. In the chaos of the Weimar years, Hitler and his National Socialists promised national rejuvenation. They also threatened violent ends for any who opposed them. Yet these explanations found a comparatively small place in the American popular press and scholarship of the time, where more cultural and characterological explanations often held sway. In 1941, for instance, William McGovern, a professor of political science at Northwestern University, published a representative if long-winded analysis of the origins of National Socialism entitled *From Luther to Hitler: The History of Fascist-Nazi Political Philosophy.* The nearly seven-hundred-page tome argued that Hitler's program had deep roots in a German society that had long embraced authoritarian ideals.[5] Somehow Hitler had managed to harvest those ideals and so transform a German cultural trait into a principle of national unity. For McGovern and others, it was not only German politics that had produced National Socialism, but something in the German mindset.

This conclusion presented a problem: If German totalitarianism was rooted in German culture, how could Americans explain the apparent rise of fascism in the United States?

Though few remember the fact today, in the late 1930s, uniformed fascists marched down American streets and their voices echoed over the radio airwaves. The Catholic demagogue Father Coughlin, for example — founder of the "Radio League of the Little Flower" — was a ubiquitous presence on American radio for much of the decade. He formed a political party to oppose Roosevelt in 1936, endorsed and helped publish the anti-Semitic tract known as *The Protocols of the Elders of Zion*, and by 1938 could be heard spewing anti-Semitic and pro-fascist propaganda on the radio to a regular audience of some 3,500,000 listeners. A Gallup poll taken in January 1939 reported that some 67 percent of these listeners agreed with his views.[6]

Alongside Father Coughlin, Americans could track the activities of William Dudley Pelley's Silver Legion of America—an anti-Semitic paramilitary group formed in 1933 and modeled after Hitler's brownshirts and Mussolini's blackshirts. Though Pelley claimed to hear the voices of distant spirits, his group still attracted fifteen thousand members at its peak.[7] Americans could also follow the Crusader White Shirts in Chattanooga, Tennessee; the American National-Socialist Party; and, of course, the Ku Klux Klan. For more than a few Americans in the 1930s, fascists were not merely threats from overseas. They lived next door.

The group that attracted the greatest notice of the American press in this period was the Amerikadeutscher Volksbund. The Bund had been created in 1936, when self-styled "American Führer" Fritz Kuhn, a German-born American citizen, was elected head of a German-American organization known as the Friends of New Germany.[8] At its largest, the Bund probably had no more than twenty-five thousand members, most of them Americans of German extraction.[9] Even so, on the night of February 20, 1939, they managed to bring twenty thousand people to Madison Square Garden for a pro-fascist rally. Though the event ostensibly celebrated George Washington's birthday, the Garden was hung with anti-Semitic and pro-Nazi banners. Speakers wore uniforms clearly modeled on the military regalia of Nazi Germany. Three thousand uniformed men from the Bund's pseudo–police force, the Ordnungsdienst, moved among the crowd, spotting and removing hecklers and soliciting donations. Throughout the rally, speakers and audience carefully proclaimed their pro-Americanism. They sang the "Star-Spangled Banner" and pledged "undivided" allegiance to the American flag. But speakers also launched a steady attack on Jews and the Roosevelt administration. One drew out the word "Roosevelt" in such a way that it sounded like "Rosenfeld." Another tried to convince the audience that Judaism and communism were essentially the same social movement.[10]

FIGURE 1.1.

Twenty-two thousand Americans rally to support fascism in Madison Square Garden, February 20, 1939. Among the banners was one that read "Stop Jewish Domination of Christian America." Photograph by FPG. © Getty Images. Used by permission.

Outside the Garden, Mayor Fiorello La Guardia stationed 1,700 policemen to keep order. City leaders feared large and violent counterdemonstrations, but the mayor had refused to prevent the rally, arguing that permitting free speech was precisely what distinguished democratic America from fascist Germany. In the end, police counted approximately ten thousand mostly peaceful demonstrators and observers, some holding signs reading "Smash Anti-Semitism" and "Drive the Nazis Out of New York." Journalists on the scene believed police estimates to be heavily exaggerated.[11] Even if they were correct, pro-fascist rally-goers outnumbered protesters two to one. To reporters at the time, it seemed entirely plausible that the Bund enjoyed substantial support, at the very least among Americans of German origin, and perhaps among other communities as well.

Even before this rally, the Bund loomed large as an emblem of the threat fascism posed to the United States. On March 27, 1937, for instance,

Life magazine published a two-page spread under the headline "The 'American Nazis' Claim 200,000 Members."[12] One photograph depicted American fascist families picnicking at "Camp Siegfried," a Bund-owned recreation and training camp on Long Island. Another image featured American men in white shirts giving the Nazi salute. Yet another depicted the German consul speaking to an audience of Bund members. Over the next two years, *Life* published a dozen photo features on American fascists and on the threat of foreign propaganda. On March 6, 1939, two weeks after the Bund staged its rally in Madison Square Garden, *Life* published a seven-page spread under the headline, "Like Communism It Masquerades as Americanism." There on the first page of the piece, Americans could see a Bundist color guard at the Garden wearing imitations of Nazi brownshirt uniforms and standing in front of a massive portrait of George Washington. Another headline in the same feature underlined the visual point: "It Can Happen Here."[13]

The actual number of fascists in the United States never came anywhere near to becoming a sufficiently critical mass to challenge, let alone overthrow, the state. Yet in the late 1930s analysts across much of the political spectrum feared that it soon might.[14] If it did, they reasoned, it would be because of one or both of two social forces. The first was a fascist fifth column inside the United States. In the 1930s, American journalists and politicians believed that Hitler's Germany was engaging in a massive propaganda campaign inside the United States. Reporters noted that Germany had established active propaganda networks in European nations such as France, Norway, and the Netherlands, and suggested that they were exporting those tactics to American shores.[15] In June of 1940, *Life* magazine announced, "These Are Signs of Fifth Columns Everywhere," and published pictures of fascists congregating in South America, Asia, and Long Island.[16] And despite the fact that Hitler's regime had tried to distance itself from Fritz Kuhn, many Americans assumed that the Bund was as much as anything a front for Nazi interests in the United States.[17]

The presence of Nazi agitators was only one part of the problem, though. The other was the power of language and of mass communication. Consider the national popularity of two groups that sought to challenge that power: the Institute for Propaganda Analysis and the General Seman-

FIGURE 1.2.

German-American Bundists parade swastikas and American flags down East 86th Street, New York, October 30, 1939. Photograph from the *New York World-Telegram*. Library of Congress, Prints and Photographs Division, NYWT&S Collection, LC-USZ62-117148.

tics movement. Each presented a view of the individual psyche as vulnerable to irrational impulses and false beliefs. Each also suggested not only that communication could be manipulated by unscrupulous leaders, but that the media of communication—pictures, verbal language, symbols— were themselves naturally deceptive. Both agreed that the technologies of one-to-many communication amplified this power enormously. The individual American mind had become a battleground, and it was their mission to defend individual reason from the predations of fascism, of communication, and, potentially, of the individual's own unconscious desires.

The Institute for Propaganda Analysis emerged in 1937 out of a class in "Education and Public Opinion" taught by Dr. Clyde Miller at Columbia's Teacher's College.[18] Thanks to a $50,000 grant from Boston businessman Edward A. Filene, Miller, a number of New York-area colleagues, and a board of advisors that included leading sociologists Hadley Cantril, Leonard Doob, and Robert Lynd began creating study materials for a group of high schools in Illinois, New York, and Massachusetts. They also began publishing a monthly newsletter aimed primarily at teachers; it soon had almost six thousand subscribers.[19]

The newsletter offered its readers a detailed training regime designed to help Americans achieve a heightened state of rational alertness. In the Institute's materials the words and pictures of the mass media were scrims that obscured the motives and actions of distant powers. The source of their power to persuade lay primarily in their ability to stir up the emotions. The Institute implied that Americans could build up a psychological barrier to such manipulation by wrestling with newspaper stories and radio news accounts. An Institute-sponsored guide for discussion group leaders published in 1938 noted that propaganda analysis should proceed in four stages: "1) survey the contents 2) search for evidence of the statements or claims 3) study the propagandist's motive [and] 4) estimate the content's persuasive force."[20] This work could be done alone or in groups, and it was a species of intellectual calisthenics. Much as members might exercise their bodies to ward off disease, so might they also exercise their reason so as to ward off the inflammation of their unconscious desires and its potentially authoritarian consequences.

For the members of the General Semantics movement, the fight against propaganda depended on decoupling symbols and words from their objects of reference. If "semantics" referred to the study of meaning, "general semantics" referred to the more specific and, in the minds of its practitioners, scientific study of language and reference. The term "general semantics" was coined by Polish philosopher and mathematician Alfred Korzybski in the early 1920s. Korzybski had published a series of articles and books in which he argued that human beings' ability to pass knowledge down through time via language was what made them unique as a species. In 1933 he published an exceptionally influential extension of his early theories, entitled *Science and Sanity: An Introduction to Non-Aristotelian Systems and General Semantics*. At its core, the book argued that much human unhappiness in both the psychological and social realms could be traced to our inability to separate the pictures in our heads and the communicative processes that put them there from material reality itself. To solve this problem, Korzybski offered a course in close scientific reasoning and linguistic analysis. To alleviate the power that symbols and their makers have over us, he argued, human beings needed to parse the terms in which language presented the world to them. Having done so, they could begin to recognize the world as it was and thus to experience some degree of mental health.

General Semantics enjoyed a three-decade vogue among American intellectuals and the general public. In the years immediately before World War II, it seemed to offer new tools with which to confront not only the psychological threats posed by propaganda but a whole panoply of social and psychological ills. In his popular 1938 volume *The Tyranny of Words*, economist Stuart Chase summed up the historical importance of semantic analysis thus: "First a war that killed thirty million human beings. Then a speculative boom which, after producing more bad language to sell more fantastic propositions than in the entire previous history of finance, exploded like the airship *Hindenburg*. Finally, when a little headway has been made against economic disaster, the peoples of Europe, more civilized than any other living group, prepare solemnly and deliberately to blow one another to molecules. . . . Confusions persist because we have no true picture of the world outside, and so cannot talk to one another about how to stop them." [21]

To be able to understand the world and change it, Chase argued, Americans needed to break down language itself, to dissolve its terms from their material-world referents, and so distinguish the pictures in their heads from reality. And nothing made the importance of that work clearer than the omnipresence of mass communication, propaganda, and the threat of a second world war. In 1941, linguist and future Senator S. I. Hayakawa's volume *Language in Action* brought Chase's argument and Korzybski's theories into the public eye. Like Chase, Hayakawa argued that "we live in an environment shaped and partially created by hitherto unparalleled semantic influences: commercialized newspapers, commercialized radio programs, 'public relations counsels,' and the propaganda technique of nationalistic madmen." [22] To survive this onslaught, citizens needed scientific techniques for interpreting and resisting semantic assaults.

They especially needed techniques for disabling their immediate emotional responses to individual symbols. Hayakawa argued that human nervous systems tended to translate flows of experience into static pictures. Without training in General Semantics, it did so automatically. This in turn led quite literally to individual and collective madness. That is, words like "Nazi" and "Jew" conjured instant emotional responses; individuals lost track of the fact that the terms lacked immediate referents and were in fact so general as to be practically meaningless. Moreover, in their rush to emotional judgment, Hayakawa feared that citizens would rush to war as well. The only solution was a deep study of language and, with it, of our own roles in the communication process. As Hayakawa put it, "Men react to meaningless noises, maps of non-existent territories, as if they stood for actualities, and never suspect that there is anything wrong with the process. . . . To cure these evils, we must first go to work on ourselves. . . . [We must] understand how language works, what we are doing when we open these irresponsible mouths of ours, and what it is that happens, or should happen, when we listen or read."[23]

MODERNITY AND MASS MEDIA

The Institute for Propaganda Analysis and the General Semantics movement focused on making visible the mechanics of representation and interpretation. But for many analysts, the fear of communication that drove their work extended well beyond the individual encounter with language to encompass mass media technologies, capitalism, and modernity itself. In the decades leading up to World War II, Americans had witnessed enormous social and technological change. Between 1900 and 1940 the population of the United States had nearly doubled, from approximately 76 million to 132 million. Wave after wave of immigration, coupled with ever-increasing industrialization, had made America a much more urban society as well. In 1900 almost two out of three American citizens lived in rural areas; in 1940 more than half lived in cities.[24] America had undergone a technological transformation too. In the single lifetime between the end of the Civil War and the start of World War II, Americans had seen the arrival of the telephone, the electric light, air conditioning, the automobile, the snapshot camera, silent film, sound film, and radio. In the mid-1920s movie houses saw an average of 50 million visits a week—in a country of just over 100 million citizens.[25] Radio, too, had become ubiquitous. In 1924, just four years after the first commercial radio broadcast, Americans had some 3 million radio sets in their homes; by 1937 that number stood nearer to 30 million.[26]

The 1920s in particular saw a dramatic acceleration in industrial capitalism and its attendant hype. America's first self-styled "public relations counsel" and Sigmund Freud's nephew Edward Bernays recalled the 1920s thus:

> Hordes of publicity agents served products and causes. And causes, worthy and unworthy, rushed to take advantage of the new techniques. Any idea could be built up if dealt with skillfully.
>
> Mahjongg, crossword puzzles, Valentino, and Lindbergh's flight were some of the focal points of the era's interest.
>
> Intense attention was given to wooing the public and bringing about adjustment between people and causes. People, tired of war issues, became interested in ballyhoo. Waves of contagious excitement spread over the land in fashions and public issues.[27]

To a number of commentators, and particularly to those on the left, the political propaganda of the 1930s extended the manipulative tactics of commercial advertising into a new and dangerous realm. "Capitalism has developed to the full the techniques of advertising and high-pressure salesmanship in order to get unwanted products into the hands of buyers," wrote popular left-leaning columnist Max Lerner in 1939. "Is it any wonder that those techniques have been taken over by the fascists? Is it any wonder that Hitler should have done us the honor of borrowing our most highly prized manipulative techniques in order to turn them to purposes we never dreamt up? In terms of the swaying of mass emotions Nazism may be summarized as the application of American capitalist techniques to German and middle-class docility."[28]

Lerner and Bernays had lived through the commercial frenzy of the 1920s and the depression that followed. But their writings also embodied a deep fear of a more broadly modern crowd. In the 1920s and 1930s, American intellectuals read a great deal of Freud, but for explanations of collective psychology, many turned back to the writings of French physician Gustave Le Bon. In 1870 and 1871, Le Bon had lived through the defeat of Napoleon's armies, the siege of Paris, and the mob violence of the Paris Commune. In the chaotic decades of the Third Republic that followed, Le Bon came to see crowds as an increasingly common social phenomenon and as emblems of a new mass society. He also saw them as a threat—to collective social order and to individual reason.

In his 1895 volume *The Crowd: A Study of the Popular Mind*, Le Bon linked their rise to the coming of modernity itself. The rise of industry and science had challenged the religious and political structures of the pre-modern world, he explained. Cut loose from these institutions, the modern individual found himself swept up into a sea of people who had left their villages, moved into the jammed tenements of the city, and labored in its innumerable factories. Le Bon feared these masses would soon drag France down into barbarism by becoming crowds. By a crowd, Le Bon meant not a simple gathering of people, but what he called "a psychological crowd."[29] Such a gathering had a "mental unity" and was characterized by two distinct features. First, the individuals in such groups had suffered "the disappearance of conscious personality"; and second, they had seen "the turning of their feelings and thoughts in a definite direction."[30]

Both of these features would become important elements of the dominant critique of mass media in America in the years leading up to World War II. In Le Bon's view, a leader could analyze the hidden desires of the individuals in a group and speak to them in a way that would undermine their ability to reason—that is, their "conscious personality." Once exposed to the leader's messages and to the contagious enthusiasm of the group, the individual would enter "a special state" like that of "the hypnotized individual . . . in the hands of the hypnotizer." In hypnosis, he explained, and by analogy, under the sway of the leader and his communicative technique, the individual would become "the slave of all the unconscious activities of his spinal cord, which the hypnotizer directs at will. The conscious personality has entirely vanished; will and discernment are lost. All feelings and thoughts are bent in the direction determined by the hypnotizer."[31]

While Le Bon noted the power of a leader's charisma, he ultimately located the capacity to bind a crowd together in the process of communication and in mass media. The leader, he explained, could be "replaced, though very inefficiently, by the periodical publications which manufacture opinions for their readers and supply them with ready-made phrases which dispense them of the trouble of reasoning."[32] In Le Bon's view, either a live speaker or a paper-and-ink magazine could shut down the individual's reason. The media need only "affirm" and "repeat" a particular message. Over time, the individual would simply forget the origins of the message and would melt into the crowd.[33] Le Bon also harbored a grander, darker notion: "Given the power possessed at present by crowds," he wrote, "were a single opinion to acquire sufficient prestige to enforce its general acceptance, it would soon be endowed with so tyrannical a strength that everything would have to bend before it, and the era of free discussion would be closed for a long time."[34]

WHEN MASS MEDIA MADE MASS MEN

This was in fact Hitler's plan. As Shepard Stone and others noted, Hitler's 1925 memoir *Mein Kampf* argued that the German masses lacked the ability to comprehend complex messages and forgot them almost soon as they did. Thus, propaganda should present simple, single messages over and over again. Above all, it should appeal to the emotions of individual citizens and so enlist their feelings in support of the state. Mass media should be used to centralize the distribution of opinions, to help them flow from the top of the national pyramid down to its wide popular base. They should guarantee that every member of the radio audience should hear the same voice that others heard in person at mass rallies, and that they should feel the same irrational bond to one another and to the Führer.

In part, then, the power of mass media derived from its ability to centralize and distribute the ideas and emotions of a single person or institution. If Hitler and his circle were insane, Nazi-controlled newspapers and radio threatened to pass their madness to their audiences. But for a number of critics, mass media mattered not only for their ability to deliver infectious messages, but also for the patterns of interaction they demanded of their audiences. To those who believed that Hitler's vision of mass media simply took up where American commercial media left off, the one-to-many dynamic of broadcasting and publishing and moviemaking modeled the top-down, one-to-many power structure of mass society—whether that society was fascist, as in Germany and Italy; communist, as in the Soviet Union; or capitalist, as in the United States. Simply by engaging with mass media, individuals entered into a temporary psychological contract with the forces of mass society. As they watched or read or listened, they couldn't help but turn their minds and feelings in the direction of their society's central powers. At a psychological level, mass media asked them to practice the sort of unreasoning fealty to a single source of illumination demanded of citizens in totalitarian states. Moreover, despite the clear differences in their philosophies, authoritarian regimes were themselves representatives of deeper social forces such as industrialization, modernization, and bureaucracy. For these critics, modernity itself had spawned both the fascist state and mass media, and interaction with each promoted allegiance to the other.

In the 1930s, few critics expressed this view more articulately than Theodor Adorno. Like many of his colleagues at Frankfurt's Institute for Social Research, Adorno had fled Nazi Germany in the early 1930s. In 1938, he made his way to the United States, where the Institute's director, Max Horkheimer, found him a research position at the Princeton Radio Research Project in Princeton, New Jersey, alongside Austrian refugee Paul Lazarsfeld, American sociologist Hadley Cantril, and CBS Research Director Frank Stanton. After his arrival, Adorno penned a series of essays on music and radio, some published and others not, in which he limned the power of the mass media to indoctrinate audiences in the ways of authoritarian society. In the process, he transformed the critique of mass society articulated by Le Bon into a critique of mass *culture* and, specifically, mass *media*. Though his writing in this period would remain largely out of the public eye, much of it would be read by sociologists, social psychologists, and other intellectuals gathering in New York just before the war. Its terms would frame the American debate on mass culture well into the 1960s. And when they were finally translated into English in the early 1970s, several of the essays would help set off a new wave of critical media analysis.

FIGURE 1.3.

As early as the 1930s, theorists on the left and right imagined mass media as a force that could penetrate the home and the mind alike, bringing with it state propaganda. Poster by Lester Beall, 1937. © Dumbarton Arts, LLC / Licensed by VAGA, New York.

Adorno began reading Freud at least as early as 1926.[35] Yet his first essay for the Institute's *Zeitschrift*, "On the Social Situation of Music," published in 1932, took a strictly Marxist line. The social situation of music was the social situation of capitalism in miniature, he explained. Music had become commodified, and mass media had become mechanisms of industrial distribution. "The islands of pre-capitalistic 'music making'—such as the nineteenth century could still tolerate—have been washed away," he argued. "The techniques of radio and sound film, in the hands of powerful monopolies and in unlimited control over the total capitalistic propaganda machine, have taken possession of even the innermost cell of musical practices of domestic music making."[36] Even from a distance of many decades we can almost hear Hitler's soldiers knocking on the door, breaking down cells of musical resistance, flattening German society. But for all its emphasis on the cultural violence wrought by mass media, Adorno's essay left out issues of individual psychology.[37]

In 1936, however, Adorno began to integrate Freud into his essays on music. In his essay "On Jazz," published that year in the *Zeitschrift*, Adorno described jazz as the musical equivalent of a detective novel: generic, hyperstylized, commodified. Jazz was also very much about sex, he thought. Jazz played on the listener's unconscious libidinal desires—so much so, wrote Adorno, that "one would like to designate the symbolic representation of sexual union as the manifest dream content of jazz." Behind that dream content lurked another, more sinister reality: the transformation of the seemingly pleasant experience of listening into the work of aligning one's psyche with the social order. For Adorno, the conventional structure of the jazz tune modeled both the structure and the affective content of interpersonal relations in industrial society. The verse of a traditional jazz tune, he explained, spoke in the voice of "the individual . . . as if in isolation"; the chorus, by contrast, spoke of the pleasures of joining the social whole. During the course of listening, Adorno theorized, the individual experienced himself as a "couplet-ego"—that is, as a follower of the emotional lead taken by the song itself. According to Adorno, the individual listener first identified with the solitary voice of the verse, then melted into the crowd. He "feels himself transformed in the refrain," wrote Adorno. "He identifies himself with the collective of the refrain, merges with it in the dance, and thus finds sexual fulfillment."[38]

In short, like the children of authoritarian parents, listeners to jazz found their individual desires bound to the will of the social collective through their participation in communication. Yet music did not simply manipulate their unconscious minds. It also restructured them. As Adorno put it, "The person of the amateur [listener] is the subjective correlative of an objective formal structure [in the music]."[39] That is, through its conventional structuring of sound, the jazz tune brought to life a conventional structure of feeling in the listener—one that mirrored the structure of the individual mind in mainstream society, and one that helped shape and maintain that mind's likeness to the mainstream ideal. By playing on the unconscious emotions of a listener, jazz helped turn his feelings in the direction of allegiance to the dominant structures and ideologies of the listener's society. In other words, it helped make a listener a certain kind of *citizen*.

During the three years that Adorno worked on the Princeton project, he applied his critique of the psychological power of media with a ferocious rhetorical bite.[40] He steadily attacked both popular music and the radio as if they were themselves the Nazi forces that had driven him from Europe. "The liquidation of the individual is the real signature of the new musical situation," he exclaimed in a 1938 essay for the reconstituted Institute for Social Research's *Zeitschrift*, "On the Fetish Character in Music and the Regression of Listening."[41] Written in the same year that saw the anti-Jewish pogrom of Kristallnacht and the German annexation of Austria, Adorno's essay echoed with despair:

> It can be asked whom music for entertainment still entertains. Rather, it seems to complement the reduction of people to silence, the dying out of speech as expression, the inability to communicate at all. It inhabits the pockets of silence that develop between people molded by anxiety, work and undemanding docility. Everywhere it takes over, unnoticed, the deadly sad role that fell to it in the time and the specific situation of the silent films. It is perceived purely as background. If nobody can any longer speak, then certainly nobody can any longer listen.[42]

According to Adorno, the power of music to silence the individual grew out of its power to undermine the individual reason—a power that itself grew out of the industrial structure of the music industry. Building on his Marxist critique of 1932, Adorno suggested that industrial music production had managed to produce the illusion of "impulse" and "subjectivity" that characterized true art, but only that.[43] In the process it had brought out the most infantile impulses in its listeners. Tucked comfortably into beds of popular sound, Adorno's listeners became children and, at the same time, the sorts of unconscious denizens of the crowd described by Gustave Le Bon:

> Not only do the listening subjects lose, along with the freedom of choice and responsibility, the capacity for conscious perception of music, but they stubbornly reject the possibility of such perception. They fluctuate between comprehensive forgetting and sudden dives into recognition. They listen atomistically and dissociate what they hear, but precisely in this dissociation they develop certain capacities which accord less with the concepts of traditional esthetics than with those of football and motoring.[44]

In Adorno's essay, popular music not only speaks for the larger social order but—in its generic, mass-produced structures—actually *models* that order. When it engages listeners, it forces them to *imitate* its own dissociation from authentic feeling and authentic art. Listeners become unaware of their own predicament even as they become ever more standardized parts in a mechanistic social order. And if they start to come to adult awareness, the entertainment industry will quickly put them back in the nursery: "Together with sport and film, mass music and the new listening help to make escape from the whole infantile milieu impossible," declared Adorno.[45]

In 1938 the political consequences of infantilization were clear: in a sense, all of Germany seemed to be playing a horrible game of follow-the-leader. Adorno drove the point home in a 1941 article for the English-language edition of the *Zeitschrift*, *Studies in Philosophy and Social Science*, entitled "On Popular Music." As he and his coauthor, George Simpson, pointed out, Americans had endowed popular music "with the halo of free choice" even as the music industry had limited and standardized the choices available.[46] With its glamour and banality, popular music sparked "child-behavior."[47] It also gave rise to particular character types. According to Adorno and Simpson, music facilitated "adjustment" to mainstream society in two ways, each "corresponding to two major socio-psychological types of mass behavior toward music in general and popular music in particular, the 'rhythmically obedient' type and the 'emotional' type."[48] By the first group, Adorno meant young radio listeners and especially those who danced the jitterbug. For Adorno, dance was a mode of accommodation. To dance to popular music was to rehearse one's alienation and at the same time, by attaching oneself emotionally to the pleasure system of the existing society, to increase that alienation. In the frantic footwork of the jitter-bugs, Adorno seemed to hear the mechanical drumbeat of goose-stepping soldiers. The "rhythmically obedient" types, he wrote, were the "most susceptible to a process of masochistic adjustment to authoritarian collectivism."[49] They were not the only ones, however. Adorno's "emotional type" also put himself under the sway of the social order. In the jazz hall as well as the movie theater, Adorno explained, emotional individuals could experience the possibility of happiness denied in real life. Having thus had their wishes satisfied, albeit by an illusion, citizens would retreat from the barricades of political change to the safety of their fantasies.

Adorno's essay offered an early model of how communication could shape individual character and be shaped by it. It substantially extended the range of forces that Freudian psychiatrists had described as shaping the libidinal structure of the individual. In Adorno's theory of popular music, Le Bon's theory of mass media as thought leader returned as well: affirmed and repeated, the emotional messages of pop music had undermined the reason of listeners and opened them up to the pleasures of masochistic obedience. Moreover, the listener had become always and everywhere a citizen. In his late 1930s writings on popular music, Adorno politicized the psychological process of listening. To hear, to dance, to drift off to sleep while the radio played—at the edge of World War II, Adorno depicted these bits of everyday life as political acts. In his writing, as in that of many of his American contemporaries, the psyche itself had become a battleground in the struggle against fascism. And for Adorno at least, mass culture and mass media were on the wrong side.

FIGURE 1.4.

Hermann Goering at the microphone, 1935. American press reports in the late 1930s often suggested that Hitler and his colleagues were perverse, mentally unstable, or insane. Many Americans feared that mass media might provide conduits through which such leaders could infect an entire population with their madness. Photograph by Three Lions. © Getty Images. Used by permission.

THE WAR OF THE WORLDS

In the late 1930s, no event brought Adorno's point home to more Americans than the CBS radio network's broadcast of *The War of the Worlds*. At eight o'clock in the evening on the night before Halloween, 1938, Orson Welles's Mercury Theatre on the Air set loose a nationwide panic by broadcasting its adaptation of H. G. Wells's famous novel. Across the country, listeners could hear what purported to be eyewitness accounts of Martian landings in and around New Jersey. The ferocious aliens shot off heat rays, launched gas attacks, and marched across the landscape in hideous spider-like machines. American bomber pilots dove to their deaths as they tried to destroy the invaders. Local police and military forces were completely overwhelmed. Only after the aliens succumbed to a massive bacterial infection did the assault come to an end.

According to what remains the most authoritative study of events that evening, Hadley Cantril's *The Invasion from Mars*, somewhere between four and twelve million people heard the broadcast.[50] At the start of the show, an announcer clearly stated that it was a radio drama and not a news account. CBS also interrupted the hour-long broadcast four times for station announcements and other business. Some 60 percent of local stations carrying the show also interrupted it on their own initiative to remind listeners that it was a play.[51] Despite these reminders, though, citizens from Newark to Omaha mistook the play for news, and panicked. The next day, the *New York Times* reported that during the broadcast, weeping citizens had flooded the switchboard of the *Providence Journal* in Rhode Island; hundreds of doctors and nurses volunteered for hospital service in Newark, New Jersey; and in that same town some twenty families on a single block had fled their homes, wet towels over their faces, believing that a gas raid was underway.[52]

In the wake of the broadcast, Cantril and his colleagues interviewed many who had panicked. Their interview with Sylvia Holmes, a housewife in Newark, gives some feel for the fears they uncovered:

> We listened, getting more and more excited. We all felt the world was coming to an end. Then we heard "Get gas masks!" That was the part that got me. I thought I was going crazy. . . . I guess I didn't know what I was doing. I stood on the corner waiting for a bus and I thought every car that came along was a bus and I ran out to get it. People saw how excited I was and tried to quiet me, but I kept saying over and over again to everybody I met: "Don't you know New Jersey is destroyed by the Germans—it's on the radio." I was all excited and I knew that Hitler didn't appreciate President Roosevelt's telegram a couple of weeks ago. While the U.S. thought every-

thing was settled, they came down unexpected. The Germans are so wise
they were in something like a balloon and when the balloon landed—that's
when they announced the explosion—the Germans landed.

When Holmes finally turned the radio to another station, she remembered, "It was eleven o'clock and we heard it announced that it was only a
play. It sure felt good—just like a burden was lifted off me."[53]

Holmes's response was somewhat extreme, but her illogic was common
among those who thought the broadcast had been news. In the wake of
the panic, newspaper columnists, government officials, and media analysts such as Cantril all struggled to make sense of what had happened.
Many commentators pointed to the international political situation as
a key source of the confusion. In the weeks leading up to the broadcast,
Neville Chamberlain had visited Hitler in Berlin on his infamous mission
of appeasement. The Nazis had occupied Austria some months before;
then, on October 15, they had occupied Czechoslovakia. In America these
events had been accompanied by a series of news flashes—the same for-
mat in which Welles had couched his radio play. The editorial committee
of the *New York Times* made the connection explicitly. In a column entitled
"Terror by Radio," they opined: "Common sense might have warned the
projectors of this broadcast that our people are just recovering from a psychosis brought on by fear of war. But the trouble goes much deeper than
that. It is inherent in the method of radio broadcasting as maintained at
present in this country."[54]

The editorialists of the *Times* went on to argue that by blurring entertainment and news, Welles and company had made it all too easy for listeners to mistake one for the other. Yet their use of the word "psychosis"
is revealing as well. For journalists as for social psychologists in this period, the primary terms in which to interpret the power of mass media
and particularly radio were psychological. In perhaps the most widely
circulated contemporary response to the panic, nationally syndicated columnist Dorothy Thompson argued that the *War of the Worlds* broadcast
had proven "how easy it is to start a mass delusion."[55] Its producers, she
explained, "have uncovered the primeval fears lying under the thinnest
surface of the so-called civilized man." According to Thompson, the radio

broadcast had circumvented and thus subverted the reason of listeners. It had triggered their deepest fears. And it had left them crazed for some sort of salvation by those in authority. By revealing this process, she argued, "Mr. Orson Welles and his theater have made a greater contribution to an understanding of Hitlerism, Mussolinism, Stalinism, anti-Semitism and all the other terrorisms of our times than all the words about them that have been written by reasonable men."

In Thompson's view, the broadcast had revealed a key mechanism of fascist formation in action, and one that threatened American democracy from within as well as without. Thompson explained that "the technique of modern mass politics calling itself democracy is to create a fear—a fear of economic royalists, or of Reds, or of Jews, or of starvation, or of an outside enemy—and exploit that fear into obtaining subservience in return for protection." And as the broadcast of *War of the Worlds* had demonstrated, the radio could be an ideal instrument for the transmission of terror. "The power of mass suggestion is the most potent force today," Thompson explained. It had brought the dictators of Europe to power, and it kept them there too. What's more, Thompson feared that it could easily turn Americans not simply into hysterics, but into political fanatics. "If people can be frightened out of their wits by mythical men from Mars, they can be frightened into fanaticism by the fear of Reds."

In Adorno's view, fanaticism was a feature of the listening situation itself. Radio and popular music bypassed reason, reached down into the unconscious emotions of listeners, and bound them to the distant rhythms of the jitterbug and the dictator's speech. For Thompson, the atomizing tendencies of modern industrial society and the terrific political and economic upheavals of the 1930s had created a vulnerable individual. Modern social conditions had untethered individuals from the local social worlds that sustained their identities. And in both Nazi Germany and the panic-stricken, demagogue-fearing United States of 1938, mass media amplified the individual's fear of his or her own vulnerability. At the same time, in the sorts of listening situations analyzed by Adorno, mass media presented individuals with opportunities to escape their isolation, to submit themselves to a higher authority, and to join other sufferers in a single mass. In these ways, to these and many other critics, radio and other mass communication media threatened to turn American citizens into fascists. Adorno, Thompson, and their fellow journalists and scholars varied in their accounts of how the transformation would occur, but by 1938, virtually all agreed: Mass communication could turn the individual personality and, with it, the structure of society as a whole in a totalitarian direction.

2
World War II and the Question of National Character

As America edged closer to World War II, the fear that mass media could make mass men forced intellectuals and policy makers to confront two questions: First, how could they convince democratic Americans to go to war without turning them into the sort of unthinking authoritarians they would be trying to defeat? And second, what kinds of media could they use to do it? These questions in turn raised the question of national character. In Germany—which remained the touchstone case for American intellectuals, despite Japanese predations in Asia and Italian advances in Africa—Hitler's astute use of mass communication seemed to have amplified authoritarian tendencies already alive in German society. Analysts began to wonder what psychological tendencies might be native to American society. Was there such a thing as a "democratic personality?" And if so, what were its characteristics? And what forms of communication might strengthen it sufficiently to confront its increasingly battle-hardened totalitarian counterpart?

In the first years of World War II, two groups of social scientists began to develop answers to these questions. One group, consisting of psychologists and psychiatrists, had already turned away from Freudian orthodoxy toward developmental models of the self and, with them, visions of a flexible, collaborative personality. The other group, consisting of cultural anthropologists, had ventured into the Native American West and the wilds of Polynesia in search of alternatives to modern industrial societies and had begun to rethink the whole of American culture. Together these communities began to imagine an American society that would acknowledge and tolerate differences in race, sexual preference, and cultural style. Some also began to experiment with film, photography and new multimodal forms of communication that they hoped would promote American morale and a democratic mode of unity. As they did, they laid the intellectual foundation for a mode of communication and a vision of an egalitarian world that would long outlive the war.

THE WAR OF NERVES AND THE PROBLEM OF MORALE

To many writers, the months leading up to the explosion of military conflict across the European continent served as yet another demonstration of the power of propaganda campaigns to undermine national unity. American journalist Edmond Taylor, for instance, was stationed in Europe. In 1942 he published a chronicle of the prewar years, together with fragments of his own and his wife's diaries. Their account depicts prewar France as foggy with fear. Taylor recalled "those inhuman diplomatic crises, more unnerving than war . . . I remember all the false hopes, all the bitter disillusionments. Above all I remember the paralyzing political despair which grew and grew until it almost overshadowed our private lives, the feeling that this world of ours would always be a madhouse and a jungle, that collective efforts to bring reason into it were fruitless, that individual escape was impossible."[1] Starting in 1938, Taylor and his neighbors found themselves seesawing between the fear that fighting would erupt momentarily and the confidence that it would not. "After Munich," wrote Taylor, "France seemed to be stricken with something like collective locomotor ataxia; she was visibly throwing out from the knees. Defeatism, demobilized like the army, put on civilian clothes and entered every phase of life."[2]

Taylor argued that the French paralysis of 1939 stemmed from a coordinated fascist propaganda campaign. Before they sent their armies into the field, the Nazis engaged in "nerve-tactics," he explained.[3] They sent out spies, delivered radio broadcasts, planted news stories and rumors—all in an effort to dissolve the morale of their enemies. So too, of course, did the British and the French. Taylor described the seven months between the Germans' attack on Poland and their invasion of France and the Low Countries as one in which armies of communication specialists from every nation dueled with one another on "the front of the mind."[4] Many of Taylor's readers feared that the psychological fight had come to them as well. The rise of native demagogues, the ability of the German-American Bund to stage rallies in Madison Square Garden, a daily diet of hyperbolic newspaper headlines threatening war or promising peace—all suggested that Americans might already be under the sort of attack that had preceded German military assaults in Europe.[5]

In the two years before American troops entered the fray, civic groups, celebrities, and intellectuals mustered to resist the onslaught.[6] Some of these groups were explicitly interventionist.[7] Others focused on the more nebulous goal of building American morale. One of the most influential of these was the Committee for National Morale. Founded in the summer of 1940 by Arthur Upham Pope, a Manhattan-based curator of Persian art, the committee gathered many of the era's leading psychologists, sociologists, anthropologists, and journalists into a single organization. Members included journalists Edmond Taylor and Ladislas Farago, psychologists Gordon Allport and Kurt Lewin, and anthropologists Ruth Benedict, Gregory Bateson, and Margaret Mead, among more than sixty others. Committee members aimed to serve as expert advisors on questions of morale to President Roosevelt and the public. Over the next two years the committee published reports on German propaganda and strategy, as well as a white paper on American foreign policy across the preceding decade. Individual members also wrote extensively on morale for both the popular and the professional press.

A survey of that writing reveals a deep tension between a desire for and a fear of American unity. By and large, committee members' statements, like those of the leaders of other civic organizations, stuck to a relatively hazy definition of morale. In a 1941 article, Arthur Upham Pope articulated the consensus view when he wrote, "High morale shows itself by enthusiasm, confidence, teamwork, endurance. . . . In essence morale is a state produced by a clearly envisaged value of such commanding power and authority that it evokes all the capacities of a man or a group, fusing them into an intense and durable emotional and ideational unity that increases, sustains, and organizes all effort."[8] At an everyday level, this sort of formulation must have been quite appealing to Americans working their way out of the Great Depression. The vision of a nation united behind a single optimistic purpose presented a glowing alternative to the fact of ongoing labor and racial strife. But to ears tuned to the threat of totalitarianism, visions of a force that might melt the nation into a single mass must have been frightening as well. Pope acknowledged as much later in his essay, when he wrote, "Above all, it must be remembered that . . . morale is not something to be imposed by a central organization, but something that demands the initiative and response of the people in every type of activity and grouping." In other words, propagandists needed to be careful not to make Americans *too* obedient. Only with the active engagement of the people could American leaders knit together a "resilient fabric of morale that represents the whole character of the whole nation and involves the total personality of each citizen."[9]

The tension in Pope's article echoed a debate within the Roosevelt administration.[10] In the wake of the German advance in Europe, Roosevelt was considering inviting George Creel, leader of the infamous Committee on Public Information, to return to government service. During World War I, Creel had managed to stir up a pro-war frenzy by managing perhaps the most far-reaching domestic propaganda campaign ever undertaken in America. Roosevelt's secretary of the interior, Harold Ickes, was dismayed to think that he might repeat his earlier performance. These social scientists, Ickes hoped, might provide an alternative to Creel's return. He arranged for the Committee for National Morale to receive a five-thousand-dollar appropriation in order to develop a plan for a national morale service.[11] The committee delivered its recommendations—more than five hundred pages of them—to the Cabinet in February 1941.[12] In the end, Roosevelt declined to appoint Creel or even to establish a national morale agency. The debate within the Cabinet however, marked a quandary for American leaders: Should they build a propaganda ministry of their own, so as to harness the power of mass communication to boost morale? And if they didn't build such a ministry, how would they promote morale at all?

For the members of the Committee for National Morale, these debates reflected more than a disagreement about the mechanisms of propaganda. They reflected fault lines in the concept of morale itself. Gordon Allport, a professor at Harvard University and one of America's foremost theorists of personality, echoed Arthur Upham Pope when he explained, for the readers of *The Christian Science Monitor*, "Morale is a condition of physical and emotional well-being residing in the individual citizen." But he went a step further too in explaining that "national problems . . . are nothing but personal problems shared by all citizens."[13] For Allport, as for the other members of the Committee for National Morale, the nature of well-being within the individual mirrored and shaped the well-being of the state. In defining American morale, they also hinted at a definition of an ideal American personality and, through it, an idealized vision of the nation as a whole.

In part for that reason, Committee members did a great deal of work to distinguish fascist from democratic morale. In his 1941 Committee-sponsored study *German Psychological Warfare*, Ladislas Farago pointed out that many Americans believed that "the German is a robot." In

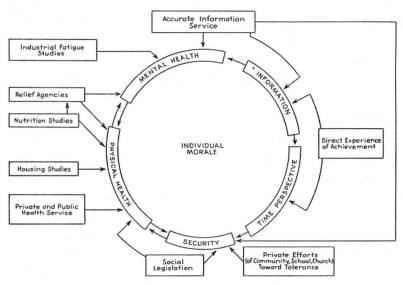

Fig. 1. *Interrelations in morale research.*

FIGURE 2.1.

At the start of World War II, American social scientists imagined individual morale as the center of an enormous multidisciplinary research effort. As this diagram shows, they imagined the internal psychology of individual Americans as both a function and a source of the social order around them. Source: Gardiner Murphy, "Essentials for a Civilian Morale Program in American Democracy," 435. Used by permission of the Society for the Psychological Study of Social Issues.

fact, he explained, "the Nazis intend him to be exactly that in the mass-psychological sense." To achieve that slavishness, the Nazis instilled their citizens with a spirit of collectivity that would have been familiar to Gustave Le Bon: "Mass morale," wrote Farago, " is produced along classic Prussian lines. It is synthetic, artificial, based on habit, coercion, intimidation, uniform thinking and the community feeling of 'military socialism'. . . ."[14] Even so, German morale was clearly high. Farago's Nazis appeared to have succeeded in fusing the individual desires of German citizens into a single mass, arrayed behind a single flag and serving a single cause. And in this respect, Nazi morale did not look so different from the sort of American unity called for by Arthur Upham Pope. Perhaps for that reason, Farago aimed to distinguish fascist from democratic unity in terms of its *effect* on the psyche of the individual. The Nazi type of morale resulted in "conformity" but not in an "inner strength" that might outlive the regime itself, he argued.[15] Nazi morale might have looked like the sort of national unity Americans needed, but it wasn't: it was too brittle.

Gordon Allport grounded his critique of Nazi morale even more thoroughly in its relationship to personality. In the early years of World War II, Allport was one of the most visible analysts of morale. He compiled bibliographies on the subject, ran a seminar on morale at Harvard, and wrote numerous essays on the theme. In a 1942 volume edited by a fellow member of the Committee for National Morale, he summed up many of his views in an essay entitled "The Nature of Democratic Morale." "In a democracy," he wrote, "every personality can be a citadel of resistance to tyranny. *In the co-ordination of the intelligences and wills of one hundred million 'whole' men and women lies the formula for an invincible American morale* [italics original]."[16] For Allport, the defining problem of fascist morale was that it depended on a fracturing of the psyche. Totalitarian propaganda worked to divide the emotions from the reason. It amplified the sentiments and muted the voice of logic. The totalitarian thus became a fractured person. He or she would be blown here and there by the voice of the Führer, on the wind of feeling alone. Intelligence and will would be decoupled, and the self would be crippled as a person and as a citizen. Democratic morale, on the other hand, worked to integrate the personality. Emotion and reason, intellect and will, evaluation and action—all would be one.

In part, Allport's democratic morale foreshadowed the liberalism of the 1950s. The individual with high morale in 1940 or 1941 was a person who could act independently on the basis of reason, and who was, in that sense, free. It also pointed backward, to a nineteenth-century preoccupation with "character." A person with democratic morale could fuse emotion and intellect into a powerful form of principle-driven agency. But Allport's democratic morale also pointed toward the concerns with personal fulfillment that would come to dominate both humanistic psychology and the American counterculture in the 1960s. To boost American morale was to help make individual personalities "whole" and "integrated" in Allport's terms. Only a coalition of such whole people, linked in voluntary cooperation and not managed from above, could sustain American democracy in the face of the fascist threat.

For Allport, the concept of morale linked practices of communication to individual psychological development and to the welfare of the nation. For that reason, he and others associated with the Committee for National Morale helped *define* the national drive for morale as a drive for a particular kind of personality. The fight for morale became the fight for a "whole" self—and for a propaganda strategy and a set of communication tactics that would help foster the development of such a self. Psychologist Lawrence Frank stated the point succinctly in his 1940 essay, "Freedom for the Personality":

> We are, somewhat reluctantly, realizing that the democratic aspirations cannot be realized nor adequately expressed in and by voting and representative government; democracy, or the democratic faith, is being reformulated today in terms of the value and integrity of the individual, not as a tool or as a means, but as an end or goal for whose conservation and fulfillment social life must be reoriented. . . . Thus freedom for the personality may be viewed as the crucial issue of a democratic society . . . .[17]

THE QUESTION OF CULTURE AND PERSONALITY

But what exactly was a free personality? And what did it have to do with American democracy?

These questions exploded into view even before the attack at Pearl Harbor with the publication of fascist and especially Nazi theories of racial superiority. For the Nazis, as for the Japanese, the character of individuals reflected the character of their "race." Perhaps no single volume expressed the Nazi theory of personality as succinctly as *The Nazi Primer,* an official handbook for the Hitler Youth that was translated into English and published for a general American audience in 1938. "The foundation of the National Socialist outlook on life is the perception of the unlikeness of men," its authors announced in its very first line.[18] In the Nazi view, body and character were one, and both were determined by racial genetics. *The Nazi Primer* distinguished six racial types—the Nordic, Phalic, Western, Dinaric, Eastern, and East Baltic—by the shape of their skulls, their hair and eye colors, and their typical character features. The Eastern race inclined "to craftiness" but made for "compliant and submissive subjects."[19] Dinarics had "a great gift for music."[20] East Baltics lacked "a real power of decision in conflicts of conscience" and were "never resolute."[21] The Nordic race, however, was "uncommonly gifted mentally" and "outstanding for truthfulness and energy." In contrast to all of the other races, Nordic men "were predisposed to leadership by nature."[22]

From the point of view of American social scientists, the fact that the Nazis had divided individuals into clusters and assigned them typical physical and personality traits was not in itself a problem.[23] Anthropologists and social psychologists had long worked to link the individual to his or her culture, and even to think about culturally specific character types (such as the authoritarian personality). The problem was the question of race and, specifically, its account of the *origin* of personality. As *The Nazi Primer* put it, fascists believed that "inheritance is in the long run always victorious over environmental influences."[24] A German was a German, by blood; a Jew, a Jew.

In the 1930s, the Nazis did have sympathizers in American academe.[25] But the psychologists and anthropologists of the Committee for National Morale were not among them. To these intellectuals, fascist views on race represented a gross misuse of science. They also forced a confrontation with the racism and, to a less widely acknowledged extent, the anti-Semitism that existed in the United States. Finally, they challenged the tenet that more than any other had come to unify understandings of the personality among members of the Committee and their circles: that individual personality was a dynamic product of lived history and, thus, malleable. Each analyst had his or her own view of *how* social situations shaped the individual psyche, but all agreed that they did shape it. Whether they emphasized early familial socialization, adult encounters with the social world, or both, the men and women associated with the Committee for National Morale tended to imagine the self and the social world as shaping each other through a process of communication. From this perspective it was a relatively small step for those who had studied personality and culture—and particularly for Margaret Mead and Gregory Bateson—to begin to prescribe communication strategies that might promote American morale alongside the development of nonauthoritarian personalities.

To understand the appeal of their prescriptions early in the war and their power in the decades after it, we need to first explore what the psychologists associated with the Committee and with Mead and Bateson meant by "personality," and especially by its democratic variant. In the early years of World War II, the notion of "personality" was still relatively young. In the later decades of the nineteenth century and the first two of the twentieth, intellectuals talked more often of "character"—that is, of the notion of what Emerson called the "moral order seen through the medium of individual nature."[26] By the 1930s, Americans had become dramatically more cosmopolitan. Intellectuals had embraced Freud; so too had advertisers, department store owners, and the consumers of the suddenly ubiquitous mass culture of the 1920s. This new world seemed to require a new understanding of the self.[27] An individual's character grew out of his debts to others and his willingness to service them; a personality could be something else—something more expressive, more unique, more flexible.[28]

Two intellectual traditions dominated American psychology in the early twentieth century: behaviorism and psychoanalysis. For the former, personality consisted of the sum of responses to external stimuli. For the latter, the individual psyche grew out of the interaction of universal human drives with a person's individual life experience. Key members of the Committee for National Morale embraced neither of these views in their entirety. Rather, they developed alternative perspectives: a humanistic psychology, in the case of Gordon Allport, and a field psychology, for Kurt Lewin. Their views in turn accorded well with critiques of Freud penned by well-known psychoanalysts such as Harry Stack Sullivan, Karen Horney, and Erich Fromm. They also meshed with new theories of the relationship between culture and personality that were emerging among anthropologists such as Ruth Benedict, Abraham Kardiner, Margaret Mead, and Gregory Bateson. To all of these critics, behaviorism and psychoanalysis seemed to present relatively static and one-dimensional pictures of the individual psyche. As they challenged these views, psychologists and psychoanalysts turned to questions of culture and to the sociologists and anthropologists who studied them. Together, these communities set the terms by which they and later analysts would come to define particular personalities as "democratic."

For Gordon Allport, each group presented an inadequate account of the parts of personality formerly associated with the concept of character. Allport and his brother Floyd, also an influential psychologist, had grown up in a religious family—so religious that his mother had hoped Gordon would become a minister.[29] In the 1920s he had traveled to Europe, where he met Freud and studied with Gestaltists Max Wertheimer and Wolfgang Köhler, among others.[30] By 1937, when he published his highly influential book *Personality: A Psychological Interpretation*, Allport had become one of the foremost American theorists in the field. But he had not become a Freudian or a behaviorist. On the contrary, he rejected Freud's theories of drives as too biocentric and too unable to account for changes in the personality over time. And he rejected behaviorism as offering an entirely too mechanistic account of human agency.

Allport preoccupied himself with a question that had also engaged nineteenth-century theorists of character: How did an individual achieve autonomy, in a given moment and over a lifetime? His 1937 definition of personality provided an answer to that question. "Personality," he wrote, "is a dynamic organization within the individual of those psychophysical systems that determine his unique adjustments to his environment."[31] To Americans today, the word "adjustment" may smack of psychology's role in enforcing Cold War conformity. But in 1937, Allport's definition of the self allowed the individual to emerge as a creative being. The individual personality could change in response to the situations in which it found itself. And the individual could make choices as well, in response to those changes. A person was not the prisoner of his or her childhood. Moreover, the individual's ability to change altered with age. In the Freudian account, the socialization of the infant together with the child's own drives structured the personality for a lifetime. In Allport's, the psyche changed as the person aged—often in ways dictated by his or her culture. Moreover, the individual could *be* changed by shifts in his or her social and symbolic surroundings.

Allport's views paralleled those of his friend and colleague the German refugee psychologist Kurt Lewin. In World War I, Lewin had served as a lieutenant in the German army. One of his earliest papers described his own march from the rear to the front lines and the psychological changes he underwent along the way.[32] These movements ultimately became the foundation of what Lewin called his "topological" theory of personality.[33] Lewin saw individuals moving through a field of phenomena that he called the "life space." This field transformed individuals as they moved through it—it gave them energy, increased psychic tension, and offered release for pent-up anxiety. Like Allport, Lewin was an early and avid reader of Gestalt theory. And like Allport, he saw the individual personality as a whole system that lived and changed in relation to the systems around it. As the environment changed, so did the individual's perceptions of it. Those perceptions in turn became the foundation of the individual's inner life. The process of communication brokered this exchange between the inner and outer worlds—at the interpersonal level within the social group, but potentially at the intercultural and even international levels as well.

In 1938, Lewin and two colleagues at the State University of Iowa's Child Research Station conducted a study that seemed to demonstrate the parallels. They began by asking how phenomena such as scapegoating, submission to authoritarian leaders, and even rebellion against authority might be linked.[34] To answer these questions, they staged an experiment designed to compare the social-psychological dynamics of three kinds of society: authoritarian, democratic, and anarchic.[35] They gathered groups of ten-year-old boys into five-member after-school clubs where they would make masks and play games. They gave each group an adult leader who was instructed to take charge in an authoritarian, democratic, or laissez-faire manner. In the first mode, the leader made all decisions and demanded that the boys simply follow them. In the second, the leader engaged the boys in collaborative discussion to choose their activities. And in the third variation, the leader simply let the boys do whatever they liked with no interference. The results were tellingly consistent with liberal American views of contemporary geopolitics: under the authoritarian condition, the boys either became passive and obedient, or imitated their leader and became aggressively domineering toward each other. They also chose scapegoats and turned on them in unison—not unlike the Germans under Nazi rule. Democratic leaders, by contrast, engendered affection and a moderate level of aggression in the boys—something closer to the energetic civic participation expected of Americans than to the sort of dominance/submission dynamics seen in dictatorships. Under laissez-faire conditions, most boys were similarly active and described themselves as quite happy—a finding that Lewin and his colleagues acknowledged but did not dwell on.

According to Lewin and his colleagues, all three political structures allowed groups to become aggressive toward outsiders, but an autocratic structure produced the most extreme kinds of aggression. Lewin and his colleagues theorized that the autocratic mode of management restricted the boys' psychological liberty. This in turn generated tensions within their individual psyches and within the groups. These tensions found release in aggression. Though Lewin and his colleagues reported their findings with typical academic cautions—experiments did not necessarily predict social reality, more studies were needed, et cetera—they clearly believed that they had modeled the pressures at the heart of the international situation. Other scholars and policy makers agreed. The Iowa study became widely known in subsequent decades. And Lewin's focus on fields of energy and tension within and between groups, and on the relationship of the individual psyche to those collective patterns, would go on to suffuse later American attempts to manage the international tensions of the Cold War.

In the run-up to World War II though, Lewin's field approach, like Allport's dynamic humanism, presented a powerful framework with which to challenge fascist notions of an unchanging, genetically determined individual. So too did new modes of psychoanalysis developed by Harry Stack Sullivan, Karen Horney, and Erich Fromm. Although each of these theorists had embraced Freudian psychoanalysis to varying degrees, each also challenged Freud's theoretical allegiance to internal drives and universal if invisible psychic structures such as the id, the ego and the superego.[36] Together they turned outward from the self and toward culture, society, and history as sources of personality change.

They did so to different degrees and for different reasons. Having trained in the Marxist-Freudian hothouse of Berlin in the 1920s, Fromm became fascinated with the ways in which historical circumstance shaped the personality, first through the family and later through larger social formations. Born in Frankfurt in 1900 to Orthodox Jewish parents, trained in sociology and psychoanalysis, Fromm joined the Institute for Social Research in Frankfurt in 1930. When Hitler came to power, he fled to the United States, where he soon acquired a national reputation as both a psychoanalyst and a popular social theorist. Just before he crossed the Atlantic, Fromm penned a series of papers that set the stage for rethinking the relationship between the personality and mass communication.[37] Like Wilhelm Reich and other Marxist psychoanalysts, Fromm believed that the economic conditions of everyday life shaped the psychological structure of the individual. Society and psyche formed a feedback loop. Society shaped the roles and the emotional life of the family; the family shaped the libido structure of its children; and when the children grew up, they repeated the process. Since members of a given community underwent similar social pressures, they tended to develop similar habits of mind and feeling, habits which Fromm later gathered together under the umbrella concept of "social character."[38] "Every society," wrote Fromm in 1932, "has its own distinctive libidinal structure, even as it has its own economic, social, political, and cultural structure."[39] The sociological job of the psychoanalyst was "to explain the shared, socially relevant, psychic attitudes and ideologies—and their unconscious roots in particular—in terms of the influence of economic conditions on libido strivings."[40]

Fromm took that assignment literally, launching an extensive survey of German workers in 1929.[41] Over the next two years, he and his colleague Hilde Weiss presented a questionnaire to 3,300 skilled laborers and clerks.[42] In 1931, as he worked with the 700 surveys that came back completed, Fromm mapped the relationship between his subjects' emotional orientation to authority and their party affiliation. He began by identifying three dimensions of personality and associated patterns of response: "authoritarian vs. nonauthoritarian," "individualistic vs. collectivistic," and the degree of "consistency of an individual's political ideas."[43] As he analyzed survey responses in terms of these dimensions, he developed a way of mapping character structures and comparing them to party affiliation. Ultimately, the survey led Fromm to identify three core character types, each matched to a likely political orientation: "the authoritarian, the revolutionary, and the ambivalent."[44]

These types, as well as Fromm's empirical methodology, would ultimately form the foundation of the far better known study of 1950, *The Authoritarian Personality*, penned by Theodor Adorno and a team of researchers.[45] But before World War II, Fromm and Weiss's work helped establish two important ideas: first, it suggested that individual character was at the very least substantially shaped by social structure; second, it seemed to demonstrate that the rising authoritarianism of Germany had its roots in the German family, and in that sense, in German culture.

By the 1930s, Fromm's psychoanalytic and sociological insights had become so entwined that some more orthodox Freudians rejected his work outright.[46] Freudian loyalists also challenged the work of his lover, Karen Horney. Horney was fifteen years older than Fromm and had helped found the Berlin Psychoanalytic Institute, where he trained and where they met. Originally a relatively orthodox Freudian, in the 1920s Horney began to critique Freud's account of what she called "the masculine complex" in women.[47] Penis envy, a sense of genital and personal inadequacy, a desire to actually be a man—Horney argued that these elements which Freud had suggested were somehow built into the psyche of all young girls were in fact at least in part the products of lived experience. And if they were, she concluded, then Freud's own account, while brilliant, was also a product of its culture. By the mid-1930s, when Horney had moved to America, she had completely dismissed Freud's claim that the Oedipus complex was a universal human phenomenon. It was a part of the European culture in which he worked, she wrote.[48] To even identify some elements of the individual psyche as "feminine," she argued, was to create the intellectual conditions under which women could be rendered socially and politically inferior.[49]

Horney's very public cultural turn triggered a hailstorm of attacks from more mainstream Freudians. But she was hardly alone in her views. A decade earlier, her friend Harry Stack Sullivan had made a parallel defection. Stack Sullivan was a medical doctor who began working with schizophrenics in Washington, DC, in the 1920s.[50] His colleagues were steeped in the writings of Freud and his students and in the early 1930s; Stack Sullivan himself underwent three hundred hours of psychoanalysis. But Stack Sullivan never became a thoroughgoing Freudian. On the contrary, in 1927 he began to analyze his patients in terms of what he called their "interpersonal relationships."[51] Destructive interpersonal relationships had largely helped make his patients ill, he believed. What bound the individual to the collective was the process of interpersonal communication. As individuals interacted with the group—physically and socially, in action and in language—their minds wedded the experience of those interactions to internal emotional states. In the process, individuals transformed these experiences into what Stack Sullivan called "signs and signals for . . . satisfactions, frustrations, security, or insecurity."[52]

Stack Sullivan's papers circulated very widely among psychiatrists in the 1930s, and his views gained substantial traction in debates of the day. But Stack Sullivan wielded much of his influence socially. In 1930, when he moved to New York City and entered private practice, he retained close working links with political scientist Howard Lasswell and linguistic anthropologist Edward Sapir, both of whom taught at Yale in the early 1930s.[53] In 1933, Stack Sullivan, Lasswell, and Sapir joined psychoanalyst Ernest Hadley in founding the William Alanson White Foundation in Washington, DC, an organization that would go on to train generations of psychiatrists and publish one of the foremost journals in the field, *Psychiatry*. In New York, Stack Sullivan also convened a weekly dinner group that called itself the Zodiac Club.[54] The group met in a speakeasy until Prohibition ended, whence they decamped for restaurants and one another's homes. The original group consisted of four psychoanalysts—Stack Sullivan, his own analyst Clara Thompson, William Silverberg, and Edward Shipley—and a former patient of Stack Sullivan's named Jimmie. Karen Horney joined in 1934, and Erich Fromm attended off and on as well. Other regulars included anthropologist Hortense Powdermaker, photographer Margaret Bourke-White, several attorneys, and various local actors and directors.

By the late 1930s, the social world of the Zodiac Club overlapped with that of Margaret Mead, Gregory Bateson, and the anthropologists of the "culture and personality" school.[55] During the same years in which psychologists and psychiatrists began to push back against determinist accounts of the origins of personality, cultural anthropologists took a disciplinary turn away from biological theories of cultural evolution. By the late 1930s, Mead and Bateson in particular had embraced a vision in which personality and culture shaped one another as a society moved through time. They also embraced the flexible, tolerant personality styles described, and in some ways lived, by analysts such as Stack Sullivan, Horney, and Fromm. Finally, as American soldiers entered the fray, they transformed these nonauthoritarian character styles into the specifically *American* personalities for and by whom World War II must be fought.

The cultural anthropologists of the 1930s had inherited a discipline in which biology seemed to explain social differences. In the late nineteenth century, social scientists had argued that geography largely shaped the nature of culture and that evolution had caused some races to be more advanced than others. In the early years of the twentieth century, anthropologists had set out to challenge that account. Franz Boas led the charge. His studies of Eskimos, Northwest Indians, and even immigrant populations in American cities undermined theories of racial purity and cultural superiority based on genetics. They showed instead, he argued, the power of cultures to shape their inhabitants.

In later decades Boas's work so infuriated the Nazis that they burned his books in the street when they came to power. It also became a foundation on which two of his students built a vision of a tolerant, democratic society. The first was Margaret Mead. In 1925, at the age of twenty-three and at the urging of Boas, Mead set sail for American Samoa. When she arrived, she found what she described as a palm-fringed society of smiling adolescents who fished and chatted during the day and slipped surreptitiously into adventurous lovemaking at night. Mead's account of Samoan life has since been challenged by a number of anthropologists, but in 1928, when *Coming of Age in Samoa* arrived in bookstores, it presented readers with a tremendously compelling alternative to prevailing views of human nature and even of American society. It showed that adolescence need not be a time of struggle and stress. Premarital sex need not ruin a woman. Families need not even consist simply of a mother and father and children in order to be happy. Mead's Samoans took pleasure from parts of life and from social structures that would have caused their American counterparts grief. What made the difference in their responses, Mead argued, was culture itself. With vivid and often lyrical prose, Mead brought to life the ways in which the rules of Samoan life shaped how individuals actually *felt*; in her account, the structure of Samoan society structured the emotional responses of its members.

Mead knew something about the power of culture to shape a society's expectations of women. Bisexual, intellectually omnivorous, tremendously ambitious, and at the same time hungry for the sort of intimacy that a home and family might provide, Mead sought throughout her life to find a combination of social relationships that could sustain her own desires. Reading *Coming of Age in Samoa* today, it is easy to dismiss her accounts of island life as the starry-eyed misperceptions of a neocolonial scientist. But in light of her biography, and of the racism and homophobia that permeated mainstream American society at the time, her book was also a provocation: If an ostensibly primitive society of Samoans could offer the kinds of romantic flexibility, interpersonal warmth, and collective benevolence that she described, why couldn't a modern America? If Samoans could be psychologically free, why couldn't Americans?

For Mead and her colleagues in cultural anthropology, the answers to those questions lay in understanding how individual personalities and cultural structures shaped each other. In 1934, Mead's teacher, colleague, and friend, Ruth Benedict, published a best-selling book that would shape debate in this area well into the 1960s, *Patterns of Culture*.[56] Benedict had also studied with Boas and, like him, she believed that by comparing cultures she might be able to explain their unique individual features. In *Patterns* she reported her research among the Pueblo Indians of New Mexico, the Native Americans of the Pacific Northwest, and the Dobu people of New Guinea. Like Mead, she had found successfully functioning societies that embraced sexual behaviors many Americans considered deviant, including homosexuality and transvestitism.

As she attempted to account for these consistencies and, at the same time, for differences from the American mainstream, Benedict argued that the individual personality tended to mirror the culture in which it had emerged. Personalities and cultures emerged and changed primarily through social processes, she argued. Even so, she pointed out that each culture had a unique and identifiable character—that is, a pattern of psychological organization that could be found within both the individual and the culture as a whole—which she labeled Apollonian in the case of the Zuni, Dionysian in the case of the Kwakiutl, and paranoid in the case of the Dobu. Cultures reproduced themselves, she suggested, by imbuing individuals with psychological habits that allowed them to adapt to social forms around them. Those habits, in turn, drove them to later reproduce the forms and so perpetuate their cultures.

Benedict's views fit well with those of Erich Fromm and the sociologists of the Frankfurt School. Like Fromm and other psychoanalysts critical of Freud, Benedict saw the individual psyche as exceptionally malleable. Cultures acquired their consistency, she argued, because they succeeded in molding the individual personality in terms of collective tradition. Every human individual entered the world with a broad array of capacities and motivations. As families and communities socialized the individual, they drew out particular cognitive and emotional elements of the personality and celebrated them as especially effective.[57] In this way, the configuration of a given culture dramatically shaped the configuration of the personalities within it. Not all individuals would be alike in all ways, she noted. But they would need to strike an accommodation between their psychological needs and the institutions of their society. And that process would tend toward making the individual psyche and its collective cultural surroundings isomorphic. As she put it in a 1932 article, she believed that "cultures . . . are individual psychology thrown large upon the screen, given gigantic proportions and a long time span."[58]

A number of researchers would take issue with the scope and precision of Benedict's claims. But by the early years of World War II, few social scientists ignored them. Benedict and Mead were only two of many researchers preoccupied with culture and personality. Others included Edward Sapir, Abraham Kardiner, John Dollard, Ralph Linton, Cora DuBois, and Gregory Bateson. These researchers, in turn, read and responded to the work of Erich Fromm, Harry Stack Sullivan, Karen Horney, Kurt Lewin and Gordon Allport. Virtually all of these scholars wrote regularly for the popular press. Benedict, Mead, Fromm, and Horney wrote books that reached very wide public audiences and still do today. Though they disagreed somewhat on the mechanics of the process, they agreed that culture shaped personality, that childhood represented a particularly influential period for that work, and that the patterns of personality in a culture shaped its institutions, its development over time, and the forms of mental illness its citizens endured.[59] The process of communication—interpersonal and mediated, local and international—was the gravitational force that held this simultaneously psychological, social, and cultural constellation together.

THE DEMOCRATIC PERSONALITY AS
AMERICAN NATIONAL CHARACTER

At the outset of the fighting in Europe, the culture and personality tradition presented a robust, scientifically legitimate challenge to the race science of the Nazis and the Japanese—and to the racism of American society as well. It identified a psychological explanation for the transformation of one of the great citadels of European culture, Germany, into a fortress of bigotry, scapegoating, and violence. It offered a clear-eyed analysis of the social and cultural structures that helped render individuals psychologically vulnerable to fascism. And it suggested both a democratic alternative and a prescription for the structuring of social interaction that would help produce one.

Soon after Germany invaded Poland, broad contentions about the authoritarian personality became specific claims about National Socialists. At one level, analysts suggested that Hitler had infected the German populace with his own unique madness via mass rallies and radio broadcasts. At another, though, they argued that the Nazis had simply embraced the sadomasochistic excesses of German culture. Nazis longed for nothing more than to obey, and so to lose their individuality in the great mass of the crowd. They wanted only to follow and to attack those who wouldn't or couldn't also obey. Under the Nazis, the Germans had given up their powers of intellectual discrimination, of moral choice, of psychological independence. Above all, they had ceased to tolerate racial and cultural differences.[60]

For analysts focused on questions of culture and personality, theories of the Nazi personality provided a set of terms with which to articulate a democratic, American alternative. Abraham Maslow spoke for many when he wrote, "The democratic person . . . tends (in the pure case) to respect other human beings in a very basic fashion as *different* from each other, rather than better or worse [italics original]. He is more willing to allow for their own tastes, goals, and personal autonomy so long as no one else is hurt thereby. Furthermore, he tends to like them rather than dislike them and to assume that probably they are, if given the chance, essentially good rather than bad individuals." This good-natured tolerance depended in turn on a particular way of seeing other people. "We shall give the name 'perception and appreciation of difference' to the democratic way of viewing individual differences (in contrast with the authoritarian tendency to hierarchy)," Maslow wrote. "Here the stress is first of all on the fact that people are human beings and therefore unique and respectworthy [sic]."[61]

Maslow's vision of the democratic personality would echo down across the 1950s and well into the 1960s. So too would his focus on the importance of *perception* in shaping social relations. But at the start of World War II, tolerance was only one element of the kind of psyche that could stand in opposition to the Nazis. Under Hitler the Germans appeared to have become blindly obedient machines. The democratic personality, by contrast, would be an organic whole, independent and creative. Erich Fromm put this view succinctly, if abstractly, in his 1941 bestseller *Escape from Freedom*. In the modern world, he explained, individuals found themselves freed from the strictures of church and village that had constrained the individual in the pre-industrial era. This freedom, however, bewildered many and caused them to seek shelter under the powerful wing of authoritarian leaders. In that sense, sheer liberty represented a negative form of freedom. "Positive freedom," wrote Fromm, "consists in the spontaneous activity of the total, integrated personality."[62] Spontaneous action gave voice to that unity in a way that simultaneously acknowledged the uniqueness of the individual self and allowed it to contribute to the good of the entire society. "Spontaneous activity is the one way in which man can overcome the terror of aloneness without sacrificing the integrity of his self; for in the spontaneous realization of the self man unites himself anew with the world—with man, nature, and himself."[63]

Fromm believed that it was the role of the state to facilitate individual self-realization and the forms of political unity it sustained. The Nazis had become automata in large part because of the hierarchical structure of their society. The authoritarian personalities of wartime Germany reflected the authoritarian structure of fascist society and, behind that, the authoritarian socialization practices of German culture. The American state would need to create structural conditions that could simultaneously sustain the *individuality* of its citizens and their power to act *collectively* toward the common good. Fromm did not advocate that the state abandon its authority. Rather, he argued that it should use its power to plan an economic system in which citizens could "share responsibility and use creative intelligence."[64] The key, he wrote, was to avoid the rigid hierarchies of fascism. A democracy must aim to blend planning from above with the "active participation" of citizens.[65]

The ultimate test of a democracy, Fromm suggested, would be its ability to promote individual psychological growth. Modernity had freed people from medieval superstitions and feudal social structures. But it had also made them so anxious about their new solitude that entire nations had sought refuge in fascism. True freedom, Fromm explained, resided not in submission to a higher order, but in "the full realization of the individual's potentialities."[66] It was the duty of the state to enable the spontaneous, collaborative efforts of its citizens toward the goal of individual psychological growth. To do so, it would need to deploy its power in a new way. The fascist mode of social organization embodied an instrumental model of influence. So too did fascist forms of communication. In both cases, power flowed down from the top, encoded in hysterical messages on the radio and in violent military assaults, first on scapegoats within Germany, and later on the peoples of Europe. Fromm proposed an alternative. In his view, the state should not direct the drama of society; rather, it should simply provide a well-ordered stage on which individuals might pursue self-realization in a spirit of tolerance. They might thus form not an un-thinking mass, but a reasoning, affectionate collective.

PROPAGANDA AND THE DEMOCRATIC PERSONALITY

Fromm's views largely echoed those of Maslow, Allport, and the social scientists of the Committee for National Morale. By 1941 a broad consen-sus had emerged: a democratic personality was psychologically whole and able to make rational, independent choices. It acted spontaneously, it changed in response to life circumstances, and it recognized and accepted cultural and racial differences. It also required a different form of govern-ment: not rule from above, but the creation of structures within which individuals could act independently for the common good, from below.

In 1942 Margaret Mead took up this vision, fused it with the political ideals embodied in her own work, and presented it to the American public as a definition of their *national* character. In her widely read book *And Keep Your Powder Dry . . .* , Mead argued that the Nazis had brought forth a new and total kind of warfare. As German Panzers rolled across Europe, they attacked civilians and soldiers alike. So too did the fascist propaganda apparatus. Under these conditions, the cultural personality of the Amer-ican people took on a new importance. "The strengths and weaknesses of the American character," she wrote, are "the psychological equipment with which we can win the war."[67]

The first of those strengths should be tolerance. Americans, Mead wrote, "repudiate with all our strength the idea that a man's manners or his morals, his IQ or his capacity for democratic behavior, might be limited by race, that the color of a man's skin, the shape of his head or the waviness of his hair might carry with it either an ability or a disability . . . ."[68] In the segregated United States of 1943, this was hardly a universal view. But it set the terms on which Mead could simultaneously invoke American patriotism and call for social change. The American personality could change over time, she explained. The unity of the fascist mass was fragile. The American ability to preserve individual differences while acting in concert gave it an entirely different kind of strength. To win the war, Americans would need to draw on that strength in combat and, at the same time, sustain it at home. After all, she explained, "we are the stuff with which this war is being fought."[69]

But how could American leaders promote national unity without setting loose the demons of mass society?

For some analysts, the question was beside the point. In their view, the national emergency was sufficiently acute that it justified any and all modes of propaganda. Journalist Edmond Taylor argued that Americans should "fight Hitlerism with Hitler's favorite weapons."[70] The Nazis had launched a propaganda assault on the United States. Americans should fight back wherever and however they could. With their special knowledge of the mind and of the effects of communication, some psychologists believed they had a unique role to play in such work. In 1942, psychiatrists Edward Strecker and Kenneth Appel urged their colleagues to deploy their understanding of human emotions to stir American morale. They did so however, in terms set by the Nazis. "We need more patriotic music and pageantry; more festivals and rituals," they wrote, calling for events much like Nazi mass rallies. "[C]eremonies should be rich in symbols. It might be objected that symbols are belittling; that they enslave intelligence by chaining it with emotional bonds. In propaganda as elsewhere, symbols are as bad or as good as the things they symbolize."[71]

The question of whether or not to imitate the instrumental communication techniques of fascist propaganda haunted many of Mead's friends and colleagues.[72] In 1939, Rockefeller Foundation officer John Marshall gathered an exceptionally influential group of communications researchers into a monthly "Communications Seminar." Members included Paul Lazarsfeld, Hadley Cantril, Lyman Bryson, Geoffrey Gorer, and Harold Lasswell. Marshall tasked them with two entwined projects: first, identifying and combating fascist propaganda in the United States, and second, identifying a research paradigm for the new field of communication analysis. In the seminar, both projects converged around an instrumental model of the communication process.

According to Marshall, mass media could not help but turn many minds in a single direction. "When millions of people, through the press, the radio, or the motion pictures, are all told the same, or approximately the same thing, at the same time," he argued, "something relatively new in the history of communication happens. . . ." Individual audience members experienced "some response, *en masse*."[73] The challenge was to prevent the Germans from using that fact against Americans, and to empower Americans to use it against their enemies. For these purposes, an essentially ballistic model of communication, in which messages travelled from sender to receiver and had effects when they arrived, seemed ideal.[74]

Not all members of the seminar agreed with this view, however. In late September 1939, Donald Slesinger, a former dean of the social sciences at the University of Chicago, wrote to other members of the seminar, "We have used the language of students and practitioners of propaganda, and have tacitly accepted their objectives. . . . We have been willing, without thought, to sacrifice both truth and human individuality in order to bring about given mass responses to war stimuli. We have thought in terms of fighting dictatorship-by-force through the establishment of dictatorship-by-manipulation."[75] The seminar's July 1940 report called for two-way interactions between leaders and the public, but even this failed to ease the fears of some seminar members. "I suppose we are all jittery these days but [one argument] looks to me like something that Herr Goebbels could put out with complete sincerity," wrote Lyman Bryson. "I believe that the assertion of the democratic principle should be made without any . . . qualification."[76] Rockefeller Foundation officer Joseph Willits agreed. "Our government may be forced to go in as completely for propaganda as has Mr. Goebbels, especially if it goes to war. But the techniques it needs to employ to make its propaganda effective ought not to be described as a vitalizing of democratic procedure. It too much resembles the methods by which democracy has been destroyed."[77]

For Margaret Mead in 1942, instrumental modes of communication, like hierarchical modes of authority, threatened to injure the democratic personality at the heart of the American character and so also America's chances of winning the war. "We must fight and win the war as Americans, not as hastily streamlined, utterly inadequate, imitation Germans or Japs," she wrote. "It's a safe bet that an attempt to make an American adult into an imitation of a Nazi soldier will produce something inferior to a Nazi soldier. We believe that the strength of those who are reared to freedom is greater than the strength of those reared in an authoritarian state."[78]

A THEORY OF THE DEMOCRATIC SURROUND

Mead did not simply critique attempts to imitate fascist propaganda techniques. She and her husband Gregory Bateson proposed a democratic alternative. Drawing on their research and travel, especially in Bali, and on their use of photography and film there, they developed a theory of communication designed specifically to train the perceptual apparatuses of American citizens. Building on field-based, dynamic theories of personality drawn particularly from the work of Kurt Lewin, Gordon Allport and Harry Stack Sullivan, they sought to teach Americans to make and review images and systems of images that would reveal the cultural character of alien others. In place of instrumental, message-driven modes of communication, they developed a theory of what I will call *surrounds*—arrays of images and words built into environments that their audiences could enter freely, act spontaneously within, and leave at will. They also created early examples of such environments in two venues: their massive, illustrated 1942 book *Balinese Character* and their wartime programming for the Museum of Modern Art in New York. In each case, they believed that their work would promote tolerance and psychological flexibility. And it would require their audiences to practice the acts of rational, spontaneous choice that defined the democratic personality.

Margaret Mead and Gregory Bateson first met in 1932 on the shores of the Sepik River in New Guinea, where Mead and her then husband, Reo Fortune, were doing research on a local tribe.[79] Mead soon divorced Fortune and, in 1936, married Bateson. By 1940 the couple was living in New York City, where Mead had worked as a curator of ethnology at the Museum of Natural History. In the wake of the Nazi invasion of Poland, Bateson, a British citizen, started looking for ways to put his experience of other cultures to work somehow for the Allies. He soon found his way to Arthur Upham Pope and was elected secretary of the Committee on National Morale. He also found a position in the film program at the Museum of Modern Art, where he rapidly began to develop film-based training programs for American troops. Over the next two years, Bateson and Mead immersed themselves in the push for morale. Early on, they each wrote and lectured widely, working particularly to distinguish democratic from fascist modes of propaganda. As the war progressed, they found the Allies in a predicament: on the one hand, Allied soldiers very much needed information on the enemy and allied national cultures they would encounter in the field. On the other, because of the fighting, they could hardly send researchers to those places. To solve this problem, Mead and Bateson began to assemble cultural materials from overseas and to study what they called "culture at a distance."[80] They also began to design museum exhibitions and even board games that might help Americans exercise the democratic elements of their personalities.

In all of their ventures, Mead and Bateson sought to combat the instrumental modes of communication and power associated with fascist propaganda. They first laid out their positions on these issues in a series of articles and lectures in 1941 and 1942. Writing jointly, they argued that the state could influence its citizens by three means: "education, morale building, and propaganda."[81] The educator and the morale builder, they argued, worked to develop individual character in ways that supported the patterns of individual cultures as a whole. In keeping with the social psychology of Stack Sullivan, Allport, and others, they asserted that educators and morale builders should attempt to shape individual personalities by shifting the structures of the social relations around them. The propagandist, however, worked differently. As the German example suggested, the propagandist sought to fracture the psyche so as to render the citizen more malleable. "Such manipulations," they wrote, would only "tend in the long run to debase and confuse [propaganda's] victims."[82]

Bateson and Mead nevertheless strongly supported government promotion of American morale. Like Fromm, they sought to balance the need to produce spontaneous, creative individuals with the political imperative of taking concerted national action against fascism. And like Fromm, they suggested that the state could best strike this balance with a mode of communication oriented toward setting a stage for action. If propaganda was a system of messages sent down from above and aimed at shattering the psyche, then the system Mead and Bateson sought was its opposite. "The essential thing," they wrote, "is that this central [state] agency [for morale building] shall not see itself as 'manipulating people.' The moment the central agency begins . . . to see itself as a manipulator of puppets, propaganda becomes inevitable. The only way to avoid this result is to organize the whole system so that the central agency is firmly oriented toward discovering, encouraging, and servicing local initiative."[83]

For Mead and Bateson, though, even the generation of morale-boosting activity from the grass roots wasn't enough. Social scientists had learned that personality structure and social structure were inextricable. In wartime, the success of America's armies would depend on the strength of its psychosocial fabric. The challenge was thus not simply to convince Americans that they should *believe* in an egalitarian, individualistic, and yet unified society. Rather, it was to help Americans *build* one. In September 1941, Mead and Bateson took part in an annual symposium on science, philosophy and religion at Columbia University. In an essay she wrote for the meeting, entitled "The Comparative Study of Culture and the Purposive Cultivation of Democratic Values," Mead argued that social science could help empower the individual, even in a war that would require the exercise of substantial state power:

> Have we then reached a point at which freedom of the individual will and scientific procedure clash? Does not the implementation of a defined direction call for control, and does not control—measured, calculated, definite control; control which really attains its ends—by its very existence invalidate democracy, necessarily raising up some men to exercise the control and degrade all others to be its victims? You can implement loyalty to the state, or rigid conformity to law, habits of uncomplaining industry or absolute obedience to a religious functionary. This has often been done without the aid of science. Fascism is showing us how much more efficiently it can be done with scientific aid. But to implement moral responsibility for the individual means, in effect, the development of a kind of

social order within which moral responsibility will be developed in every child and given free flexible play in the adult. This task is a far more complicated one, yet I think it is possible.[84]

In Mead's view, and in Bateson's, the work of rebuilding society required two unusual efforts on the part of the state. First, political leaders and the scientists who informed them had to set aside particular behavioral targets, as well as instrumental means for producing them. They needed to focus on a *direction* for change rather than on writing a recipe for specific changes. "Only by devoting ourselves to a direction, not a fixed goal, to a process, not a static system, to the development of human beings who will choose and think the choice all-important and be strong, healthy and wise in choosing, can we escape this dilemma," wrote Mead.[85] Second, leaders needed to focus on transforming the perceptual capacities of citizens. As Mead put it, "Cultures have no real existence outside the habituated bodies of those who live in them."[86] For that reason, those who sought to create democratic people and democratic social structures needed to focus on their citizens' abilities to perceive and interact with the social world around them.

In a response to Mead's article printed alongside it in 1942, Bateson made this point with some force. The citizens of the future needed to think of their relations with one another in a noninstrumental and, in that sense, democratic manner. To make that possible, American intellectual and political leaders needed to train citizens' "apperceptive habits, [our] habitual ways of looking at the stream of events of which our own behavior is a part."[87] Part of this work meant training the senses in the arts of seeing and hearing the social world. But it also meant training a deeper faculty, one that could perceive the layers of order underlying society, nature, and the material world. These layers might be formally invisible to the senses, but they could be sensed nonetheless, in the process of interaction.

For Bateson, the key to building both a democratic personality and a democratic culture was the transformation of apperception. This was not the same thing as abandoning political control to grass-roots groups. Nor was it the same as attempting to dictate social change from above. Rather, it was a species of scientific management designed to simultaneously liberate and coordinate the actions of democratic selves. Leaders needed to act like educators, Bateson suggested, and they needed to teach people how to "learn to learn." And that in turn meant reshaping communication. "The events-stream is mediated . . . through language, art, technology, and other cultural media which are structured at every point by tramlines of apperceptive habit," Bateson explained. To transform individuals into the spontaneous actors of democratic personality theory meant to transform the communicative settings in which they lived. For examples on how to do this, researchers could look to foreign cultures that had succeeded in inculcating democratic habits. Or they could turn to the laboratory. As Bateson put it, "We may be able to get a more definite—more operational—definition of such habits as 'free-will' if we ask about each, 'What sort of experimental learning context would we devise in order to inculcate this habit?' 'How would we rig the maze or problem-box so that the anthropomorphic rat shall obtain a repeated and reinforced impression of his own free-will?'"[88]

Though the vision of human beings as rats in a box may chill today, Bateson and Mead both hoped to liberate their fellow citizens. They argued that scientists, and by implication politicians should set a direction for change, build a set of institutional settings in which it might occur, and engage the senses of individuals in seeing into the needs of one another and into the shifting relations of culture, social structure, and their own changing psyches. If fascist society was static and ruled from above, democratic society would be ever-changing and managed via the interplay of the senses. In place of dictators who perverted science to their own instrumental ends, it would feature managers and scientists who could work as partners to free the personalities of citizens and so the culture as a whole. If Nazi Germany's morale was rigid and brittle, America's unity would be muscular and dynamic. If German society and German psyches were authoritarian, American society and American personalities would be egalitarian. They would see and appreciate and tolerate others different from themselves and would be stronger thereby.

In the early years of the war, Bateson and Mead began to design media and communication settings in which to offer American citizens the chance to practice these values. In March 1936, immediately after they married in Singapore, Mead and Bateson traveled to Bali. They intended to study both what Bateson called the "ethos" of the culture and, more specifically, a type of schizoid psychological process they believed characterized the Balinese personality and might shed some light on the roots of schizophrenia in the United States. After two months in the artistic center of Ubud, they moved to the mountain village of Bajoeng Gede, where they worked steadily for a year. They continued to visit Bajoeng Gede off and on, even as they set up households in two other towns, until they left Bali in 1938.

For Mead and Bateson, the Balinese served as a sort of mirror culture against which the anthropologists could test the psychological and social styles of their own. In this respect they resembled Mead's Samoans of a decade before. Yet in the wake of their reading of Benedict's *Patterns of Culture,* Bateson and Mead also saw Bali as a place to explore the relationship of the individual psyche to culture, and of both to media. Ten years earlier, Mead might have done that work as she had in Samoa: by hanging around and interrogating locals. While she certainly did that in Bali as well, she also began to observe the Balinese with a new visual rigor. Franz Boas had once told Mead that if he studied the Balinese, he would focus on their gestures.[89] And so Mead began to observe the movements of her subjects especially closely. She sat and watched for hours as mothers tended their children, children played with one another, and the village went about its daily business. Bateson went further. While Mead scribbled notes, he moved among the villagers with two cameras, one a 35-millimeter Leica for still images and the other a 16-millimeter motion picture camera. Over the course of their years in Bali, he and Mead would create some twenty-five thousand still pictures and about twenty-two thousand feet of film footage.[90]

They recorded their work in a 1942 volume entitled *Balinese Character: A Photographic Analysis*, published by the New York Academy of Sciences. The book included 759 photographs—only eight of which, the authors noted, had been "posed."[91] Their subjects ranged from babies nursing to men grooming fighting cocks to crowds massing on the beach and dancers waving in trance, and each featured a caption describing the action, largely written by Bateson. The book opened with a long essay by Mead entitled "Balinese Character." In it, Mead makes clear that she and Bateson subscribed to neither Freudian nor strictly behaviorist accounts of personality. Rather, they subscribed to a vision of the self much in line with the topological psychiatry of Kurt Lewin and the social psychology of Harry Stack Sullivan.

Mead organized her essay in the same nine categories in which she and Bateson would next array their images: "Spatial Orientation and Levels," "Learning," "Integration and Disintegration of the Body," "Orifices of the Body," "Autocosmic Play," "Parents and Children," "Siblings," "Stages of Child Development," "*Rites de Passage.*" In each case, she refused to separate the development of an individual subject's personality from the cultural context in which she met it. Balinese character, in Mead's view, could only be perceived at the moment when the structures of social relations met patterns of bodily movement and emotional expression. Like Stack Sullivan, Mead and Bateson worked only with what they could see. They made no claims about invisible, biologically driven psychological forces such as the ego, the superego, or the id, or for ostensibly universal psychosocial patterns such as the Oedipus conflict. Rather, they sought to observe individual behavior and cultural structures as interlocking patterns at the moments in which they came together.

In her essay, Mead pointed to dance training as one of the richest of these patterns. The Balinese had long cultivated complex, difficult dances, and had trained children to perform them. Sometimes the children danced while in trances—a phenomenon especially interesting to Mead and Bateson because of their belief that trance and schizophrenia were related. For Mead, the training of the dancer modeled the entire process of personality formation among the Balinese. It was, as she put it, "the prototype of Balinese learning."[92] Dancers learned through all of their senses simultaneously. "The flexible body of the dancing pupil is twisted and turned in the teacher's hands," she wrote. "Teacher and pupil go through the proper gesture, then suddenly the teacher springs aside, leaving the pupil to continue the pattern to which he has surrendered himself, sometimes with the teacher continuing it so that the pupil can watch him as he dances. Learning with the eyes flows directly from learning passively while one's own body is manipulated by another."[93] Culture entered the young dancers through their eyes and through the touch of their teachers; as they danced in the village, their bodies moved in patterns set not by a universal human physiognomy, but by the patterns of Balinese culture. For Mead and Bateson, to have a "Balinese character" was just this: to literally embody the symbolic order of Balinese culture and to choose its patterns as your own.

In other words, Mead's Balinese were both well adjusted to their societies and free. A firm and complex social structure set a stage on which they could enjoy rich creative lives, strong families, and healthy communities. This was not paradise—as Mead and Bateson pointed out, the children were filthy by urban American standards; the mothers often taunted their children and pushed them away; fear and passivity haunted the villagers. But it was a culture organized around noninstrumental modes of control and communication. The Balinese did not make each other do things, in Mead's account; rather, they showed each other how things were done. The distinction came clearest in Mead's account of Balinese storytelling. Whereas in America, one person generally told a story while another listened, in Bali, storytellers and their audiences recounted tales together. "The Balinese story teller does not continue gaily along through a long tale," wrote Mead, " . . . but he makes a simple statement, 'There was once a princess,' to which his auditors answer, 'Where did she live?' or 'What was her name?' and so on, until the narrative has been communicated in dialogue."[94]

To an American audience threatened by the hierarchical, instrumental power of fascist propaganda and fascist armies, a vision of a community living in dialogue must have held enormous appeal as a political prototype. Mead and Bateson and their publishers, the New York Academy of Sciences, certainly thought it did. On the volume's first page, they conspicuously dated its publication to the first anniversary of Pearl Harbor: December 7, 1942. By studying the Balinese, Bateson and Mead had made visible a society that differed vastly from the United States, and which at the same time could be known, enjoyed, and learned from by Americans. In their book they offered their own ethnographic tactics as models of the sort of apperceptive habits that could produce democratic personalities. In other words, they taught their readers to look with their eyes at Balinese individuals so as to see more deeply with their minds into the cultural order that animated them. In the process, they gave their readers a glimpse of the sort of postwar world they might be fighting for, and of the role Americans might play in it.

They also introduced photography and film as tools for making visible the character of alien cultures, and for training Americans in a democratic mode of seeing. In a long set of notes to the photographs and captions in *Balinese Character*, Bateson explained that he and Mead had tried to work in a way that would erase their subjects' self-consciousness. "We tried to shoot what happened normally and spontaneously, rather than to decide upon the norms and then get Balinese to go through these behaviors in suitable lighting," he wrote. "We treated cameras in the field as recording instruments, not as devices for illustrating our theses."[95] In this respect, their work differed from common documentary practice at the time. But it was in keeping with the understanding of the relationship between culture and personality both brought with them from their time in New Guinea. Personality and culture revealed themselves in patterns. That is, the interactions of individuals served as visual emblems of the ethos of their group. Thanks to its technological affordances, the camera could record visual patterns with a scientific neutrality. Suddenly it could transform the scientific gaze of the anthropologist into a two-dimensional representation—of visible behavioral patterns and, behind them, of cultural patterns too.

Recording the scientific insights of the anthropologist in visual form was only half the battle, however. In *Balinese Character*, Mead and Bateson sought to present these images in a way that would transform readers into pattern-recognizers in their own right. Photography promised to make the Balinese cultural ethos visible with minimal distortion. Individual images revealed standard postures and poses. But Mead and Bateson arranged their images in densely patterned sequences across their book. Each page of images faced a page of captions. Though each pairing is part of the larger analytical framework outlined by Mead in her opening essay, each pairing also stands independently, as a visual and linguistic array. No image is given precedence over any other. The moments themselves appear exceptionally ordinary. Far from the nostalgia conjured up by, say, a tourist snapshot, these images draw the eye in several directions at once. The reader, like the anthropologist, must take in a stream of moments and,

FIGURE 2.2.

Margaret Mead and Gregory Bateson hoped that photographs could reveal expressions of Balinese character, and that patterns of photographs on the page could help readers synthesize an understanding of Balinese culture as if they were anthropologists themselves. This page was labeled "Female Adolescence I." Photographs by Gregory Bateson. *Balinese Character*, 217. Courtesy of the New York Academy of Sciences and the Bateson Idea Group.

at the same time, pay attention to each individual image. They must see the behavior of the Balinese with their eyes and, at the same time, come to know the order of Balinese society by immersing themselves in the paginated village of the book itself.

With *Balinese Character*, Mead and Bateson groped toward a new and specifically democratic genre of communication. No instrumentally powerful narrator demanded that the reader glance at one image or another.

No dictator tugged at the reader's heartstrings or tried to paint a picture of racial differences. No one perverted the scientific gaze. Mead and Bateson simply presented images and captions as a form of evidence. They set a visual and textual stage and, with constraints, left it up to the reader to decide what script to act out on it. The default point of view would be their own: the images and captions called for the reader to play anthropologist. But it would also demand that the reader practice the skills on which the democratic personality depended in the early years of World War II: spontaneous choice, the recognition and appreciation of the cultural and personality patterns of others, the ability to see unity in diversity.

The understandings and uses of photography and text that they developed in *Balinese Character* formed the basis of much of Mead and Bateson's morale-building work during the war. In the Museum of Modern Art's film department, Bateson worked alongside German refugee film critic Siegfried Kracauer reading German films in the same terms in which he urged readers to examine his photos of Bali.[96] In part, like Kracauer, he sought to understand what made Germany and other nations unique. But he also aimed to turn the museum's film collection into a tool for training military specialists before they went abroad. In Bateson's view, even fictional films encapsulated the cultures of their makers. They were made by teams, after all, and if they were to be popular at all, they would need to express widely shared assumptions. Moreover, they granted American audiences a glimpse of the ways in which patterns of individual behavior echoed those of national cultures. For Bateson, as for Ruth Benedict, national culture and individual personality seemed to mirror each other; film provided a window on this process. It did so, however, for political ends. After the war, Bateson explained in one memo, Americans might need to create "fundamental changes in the underlying structures of some of these cultures."[97] To do so, they needed to transform soldiers into what amounted to military anthropologists.

In his lectures and writings on German film, Bateson managed to defuse its propaganda power. Far from being the hypnotic medium so feared in the American press of the late 1930s, film became the ground of culture itself, a landscape open to observation. The viewer in turn became not a victim of the enemy's hysteria, but its analyst. In 1943, Bateson created that experience in three dimensions at the Museum of Modern Art. Working with Bauhaus refugee designer Xanti Schawinsky, he took images and artifacts depicted in *Balinese Character* and arrayed them into an exhibition entitled *Bali, Background for War: The Human Problem of Reoccupation*. The show included many of the images and notes he had created for the book, but this time, Bateson aimed them at an audience that might soon be going overseas. One of the first labels in the exhibition alerted Americans that when they occupied foreign lands they would need to pay special attention to how people learned. Only by doing so—first by examining media here, and second by observing people in the field—could Americans learn enough about foreigners to "teach them."[98]

By 1943 Mead and Bateson were part of an enormous wartime transfusion of social scientists into the business of analyzing and making propaganda. Yet they sought not so much to influence the attitudes of citizens by delivering pro-American messages as to build symbolic environments in which Americans could make meanings for themselves. Mead made the distinction most clearly in a wartime discussion of American eating routines. Because they had come from so many different cultures, she explained, Americans could not be served by a single restaurant; rather, they would need to have their food choices arrayed before them cafeteria-style, and pick and choose their own diets. In a sense, Mead and Bateson helped pioneer a "cafeteria" style of media representation based on just this understanding of American character. If instrumentalists believed that mass media delivered messages on a single theme and tended to turn their audiences into automata, Mead and Bateson argued that multi-image, multi-text environments like the one they had constructed in *Balinese Character* or the one Bateson and Schawinsky mounted in their exhibition gave viewers the chance to exercise democratic choice.

They also identified museums as key sites at which to do that work. In 1941, Mead drafted an article entitled "Museums in the Emergency" for *Natural History* magazine. Americans, she explained, had been bombarded by advertising and by propaganda. They had grown suspicious of all mass media. But they still trusted museums. Unlike their mass media cousins, museums did not distort the truth of science. Nor did they even attempt to communicate it instrumentally. Rather, they created settings in which audiences could explore the world around them and, through interaction with it, experience themselves as independent truth seekers. As Mead put it, "They go out from the doors of the Museum believing in one of the foundations of democracy, that it is possible, by slow, honest, exact study to find out more about man and the world in which he lives. For an hour or so they have been able to trust their eyes and let their minds rove over materials which have not been arranged to impress, to convert, to push them around, but merely to tell them as much of the truth as is now known, and that quietly."[99]

For that reason, Mead and other members of the Committee for National Morale envisioned the museum as the proper setting for a new kind of propaganda: one that would nurture both the individual democratic personality and the collective sense of national purpose. In 1941, Mead and her colleagues on the committee planned an exhibition on the theme of "democracy" for the Museum of Modern Art. The exhibition was never built, but the planning documents still serve as a comprehensive statement of the logic behind developing surround-based media for propaganda purposes. In an unpublished manuscript entitled "The Psychology of Such an Exhibit," most likely drafted by Mead, the members took a strong line against appealing to the emotions of their audience. To do so, they argued, would be to ape the fascists. Rather, they ought to do what museums did best. "In the movies or in listening to the radio, the spectator is the passive recipient of whatever stimuli are flung at him, and, whatever he may digest of the message, he will at least spend his hour learning passivity," they wrote. In a museum, the spectator was active. And in the months before the United States entered World War II, the need to activate Americans was uppermost in the committee's mind. "The primary need at the moment is . . . to free the individual citizen from his fear of being moved, to restore to the individual his belief that HE CAN MAKE CHOICES, HE IS NOT JUST A HELPLESS MUSICAL INSTRUMENT ON WHICH THE PROPAGANDIST PLAYS WHATEVER TUNE HE WISHES" [capitalization original].

Here, then, Mead and the committee found a prescription for the democratic surround. A visitor to an exhibition on democracy, they wrote, "should be able to choose his own pace; to pull levers to make machines work; and to express his opinion of exhibits and of their meaning (e.g. as in voting for the 'best' picture at [the] World's Fair). It is very important that in an exhibit of democracy, the spectator should *not* be and should not feel himself to be under the thumb of the exhibitor." And the exhibition itself should be a multi-mediated affair. If it brought together pictures, sculptures, words, and music, it could "invoke a fuller response from the personality. It can appeal simultaneously both to the intellect and to the emotions, and is therefore specially appropriate as a medium for encouraging the view that democracy might be an expression not only of emotions (as in totalism) nor of the intellect (as in Machiavellian political planning) but of the whole personality."[100]

3

The New Language of Vision

The social scientists of the Committee for National Morale were excellent theorists. They could articulate the nature of a democratic personality, of democratic morale, and of communication practices that might encourage both—in *words*. With the exception of Mead and Bateson, however, they lacked hands-on familiarity with the media technologies that could transform their ideas into visual modes of communication. For that, they would have to depend on another community: the refugee artists and designers of the Bauhaus. At the same moment in which American government officials and social scientists were focused on developing Americans' will to confront fascism, the former members of the Bauhaus were busy integrating themselves into America's intellectual and artistic elites. As they made their way in the New World, these artists turned the theoretical and practical tools they had developed in Germany toward the work of promoting American ideals and American morale.

Today the designers of the Bauhaus are perhaps best remembered for fusing art and technology and for spawning the mass-produced modernism that dominated the design of much American architecture, furniture, and advertising in the second half of the twentieth century. The glass-and-steel-box office buildings of Walter Gropius, the aluminum-tube chairs of Marcel Breuer, the simplified "universal alphabet" typescript of Herbert Bayer—each has become a ubiquitous memento of a time in which the artists of the Bauhaus glimpsed the possibility of an industrially manufactured utopia. When they established their school in 1919, however, the founders of the Bauhaus conceived of their project in terms that were simultaneously therapeutic and communalist as well as aesthetic. That is, they wanted their school to produce not only a new kind of design, but a new community of designers, and above all a new kind of person.

First, its founders hoped to train craftsmen who might integrate the many specialties associated with industrial design. Such transdisciplinary workers might then design material goods in such a way as to help break down the fractured, isolating social order of the modern industrial era and restore to its members a sense of community. Second, as part of that project, the founders of the Bauhaus hoped to transform the psychology of their students. The hyperspecialization of the industrial world had driven their students toward a psychological narrowness and an inability to integrate sensations, emotions, and analytical thought. Bauhaus teaching thus needed to help develop a student's "whole personality."[1] Bauhaus products, too, would ideally promote the integration of the psyche. Whether in architecture, in photography, or on the stage, Bauhaus leaders created environments in which they required individual viewers to knit together a diverse array of visual experiences and so come to a coherent sense of the world around them and of themselves.

In 1933 the Nazis closed the Bauhaus, objecting to its members' ostensibly degenerate penchants for abstraction and collectivism. By the end of the 1930s, many of the most prominent members had migrated to the United States. As World War II got under way, the former teachers of the Bauhaus, and particularly László Moholy-Nagy and Herbert Bayer, applied these techniques to helping make the personalities of American citizens more democratic and the nation as a whole more committed to confronting fascism. Drawing on tactics first developed to challenge the visual and social chaos of industrial Europe, they built environments—in books, in museum exhibitions, in classrooms, and in their own photographs, paintings, and designs—that modeled the principles of democratic persuasion that were being articulated by American social scientists at the same moment. These environments became prototypes for the propaganda pavilions that the United States government would construct overseas throughout the Cold War. Ultimately, they helped set the visual terms on which the generation of 1968 would seek its own psychological liberation.

THE BAUHAUS: TRAINING THE SENSES OF THE NEW MAN

To understand how former members of the Bauhaus might have turned toward the promotion of American morale in the early war years, and to understand why their aesthetics might have appealed to an American public not then known for its embrace of the European avant-garde, it is important to remember that from its earliest days the Bauhaus was preoccupied with creating what Walter Gropius called "the new human type of the future" and what Moholy called simply "the whole man."[2] At the professional level, this new man would integrate skills that had become the property of narrow specialists. Having done so, he would then be prepared to reintegrate form and function. He could do away with the frivolous decorations of nineteenth-century architecture and, for that matter, with his own frivolous attachment to the identity of the Romantic artist. "The work of the new man will become an organic part of unified industrial production," wrote Gropius.[3] And ideally, it would do for ordinary citizens what it had already done for the designer himself: restore their visual and thus psychological balance. The ultimate aim of the Bauhaus, Gropius later wrote, was to achieve "a new cultural equilibrium of our visual environment," and so to improve the health and happiness of its inhabitants.[4]

For Gropius and the other early Bauhaus masters, the objects of industrial design and of art, plagued as they were by divisions between the functional and ornamental, mirrored the structure of the design professions, which had also become overspecialized. The gaps between specialties, in turn, mirrored a larger pattern of fractures in modern society and within the modern individual as well. Just as industrial society had detached individual artisans from the community of craftsmen, so the industrial world had driven modern individuals to let go of their own authentic impulses and of the natural unity between their sense-experience and their reason.

In the school's early years, the professors of the Bauhaus hoped to heal all of these fractures simultaneously. The Bauhaus was to be a living example of a classless society of creative individuals. These workers were to create *Gesamtkunstwerke*—works of art that integrated multiple production techniques and spoke to the multiple perceptual faculties of their audiences. Nineteenth-century society had broken Germany apart; in the years after World War I the Bauhaus hoped to put it back together again, as a collective built around individual creativity and managed through design. "Let's create a new guild of craftsmen, without the class distinctions which raise an arrogant barrier between craftsmen and artists," they announced in a founding manifesto. "Together let us conceive and create the new building of the future, which will embrace architecture and sculpture and painting in one unity which will rise one day toward heaven from the hands of a million workers like the crystal symbol of a new faith."[5]

For Gropius and his colleagues, the key to building a unified, classless society and to creating the whole man was design. To the founders of the Bauhaus, the Romantic artist, standing on the ramparts, daring society to return to an agrarian idyll, cut a ridiculous figure. So too did the artist's mode of agency. In the Romantic account, an individual of genius reached into his soul, pulled forth some unique, indwelling bit of character, and gave it form in a singular work of art. The essence of the Romantic mode, as least as understood by the Bauhaus, was instrumental and individualistic: geniuses transformed spiritual raw material into polished art in order to express themselves. The Bauhaus mode, on the other hand, depended on an environmental model of power and a collective form of agency. As Gropius put it, many in the Bauhaus believed that "creative freedom does not reside in the infinitude of means of expression, but in free movement within its strictly legal bounds."[6] Unlike the Romantic artist, the Bauhaus designer would integrate himself into the industrial process—and accept its limitations on his range of expressive options. What he made would in turn set boundaries for the movement of individuals and so, paradoxically, free them to express themselves within society and not only as rebels against it.

Both the design of materials that might free their users and the training of designers themselves required an education of the senses. The professors of the Bauhaus did this work primarily in their required first-year course. The class was first taught by a mystic, Johannes Itten, and after 1923 jointly by Moholy-Nagy and painter Josef Albers. Under Moholy and Albers the course covered work in basic visual forms and in particular media: stone, wood, metal, clay, glass, color (conceived as a medium), and textiles. The workshop was not meant to be a ladder up which the student climbed toward a mastery of certain skills, though in part it did accomplish that. Rather, it was meant first and foremost to enable students to discover their own authentic interests and abilities—the inner core of their creative selves. "The preliminary course concerns the student's whole personality," explained a 1922 summary, "since it seeks to liberate him, to make him stand on his own feet, and makes it possible for him to gain a knowledge of both material and form through direct experience."[7]

For the masters of the Bauhaus, the liberation of a student's creative potential depended on his ability to *recognize* his affinity with some element of the world outside him and to *choose* to pursue it. Bauhaus publications of the 1920s routinely visualized this understanding by depicting the preliminary course as a circle, with the student implicitly at its center. In the first ring he would find new materials to work with: clay, stone, and the like. Beyond that, he would engage the abstract, elemental forms on which visual harmony depended. And still further out, in a third ring, he would encounter more traditional academic subjects: the analysis of nature, elements of engineering, and issues in what we would now call materials science. In each case, Bauhaus instructors would set these subjects out like a banquet and watch as individual students moved freely among them, choosing and so developing psychologically and professionally. To put it another way, at a curricular level the teachers of the early Bauhaus did not tell their students what to do so much as they created the conditions under which they could choose what to do from a cafeteria of options. Students could thus find their way to authentic free expression of their innermost selves, but in terms set by the needs of industry and society. At the same time, students could also integrate their exposure to various skills into their professional practices, and their exposure to different sensations into their personalities. They could, in short, become whole.

Of all the senses addressed in the preliminary course, the one that would go on to have the greatest impact on Americans in search of morale was vision. In the years before the Bauhaus instructors moved to America, two who would have an extraordinary influence here—Moholy and Bayer—developed modes of visual display that echoed the experiential ideals of the preliminary course. In the first mode, which he called the "New Vision," Moholy mingled the utopian ideals and montage aesthetics of Russian Constructivism with new photographic and typographic techniques to produce a wildly vertiginous aesthetic. In the second, which built on both Moholy's work and its Constructivist origins, Bayer developed a new mode of museum display. Whereas museums had traditionally hung images at eye level, Bayer began to enlarge photographs and words, to hang them above and below the viewer's line of sight, and so to expand the viewer's array of visual choices.

These techniques would become tools for democratic modes of propaganda during and after World War II for two reasons. First, artists like Moholy and Bayer had to make a living in mid-century America, and to do so, they aggressively applied the techniques they brought with them to intellectual and professional opportunities they found here. Second, Moholy's "New Vision" and Bayer's "field of vision" techniques solved a problem for American promoters of morale. If fascist communication worked instrumentally and molded individuals into a single, unthinking mass, these Bauhaus modes of seeing were designed to do the reverse: like the preliminary course, they demanded that individuals reach out into an array of images and knit them back together in their own minds. In the process, they could reform both their own fractured psyches and, potentially, society itself. For Moholy and Bayer, as for Gropius, art and the technologies of artmaking offered environments in which individuals could experience themselves as simultaneously more completely individuated *and* more integrated into society.

LÁSZLÓ MOHOLY-NAGY AND THE NEW VISION

As a young man, Moholy embraced Russian Constructivism and, with it, the notion that making art meant making social revolution.[8] A painter and graphic designer born and raised in Hungary, Moholy left Hungary in 1919 and moved to Berlin, where he travelled in circles that included Dadaists, various modernist literati, and the Russian Constructivists El Lissitzky and Naum Gabo.[9] Together, the Constructivists turned away from academic realism and toward the construction of abstract forms. They were to imitate the shapes of industry if they imitated any shapes at all, and they were to make their peace with machines. "To be a user of machines is to be of the Spirit of the Century," wrote Moholy in 1922. "Before the machine, everyone is equal. . . . This is the root of socialism, the final liquidation of feudalism."[10] For Moholy and other Constructivists, to create abstract assemblages was to turn the senses and the intellects of their viewers toward utopia. Theo van Doesburg, a Dutch artist living in Berlin at the time and a friend of Moholy, celebrated the Constructivists' goals in a 1921 manifesto: "Theirs is the language of the mind, and in this manner they understand each other. . . . The International of the Mind is an inner experience which cannot be translated into words. It does not consist of a torrent of vocables but of plastic creative acts and inner or intellectual force, which thus creates a newly shaped world."[11]

Moholy brought this twinning of psychological and social revolution to the Bauhaus when he joined the faculty and began teaching its preliminary course in 1923. Under the previous instructor, Johannes Itten, the preliminary course had included exercises in breathing and meditation as well as craft technique.[12] Under Moholy, the course lost its mystical tone but retained Itten's insistence on the unity of artistic and psychological development. That fusion, Moholy believed, could transform the organization of society. "Through technique man can be freed, if he finally realizes the purpose: a balanced life through free use of his liberated energies," wrote Moholy some years later.[13] Technique, he suggested, could help individuals bring together the senses of their biological organisms and the critical impulses of their reasoning minds. Thus strengthened, individuals could resist the imperatives of received authority and the demands of narrow specialists. They could find what Moholy called "a plan of life which places the individual rightly within his community."[14]

Moholy taught at the Bauhaus from 1923 to 1928. Outside the classroom in the same years he explored photography, typographic montage, and the sculptural powers of light. These new modes of communication represented a qualitative break from the realistic representation offered by painting, he believed. Photography in particular made it possible for a person to see objectively for the first time. No longer would the viewer have to behold the world through the sensibility of the painter. Instead, the camera could so automate vision as to extend the viewer's senses in the direction of reason: "The camera is the objective presentation of facts,"

Moholy explained, and so "makes [the onlooker] more apt to form his own opinions" about reality.[15] As such, the camera could become an instrument of public mental health: thanks to its objectivity, wrote Moholy, "the hygiene of the optical, the health of the visible is slowly filtering through."[16]

For Moholy, as for a range of American critics in the 1920s and 1930s, the mass media were enemies of visual and mental health. In a 1934 letter to his Hungarian friend and sometime editor Frantisek Kalivoda, Moholy explained that "a widely organized and rapid news service today bombards the public with every kind of news. . . . Without interest in evolution it overwhelms its public with sensations. If there are no sensations, they are freely invented or deliberately improvised." The average newspaper reader encountered its daily texts with little more than a mild interest, Moholy believed; its stimuli made the reader numb.[17] In his attack on newspapers and radio, Moholy identified an instrumental mode of communication much like the one that American critics of the late 1930s would associate with German propaganda. In his view, mass media sent out messages to which readers responded like puppets: they became unable to think and unable to resist the authorities around them.

Moholy's critique of the mass media contained within it an implicitly Freudian understanding of the mass media's power. In his account, mass media stimulated the internal regions of the psyche in ways of which the individual was unconscious. By contrast, his own work manifested a Gestaltist understanding of the mind. In this view, perception itself became the means by which a person created his or her inner life. As in the field psychology of Kurt Lewin or the personality theories of Gordon Allport and the neo-Freudians Horney, Stack Sullivan, and Fromm, Gestaltists like Moholy believed that the person was always a work in progress, and that the individual psyche changed and grew in relation to the environment around it. This process depended on the ability of the person to apprehend that environment through the sense organs—the eyes, ears, nose, fingertips, and tongue. It was the senses, after all, that tugged on the individual threads of experience and drew them inward to be woven into the psyche.

For Moholy, media technologies could serve as extensions of the sense organs. The 35-millimeter camera, for example, enabled viewers to extend their range of vision. As it did, it presented viewers with opportunities to become more conscious of their places in space and time. When they looked at his photographs, and so in a sense looked through his camera's lens, Moholy believed his viewers could not only see more of the world around them, but integrate what they saw into a more complete picture of reality.

Moholy's photographs showed little resemblance to the straight documentary gaze that Americans would associate with "reality" in coming years. On the contrary, he aimed his lens downward from dizzying towers and outward through patterns of girders. He made strange patterns of objects on paper, called photograms, that seemed to be half X-ray and half ghost. He also began to mingle typographic designs with photographic imagery in a style he called "typophoto."[18] Like his photographs, his typophoto images transformed two-dimensional surfaces into seemingly three-dimensional environments. They were not pictures *of* a three-dimensional world so much as worlds unto themselves. Moholy's desire to spatialize visual experience extended to his work with light. For Moholy, light did not simply illuminate the material world; it could be a materially structuring force in its own right. Light could surround individual people and free their senses to such a degree that they could finally comprehend their places in the universal space-time continuum.[19] In a 1917 poem, Moholy foreshadowed the ecstasies of the countercultural light shows of the 1960s when he exclaimed, "Light, total light, creates the total man."[20]

In 1928, Moholy published a volume in which he summarized his ideals and which in its design exemplified them, *The New Vision*. The volume outlined the stages of the preliminary course as Moholy taught it, and it included photographs of students' work. But it was much more than an aesthetic primer. According to Moholy, it was a guide to human evolution. Before the industrial era, he argued, "primitive man" had used all of his faculties constantly.[21] Now he had to specialize. As a result, he could no longer see reality whole, nor could he see, feel, and think simultaneously. The preliminary course at the Bauhaus aimed to restore those abilities; so too did *The New Vision*. In its pages, photographs and text mingled promiscuously. Photographs might be straight documentary images, or they might be montages. Text might be ordinary, bold, or a mixture of the two.

And the images depicted everything from tabletop constructions to the frame of a dirigible. Taken as a whole, the book was more collage than linear text. Like the preliminary course, it offered readers a way to stand in a circle of visual and textual signs, selecting those that engaged them, and pulling them together into a whole and substantially enlarged view of their place in the world.

HERBERT BAYER AND THE EXTENDED FIELD OF VISION

The New Vision was translated into English and republished soon after Moholy migrated to America in 1937, and it went on to have an extraordinary influence on American photography and design. In the years in which he was writing it, though, Moholy's visual tactics and the Constructivist ideals they embodied had a substantial influence on a Bauhaus student and later instructor, Herbert Bayer. Born in Vienna in 1900, Bayer came to the Bauhaus as a student in 1921. He had read Wassily Kandinsky's book *Concerning the Spiritual in Art,* in which Kandinsky called for a new kind of art, one that would turn away from materialist concerns and toward the cultivation of spirituality in its makers and its audiences. Bayer mistakenly believed that Kandinsky was already teaching at the Bauhaus (he wouldn't join the faculty until 1922) and he hoped to study with him.[22] Bayer stayed at the Bauhaus until 1923, traveled for a year, and then returned to the Bauhaus as the head of the typography workshop. He would teach there until 1928.

As an instructor at the Bauhaus, Bayer absorbed the aesthetic theories of his colleagues, and especially Moholy, as well as their social-utopian and pro-industrial orientations.[23] Before Bayer took over the typography workshop, it had focused on hand printing and small-scale letterpress work.[24] Bayer quickly found industrial printing gear and oriented the students' work in a more pre-professional direction. At the same time, he turned his own work in the direction of Moholy's typophoto aesthetics. Like Moholy, he aimed to make type easier for readers to read and for printers to work with. He thus turned away from the Gothic German script of the period and developed the "universal alphabet" that would become a hallmark of Bauhaus publications after 1925.[25] At the same time, he experimented with ways in which to combine typography and photography and to spatialize the two-dimensional picture plane. His posters for Bauhaus dances, for example, layered images and text one on top of the other in ways that transformed the surface of the paper into a well in which the visual elements of Bayer's compositions seemed to float at different depths. Even his more two-dimensional works such as letterheads featured a geometric, architectural sensibility. His images and texts did not look as if they had been drawn or even printed; they looked as if they had been built.

Such designs matched well with both Bauhaus director Gropius's emphasis on architecture and Moholy's Constructivist ideals. Just how well would not become clear, however, until all three had left the Bauhaus. In 1930, art critic and curator Alexander Dorner asked Walter Gropius to organize Germany's contribution to the pan-European *Exposition de la Société des Artistes Décorateurs* at the Grand Palais in Paris.[26] Gropius in turn commissioned former Bauhaus colleagues Bayer, Moholy, and Marcel Breuer to assist him. Together they designed a "community center" to be included as part of an apartment building.[27] Gropius designed the public spaces; Breuer furnished an imaginary apartment; Moholy created exhibitions of stage and ballet materials, architectural photography, and lighting fixtures. Bayer created installations of everyday objects that could be mass-produced.

Conventional exhibition practice of the time suggested that Bayer should arrange his objects and images either at eye level or as they might be seen in an actual living room. Building on the Gestaltist visual sensibility outlined in Moholy's *New Vision*, as well as in an earlier exhibition by El Lissitzky, Bayer took a radically different tack. As he prepared the blueprints for his part of the exhibition, he drew a picture of man whose head was nothing but a giant eyeball. In front of the man he drew some seventeen screens—some arrayed at eye level, but others angled down from the ceiling and still others angled up from the ground. Entitled "Diagram of Field of Vision," the image was later reprinted in a catalog of the exhibition. It also became the basis of Bayer's installation for the Paris show. In his gallery of furniture and architecture, Bayer hung rows of chairs from the walls and arrayed enlarged photographs of buildings in front of, above, and beneath the eyes of the spectator.

By today's standards, such an innovation might seem mild, even trivial. In a time in which digital screens bombard us with images from every conceivable angle and in places as diverse as football stadiums, airplanes, and bedrooms, it is difficult to imagine how important Bayer's new strategy actually was. In essence, he had found a way to transform Moholy's New Vision into a three-dimensional environment. In the early 1920s, fans of the Bauhaus or of Moholy might have celebrated the ways in which they blended text and image to create the illusion of depth on the page. But in Paris, Bayer created something that was no illusion; it was an actual, three-dimensional space into which the viewer could walk. Five years later, he extended that environment to include the ground below the viewers' feet and the area over their heads. In 1935, Bayer worked again with Gropius, Breuer, and Moholy, this time to construct the *Baugewerkschafts Ausstellung* (Building Workers' Unions Exhibition) in Berlin. Once again, he designed an environment that would extend the range of the visitors' visual field. And once again, as he planned, he drew a man whose head had been transformed into an eyeball. This time though, the viewer stood on a slightly raised platform and screens surrounded him on all sides. They looked up from below and down from above. They hung in front of him and behind him. In this new drawing, the visual field and the three-dimensional world itself were virtually contiguous.[28]

In both exhibitions, the material world of chairs and buildings had been transformed into a semiotic universe. Wrenched from their ordinary, everyday physical places, chairs on the wall and oversized photographs became a kind of three-dimensional typescript. But they produced no message, no instrumental instructions for their viewers. Rather, like Moholy's photomontages, or like the different materials from the preliminary course at the Bauhaus, they offered observers the chance to identify and integrate into their psyches those elements of the visual field they found most meaningful. By the mainstream standards of the time, hanging chairs on the wall might have looked like a bit of visual cacophony; yet in the context of the New Vision, it gave viewers the chance to synthesize their perceptions and so create in themselves a state of visual and emotional balance. If mass media tended to trigger the unconscious desires mapped by Freud and thus

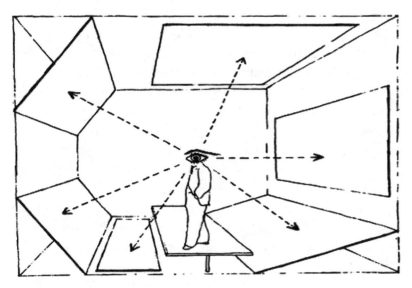

FIGURE 3.1.
Herbert Bayer, "Diagram of 360 Degrees of Vision," 1935. © 2011 Artists Rights Society (ARS), New York / VG Bild-Kunst, Bonn.

make viewers numb, the displays pioneered by Bayer were meant to make museumgoers active synthesizers of the world around.

Part of the appeal of Bayer's work for Americans grew out of the ways in which Bayer situated his installations in relation to the two political extremes of avant-garde display in the 1930s: the communist and the fascist. Bayer was not the first designer to enlarge photographs or to array them top to bottom on a wall. In 1928 he had attended the International Press Exhibition in Cologne, where he saw El Lissitzky's massive photo mural "The Task of the Press Is the Education of the Masses" in the Soviet pavilion, as well as photographs hung on wires dropped from the ceiling and towering pillars bedecked with images. Bayer later recalled that it was Lissitzky's installations that inspired him to take up exhibition design.[29] At the same time, however, he thought Lissitzky's design was "chaotic."[30] Though Bayer adopted Lissitzky's environmental orientation, he fused it with a Gestaltist visual sensibility and, beyond that, a desire for artistic control. "An exhibition can be compared with the book," he later wrote, "insofar as the pages of the book are moved to pass by the reader's eye, while in an exhibition the visitor moves in the process of viewing the displays."[31]

Though Bayer thought of himself as an author and, in that sense, sought to control his audience's movements and point them to certain conclusions, he was also careful to leave plenty of room for the reader to interpret his text. "The physical means by which the content of exhibits is brought to the attention of the visitor should not in themselves be autocratic or domineering," as he later put it.[32] In the 1930s, utopian Constructivists were not the only ones staging spectacular exhibitions. Fascists, and particularly Italian fascists, were equally fascinated by the power of surrounding viewers with images to influence their ideals. Like Bayer, they arrayed images from floor to ceiling in such a way that they required viewers to crane their necks to see what was above them, or to peer down to their toes to see the imagery there.

Yet despite the fact that they shared a totalizing, environmental orientation toward display, Bayer's images extended the viewer's field of vision to present a distinct alternative to fascist aesthetics, politics, and psychology. In 1932, for instance, the Italians mounted a massive exhibition in Rome to celebrate the tenth anniversary of the fascists' march on the Italian capital.[33] Along one wall, designer Giuseppe Terragni installed a huge photomontage that featured many of the elements common to El Lissitzky's pro-communist imagery: large crowds, a blending of text and image, a mix of abstraction and realism. But far from offering the eye a set of images for the viewer to bring together in his own independent mind, as Bayer recommended, Terragni's wall did the work of integration *on behalf of* the viewer. As the viewer moved from right to left along the wall, he saw crowds of individuals slowly morph first into turbines and then into an abstract field of hands raised in the fascist salute.

Like Bayer—and, for that matter, like Moholy, Gropius, and many at the Bauhaus—fascist designers like Terragni were preoccupied with the relationship of the individual to the social whole. But unlike their Bauhaus counterparts, the fascists sought to *de*-individuate their viewers and help them join the undifferentiated social mass that they believed to be the source of their political power. Bayer, on the other hand, had designed his exhibitions to resemble books. Each image was a separate page, cut off

FIGURE 3.2.
Giuseppe Terragni, *Tenth Anniversary Exhibit of the Fascist Revolution, Sala O*, a 1932 installation dedicated to the 1922 fascist march on Rome. The exhibit ("Mostra della Rivoluzione Fascista") was held in the Palazzo delle Esposizioni on the Via Nazionale in Rome.

from the others by a bit of space across which the viewer would need to make both a physical and perceptual leap. Bayer's images needed interpretation and integration into a larger narrative. Fascist exhibitions presented looming environments dominated by a single idea: the people should be one, fused into a single engine-like machine, empowering and empowered by their leader. To disappear into the crowd was a glory. Bayer's work, in contrast, arrayed a mass of carefully separated individual images. It asked viewers to move from picture to picture, to recognize those of particular value to themselves, and to choose to integrate them into their own individual psyches. If fascist artists encouraged viewers to turn their individual agency over to dictators, Bayer encouraged his viewers to practice psychological self-sufficiency as they chose dishes from the visual banquet he had laid out. If the fascists hoped to dissolve the individual into a single social whole, Bayer, like Moholy and the founders of the Bauhaus, aimed to build a diverse social collective out of psychologically complete individuals.

THE NEW VISION COMES TO AMERICA

In the late 1930s, Bayer was working as a creative director at an advertising agency in Berlin. In 1936, the Ministry of Propaganda demanded that he insert a picture of Hitler in an exhibition catalog; later that year, they required a two-page photomontage celebrating the Nazified nation.[34] While Bayer himself wasn't Jewish, his wife and daughter were, and so were many of his clients.[35] He began to seek a way to leave the country. So too did Moholy, Gropius, and many other former Bauhaus faculty. They soon became part of an extraordinary migration of German intellectuals and artists that would transform American social thought and American art.[36]

As the veterans of the Bauhaus arrived in an America that still struggled with economic depression, deep racism, rampant demagoguery, and increasingly, a fear of war, they found that their earlier preoccupations could be made to serve new ends. Their fascination with the role of the individual in industrial society became a fascination with self-actualization in democratic society. Their critiques of industrial bureaucracy took on an antifascist tinge. And perhaps most powerfully, Bayer and Moholy began applying the same techniques that had been aimed at making the personalities of Bauhaus students whole toward promoting American morale and, once American troops entered combat, toward helping veterans recover from its effects. In the late 1930s and early 1940s, aesthetic strategies rooted in socialist utopianism became tools with which to make a more democratic America.

Moholy began to articulate his utopian aesthetic agenda in American terms almost as soon as he arrived. In 1937 a group of Chicago businessmen known as the Association of Arts and Industries invited Walter Gropius to establish a design school in their city. Gropius recommended Moholy for the job and in summer of that year, Moholy moved to the American Midwest.[37] In August he wrote to his wife Sybil, "You ask whether I want to remain here? Yes, darling, I want to remain in America. There's something incomplete about this city and its people that fascinates me; it seems to urge one on to completion. Everything seems still possible. The paralyzing finality of the European disaster is far away. I love the air of newness, of expectation around me. Yes, I want to stay."[38]

With the support of the Association, Moholy established the New Bauhaus, and on October 18, 1937, he admitted some thirty-five students. The opening drew nationwide press coverage. Reporters celebrated Chicago's embrace of the forward-thinking Bauhaus modernists whom Hitler had rejected. Few Americans, however, quite grasped the socialist inclinations of the original Bauhaus.[39] Nor did they have to. Even as he reinstituted much of the original Bauhaus curriculum, Moholy reframed its mission in American terms. "Now a *new* Bauhaus is founded on American soil," he announced in a new American edition of *The New Vision* (italics original). "America is the bearer of a new civilization whose task is simultaneously to cultivate and to industrialize a continent. It is the ideal ground on which to work out an educational principle which strives for the closest connection between art, science, and technology." Having linked the intellectual mission of the German Bauhaus to the practical, industrial orientation of the school's original backers, Moholy went on to stress the importance of personal psychological development. "To reach this objective one of the problems of Bauhaus education is to keep alive in grown-ups the child's sincerity of emotion, his truth of observation, his fantasy and his creativeness."[40]

As he established the New Bauhaus, Moholy dropped the socialist rhetoric of his youth but preserved its techniques: the New Bauhaus, like the old, would be a place for personal transformation. Once again, craftsmen would integrate skills, work to become whole people, and develop a community of shared labor. But this time, they would become part of a long American tradition. "The characteristic pioneer spirit which we find unimpaired in our American students" equipped them well to invent new visual and social forms, he explained.[41] As once he had hoped that the abstract constructions of German students would help them glimpse utopia, so now he argued that the works of his new American students exemplified traditional American ideals. He printed images of their work alongside his own; they too, he argued, had obtained a new way of seeing. But this time the future they glimpsed had a nationalist cast.

Moholy's embrace of things American increased as Hitler's armies swept across Europe. In a 1940 article entitled "Relating the Parts to the Whole," Moholy argued that design schools offered the kind of training that would strengthen individual American character and American society as a whole in the face of fascism. His case is worth quoting at length:

> THE PRESENT WORLD CRISIS will bring unforeseen problems to all of us. We shall have to make decisions of great consequences, both to ourselves and to the nation. Whether or not Hitler wins, whether or not we get into the war, we shall undergo great strains because an equilibrium has been disturbed. Europe has lost the leading position which it had in culture and technics. America is now the country to which the world looks.
>
> AMERICANS, A MOST RESOURCEFUL PEOPLE in technology and production, have in one respect over-done specialization. Processes and institutions have developed which, however ingenious, are wasteful because they are poorly related, each to the other.
>
> WE NEED IN LARGE NUMBERS a new type of person—one who sees the periphery as well as the immediate, and who can integrate his special job with the great whole of which it is a small part. This ability is a matter of everyday efficiency. It will also contribute to building a better culture [capitalization original].[42]

Moholy's account clearly marks his own attempt to market Bauhaus training and theory to an America on the brink of war. At the same time, though, it offers a new way to meet the psychological challenges posed by the theorists of the Committee for National Morale. Like psychologist Lawrence Frank, Moholy here recasts the battle against fascism as a battle *for* personality. By creating a new kind of person, endowed with a new kind of sight, Americans can build not only a more efficient society, but a better one. From a distance of half a century, Moholy's language may look curiously abstract. But in the context of American society at the end of the 1930s, that abstraction made it possible to point to the ferocious racial, regional, economic, and political divisions plaguing American society without naming them. Moholy could simultaneously acknowledge problems in American society, obscure their social-structural roots, and shift the site of their solution from the governmental to the personal level. In other words, like the psychologists and sociologists of the Committee for National Morale, Moholy found a way to transform political problems into psychological ones.

In Moholy's thinking, the practice of design in turn became the link between the making of better selves and the making of a better America: "A designer trained to think with both penetration and scope will find solutions, not alone for problems arising in daily routine, or for development of better ways of production, but also for all problems of living and working together. There is design in family life, in labor relations, in city planning, and living together as civilized human beings. Ultimately all problems of design fuse into one great problem of 'design for living,'" he wrote. His own school in Chicago served as a prototype both for the teaching of this new way of changing the world and for the kind of world such teaching might produce. It modeled, "on a small scale, what might happen on a large scale as the ability to think and work relatedly extends," he explained.[43]

THE EXTENDED FIELD OF VISION
AT THE MUSEUM OF MODERN ART

At the same time that Moholy was working to Americanize the New Vision in Chicago, Herbert Bayer was bringing his extended field of vision to the Museum of Modern Art in New York. The museum had been founded in 1929 by three society doyennes, the most prominent of whom was Abby Aldrich Rockefeller, wife of John D. Rockefeller and mother of future vice president Nelson Rockefeller. It quickly became a primary gateway for European art and artists seeking entry into the United States. In its first ten years it helped introduce Americans to impressionism, Futurism, and cubism, as well as to modern architecture, photography, and typography. In 1939 after Hitler invaded Poland, its director, Alfred Barr, and his wife immediately launched an effort to rescue avant-garde artists. With the prestige of the museum and the Rockefeller family name behind them, they managed to help bring half a dozen leading figures to the United States, including Marc Chagall, Max Ernst, and Jacques Lipschitz. Even before Pearl Harbor, Barr and the Rockefellers began to transform the museum into an engine of ideological production that would support American propaganda efforts across the Cold War.

Herbert Bayer's extended field of vision would play an important role in that process. Bayer first came to the Museum of Modern Art at the invitation of John McAndrew, the museum's curator for architecture and industrial art. In the summer of 1937, the museum was planning to mount a comprehensive historical exhibition of the Bauhaus's work from 1919 to 1928. In those same months, Bayer and Marcel Breuer were visiting the United States with an eye to preparing for emigration. They joined Gropius, Moholy, McAndrew, and others for a meeting to discuss the upcoming exhibition, and by the end of it, Bayer had been enlisted to design the show.[44] Bayer then returned to Germany to help find Bauhaus artifacts and ship them to New York. The materials that he and Gropius gathered spanned the panoply of Bauhaus productions. They included paintings, sculptures, photographs, drawings for stage sets, and typophoto posters. They also featured shiny Bauhaus tea sets, Marcel Breuer's aluminum-railed armchairs, and even an architectural model of the Gropius-designed Dessau Bauhaus. When the show opened on December 7, 1938, it was the most complete representation of the early Bauhaus seen outside of Germany.

For American art critics, the most surprising element of the exhibition was not its content but its installation. Because the Museum of Modern Art was then constructing a new home for itself at 11 West 53rd Street in Manhattan, Bayer installed the show in the museum's temporary space in the concourse of Rockefeller Center. He and Gropius broke the show up into six sections, each with its own gallery: "The Elementary Course Work," "The Workshops," "Typography," "Architecture," "Painting," and "Work from Schools Influenced by the Bauhaus."[45] Bayer then transformed these areas into variations of the extended visual environments he had built in Paris in 1930 and in Berlin in 1935. In Berlin, Bayer had been unafraid to attach chairs to the wall. Here, he became more conservative, confining furniture to the floor and most images to a range fairly near eye level. At the same time, however, he transformed the galleries of Rockefeller Center into spaces that would surround viewers with visual information and guide their experience of the exhibition.

As viewers entered the first gallery, they encountered Lyonel Feininger's painting *Cathedral of Socialism*—an image that had been printed alongside the first manifesto of the Bauhaus in 1919. The painting hung by strings from the ceiling. Moving from room to room, viewers found footprints on the floor and graphic hands on the wall, pointing them to new parts of the exhibition. A giant egg hung from one wall, representing a teaching form from the first-year curriculum. Photographs arched downward from overhead; diagrams of color wheels dangled from the ceiling. In one room a giant eye stared outward from the wall at the viewer from underneath a slot. When the viewer peered through the hole in the wall, he saw a cluster of spinning, humanoid automatons in costumes created by Bauhaus theater master Oskar Schlemmer. Finally, throughout the exhibition, Bayer had painted the floor in geometric shapes, as if it too were an abstract construction.

From the point of view of early Bauhaus ideology, Bayer's design transformed the exhibition into a *Gesamtkunstwerk*. In accord with his theories of the extended field of vision, it surrounded viewers, gently nudging them here or there, encouraging them to go with the flows painted on the walls and floors. In keeping with the Gestaltist psychology underlying Bayer's theories, viewers would need to synthesize the elements presented to them into coherent internal pictures of their own. The exhibition itself could suggest, could present, could house and frame—but viewers would ultimately have to put together their own pictures of the Bauhaus as a whole.

In 1938 more than a few viewers found this degree of agency disconcerting. Some seventeen thousand visitors passed through the museum during the show's seven-week run.[46] Museum records suggest that many in the audience especially enjoyed seeing everyday objects designed by the Bauhaus, and that response to the show among the broad public was quite favorable.[47] The exhibition set off something of a firestorm among art critics, though. Some, most notably Lewis Mumford in *The New Yorker*, applauded the show and the work of the Bauhaus more generally.[48] Many appreciated the individual works on display. But in a report for museum trustees, Alfred Barr noted that many who admired the work of the Bauhaus found the exhibition installation confusing.[49] The *New York Times* critic Edward Alden Jewell, for instance, praised the Bauhaus for its forward-looking designs but condemned the exhibition as "chaotic," as "voluminously inarticulate," and as suffering from "disorganized promiscuity."[50]

Not every critic agreed with Jewell. But his review serves as an important chronological marker. In 1938, even some of the most experienced museumgoers in America found Bayer's extended field of vision techniques utterly alien. Since most American critics lacked the utopian impulses of the early Bauhaus, its faith that a change in perception could change the social order, and even a basic familiarity with Gestalt psychology, few saw the need to knit together their own visual experiences from a visual surround as being a liberating experience. On the contrary, they found themselves at sea.

Only a few years later, however, as the Museum of Modern Art became a central hub for the boosting of American morale, critics came to see the flexibility and independence that Bayer offered his viewers, coupled with his environmental mode of governing the viewers' movements, as a uniquely pro-American mode of propaganda making. Bayer's extended field of vision solved the problem posed by fascist propaganda and mass media: by granting viewers high degrees of agency with regard to the visual materials around them, and by at the same time controlling the shape of the field in which they might encounter those materials, the extended field of vision could lead American viewers to remake their own morale in terms set by the field around them. That is, they could exercise the individual psychological agency on which democratic society depended, and so avoid becoming the numb mass men of Nazi Germany. At the same time, they could do so in terms set by the needs of the American state, articulated in the visual diction of the Bauhaus.

In the years between its *Bauhaus 1919–1928* exhibition and Pearl Harbor, the Museum of Modern Art became an extraordinary forum for the development of pro-democratic propaganda and for debates about what forms it should take. In 1939, the museum's board appointed Nelson Rockefeller president of the museum; within a year, he would serve as President Franklin Roosevelt's point man in the effort to keep Latin America from supporting the Axis. The board also soon included Archibald MacLeish, the librarian of Congress and occasional speechwriter for President Roosevelt, who would go on to briefly help lead America's wartime propaganda efforts as director of the deceptively blandly named Office of Facts and Figures. Roosevelt himself acknowledged the museum's importance as a bulwark against fascism when he gave a radio address celebrating the opening of the museum's new building on May 10, 1939. The museum, he explained, would be an emblem of freedom, artistic and political. "The arts cannot thrive except where men are free to be themselves and to be in charge of the discipline of their own energies and orders," he said. "The conditions for art and democracy are one and the same."[51]

In June 1940, Abby Rockefeller had become incensed by the fall of Paris and the rise of Mussolini in Italy, and sought to create an exhibition that would awaken isolationist Americans to the dangers they posed.[52] She recruited the museum's director, Alfred Barr, writer Lewis Mumford, librarian of Congress Archibald MacLeish, and eminent curator Leslie Cheek to design the show. They and several others labored for four months to craft an enormous, immersive multimedia environment that would persuade Americans to take action. The project was known first as *Exhibition X* and later as *For Us the Living*. In their scenarios, the authors proposed to double the museum's floor space by constructing an entirely new building to house the exhibition. Cheek wrote, "Into this carefully designed structure would go the display, which was really an 'experience' through which groups of the public were to be taken, via an automated taped voice, through a series of areas of varying size, color, texture, lighting, smell, and sound to view the displays of illumined texts, movies, mannequins, motion pictures, etc."[53]

The drafts of scenarios that remain in the museum's archives reveal that Cheek and his colleagues hoped to immerse their audiences in what they called a "drama."[54] They imagined dividing their building into a series of thirteen halls, which they called "scenes." The viewer would enter a "waiting room" with questions written in giant letters on the wall:

"How far can I plan ahead?

Will I have a job tomorrow?

Dare we have children?

Will democracy hold its own against fascism?

What would life be like in an undemocratic and enslaved world?"[55]

Thus primed, viewers would hear a voice on a loudspeaker inviting them to enter the next room. There they would see projections of America and Europe at peace. They would listen to a narration, backed by music, of American history. Suddenly a voice would announce: "And now, today, November 15, 1940, every man and woman in this room faces a crisis. We must choose between (music stops, dramatic pause by voice) *Democracy and Freedom or Fascism and Slavery*."[56] Hidden projectors would then post an image of Lincoln on one wall and a portrait of Hitler on another.

The authors continued in this vein as they drew visitors first down the "Avenue of Fascism"—a hall lined with dummies dressed as storm troopers, workers, mothers, and children—and into an imaginary fascist future. Having frightened their visitors with that possibility, the authors then welcomed them to the "Hall of American Character." "This room is an esthetic and emotional contrast to the dynamic humbug of the faceless men," wrote the authors. "It is quiet, assured, full of character. . . . It is lined on both sides with pictures of Americans, of uniform size; portraits of head and shoulders." These would be "pictures of real people, with real biographies . . . drawn from each state." Together they would represent "the essential principle of democracy—the worth of the individual personality."[57]

These images would also introduce visitors to halls featuring the history of the American people and their achievements before sending them on to confront "the job in hand." This included not only confronting Hitler, but remaking American democracy so that it would be something worth confronting Hitler with. The authors advocated four principles, which they labeled "goals for tomorrow" and proposed to post as signs reading "Rededication to Natural Resources," "Transformation of Work," "Renewal of Family and Personality," and "Revitalizing of Democratic System [sic]."[58] Thus sequenced, the goals served as a road map out of the Depression and toward the strengthened faith in the nation that was required by the impending war. Finally, the show's designers released visitors into the final exhibition room, the "Hall of Human Values." There they would stand on a balcony, gazing down onto "a great, simple room, flooded with cool light and fine music." Across from the balcony they would see gigantic tablets, each with a bit of wisdom from "the high religions and philosophies of mankind," and a sign illuminating "the highest goal of effort: Rededication to the Enduring Truths and Values of Mankind." Ideally, wrote the authors, visitors would experience feelings of "composure and elevation, too deep for mere brassy self-confidence and egoistic national assertiveness, but capable of being translated into sustained thought and action." Upon leaving the hall, they might even be confronted with tables soliciting their active support for the antifascist Allies—and thus, an opportunity to benefit all mankind.[59]

In all of these ways, the designers of *For Us the Living* hoped not only to strengthen Americans' faith in their democracy, but to prepare the nation to go to war. The discussions at the Museum of Modern Art that surrounded their work, however, reveal a deep distrust of propaganda, and of instrumental communication more generally. When Alfred Barr presented the group's scenarios to the museum trustees in July 1940, he explained that they had designed the exhibition to show that Americans had a responsibility to confront fascism. At the same time, he argued, it would "ostensibly not be a propaganda exhibition."[60] That is, it would lead visitors to certain views, but do so in a way different from both the propaganda masters of Nazi Germany and the American propagandists of World War I. Leslie Cheek seconded this view. Even as he described the exhibition as a drama and structured it like one of the most prominent and most suspect mass media, a film, Cheek argued that the exhibition would not overwhelm viewers or deprive them of agency. "In this exhibition, the visitor is not a passive spectator but an actor; and the aim of it is to indicate the character and scope of further activity that demands his participation as a citizen."[61]

In other words, Cheek argued that the exhibition served as a space in which viewers could practice the skills on which the future of democracy depended. But Abby Rockefeller was having none of it. In October 1940, she and the board turned the project down flat. In part she must have objected to the exhibition's $750,000 budget—though if she did, she didn't say so. In a letter to Cheek, she explained that she would not support the exhibition because to her it seemed too much like a movie.[62] Rockefeller didn't expand on the point, but in 1940 America she didn't have to. For those concerned with propaganda, movies smacked of the instrumental mode of communication employed by Hitler and Mussolini. They seemed to work as dictators did, by turning off the reason of their viewers, by making them numb and obedient. This exhibition, Rockefeller implied, was trying to do the same thing.

The failure of *For Us the Living* notwithstanding, it is hard to overstate the depth of the Museum of Modern Art's ties to the American government and the strength of its propaganda efforts just before and during World War II. The museum not only developed exhibitions but served as an intellectual and inter-institutional hub. Within its walls, artists met diplomats, anthropologists developed materials for cultural training, and soldiers sought solace for the psychological wounds of combat. At a self-congratulatory gathering in November 1945, museum officials summarized their accomplishments during the war.[63] They had provided three kinds of support, they concluded: direct work for the government, the creation and circulation of exhibitions that supported American policies, and the development of an Armed Services Program to support soldiers in the field and after their return home. They had carried out thirty-eight contracts for Nelson Rockefeller's Office of Inter-American Affairs, for MacLeish's Library of Congress, and for what came to be the nation's premier propaganda agency in this period, the Office of War Information. They had brought in more than a million and a half dollars from these contracts alone. They had staged some thirty exhibitions directly connected to the war. They had transformed the exhibitions they created at the Museum of Modern Art into traveling kits and sent these to London, Cairo, Stockholm, Rio de Janeiro, and Mexico City—anywhere, in short, that an alliance needed shoring up. And they had developed a host of programs and tools to help soldiers regain their psychological balance in the wake of combat.

Of all the work they undertook, the museum officials were proudest of a single exhibition, the 1942 propaganda blockbuster *Road to Victory*. The exhibition "was not only a masterpiece of photographic art but one of the most moving and inspiring exhibitions ever held in the museum," they wrote.[64] Curated by photographer Edward Steichen and designed by

Herbert Bayer, *Road to Victory* borrowed the immersive impulse behind *For Us the Living* but did so in terms set by Bayer's extended field of vision. Suddenly the same critics who had found Bayer's exhibition techniques confusing in 1938 found them to be the epitome of creativity. And the museum officials who had so feared the pseudocinematic power of Leslie Cheek's design of *For Us the Living* now embraced a directive, immersive multiscreen environment as a means of bringing visitors to an understanding of America's wartime mission.

In September 1941, at the same time that Mead and the Committee for National Morale were trying to develop their exhibition on democracy at the Museum of Modern Art, trustee David McAlpin approached photographer Edward Steichen. The museum had begun to host small exhibitions devoted to the fighting in Europe and to American ideals here at home, and McAlpin hoped that Steichen might stage another in the sequence.[65] Steichen was sixty-one at the time, with a long career as a gallery owner, portraitist, and advertising photographer behind him. His work showed none of the preoccupations with the extension of the human senses that preoccupied Europeans like Moholy. On the contrary, his images partook of an aestheticized realism. Despite a little soft focus here and a slightly off-center composition there, Steichen's images were the visual equivalent of American realist fiction: they presented straight-on views of American characters in a largely plainspoken visual idiom.

Steichen accepted McAlpin's invitation and, in October 1941, began selecting images for the show. He trolled through thousands of photographs, almost all from government collections, and the great majority from the Farm Security Administration (FSA). Across the 1930s the FSA had been the premier chronicler of the Great Depression, but by the end of the decade, hoping to maintain government funding in a changing political climate, the agency's director asked his photographers to turn away from dark depictions of poverty and toward images and individuals who might provoke a feeling of hopefulness in viewers.[66] Of the 150 images that Steichen eventually chose, more than 130 came from the FSA.[67] The rest came from the Army and Navy, various press agencies, and several other government bureaus. Like Steichen's own work at the time, they tended to be "straight" photography—that is, they mostly depicted their subjects in a head-on, straightforward manner, with clear, sharp lines and a strong documentary flavor.

Steichen in turn recruited his brother-in-law, poet Carl Sandburg, to create a text for the show. Like Steichen's photographs, Sandburg's poems portrayed the everyday life of Americans in ordinary, seemingly documentary speech. But like Steichen's pictures, and like the pictures Steichen chose for *Road to Victory,* Sandburg's verse elevated its subjects to creatures of myth. In his most famous poem, for instance, Sandburg transformed the notoriously bloody and impoverished stockyards of Chicago into the object of an encomium: Chicago wasn't a gore-ridden mess; it was the "city of the big shoulders" and "hog butcher for the world." Finally, in what turned out to be an inspired decision, the Museum of Modern Art's director of exhibitions, Monroe Wheeler, paired these two middlebrow American realists with a representative of the European avant-garde, Herbert Bayer. The resulting exhibition fused the familiar photorealism of *Life* magazine with the Gestaltist tactics of Bayer's extended field of vision — and the utopian ideals of the Bauhaus with the propaganda needs of wartime Americans.

Bayer designed the exhibition as a road, curving through the entire second floor of the Museum of Modern Art and winding by images and texts of varying sizes. When they entered, visitors encountered a floor-to-ceiling photograph of Utah's Bryce Canyon and huge portraits of three Native American men. The words "Road to Victory" floated over their heads on nearly invisible wires, a look that would have been familiar to El Lissitzky a decade earlier. A text by Carl Sandburg translated the images into words: "In the beginning was virgin land and America was promises — and the buffalo by thousands pawed the Great Plains — and the Red Man gave over to an endless tide of white men in endless numbers. . . ." From there, visitors could meander by vistas of grain waving in wide-open fields, to views of small-town life: a farmer carrying a bushel of corn, a view of grain elevators in Montana, a glimpse of a middle-aged woman out front of her clapboard house. Visitors found the sheer number of such images powerful and their meaning clear. Elizabeth McCausland, reviewing the show for the *Springfield Sunday Union and Republican,* spoke for many when she

FIGURE 3.3.

Entrance to *Road to Victory*, Museum of Modern Art, New York, 1942. Photograph by Albert Fenn. Digital image © The Museum of Modern Art, licensed by SCALA / Art Resource, New York. Used by permission.

wrote, "All these are familiar aspects of American life. . . . This is the stuff of which we build a people and its traditions."[68]

Having explored the American nation's roots in its landscape and the character of its people, visitors then moved on to images of the war itself. As they rounded a curve, they came on a uniquely jarring juxtaposition: a huge photograph of a warship exploding at Pearl Harbor while underneath it, in a separate photograph mounted in a bit of montage, two Japanese government officials laughed above the inscription "Two Faces." A temporary wall met these images at ninety degrees. On it, an American farmer looked bravely into the distance. Below him, Bayer, Steichen, and Sandburg had written, "War—they asked for it—now, by the living God, they'll get it." In fact, Steichen had repurposed a 1938 Dorothea Lange image from the FSA archives, one in which this same farmer, a migrant, had been shown confronting his utter destitution.[69] Here, Steichen turned the farmer's endurance in the face of poverty into visual evidence of American resolve in the face of war.

The exhibition then opened onto scenes of American troops in training, of airmen raining down in parachutes on an unseen enemy, and of bombs doing the same. "Smooth and terrible birds of death," captioned Sandburg, "smooth they fly, terrible their spit of flame, their hammering cry, 'Here's lead in your guts.'" Visitors passed vistas of American warships sailing windblown, choppy seas—in Sandburg's words, "hunting the enemy, slugging, pounding, blasting . . . ." At last, at the end of the exhibition's road, visitors confronted an enormous, floor-to-ceiling, panoramic overhead photograph of row upon row of American soldiers marching. These soldiers might well have looked like the anonymous masses of fascist exhibitions from the thirties, had they not featured inset images of middle-aged, white, and mostly rural American couples—clearly meant to be the symbolic parents of the marchers—sitting in front of their houses, on their sofas, and in one case outdoors on what looked like a reviewing stand. Visitors to this final scene were surrounded—by American troops, but also by the same sorts of American citizens they had seen at the start of their journey through the show. If a fascist exhibition asked its viewers to melt into an anonymous mass, this final set of images asked Americans to preserve their individuality, their roots, even as they formed into a fighting machine.

Such an appeal struck a deep chord in audiences. Across the summer of 1942, more than eighty thousand people visited the exhibition.[70] Reviewers fell over themselves to praise it. "It would not at all amaze me to see people, even people who have thought themselves very worldly, nonchalant or hard-boiled, leave this exhibition with brimming eyes," wrote Edward Alden Jewell, the *New York Times* critic who had disparaged Bayer's design for the Bauhaus show in 1938.[71] Jewell particularly praised the exhibition's ability to reveal essential aspects of American character and help visitors feel them as their own. If other exhibitions had simply depicted "a nation at war," this one, wrote Jewell, "reveals the very fiber of the nation itself." Much like Margaret Mead's book *And Keep Your Powder Dry . . .* , the exhibition seemed to Jewell to fuse the nature of the nation with the personality formations of its citizens and to offer that fusion as the source of America's national might. By drawing visitors down a road, by arraying images above and below eye level, and by mixing images of life at home with life in the Army, Jewell argued that the exhibition drew visitors into a new form of emotional citizenship. "I think no one can see the exhibition without feeling that he is a part of the power of America . . . ," wrote Jewell. "It is this inescapable sense of identity—the individual spectator identifying himself with the whole—that makes the event so moving."[72]

Jewell lacked Bayer's Gestaltist orientation, but his review proclaimed the success of Bayer's technique: in *Road to Victory*, Bayer, Steichen, and Sandburg had created what Moholy might have called a typophoto environment. They offered visitors the chance to experience themselves as individuals in charge of their own movements and, at the same time, to extend the reach of their senses across the American continent and all the way to foreign battlefields by means of the photographs on the walls. They could thus use their eyes to imaginatively stitch themselves into the fabric of the American nation. As once the students of the Bauhaus were to integrate art and technology so as to create a New Man, so here, *Road to Victory* brought together art and technology to create a new, more confident American.

Of all the reviewers to celebrate this achievement, Elizabeth McCausland explained it most clearly: "The exhibition may be thought of as a movie in three dimensions, with the difference that it is the spectator who moves, not the pictures. In this kinesthetic relation between the one who sees and what is seen lies the explanation of the moving psychological effect of the exhibition. It has visual activity, as life has. It speaks with a variety of accents, and it shows the various faces of remembered experience." In other words, to enter the physical environment of the exhibition was to enter a place in which one could move back and forth between the external world and one's internal state of mind, integrating the two. The medium of photography, coupled with the extended field of vision technique, provided evidence with which the visitor could simultaneously reason and feel. At the same time, even though the visual power of the exhibition put McCausland in mind of a film, the exhibition did not seem to manipulate the viewer in the ways that Abby Rockefeller had feared *For Us the Living* might. As McCausland pointed out, *Road to Victory* did not "mold" the visitor's opinions—"for that word smacks of the Fascist concept of dominating men's minds."[73] Rather, it offered visitors tools and settings with which to remake their own personalities in democratic, pro-American terms.

To appreciate the political valence of Bayer's design and its impact on visitors like McCausland, we need only look a few blocks uptown, to 57th Street. There, a few months after *Road to Victory* opened at the Museum of Modern Art, heiress and art collector Peggy Guggenheim opened a multiroom gallery to showcase her collection. Austrian-American designer Friedrich Kiesler divided the space into four themed spaces: the Daylight Gallery, the Abstract Gallery, the Surrealist Gallery, and the Kinetic Gallery. Like Bayer, Kiesler created a pathway through the exhibition. And like Bayer, he hung images at unusual levels. He configured the Surrealist Gallery like a tunnel, for example, with curved walls and unframed paintings jutting outward on struts to within a few inches of viewers. The Abstract Gallery, too, featured wraparound walls, this time made of cloth; its paintings hung from wires strung floor-to-ceiling in the middle of the room.

Like Bayer, Kiesler was trying to reinvent the traditional relationship between viewers, art, and the spaces in which they encountered one another. But Kiesler was working within a radically different psychological framework. In a press release for the show, he explained that his display technique offered "a much better possibility for concentrating the attention of the spectator on each painting and therefore a better chance for the painting to communicate its message."[74] For Kiesler, the psychological impact of the viewers' movements through the exhibition space depended primarily on their encounters with individual images rather than with the pattern of their arrangement. In his view, pictures contained messages and, when properly attended to, they could transmit them. "Man," wrote Kiesler at the time, "seeing in a piece of sculpture or a painting on canvas the artist's projected vision, must recognize his act of seeing—of 'receiving'—as a participation in the creative process no less essential and direct than the artist's own."[75] For Kiesler, the creative process was an act of communication initiated by the artist, enacted by the individual work of art, and completed by the viewer's passive reception of the message carried by the work. The role of the display was to facilitate this sequence.

Critics were quick—and largely dismayed—to catch Kiesler's drift. "To the uninitiated and unenlightened," wrote one, "most of the paintings look like pieces of canvas on which artists have wiped their brushes while the sculptured works of the chiselers look like they are a long way from being finished. The devotees of surrealism, however, insist that these works of art have real meaning if you know how to get it."[76] One writer after another echoed this view: in Kiesler's galleries, art works needed to speak to viewers; viewers needed to hear and "get" their messages; the environment itself had been designed to make it easier for viewers to passively receive the aggressive intellectual and aesthetic challenges posed by the art. Such a structure did little to promote the sort of democratic agency offered by Bayer and Steichen's *Road to Victory*. On the contrary, wrote Henry McBride of the *New York Sun*, "this scheme [of display] is too much like the 'ordered society' of the Japanese. It compels you to have the correct thought at the correct time. It is not my idea of aesthetic liberty."[77]

McBride penned these lines less than a year after Pearl Harbor. The fact that he did suggests both the intensity of his reaction to Kiesler's work and the political stakes of exhibition design in this period. *Art of this Century* remained controversial until it finally shut down in 1947. By contrast, *Road to Victory* was so popular that Monroe Wheeler and the Office of War Information teamed up with Bayer the next year to create a sequel, *Airways to Peace*. Though it did not have the public impact that *Road to Victory* did, *Airways to Peace* presented a powerful, even utopian vision of a postwar world, and a glimpse of the role that Bayer's extended field of vision would play in it. By June of 1943, when the exhibition opened, the tide of the war had begun to turn. British forces had pushed the Germans out of North Africa, American troops had begun working their way up the Solomon Islands toward Japan, and the Soviets had captured some ninety thousand German troops at Stalingrad. American intellectuals, journalists and government officials had begun to turn toward imagining a new international order—one in which a victorious America would play a leading role. They had also begun to see how the massive industrial shifts demanded by the war might become resources in peacetime. In 1943, reporters were particularly fascinated with air power: less than fifty years earlier, no one had flown; by 1943, military and commercial airplanes had traveled around the globe.

In 1942, former presidential candidate Wendell Willkie proved the point. That August he set out in a four-engine bomber piloted by an Army crew on a forty-nine-day trip around the world. The plane visited every continent save Australia, and Willkie himself used the occasion to visit military commanders and politicians in the Middle East, Russia, and China. His book-length chronicle of the trip, *One World*, became an instant bestseller. Within five months of its March 1943 release, the book had gone through ten printings and sold more than 1,200,000 copies.[78] At one level the book was simply a wartime travelogue. "America is like a beleaguered city that lives within high walls through which there passes only an occasional courier to tell us what is happening outside," wrote Willkie. "I have been outside those walls."[79]

At another level, though, the book articulated a utopian vision of a postwar world, abroad and at home. The same technologies that allowed him to travel and that were winning the war for America, Willkie argued, had transformed the globe into a single community. This fact presented Americans with the chance to pursue three possible routes after the war: a parochial nationalism, an international imperialism, or "the creation of a world in which there shall be an equality of opportunity for every race and every nation."[80] Willkie argued that Americans had to begin planning immediately, with the aid of the then-new United Nations, to build—and lead—this postwar world. At the same time, he argued, they must eliminate racism at home. "Minorities are the rich assets of democracy," he explained. "We cannot fight the forces and ideas of imperialism abroad and maintain any form of imperialism at home. The war has done this to our thinking."[81] Americans instead had to create a new social unity, one in which individuals might preserve their unique personalities and cultures and yet belong to the whole.

In the summer of 1943, just as Willkie's book was topping the bestseller lists, Wheeler and Bayer created a visual environment in which visitors could integrate Willkie's vision into their own views of the world. Like *Road to Victory*, *Airways to Peace* featured a broad path for visitors to follow and an array of images and texts—this time written by Willkie—at every level of vision through which the visitor walked. Upon entering the show, visitors confronted a floor-to-ceiling photocollage depicting an airplane flying through the clouds, its wings linked to a drawing of Icarus, beside a long introduction by Willkie. The airplane, he wrote, soared over natural landscapes and cities alike, uniting the organic and the man-made. "There are no distant places any longer: the world is small and the world is one," it explained. "The American people must grasp these new realities if they are to play their essential part in winning the war and building a world of peace and freedom."[82]

As visitors left Icarus behind, Bayer's design offered them repeated opportunities to imagine themselves flying above the earth. They first encountered some thirty globes and maps, including a clay tablet map from 2500 BCE, a globe from 1492, and Franklin Roosevelt's own Oval Office globe, which he lent to the museum for two weeks.[83] In keeping with the principles of his extended field of vision, Bayer surrounded visitors with visual elements, but in a manner designed to produce a limited range of conclusions. Here he offered visitors the chance to link the global expansion of America's military presence and its pursuit of victory to the expansion of the human race as a whole. The American project was a human project; what was good for the state was good for humankind. As a contrast, the exhibition presented "Mackinder's Famous Map," which depicted "Eurasia" at its center. The exhibitors argued that this map depicted the globe as the Nazis saw it—with North America at its outer edge—but not as it actually was. Seeing the world correctly, they implied—that is, seeing the world with America at its center—offered the key to American victory and world peace.

Lest viewers misunderstand their own roles in this process, the exhibition culminated in an area called "Global Strategy." After walking over a ramp that allowed them to peer down at photographs shot from the air as if they were looking down through the windows of a plane, visitors encountered two elements, side by side. On the left, an eleven-foot-high map of the earth, with the North Pole at its center, illustrated "major air routes of the future."[84] On the right, hung from the ceiling by cords as if suspended in space itself, they saw an enormous globe turned inside out. Through doorways cut into the lower latitudes, visitors could enter the globe and see the countries of the world painted on the dome around them. If America's global strategy to win the war meant flying men and materiel around

FIGURE 3.4.
Herbert Bayer's walk-in globe, built as part of Edward Steichen's 1943 exhibition *Airways to Peace*. With the globe, Bayer offered American viewers a chance to use Bauhaus and Gestaltist styles of perception to imagine themselves at the center of the world—and to feel, perhaps, as though they and their army were in charge of its future. Photographer unknown. *Bulletin of the Museum of Modern Art* 11, no. 1 (August 1943): 9. Digital image © The Museum of Modern Art, licensed by SCALA / Art Resource, New York. Used by permission.

the globe, its postwar strategy—at least according to Willkie—was to see the world as one. Within the globe, visitors could stand in for the American nation itself. As they moved their eyes from country to country, they could imagine themselves in a personal, psychological version of international political relations. Their own bodies could take in a vision of the globe as an interrelated whole. And they could experience themselves as Americans, coordinating the visual and, by implication, political interrelations of its many parts.

Like *Road to Victory*, *Airways to Peace* did not seek to "mold" its visitors. Rather, it presented them with an array of visual materials and three-dimensional environments within which they could mold themselves. To that extent, it offered visitors a chance to experience a democratic degree of agency. At the same time, however, it created visual conditions under which it would be nearly impossible to come to integrate a view of the world that did not accord with Willkie's vision of American dominance. To put it another way, Bayer had created an extended field of vision in which American viewers might glimpse utopia. But this time, it would not be the socialist utopia of El Lissitzky or the young Moholy-Nagy. On the contrary, it would be the liberal utopia of a world managed from afar by an all-seeing and technologically all-powerful United States.

4

The New Landscape of Sound

At the same time that Herbert Bayer and Edward Steichen were reconfiguring the visual landscape of propaganda, the fusion of Bauhaus aesthetics and democratic idealism that drove their installations was also helping to create a parallel transformation in the structure and performance of music. To see how, we need to revisit the early career of composer John Cage. Born in 1912 in Los Angeles to an inventor father and a journalist mother, Cage originally hoped to become a minister. Instead, he became an architect of a new relationship between artist, audience, and sound that would ultimately reshape the rules of both art music and social protest. At about the same time that Bayer was pulling images out of eye-level rows and displaying them over the heads and by the feet of visitors, Cage was breaking apart the structured ranks of traditional musical tonality and finding new sources of sound. Pianos with bits of rubber stuck in their strings, radios, blocks of wood, and amplified sheets of metal all became his instruments. Like visitors to *Road to Victory*, Cage's listeners found themselves surrounded by potentially significant signs—sonic rather than visual—and by the need to choose among them. Much as Bayer had expanded the visual field, so Cage expanded the field of sounds, invited his listeners to enter that field, and urged them to integrate what they heard into a new and explicitly democratic psychological whole.

Over the years, Cage has become perhaps best known for his turn to Zen Buddhism in the early 1950s and his subsequent use of chance composition methods. But almost a decade earlier, Cage began to orient his music making around the same therapeutic aesthetics that animated Bayer and Moholy-Nagy. Like them, he created environments in which could practice the psychological skills that social scientists at the time believed to be the keys to democratic citizenship. With the exception of his 1944 work *A Book of Music*, which the Office of War Information regularly broadcast to Indonesia because they thought it sounded "Asian," Cage did not make propaganda.[1] On the contrary, until the 1960s, Cage steadily denied that he or his music had anything to do with politics at all.

Yet a close look at his work from the late 1930s, when he invented his "prepared piano," to 1952, when he created his infamous "silent" composition, *4'33"*, and staged what has been widely heralded as the first-ever Happening, reveals a very different picture. In this period, Cage struggled continually with questions of agency and communication. Even as the American Army struggled to free Europe from fascism and, later, Korea from communism, Cage worked to free his listeners from subjection to the emotional manipulation of classical and popular music. He tried to negate his own power to impose his will on sounds and through them, on his listeners. And he described his efforts to do so in terms that echoed those of the larger American struggle against authoritarianism. By 1952, the musical situation became for him what *Road to Victory* had been for Herbert Bayer and Edward Steichen a decade earlier: a model of democratic political possibilities.

JOHN CAGE AND THE EXPANDED FIELD OF SOUND

Cage was hardly the first composer to break with the conventions of popular and orchestral music. Within the world of art music, composers had been challenging the patterns of dissonance and consonance, the sweeping harmonies and well-ordered counterpoint of orchestral music since the end of the nineteenth century. In Paris in the early years of the century, Erik Satie created atmospheric clouds of sweetly dissonant notes in his piano pieces. In the 1920s, Austrian Arnold Schoenberg turned away from major and minor scales entirely, began to compose using a twelve-tone system, and spawned an entire school of modern composition. Within

American popular music, bluesmen had been bending notes, running rhythmic schemes one on top of the other, and tangling up vocal and nonvocal sounds for at least a hundred years.[2] At midcentury it was their descendants, in fact, the howling improvisers of the new world of bebop jazz, who claimed most loudly to have democratized the musical experience.[3] In their multiracial ensembles, soloists traded riffs on equal terms. If the big band of swing was an industrial hierarchy, the bebop band was a conversation, a community of sound. And in the small clubs where they played, audiences were part of that community too.[4]

It was the largely white and European world of art music that appealed to the young Cage. In 1935 and 1936 he studied briefly with Schoenberg, but for the most part in this period, his compositions drew far more from the ideals of the Italian Futurists and, particularly, the work of Luigi Russolo.[5] In 1913, Russolo penned a manifesto, "The Art of Noises," in which he cheered all noises, and especially the noises made by machines, as improvements over traditional orchestral tones. Futurist musicians should select sounds from within the great cacophony of the world around them, he explained. They might bang on wood or metal, turn machines on and off, or screech and holler and hiss. Ultimately, they were to array this universe of sounds in new rhythmic and harmonic patterns. By doing so, wrote Russolo, they could teach listeners to wander through their lives taking pleasure in the variety of sounds around them.[6]

In the late 1930s, after studying briefly with Schoenberg in Los Angeles, Cage found his way to San Francisco percussionist Lou Harrison and, through him, to the Cornish School of Dance in Seattle. In 1937 he gave a talk to a Seattle arts society in which he laid out his ambitions in terms clearly set by Russolo: "I believe that the use of noise to make music will continue and increase until we reach the music produced through the aid of electrical instruments," he explained. The mission of the composer was to "capture and control" the noises of the world. In particular, musicians should turn the new technologies of sound reproduction into musical instruments. With technologies such as the "film phonograph," he exclaimed, "we can compose and perform a quartet for explosive motor, wind, heart beat and landslide."[7]

Cage stayed at the Cornish School until the spring of 1940. In that time he met and began composing for the dancer Merce Cunningham, who would ultimately become his lifelong collaborator and mate. He also began to bend his compositions toward the Futurist ideal. In 1939, for example, he created *Imaginary Landscape No. 1*. The composition mingled the sounds of the piano and Chinese cymbals with the slide-whistle electric signal hums of turntables sped up and slowed down in sequence. In 1940 he built an entire composition around the sounds produced by tapping and scraping objects found in a living room.[8] In April of that year, he also began slipping objects between the strings of the piano. Choreographer Syvilla Fort had asked Cage to provide an African-style accompaniment for her dance "Bacchanal"; he obliged by creating something like a modern update of the traditional African mbira. Cage wanted to work with a percussion ensemble, but there was no space in the dance hall to set up a drum crew. There was, however, a piano in the room. Cage began slotting bolts and screws between the strings and slipping bits of rubber and weather stripping in as well, until the piano had become a percussion instrument—the "prepared piano" with which he would work for more than a decade to come.[9]

In each of these cases, Cage appears to have sought to expand the range of sounds that might be called musical primarily for aesthetic reasons. On the verge of World War II, however, as Russolo and other Futurists embraced fascism, Cage began to recast his musical efforts in the emerging language of antifascist emancipation. In a 1939 essay entitled "Goal: New Music, New Dance," he argued, "Percussion music is revolution. Sound and rhythm have too long been submissive to the restrictions of nineteenth-century music. Today we are fighting for their emancipation. Tomorrow, with electronic music in our ears, we will hear freedom." As he dumped the orchestral past into the cultural wastebasket and glorified the electronic and noise-based music of the future, Cage spoke in terms that would have been congenial to Russolo. But in the America of 1939, the notion of fighting to free the oppressed had another valence as well. Thanks to a steady stream of popular commentary, many had come to see Hitler's Nazi regime as a product of nineteenth-century German culture. To turn away from the orchestral music of nineteenth-century Europe and toward

FIGURE 4.1.
John Cage preparing a piano, ca. 1960. Photograph by Ross Welser. Courtesy of the John Cage Trust.

percussion and electronic music, Cage's rhetoric implied, was to go to war on behalf of a muscular American future. "The conscientious objectors to modern music will, of course, attempt everything in the way of counter-revolution," he wrote.[10] But never mind: the implicitly American armies of freedom would march on.

CAGE AND THE BAUHAUS

During the same years in which he was exploring noise, Cage was also encountering the Bauhaus. In 1930, at the age of seventeen, Cage dropped out of college and, with his parents' help, traveled to Europe for a year and a half. He visited Paris and may well have attended the Society of Decorative Arts Exhibition in which Herbert Bayer hung Marcel Breuer's chairs from the wall.[11] From Paris, Cage traveled to Berlin and to the Dessau Bauhaus; when he returned to the United States he was carrying a copy of the school's course catalog.[12] By 1934, in a brief article written for fellow avant-garde musicians, he could be heard espousing a version of the Bauhaus call for collective craftwork and the submersion of the individual ego. He hoped, he wrote, that there would soon be "a period of Music and not Musicians, just as during the four centuries of Gothic, there was Architecture not Architects."[13]

In the late spring of 1940, Cage left Seattle for the San Francisco Bay area and a summer teaching at Oakland's Mills College alongside László Moholy-Nagy, Gyorgy Kepes, and other former members of the Bauhaus who now taught during the regular school year at Moholy's institute in Chicago. As the college's summer catalog explained, the summer school was devoted to helping each student become an "integrated individual."[14] It offered courses not only in the visual arts, music, and dance, but in child development, psychology, and social work as well. Across all of these fields, the Mills program emphasized the power of experience to shape the individual psyche. Though this emphasis had originated in the progressive educational theories of John Dewey, it also matched the pedagogical traditions of the Bauhaus. Thus, the college trumpeted the Bauhaus faculty as the centerpieces of the summer curriculum, greeting Moholy's arrival with a school-wide party and hosting a traveling version of the Museum of Modern Art's 1938 Bauhaus exhibition for much of the summer.[15]

During their time at Mills, Moholy and six colleagues taught a compressed version of the School of Design's first-year course, while Cage taught percussion in a separate summer dance program, alongside Lou Harrison. Cage clearly got to know Moholy and his book *The New Vision*, which was recommended reading for the entire student body that summer.[16] In the wake of his time at Mills, Cage even described his work to potential funders as "a counterpart in music of the work in visual arts conducted at the School of Design, which is the American Bauhaus."[17] In 1941, Moholy offered Cage a chance to teach a workshop in sound at the School of Design, and in August of that year, Cage moved to Chicago. Cage took over the school's sound workshop, where he taught five students about "Sound Experiments." Though the school's catalog described the course as offering the chance to make new sounds with everything from hands to machines to film phonographs, the fact that Cage's classroom abutted others meant that he in fact taught the course simply by means of conversation.[18]

SOUND AS THERAPY FOR THE MODERN WORLD

Even so, during his time in Chicago, Cage began to transform the Futurist search for more and more noises into something more like an aural version of Herbert Bayer's extended field of vision. In part, as art historian Branden Joseph has shown, Cage simply adopted Moholy's therapeutic understanding of communication.[19] Much as Moholy came to see photography as a way to extend the senses of his viewers and so to help them integrate the visual cacophony of the industrial world around them, so Cage began to build compositions that might extend the range of sounds whose beauty his listeners might appreciate, and so help them hear the sonic chaos of the modern world as music.

In early 1942, for example, Cage composed an exceptionally complex sonic backdrop to accompany Kenneth Patchen's radio drama "The City Wears a Slouch Hat." In his ramblings around Chicago, Cage had listened to its rumbling traffic, car horns, and drivers' shouts with an ear for their beauty, much in keeping with the pleasures that Russolo took in ambient noise. For the radio play he created a score replete with clanging pipes, police whistles, metallic thunderings, the roar of traffic, musical saws made to sound like sirens, and gamelan-like rhythms hammered out on ash cans. Patchen's script followed a wanderer in an anonymous city along various roads, through rain, through crime scenes and phone calls; Cage's score provided an aural analog to the wandering. Sitting beside their radios, listeners faced the same challenge as the story's hero: they had to roam the urban landscape, making their own sense of the random noises around them.

On May 31, 1942, CBS broadcast the program nationwide in the same series in which they had broadcast Orson Welles's *The War of the Worlds* three years earlier.[20] Where the Welles program had had an instrumental impact on many listeners, literally driving them into the streets with fear, the Cage and Patchen program asked that they immerse themselves in sound while sitting still. As Cage would later suggest, compositions such as the one he created for "The City Wears a Slouch Hat" were meant to trigger a psychological process of personality integration. After his 1943 percussion concert at the Museum of Modern Art in New York, Cage put the case thus to a reporter from *Time*: "People may leave my concerts thinking they have heard 'noise,' but will then hear unsuspected beauty in their everyday life. This music has a therapeutic value for city dwellers . . . ."[21]

By the early 1940s, Cage clearly had absorbed Moholy's notion that the arts might serve to integrate personalities that had been fractured by life in industrial society. At the same time, Cage's turn toward the therapeutic also represented a turn toward patterns of thinking and acting specifically marked as "democratic." In our own time, a word like "therapeutic" suggests a private, medicalized realm outside the political sphere. But in 1940 and 1941, in the intellectual circles surrounding the School of Design and the University of Chicago (from which the School of Design drew part-time faculty and where Cage worked as an accompanist), the capacity to retain psychological unity and intellectual independence in relation to communication, and especially mass-mediated communication, represented a kind of freedom on which national democracy depended. To be able to integrate aural or visual stimuli into a whole psychological picture of one's own making and to act on that basis distinguished the free (and presumably American) citizen from his fragmented, irrational, and massified opposite, the fascist. In other words, for many of Cage's colleagues, therapeutic modes of communication helped create the preconditions for democracy.

Perhaps the most articulate theorist of this distinction at the School of Design in Cage's time was the University of Chicago philosopher and semiotician Charles Morris. When he established the New Bauhaus, László Moholy-Nagy not only reinstituted the German preliminary course but hired a set of local professors, including Morris, to deliver courses in what he called "intellectual integration."[22] These professors were to help students imagine themselves as free, psychologically whole individuals (in keeping with Bauhaus precepts) who were training to work within complex natural and social systems (the subjects of the visiting professors' expertise). Morris lectured at the School of Design for several years, including the time that Cage was there.[23] It is not clear how well he may have known Cage, though given the small size of the School of Design and its faculty in 1941, it seems unlikely that they never met.

What is clear is that a few months before Cage composed the backdrop for "The City Wears a Slouch Hat," Morris published an essay called "The Mechanism of Freedom" in a popular collection of writings by leading public figures called *Freedom, Its Meaning*. The essay presented many of the aesthetic choices Cage had begun to make in political terms. In Morris's view, to be "free," a person or thing had to be able to act without being blocked by other forces. To act, however, the individual had to choose a direction from a universe of possibilities that presented themselves as signs—that is, as elements not only of the material world, but of the process of communication. Like psychologists such as Kurt Lewin and Gordon Allport, Morris believed that the person achieved psychological individuation by interacting with others. Communication thus shaped both the personality of individual people and the range of life choices they enjoyed.

To be free, individuals need not enjoy unlimited choices. Rather, they needed to enjoy unimpeded access to the *process of choosing* from the possibilities arrayed before them. Morris argued that an ability to choose represented a moral ideal and, at the same time, served as the basis of political democracy. Like psychologist Kurt Lewin, he argued that small groups provided a context in which individuals could achieve psychological agency by engaging with one another. He also suggested that the principles of small group interaction could be developed on a continental scale, and that when they were, they would renew the American polity. "Democracy," he explained, " . . . would involve the extension to social relations at large of the pattern of moral relations between smaller groups of individuals. It would aim to make every individual a consciously determining factor in the evolution of society." At its heart, he wrote, "a moral democracy is a society of free men freely choosing at each moment its own future."[24] Within such a system, government consisted not of the application of force upon the individual, but of the shaping of the arena of signs from which the individual made his life choices. As Morris put it, "The character of the individual's thought processes . . . is then amenable to control by the manipulation of the social environment of the individual. . . . The implication of this fact is that men can be 'made' free or kept from being free."[25]

Cage would never have called himself a manipulator of men's thoughts. Yet his compositions and his writings across the 1940s moved ever more in the direction of creating systems of sounds and words from within which individuals might choose their own aesthetic futures at every moment. During the war years, Cage struggled to define for himself the proper role of a composer with regard to the world of sounds, as well as the proper relationship between individual tones and collectives of sound, and between sound and dance. He also wrestled with his own sexuality, with his role in the war, and, at a more theoretical level, with the relationship between the interpersonal and political spheres of everyday life. In his time in Chicago he had come to understand the making of music as a species of therapeutic labor; in the years immediately thereafter, he would fuse the techniques and aims of that therapeutic work with a broader attempt to fashion models of a communicative world in which the sorts of tensions that plagued his music and his life might fade away.

CAGE IN WORLD WAR II: THE STRUGGLE WITH AGENCY

In 1935, Cage had married the willowy, artistic daughter of the archpriest of the Eastern Orthodox Church of Alaska, Xenia Kashevaroff. In June 1942, she and Cage moved to New York City and entered a metropolis fully turned toward war. When they arrived, the Museum of Modern Art was showing Steichen and Bayer's *Road to Victory*. The Army manned an antiaircraft battery in Central Park. Even the main hall of the city's self-declared epicenter, Grand Central Station, featured an enormous patriotic mural in which images of American soldiers and sailors stood at attention between photographs of American factories, Western landscapes, and a woman surrounded by children. In an arching panel over these scenes, an enormous battleship flanked by tanks and circled by warplanes set sail over the words, "THAT GOVERNMENT . . . BY THE PEOPLE . . . SHALL NOT PERISH FROM THE EARTH."

Cage wanted little to do with the jingoism at home or the fighting overseas. When the Army tried to draft him in December 1942, he presented the draft board with a doctor's letter explaining that Xenia had suffered a crippling leg injury from tuberculosis and that he was her sole support.[26] In photographs from the time, Xenia hardly appears incapacitated, but the board excused Cage from service and allowed him to take up war-related research work in a local library. As he later explained, his encounter with the war in New York City led him to rethink the relationship between public and private scales of action. In a February 1948 lecture at Vassar that was later published under the title "A Composer's Confessions," he put it this way: "Being involved in the complexities of a nation at war and a city in business-as-usual led me to know that there is a difference between large things and small things, between big organizations and two people alone in a room together. . . . My feeling was that beauty yet remains in intimate situations; that it is quite hopeless to think and act impressively in public terms. This attitude is escapist, but I believe that it is wise rather than foolish to escape from a bad situation."[27]

At first glance, the essay might seem to suggest that Cage had fled the public world of war for the presumably peaceful private realm, and that he located the pursuit of beauty—presumably by means of making music—solely in the intimate, interpersonal arena. In fact, Cage struggled with his own relationship to the public fact of the war *by means of* his relationship to his own music making. When he arrived in New York, Cage had not yet developed the chance methods of composition for which he would become famous. In his explorations of noise he had begun to expand the range of sounds his listeners might hear, and he had begun to ask them to take an active role in knitting them together into meaningful wholes. But in wartime New York, Cage turned back toward a more representational mode of music making and toward a deliberate attempt to influence the emotions of his audience.

In 1942, for instance, he composed *Imaginary Landscape No. 3*. The piece opened with a rapid hammering on tin surfaces and the rising and falling of an electronic siren; a pounding rhythm culminated in a single siren, and then more sirens. For all intents and purposes, it might as well have been the soundscape of the London Blitz. As journalist Calvin Tomkins later reported, Cage had in fact written the piece as a sonic analog to combat.[28] In this way, Cage had constructed a representation in sound that might serve as a vehicle with which to transport his feelings about the war into the hearts of his listeners. After *Imaginary Landscape No. 3*, he composed a prepared piano piece entitled *In the Name of the Holocaust* for a dance by Merce Cunningham—a piece whose title alone reflected the ways in which Cage was struggling to find a musical language with which to communicate the violence of the war to his listeners. And in 1943, he reworked an earlier percussion piece and created *Amores*—a four-part arrangement of tapping, rustling, and occasional bell tones that was infinitely slower and quieter than *Imaginary Landscape No. 3*. Cage performed *Amores* at the Museum of Modern Art in February 1943. "My composition *Amores*, is intended to arouse, shall we say, the feelings of love," he told the reporter for *Time*.[29]

With works like *Amores, In the Name of the Holocaust*, and *Imaginary Landscape #3*, Cage aimed to manipulate sounds in such a way as to also manipulate the emotions of his listeners. Across the following decades, he would find myriad ways to disavow his control over the process of composition, from turning his musical choices over to the *I Ching* to simply designating a stretch of time to be filled by whatever sounds occurred in whatever space the performance happened to occupy. But in 1943 he was still attempting to represent experience in sound and to communicate it. The trouble was that it wasn't working. "I noticed that when I conscientiously wrote something sad, people and critics were often apt to laugh," he later recalled. "I determined to give up composition unless I could find a better reason for doing it than communication."[30]

By most accounts, including his own, Cage found that reason in Eastern philosophy. Between 1943 and 1952, he turned away from an expressive sender-message-receiver model of music making and toward an environmental, surround-based mode that simultaneously denied his own agency as composer and aimed to enhance the agency of his listeners. That turn took place in two stages. The first of these occurred between 1943 and 1948, as Cage worked his way toward a mode of compositional agency that art historian Moira Roth has called the "aesthetic of indifference"; the second, in which Cage fully embraced indeterminacy, came about between 1948 and 1952.[31] According to Cage, and according to most scholars since, he experienced a period of psychological distress between 1943 and 1945. Cage publicly attributed his unhappiness to his failure to make his music communicate effectively, yet those years also saw the end of his ten-year marriage to Xenia and his acceptance of his homosexual relationship with Merce Cunningham.[32] Cage turned in a number of directions for relief, including psychoanalysis. "When I went to the analyst for some kind of preliminary meeting," Cage later recalled, "he said, 'I'll be able to fix you so that you'll write much more music than you do now.' I said, 'Good heavens! I already write too much, it seems to me.' That promise of his put me off."[33]

In lieu of psychoanalysis, Cage explained, he embraced "oriental philosophy."[34] He had first encountered the writings of Indian art historian Ananda Coomeraswamy when he and Xenia stayed briefly with the scholar Joseph Campbell soon after they arrived in New York; Lou Harrison had shown Cage the *I Ching* in 1943.[35] But according to Cage, it was a 1946 encounter with a young Indian woman, Geeta Sarabhai, that began to transform both his compositions and his understanding of the proper relationship between music and mind. Sarabhai had been introduced to Cage by the artist Isamu Noguchi. They agreed to trade lessons, Cage teaching Sarabhai about composition, and Sarabhai teaching Cage about Indian music and philosophy. Over a period of five months they met several times a week, sometimes with Lou Harrison as well. From Sarabhai, Cage learned that Indian music dealt with "permanent emotions"—"the heroic, the erotic, the wondrous, the mirthful, sorrow, fear, anger, the odious and their common tendency toward tranquility."[36] He also claimed to have learned that "the purpose of music [is] to season and sober the mind, thus making it susceptible of divine influences, and elevating one's affections to goodness."[37]

When Sarabhai returned to India, she gave Cage a copy of *The Gospel of Sri Ramakrishna*. Over the next year and a half, Cage read voraciously about mysticism, psychology, and the East. He reread Coomeraswamy and worked through the personality theories of Carl Jung, the mystical writings of Meister Eckhart, and ultimately the *Tao Te Ching* of Lao Tze. Each seemed to reinforce the idea that turning away from intentional communication toward "indifference" was a way to achieve inner peace, for composer and audience alike. By 1948, Cage came to echo Coomeraswamy, arguing that to make art was "to imitate Nature in her manner of operation."[38] For Cage, to imitate nature meant to turn away from the "large things" of nineteenth-century orchestral music, from public life in wartime, and even from harmony, which Cage believed had "become the tool of Western commercialism."[39] In their stead, Cage sought to find musical equivalents of the permanent emotions, and especially, the state of tranquility toward which they tended.

To do so, he believed he needed to find a way to become indifferent to the patterns of sound his compositions produced and to even stand apart from the process of production. At the level of composition, this meant extending his turn away from harmony and toward rhythm as a means of organizing sound. If harmonic structures concentrated the players of music toward a single expressive end, Cage held that rhythmic ones opened up spaces between sounds and allowed for an almost universal range of tones to emerge within a composition. Perhaps most important for Cage, rhythmic structures made the composer responsible for the overall shape of the composition but not necessarily the individual sounds that might come to life within it.

As musicologist David Nicholls has argued, one piece represents the outcome of Cage's wrestling with his own agency in this period especially effectively: *Sonatas and Interludes* for the prepared piano.[40] Cage worked on the piece for two years starting in February 1946, and when it was done it featured twenty movements and lasted an entire hour. As Cage described it, the piece seemed to belong to the emotionally expressive line of his earlier work. He had drawn from Coomeraswamy's book *The Dance of Shiva* and sought, he said, "to express in music" the "permanent emotions" of the Hindu tradition it described.[41] Yet, as Nicholls has shown, Cage did not map particular emotions onto individual movements.[42] Even though each element within the composition had its own emotional tenor, the composition as a whole did not so much express the range of permanent emotions as construct a scaffolding of sound patterns on which listeners had to construct their own emotional responses. In other words, Cage built the piece in such a way that he might offer his listeners the opportunity to feel the permanent emotions even as he himself remained indifferent to whether they in fact did or not.

At the same time, Cage developed a way to configure both the composition and the piano so as to grant each an expressive agency apart from his own. Cage later explained that he structured the piece in more or less mathematical patterns: "The first eight, the twelfth, and the last four sonatas are written in AABB rhythmic structures of varying proportions, whereas the first two interludes have no structural repetitions. This difference is exchanged in the last two interludes and the sonatas nine through eleven which have respectively a prelude, interlude, and postlude. The preparation of the piano is relatively elaborate, requiring two or three hours to effect."[43] In other words, Cage built a system of proportions and arrayed them onto a machine—the prepared piano—which could simultaneously produce the broad proportions called for and, thanks to the nuts and bolts and felt between its strings, introduce more or less random tones as well.

In his 1949 essay "Forerunners of Modern Music," Cage sought to outline the rationale behind *Sonatas and Interludes*. "The purpose of music," he wrote there, was to set "the soul in operation. The soul is the gatherer-together of the disparate elements (Meister Eckhart), and its work fills one with peace and love." In this context, a rhythmic structure that allowed for atonal variety of sound served a spiritual purpose: it opened the ears of the listener to the randomness of nature and to the sounds of a world from which the use of music to intentionally transmit emotional messages—and so to manipulate the audience—had disappeared. In place of self-expression Cage had instituted a practice that he thought of at the time as a species of self-negation. Cage had turned at least some of his creative agency over to a music machine and to a system for organizing the relationship of machine to performer. He had composed a system of sound by constructing the arena of processes that might limit the range of tones it would produce. At the same time, he had left his listeners free to choose among those tones for pleasure as they saw fit. The result of this process, he believed, was spiritual transformation: "The in-the-heart path of music leads now to self-knowledge through self-denial, and its in-the-world path leads likewise to selflessness."[44]

It is this spiritual turn that critics have largely marked as the root of Cage's later turn to indeterminacy. But in the same essay in which he speaks in the terms of paths and self-knowledge, Cage also describes himself in more political terms. Atonality, he wrote, was a way to overcome harmony and to maintain a more "ambiguous tonal state." Within this state, responsibility for deciding the emotional impact of tones shifted from the makers of harmonies—whether from the nineteenth century or the present—to listeners. Indeed, Cage wrote, the job of the composer was to build a new environment within which this shift toward a more decentralized, individuated agency could take place. In that sense, the composer resembled a postwar city planner. In the world of sound, Cage argued, "just as in a bombed-out city the opportunity to build again exists. This way one finds courage and a sense of necessity."[45]

Cage's simile couches a subtle but important shift. In the early 1940s, he had embraced Moholy's understanding of art as a way to make whole psyches that had been fractured by industrial society. Here, in early 1949, he has conceived of music making as a practice of postwar reconstruction. His phrasing may reflect a private urge to build a new life out of the ruins of his earlier marriage, but it also reflects a postwar political climate of which Cage was well aware. In the mid-1940s, Cage later recalled, to take an aesthetic turn to the East meant confronting popular opinions shaped by the recent conflict with Japan: "At the end of the war, or just afterwards . . . people still said that the East and the West were absolutely foreign, separate entities. And that a Westerner did not have the right to profess an Eastern philosophy. It was thanks to Coomeraswamy that I began to suspect that this was not true, and that Eastern thought was no less admissible for a Western [sic] than is European thought."[46] In 1949, in a talk that would ultimately become his 1959 "Lecture on Nothing," Cage went even further, depicting himself as fighting for freedom in the aesthetic realm:

"I found that I liked noises even more than I like intervals. I liked noises just as much as I had liked single sounds. Noises, too, had been discriminated against; and being American, having been trained to be sentimental, I fought for noises. I liked being on the side of the underdog."[47]

At the same time that Cage was describing his work in terms shaped by the war, he was trying to bring the therapeutic orientation he had developed several years earlier alongside Moholy to bear on the postwar environment. In his essay "A Composer's Confessions," Cage once again spoke of music as a tool for psychological integration:

> I began to read Jung on the integration of the personality. There are two principal parts of each personality: the conscious mind and the unconscious, and these are split and dispersed, in most of us, in countless ways and directions. The function of music, like that of any other healthy occupation, is to help bring those separate parts back together again. Music does this by providing a moment when, awareness of time and space being lost, the multiplicity of elements which make up an individual become integrated and he is one.[48]

Though the more Gestaltist Moholy would not have cited Jung, Cage's desire to create an aesthetic context in which to promote psychological integration echoes Moholy's therapeutic ideals. It also reflects Cage's responses to the war. In 1942, the cacophony of "The City Wears a Slouch Hat" emerged from the fact of Chicago's being an industrial-age city. Car engines, sirens, even footfalls on pavement: all were sounds made possible simply by modern mass manufacturing. By the late 1940s, Cage spoke hardly at all about industrial cities; rather, he spoke about the tension between "large things" and "small things," between the public and the interpersonal realms, and about how music ought to relate to both. In the late 1940s, he argued, music makers must help their listeners turn away from the deliberately impressive public harmonies of popular music. Listeners should cease to be passive mass receivers of emotional messages sent from distant powers. "It is rather the age-old process of making and using music and our becoming more integrated as personalities through this making and using that is of real value," he explained. And for that, one needed to engage in a species of aesthetic international relations. One needed to reach out to Asia, and particularly to the newly independent nation of India, and adopt what Cage believed to be its culturally specific form of creative agency. "If one makes music, as the Orient would say, *disinterestedly,* that is, without concern for money or fame but simply for the love of making it," wrote Cage, "it is an integrating activity and one will find moments in his life that are complete and fulfilled."[49]

BLACK MOUNTAIN COLLEGE AND
THE PURSUIT OF INDETERMINACY

Cage soon turned this vision against a hierarchical musical order whose performance style and sonic structures seemed increasingly to him to be the sonic analogs of fascism. The dictators of Nazi Germany (and now, in American eyes at least, of China and the Soviet Union) had imposed their authority through mass communication and instrumental propaganda. In authoritarian societies, lines of command and lines of communication paralleled each other, and both flowed from top to bottom. In democratic societies, as in democratic psyches, egalitarian relations obtained. And they could be sustained by a mode of communication in which individuals and nations alike contributed to a field of words and images, made their own choices as to whom to believe and with whom to associate, and in the process acted out a state of freedom.

In the second half of the 1940s, this same logic infused Cage's writing and composition. He too was committed to opening the senses of his listeners, particularly to sounds of a kind that had previously been declared the enemies of music. He too aimed to create a field of opportunities that spanned international boundaries, in his case by making work that bridged the East and the West. He too was an expert—albeit an expert in aesthetics rather than social science—and as such, he was devoted to building organizational systems in which individual listeners could move freely among sounds, learning within the arenas he had created through composition how to experience the wider world outside the concert hall.

To imagine Cage's performances as political acts may seem strange to us. But if it does, it is only because we have forgotten the degree to which social, psychological, and aesthetic concerns overlapped in this period. This was especially true at Black Mountain College. Today, most writers remember this tiny institution in the rural hills of North Carolina as an art school. This is not surprising, given that a list of its alumni reads like a *Who's Who* of postwar American art and literature. Between its founding in 1933 and its closing in 1956, the school employed faculty ranging from Bauhaus refugees Josef and Anni Albers and Walter Gropius to essayist Paul Goodman and poet Charles Olson. Students included painter Robert Rauschenberg, sculptor Kenneth Snelson, filmmaker Stan VanDerBeek, and writer Francine du Plessix Gray. Particularly in the 1940s and early 1950s, despite its relative isolation and its routine financial instability, the college brought together a generation of artists who had come of age in the Depression or in interwar Europe with a set of young Americans who, with Black Mountain behind them, would shape avant-garde art for the next three decades.

What is less well remembered is that like other centers of artistic innovation such as the Museum of Modern Art or Mills College, Black Mountain also embraced the theories of personality that underlay the push for democratic morale during World War II. Black Mountain was founded by John Rice, a charismatic and controversial professor of classics who had lately left Rollins College in Winter Park, Florida, and taken several colleagues with him. Rice and his compatriots hoped to establish a school built on the pragmatic educational principles articulated by John Dewey: students would learn collaboratively, through shared experience, and so acquire both academic knowledge and personal insight. They would put the arts at the center of their curriculum precisely because they believed that the arts offered the sorts of interactive experiences on which individual psychological development depended. Just before the college opened, Rice and a colleague approached Margaret Lewisohn, whose husband served on the board of trustees of the Museum of Modern Art in New York, as well as the museum's curator of architecture, Philip Johnson, to see whether they could recommend a professor who might lead the school's efforts in the arts. Johnson recommended Josef Albers.[50] Though he spoke no English at the time, Albers had taught the Bauhaus primary course in a sequence with Moholy-Nagy. He was also looking to emigrate from Nazi Germany.

When Albers came to America, Rice hired him to run a school that was already focused on using the arts as a basis of individual personality development and democratic community. Albers recognized both of these as familiar elements of the Bauhaus. But at Black Mountain, Rice and his colleagues couched their pursuits in specifically American terms. In the fall of 1935 a correspondent for *Harper's* magazine came to Black Mountain and stayed for two and a half months. He met with Rice steadily, recording his thoughts in a notebook. In a 1936 article for *Harper's*, he reported that Rice had told him, "The job of a college is to bring young people to intellectual *and emotional* maturity; to intelligence, by which I mean a subtle balance between the intellect and the emotions [italics original]." Such work was essential to the future of democratic society, he suggested. "In great part I blame Hitlerism on German education," Rice explained. German schools had focused on "stuffing the head full of facts, and [had] thus prepared for Hitler a nation of emotional infants ready to succumb to his demaguery."[51] In a 1942 memoir, Rice recalled that from its beginning, "Black Mountain was to be education for democracy." Its classrooms and its community would need to model democratic processes. Art would provide the heat with which to forge a new kind of citizen. "The democratic man, we said, must be an artist," wrote Rice. "The integrity, we said, of the democratic man, was the integrity of the artist, an integrity of relationship."[52]

By the late 1940s, Rice was gone. He had been nudged out in the late 1930s after having an affair with a student and after offending much of the faculty with his sometimes high-handed style.[53] Even so, his emphasis on democracy and the cultivation of pro-democratic personality remained. In June 1946, a young veteran and future sociologist named Charles Perrow hitchhiked to Black Mountain and stayed for two years. When he arrived in North Carolina, Perrow remembers, "Black Mountain was . . . a hologram of the nation's pending concern with democratic governance, cultural innovations, and sexual freedom."[54] With fascism and the war behind them, students at Black Mountain sought to construct a democratic community much like the open society of open selves described by Charles Morris. They also wrestled with the demands of living in what Perrow calls "a crowded cocoon cloistered in the Bible belt."[55] They buried themselves in Erich Fromm's *Escape from Freedom* and Karen Horney's *The Neurotic*

Personality of Our Time, as well as Freud's *Civilization and its Discontents*.[56] They tolerated sex outside marriage and homosexuality too, even if the towns around them did not.[57] And as early as 1944, they sought to integrate the student body, admitting black students for the summer session that year and, later, for the regular 1945 academic year as well. [58] By the late 1940s, in the eyes of its faculty and students at least, the college had become a prototype of a new, more democratic postwar American society.

At the core of that society was a new kind of person: one who possessed an integrated, balanced psyche. From its earliest days, the college sought to produce that mindset in its students by training them not only in art but in the humanities, sciences, and social sciences as well. In the years just after the war, faculty offered classes in literature, philosophy, sociology, history, economics, biology, chemistry, mathematics, several foreign languages, and even, thanks to the college's office manager, shorthand and typing.[59] Though Black Mountain College was never accredited and few of its students stayed for more than two years, it retained strong ties to some of the most elite universities in America, including Harvard, Yale, and Radcliffe.

In 1945 the college's ties to Harvard helped intensify its focus on the relationship between democracy and personality. That year the school hired John Wallen, a Harvard PhD student whose advisor was Gordon Allport, to teach courses in psychology. In the mid-1940s, Allport's writing and research had begun to focus on the reduction of social tensions by means of psychological intervention. In 1944, for instance, Allport and his student Leo Postman convened a group of Boston policemen in order to confront them with their own racism and thereby defuse it.[60] Allport had come to see the development of the individual personality and of the good society as entirely entwined. When he came to Black Mountain, Wallen brought with him Allport's conviction that multidirectional, interpersonal communication could simultaneously empower the individual and build a more cohesive community.[61] In his psychology classes, Wallen taught Fromm and Horney and, with them, the notion that contra Freud, childhood did not irrevocably mold the individual psyche. Personalities could be shaped and reshaped over time, and societies with them. To prove the point, Wallen turned one of his classes into a collective self-analysis. Students were to

FIGURE 4.2.

Architect Buckminster Fuller (center, in long-sleeved white shirt) and his students working to raise an early model of the geodesic dome, summer 1948. Photograph by Beaumont
Newhall. © Beaumont Newhall, © 2012, the Estate of Beaumont and Nancy Newhall. Permission to reproduce courtesy of Scheinbaum and Russek Ltd., Santa Fe, New Mexico.

observe their relations with each other and Wallen himself, and so come to
understand more general truths about the psychology of groups.[62] Outside
his classes, much as Gordon Allport had attempted a sort of group therapy
for the Boston police, Wallen tried to organize students into teams that
might reach out into the surrounding hills and spur local citizens to community action.

For Wallen and the many students who rallied to his charismatic vision,
"group process" presented a possible solution to the sorts of global conflicts they had all just lived through. "Were intelligent and creative individuals able to come together, or was this doomed by inescapable human
evil?" asks Charles Perrow. "Portentous as this sounds, it was something
that gripped us."[63] For Josef Albers and students more explicitly interested
in the arts, on the other hand, the route to self- and social-improvement

would be built by artistic labor. As Perrow recalls, "BMC at this time . . . was divided. On the one hand was the idea of community, and democratic governance, announced in the BMC catalogue, but really espoused for the first time in its history by the young idealist John Wallen. On the other hand was the idea of artistic, aesthetic achievement that would make problems of governance take care of themselves, that is to say, those who achieved the ideal would be the authorities."[64]

JOHN CAGE DEFENDS SATIE

The conflict between these two positions roiled Black Mountain for more than two years. It dominated discussions about curriculum and hiring, and it reared up in conversations about the college's food plan, about its buildings, and even about its fences. By early 1948, the advocates of art had largely vanquished the Wallenites and Wallen had left the campus. Just a few weeks after his departure, John Cage and Merce Cunningham arrived at Black Mountain for a four-day visit.[65] They were on their way to the West Coast on one of their periodic tours and asked if they might stop for few days to perform and lecture. The college was delighted to have them, though it offered no pay. During their stay, Cunningham danced and Cage performed his *Sonatas and Interludes* for the first time in public. The Black Mountain College community was ecstatic. To many, Cage and Cunningham looked like kindred spirits. As one student put it, their visit "illuminated the college both in creation and in response," and provided an occasion in which "one's own deepest aims are befriended by the activity or words of another."[66]

Perhaps part of their appeal stemmed from the ways in which their work resolved the campus conflict between social activism and artistic production. After his performance of *Sonatas and Interludes,* for example, Cage gave a talk about the nature of his work. His remarks spoke directly to the concerns of the college. Rather than define musical art as a specialized area of expertise, he argued that "the highest use of music was like anything man 'made': to integrate a man's total faculties through the order of the composition." In the process, Cage simultaneously validated the power of art as a quintessentially human activity, depicted it as a key part of everyday life, *and* suggested that it could have the sort of impact on social order commonly ascribed to community organizing. The ambitions of artists need not conflict with the goals of community builders; on the contrary, they could be the same thing. Because art served as a force for psychological integration, it could even give rise to a new social order. "Since integration may recognize itself in a stranger," Cage told his audience, "a new society may one day slowly take shape out of the present schizophrenia through our self-won coordination. It begins with music and ends with a common human nature."[67]

Though it is impossible to know precisely what Cage meant by "schizophrenia," those in a Black Mountain audience at the time might well have thought he was referring to one or both of two things: first, the chaos of the industrial world for which Moholy and other Bauhaus alumni had long argued art might be therapeutic; and second, the deep psychosocial divides between the forces of authoritarianism and democracy that were then echoing through discussions of campus and global politics alike. In either case, the phrase "self-won coordination" would have described the sort of democratic society promoted at the same moment by Allport, Stack Sullivan, Morris, and others. For the social scientists, as apparently for Cage, to become psychologically integrated was to win one's psyche back for oneself alone. One could then leave behind societies organized around the top-down instrumental domination of human masses, and instead enter a new world: one in which psychologically whole individuals might recognize each other, and so coordinate their interactions as equals.

The students of Black Mountain were so taken by Cage and Cunningham that they showered them with gifts of food and with paintings and drawings when they drove away. Josef Albers was sufficiently impressed as to ask them back to teach in that year's summer session. Like the core curriculum, Black Mountain's summer programs leaned toward the arts, but also featured courses in the social sciences and the humanities. In the summer of 1947, for instance, Eric Kohler gave a particularly popular set of lectures on the themes of "world government" and "the crisis of the individual."[68] In the summer of 1948, Reichian psychologist and regular Black Mountain professor Donald Calhoun taught "Culture and Personality" and "Freudianism and the Social Sciences," while Beatrice Pitney Lamb,

FIGURE 4.3.
Buckminster Fuller and Merce Cunningham perform in Satie's *Ruse of the Medusa* at Black Mountain College, summer 1948. John Cage played piano for the performance. Photograph by Clemens Kalischer. Used by permission.

editor of the *United Nations News*, a monthly report of the United Nations' work published by the Woodrow Wilson Foundation, lectured on "Soviet-American relations with the United Nations."

In 1948, alongside these relatively internationalist courses, Albers arrayed a new faculty. The college as a whole had long had a mix of European and American teachers, most well established in their fields. In the arts and especially in music, many of the professors had come from Germany. That summer, however, Albers recruited half a dozen mostly young and exceptionally innovative Americans. In a given week, students could study dance with Merce Cunningham, music with John Cage, painting with Willem de Kooning, and architecture with Buckminster Fuller, as well as color theory with Josef Albers.[69] They could also work with an astonishingly gifted group of peers. Students that summer included sculptor Kenneth Snelson, future film director Arthur Penn, and future architect Paul Williams, among nearly seventy others.

Their time together would have an extraordinary impact on the American art world for the next twenty years and, indirectly, on the American counterculture as well. That summer, Buckminster Fuller and a team of students erected the first of his geodesic domes, an architectural form that would house both American propaganda exhibitions and back-to-the-land communes in the years ahead. Cage and Fuller became fast friends; their mutual affection would shape both their work and their public personas across the 1960s and, with them, the ideals of artists and countercultural rebels alike. Paul Williams and his wife Vera become close with Cage and Cunningham, and later funded one of Cage's first forays into making music with recording tape, the *Williams Mix* of 1952. The Williamses would also join Cage and former Black Mountain professor M. C. Richards in founding the Gate Hill Cooperative community in Rockland County, an experiment in collective living that preceded the back-to-the-land movement by a decade.[70]

Charles Perrow, who stayed for the summer, recalls that the summer session had "a glitter that made the basic conflicts of the regular season suddenly seem superficial."[71] For Cage, the summer provided an opportunity to renew his assault on harmonic uniformity in music and, in the view of many in his audience, on the nation that had lately inflicted its own dark vision of unity on the world, Germany. Over the course of the summer, Cage gave twenty-five half-hour performances of works by French composer Erik Satie. After briefly introducing the music and discoursing on Satie, Cage would play the piano, sometimes in the dining hall and sometimes in his cottage, while students and faculty lounged on the lawn outside.[72] Over those same weeks, a German-born keyboardist and new Black Mountain professor named Erwin Bodky offered a seminar on the music of Beethoven. On Saturday nights he presented recitals of other classical music as well. Until about midway through the summer, the two series, Cage's and Bodky's, ran without apparent conflict. But one evening Cage delivered a lecture before his performance that soon had the campus in an uproar.

The talk would later be published under the title "Defense of Satie." In it, Cage attacked harmony and celebrated time as the proper organizing principle for music. He argued that no less a figure than Ludwig van Beethoven, with his emphasis on expressive grandeur and harmonic unity, had led music astray. "Beethoven represents the most intense lurching of the boat away from its natural even keel," exclaimed Cage.[73] Where music should have been going, said Cage, was toward India, where rhythm and time lengths had long governed the structure of music, and toward France, where Satie had demonstrated the power of time lengths in a Western setting. Neither Satie nor the anonymous Indians of Cage's account suffered from the need to impose a single unified sound pattern on their audiences. On the contrary, each constructed a form (out of time lengths) within which all sorts of sounds could encounter one another. "Into Satie's continuity come folk tunes, musical clichés, and absurdities of all kinds," wrote Cage. "He is not ashamed to welcome them in the house he builds: its structure is strong."[74]

Only three years after the end of World War II, Cage's audience—particularly the many German refugees in attendance—could not fail to hear the political overtones of his remarks. Beethoven, the German, had bound sounds together into harmonies and made them march to the single end of expressing his will. In the process, Cage argued, he had distorted and almost destroyed the natural culture of Western music. Satie, the representative of France, together with unnamed musicians from the newly free nation of India, imposed themselves on no one. Rather, they built solid structures within which sounds could be free. The audience of a Beethoven concert, assaulted by sounds that had been de-individuated and massed into lockstep harmony, was a victim of a musical blitzkrieg, Cage implied. The free French listeners of Satie or the free citizens of India, on the other hand, were surrounded by sounds among which they could make their own choices and in the process, remake their inner lives. Lest his audience misunderstand his larger purpose, Cage concluded his remarks by announcing that "the final meaning of music may now be suggested: it is to bring into co-being elements paradoxical by nature . . . that is, Law elements . . . [and] Freedom elements. . . . the whole forming thereby an organic entity. Music then is a problem parallel to that of the integration of the personality: which in terms of modern psychology is the co-being of the conscious and the unconscious mind, Law and Freedom, in a random world situation. Good music can act as a guide to good living."[75]

With these words, Cage evoked an understanding of the relationship between psychological and social organization that dominated debates across the social sciences at virtually the same moment. Like Allport, Stack Sullivan, and even Horkheimer, Cage assumed that the individual psyche must blend conscious and unconscious elements in an organic whole, and that once it did, the individual could live well. For both Cage and the social scientists, living well meant living in a society within which persons might act independently, in terms set by their own desires, though also inside boundaries set by experts. Allport, in his writings, and Wallen, at Black Mountain College, both hoped to reform individual personalities by build-

FIGURE 4.4.
John Cage and Merce Cunningham in the summer of 1953. Cage and Cunningham were on their way back to New York from teaching in the Black Mountain College Summer Institute in the Arts. Photo taken at the home of Mrs. Ira Julian by Frank Jones. Courtesy of the North Carolina State Archives.

ing small groups whose members could communicate with one another in terms set by the limits of the experiment or project at hand. Cage hoped to transform his listeners not by unifying sounds and marching them against their ears, but by building solid houses within which a diversity of sounds might live in a unified form. In this sense, Cage's music making paralleled not only the integration of personality, but an ostensibly democratic mode of creating and managing society as a whole. To integrate the personality and to create a society that tolerated individual diversity within collective unity—in 1948, these projects equally preoccupied Cage and the American social scientists and diplomats concerned with building a new postwar international order. That summer at Black Mountain, both Cage's performances and the college as a whole became prototypes—small-scale experiments in organizing power that echoed and, in the minds of some of their participants, might someday shape political experiments underway at the national and international levels.

A WORLD OF SOUNDS, FREED

Over the next four years, Cage would expand the tactics he celebrated in his "Defense of Satie" into the set of aesthetic principles and practices for which he would ultimately become most famous: "indeterminacy." As a practice, at least in its early stages, indeterminacy usually referred to the making of music using what Cage called "chance operations." In a 1952 article, for example, Cage explained that he had recently composed his *Imaginary Landscape No. IV* for twelve radios with the aid of the *I Ching*. As in his earlier work, Cage organized the composition in terms of time lengths, each of which might serve as a structural microcosm of others, thanks to a square-root formula he had devised. This time, however, he also tossed the three coins that were meant to obtain oracular advice from the *I Ching*. These coins yielded patterns of hexagrams that Cage then used in a series of complicated mathematical transformations to convert into patterns of sound. Essentially, he determined the structure of the piece through a series of appeals to randomness.

Over the years, biographers and musicologists have generally ascribed Cage's employment of chance methods to his simultaneous encounter with Zen Buddhism. Sometime around 1950, Cage began taking classes with Zen master D. T. Suzuki at Columbia University. These classes, like his earlier readings of Meister Eckhart and Ananda Coomeraswamy, stressed the negation of the self and the opening of the senses to an entire universe of experience. For Suzuki, the universe was one and whatever happened within it was, by definition, neither good nor bad. Under these conditions, intention ceased to matter. As Cage said about *Imaginary Landscape No. IV*, "A 'mistake' is beside the point, for once anything happens it authentically is."[76]

Yet even as his turn to indeterminacy reflected his engagement with Suzuki, it also spoke to an anxiety about power and communication that Cage shared with social scientists. He wrote that in the case of *Imaginary Landscape No. IV*, for instance, the *I Ching* made it possible "to make a musical composition the continuity of which is free of individual taste and memory (psychology) and also of the literature and 'traditions' of the art. The sounds enter the time-space centered within themselves, unimpeded by service to any abstraction."[77] In other words, chance methods of composition freed sounds from the need to obey the will of a dictatorial composer or even to follow the norms of an oppressive culture. Sounds could be free to be themselves. Or, to put it in the utopian political idiom of the late 1940s, they could enjoy their diversity within the unity of the composition.

In a 1958 lecture in Darmstadt, Germany, later published under the title "Indeterminacy," Cage acknowledged the political implications of his aesthetics in an exceptionally detailed analysis of the role of chance in his compositions. He described his new method less as a way of organizing sound than as a way of leveling power relationships between people *by* organizing sound. Casting a cold eye on his own work, and particularly on the work that many consider his first fully indeterminate composition, *Music of Changes*, Cage feared that he had become an aesthetic authoritarian. Cage had composed the piece with the aid of the *I Ching* but, as he explained, the piece was only indeterminate with regard to the chance procedures used in its composition: "Though chance operations brought about the determinations of the composition, these operations are not available in its performance. The function of the performer in the case of the *Music of Changes* is that of the contractor who, following an architect's blueprint, constructs a building." The composer might enjoy the freedom of identifying himself with "no matter what eventuality," wrote Cage. But the performer suffered beneath the composition. Because he is "not able to perform from his own center," the performer "must identify himself in so far as possible with the center of the work as written." That is, he must meld his own desires into those of the composer, who may have used chance methods, but who nonetheless managed to create a set of musical instructions that almost entirely constrained the performer. "The fact that these things that constitute it, though only sounds, have come together to control a human being, the performer, gives the work the alarming aspect of a Frankenstein monster," Cage concludes. "The situation is of course characteristic of Western music, the masterpieces of which are its most frightening examples, which when concerned with humane communication only move over from Frankenstein monster to Dictator."[78]

Cage's fear that his music might have played the role of dictator reflects concerns developed well outside his engagement with Zen. Throughout this essay, as he explored his own works and those of fellow modernists such as Karlheinz Stockhausen and Morton Feldman, Cage paid almost no attention to the sonic side of music. Rather, he focused on the organization of creation and performance. He castigated himself and others for turning creative instrumentalists into obedient "workmen."[79] In fact, Cage was attacking the same forces he had critiqued in 1948. Just as Beethoven's harmonies massed sounds that should be independent, unifying them so forcefully as to erase their individuality, so now modern compositions, including his own, sometimes forced performers to submit themselves to the will of a dictatorial artist.

What was the alternative to this implicit fascism? For the audience, it was to hear an array of sounds whose interrelationships could not be predicted beforehand but, rather, had to be made on the spot by the listeners themselves. For the performer, it was to cease to obey the commands of invisible authoritarians and to enter instead into a state of "being alert in an indeterminate situation." It was turn away from his sense of himself as an agent, an ego separate from all other egos, and to turn instead toward "the ground of Meister Eckhart, from which all impermanencies flow and to which they return." In practical terms, to turn toward the mystical experience of oneness meant to enter a distributed field of performers and sounds. In his lecture, Cage argued that performers should be separated and deployed around the full performance area. Doing so would free sounds "to issue from their own centers and to interpenetrate." It would also free musicians for "independent action." Ultimately, it would prevent the massification of performers and audience alike. "There is the possibility," wrote Cage, "when people are crowded together that they will act like sheep rather than nobly."[80]

If the authoritarian composer massed sounds and people, the antiauthoritarian took the democratic tack. Like Cage's version of Satie or, for that matter, like Allport and Lewin, the composer needed to develop a structure within which every person and every sound might be wholly itself, independent and free. In the summer of 1952, Cage created two events that aimed to bring these principles to life. The first took place at Black Mountain College and has been called *Theater Piece #1* or, sometimes, *Black Mountain Event*. Four years after the triumphant summer of 1948, Cage and Cunningham returned to Black Mountain. By that time the college had become a year-round home to an array of artists who celebrated a field approach to communication, including the poet Charles Olson, who led the school, and the painter Robert Rauschenberg, a student there. In the fall of 1951, Rauschenberg completed what he called his *White Paintings*. Large canvases coated only in white paint, these images served as fields across which played the light and shadow of the room around them. As Cage acknowledged when he saw them, they seemed to blur the line between painted surface and three-dimensional space.[81] The following summer, Cage, Rauschenberg, and others read Antonin Artaud's *The Theater and its Double*, which Black Mountain poet M. C. Richards had lately translated.[82] Artaud had long advocated a theater in which, as he put it, "the actors are not performing / they are doing."[83] After reading Artaud, Cage and half a dozen compatriots created what has since been widely celebrated as the first Happening.

What actually *happened* at the event remains in some dispute, but the usually reliable Calvin Tomkins has described a gathering in the Black Mountain dining room after dinner. After members of the college had taken scattered places in chairs and at tables, a series of events occurred: Cage delivered a lecture from a ladder, Merce Cunningham danced through the audience trailed by a dog, David Tudor played a Cage piece on the piano, Charles Olson and M. C. Richards read poetry, and movie and still photographs flickered across the surfaces of Rauschenberg's *White Paintings*, which were hung from the ceiling. When the activity ended, the participants picked up a series of tea cups that had been set on clusters of chairs and walked away.

In the years since, critics have described the event as an example of Artaud's explosive vision of a theater without walls and of the field aesthetics emerging across American art.[84] But in the context of Cage's decade-long struggle with agency and authority, it also represented the migration of the surround aesthetic he had developed in his music making into the world of men and women and bodies. In his *Theater Piece*, Cage freed his performers—to the extent that they were ever *his* performers at all—to act independently, yet in concert with one another. They modeled in theater the sort of world that he had idealized in sound: a world of diverse interactions, with each individual sound and person completely individuated and yet, simultaneously, orchestrated and whole.

Over the next two decades, artists and social activists would take up the Happening precisely for the aesthetic and political freedoms it offered, and they would make it a ubiquitous prototype for a new social order. Meanwhile, on August 29, 1952, David Tudor performed Cage's composition *4'33"* in Woodstock, New York. Here is the entire score of the composition:

I

TACET

II

TACET

III

TACET

NOTE: The title of this work is the total length in minutes and seconds of its performance. At Woodstock, N.Y., August 29, 1952, the title was *4'33"* and the three parts were 33", 2'40", and 1'20". It was performed by David Tudor, pianist, who indicated the beginnings of parts by closing, the endings by opening, the keyboard lid. However, the work may be performed by any instrumentalist or combination of instrumentalists and last any length of time.[85]

With *4'33"*, as with *Theater Piece #1,* Cage freed sounds, performers, and audiences alike from the tyrannical wills of musical dictators. All tensions—between composer, performer, and audience; between sound and music; between the West and the East—had dissolved. Even as he turned away from what he saw as more authoritarian modes of composition and performance, though, Cage did not relinquish all control of the situation. Rather, he acted as an aesthetic expert, issuing instructions that set the parameters for action. Even as he declined the dictator's baton, Cage took up a version of the manager's spreadsheet and memo. Thanks to his benevolent instructions, listeners and music makers alike became free to hear the world as it was and to know themselves in that moment. Sounds and people became unified in their diversity, free to act as they liked, within a distinctly American musical universe—a universe finally freed of dictators, but not without order.

part two

The Democratic Surround in the Cold War

5

The Cold War and the Democratic Personality

Today, in journalism and film at least, Americans remember World War II as a time of national unity and its soldiers as members of "the greatest generation."[1] But in the final years of the conflict, few Americans saw themselves that way. Even as their armies pressed forward across Europe and the South Pacific and the nation's factories pumped out new ships and tanks and bombs, Americans experienced widespread social dislocation. In the wake of Pearl Harbor, the American Federation of Labor promised to prevent strikes in defense plants for the duration of the war. Even so, more than fourteen thousand wildcat strikes rocked factories and mines across the country between 1941 and 1945; more than eight million Americans took part.[2] Race riots exploded in Detroit (1942), Harlem (1943), and Los Angeles (1943). During the war years, hundreds of thousands of civilians left their homes to take up work in defense plants. Rural areas emptied out, while regions with heavily war-related employment such as California, Michigan, and even the District of Columbia boomed. At the same time, the need for troops put extraordinary pressure on American families. Between 1941 and 1945, eleven million Americans served in the military overseas, many leaving their families behind for years.[3]

On the battlefield, American soldiers witnessed and committed acts of violence out of proportion to anything most had ever known. American troops in the South Pacific marched island to island, shelling Japanese bunkers, shooting enemy soldiers at close range, and, on some islands, burning them out of foxholes and caves. As American naval forces neared the

Japanese mainland, sailors watched in horror as kamikaze pilots steered their planes toward the decks of American carriers. In Europe, American troops fought their way up the Italian peninsula, through the hedgerows of Normandy, and across the frozen wasteland of the Hürtgen Forest. Allied bombers leveled German cities, most infamously Hamburg in 1943 and Dresden in 1945. And as Allied troops closed in on Germany itself, they began to find the concentration camps, peopled by living skeletons and piled high with corpses.

The kamikazes and the camps gave evidence enough of the evils of fascism. But the war also taught Americans that they too were capable of atrocious violence. In August 1945, when the United States dropped atom bombs on Hiroshima and Nagasaki, many were naturally relieved to see the end of the war. But others were shocked at what their country had done. "The United States of America has this day become the new master of brutality, infamy, atrocity," wrote one reader to the editors of *Time.* "Bataan, Buchenwald, Dachau, Coventry, Lidice were tea parties compared with the horror which we . . . have dumped on the world."[4] In many quarters the bomb caused citizens to doubt the very democratic agency that so many had promoted as the key to wartime morale. As Dwight MacDonald, editor of the left-wing journal *Politics,* put it, "There is something askew with a society in which vast numbers of citizens can be organized to create a horror like The Bomb without even knowing they are doing it. What real content, in such a case, can be assigned to notions like 'democracy' and 'government of, by and for the people'?"[5] Novelist E. B. White summed up his own response to the bomb in a column for *The New Yorker*: "For the first time in our lives, we can feel the disturbing vibrations of complete human readjustment. Usually the vibrations are so faint as to go unnoticed. This time they are so strong that even the ending of a war is overshadowed."[6]

To the analysts who had pushed for democratic morale, the bomb unleashed not only a new understanding of humankind's ability to destroy the globe, but a vision of a relationship between psychology, communication, and politics that might save it. If Americans had become as violent as their enemies, then perhaps there was something in the *human* psyche and not only in German or Japanese minds that led to war. And if that was the case, then analysts needed to ask how it was that American psyches had been transformed into minds that could allow the kind of mass violence their country had originally gone to war to stop. The answer for many intellectuals was the psychologically destructive nature of industrial society, and especially its mass communication techniques. "The movies, the radio, the super-highway have softened us up for the atom bomb," wrote essayist Mary McCarthy in 1947. "We have lived with them without pleasure, feeling them as a coercion on our natures, a coercion coming seemingly from nowhere and expressing nobody's will. The new coercion finds us without the habit of protest; we are dissident but apart."[7]

Among social scientists and policy makers, the twinned threats of cultural massification and mass annihilation drove a return to questions of the democratic personality. In the years immediately after World War II, these questions arose in two stages. First, in the late 1940s, they emerged alongside a widespread clamor for international government within an America that was itself becoming a dominant global power. For sociologists and psychologists in particular, the democratic personality again became a model for individual psychological health, while the early-war vision of democratic unity became a model for a new world order. Second, at the end of the decade, as the Soviet Union became a nuclear power and America entered the Korean War, the one-world utopianism of the mid-1940s gave way to a new vision in which East and West were divided along psychological lines. The United States remained the home of the democratic personality, while China and the Soviet Union inherited the totalitarian mantle of Nazi Germany. By 1954, President Eisenhower could be heard telling an audience at Columbia University that "the world, once divided by oceans and mountain ranges, is now split by hostile concepts of man's character and nature. . . . Two world camps . . . lie farther apart in motivation and conduct than the poles in space."[8]

In a world that could be divided by personality types, communication took on a renewed importance. As psychologists had long argued, the family produced the characters of its children and the state produced the characters of its citizens through communication—interpersonal in the first case, and mediated in the second. At the start of World War II, analysts theorized modes of communication to produce democratic citizens and democratic morale. Now, in the wake of the war, social scientists hoped to help Americans raise a generation of democratic children, reintegrate returning veterans, and reduce racial and class conflicts at home. Together, they reimagined the democratic self in terms that echoed Herbert Bayer's design for *Road to Victory*. In their theories, at least, the democratic individual would be free to invent himself in spontaneous interaction within a field of others—individuals, corporations, and nations alike—all of whom represented themselves to him through communication. Once again, individuals would be surrounded by images and sounds, and they would be free to remake themselves—but only in terms already set by others, through the process of communication.

A DEMOCRATIC PERSONALITY FOR THE POSTWAR WORLD

To understand the power so many ascribed to communication in the Cold War, we need to revisit the 1940s, when the authority of the psychological and social sciences rose in concert with the political and military authority of the United States. Psychiatrists and psychology more generally became integral elements of the American military effort as soon as America entered World War II.[9] Psychiatrists and psychologists developed surveys of psychological fitness for service, analyzed troops' motivation to fight, treated soldiers suffering from combat-related stress, and created programs to help veterans readjust when they returned to civilian life. They also offered the results of their work to the public in highly popular volumes of advice. In 1943, for instance, Edwin Boring and Gordon Allport, professors of psychology at Harvard University, collaborated with forty-eight doctors, professors, and military officials to produce a bright orange Penguin paperback entitled *Psychology for the Fighting Man: What You Should Know About Yourself and Others.* The short book offered instruction on managing everything from the uses of one's senses on the battlefield to desires for food and sex. It sold more than four hundred thousand copies at twenty-five cents each.[10] Two years later, Boring and his team produced another widely distributed Penguin paperback, *Psychology for the Returning Serviceman,* this time offering advice on choosing a job, reentering the family, and dealing with "combat nerves."[11] By the final years of the war, books like these, together with military testing, had introduced millions of Americans to the field of psychology and to the habit of monitoring their inner lives in psychological terms.

At the same time, returning veterans confronted civilians with unaccustomed levels of psychological distress. Combat psychiatrists had found that fighting could lead to extensive psychological damage. In 1942, for instance, doctors found that 40 percent of the casualties needing evacuation from the island battlefields of Guadalcanal were suffering from psychiatric wounds.[12] In European studies, they saw psychiatric casualty rates ranging from 26 percent in units with moderate combat exposure to 75 percent in units that saw sustained and heavy fighting.[13] These statistics found reflections in the films of the day. During the war, filmmakers generally depicted GIs as sturdy, even heroic figures, loyal to their buddies on the battlefield and to their girls back home. As the fighting ended, however, filmmakers began to focus on the psychological needs of returnees. Films like *The Best Years of Our Lives* (1946), *Crossfire* (1947), *The Dark Past* (1948), and *To Hell and Back* (1955) all depicted soldiers for whom memories of combat had become ongoing nightmares. Even psychologically stable soldiers seemed to carry the taint of violence. A veteran in *Crossfire,* for instance, described coming home this way: "Now we start looking at each other again. We don't know what we're supposed to do. We don't know what's supposed to happen. We're too used to fighting. But we just don't know what to fight. You can feel the tension in the air. A whole lot of fight and hate that doesn't know where to go."[14]

To a profession that had focused for some time on producing openminded, empathetic alternatives to the authoritarian personality, returning soldiers posed a challenge. Psychiatrists had discovered that soldiers did not fight simply because of their beliefs. As the authors of the much cited 1945 volume *Men under Stress* put it, they had learned that "The will to fight must be forged out of the fiery furnaces of fear and aggressiveness . . . We have to win this war with our hearts as well as our heads and hands. Ideas alone are too pallid."[15] Such truths, however, made some fear that American troops had come to resemble their fascist enemies. Like the Germans and the Japanese, Americans had been asked to turn off their reason, to act on their most violent impulses, and to do so as a unified, uniform mass. When they returned home to the United States, they brought with them not only their recollections of the fighting but the specter of their own resemblance to the enemy.

In the wake of the war, psychiatrists who worked with veterans sought to return them to a condition of health that was defined first and foremost by their separation from the military mass. As psychologist Carl Rogers put it, soldiers in uniform were "men without faces"; to return them to health in the civilian world was to help them "resume selfhood as a specific, unique individual."[16] Once reindividuated, however, the veteran still faced a problem that he had in common with civilians: an irrational psyche. Before the war, Freud had argued that deep within every individual lay a bit of madness. To many psychiatrists, the violence of combat had proven the point. The war had shown that individual unreason could be welded into mass murder. With that legacy in mind, postwar psychiatrists and psychologists, alongside novelists and filmmakers, began to fear that every individual psyche existed in a state of tension—between the conscious and the unconscious, the rational and the irrational, the peaceful and the violent. They likewise noted that the violence that lurked inside every person could rear up even in the most rational of nations. What was worse, rationality itself could be harnessed in its service. As the war ended, many saw the trauma of combat veterans and the condition of ordinary citizens as analogous. Both lived in a state of psychological tension. Both had felt the pressure of highly mechanized, rationally irrational systems—military in the first case, industrial in the second—and in that sense, both were quintessentially modern types.

As the United States became the preeminent military, scientific, and economic power on the planet, its social and psychological theorists drew on prewar and early-war visions of the democratic personality as alternatives to this bleak view of modern man. Some, especially writers associated with the culture and personality school, sought to identify a uniquely American character type.[17] Others, many of whom were physical and social scientists, transformed collections of traits associated with the democratic personality into a model of a newly universal and ideal self. In both cases, writers sought to answer the sort of question put forward by the Pulitzer Prize-winning Harvard philosophy professor Ralph Barton Perry at the start of his 1949 volume *Characteristically American.* "What of ourselves?" he asked. "What is it to be American—in thought and deed and feeling?"[18]

For Perry, the answer lay in reclaiming the individuality and unity-in-diversity idealized by World War II proponents of democratic morale for a newly powerful postwar America. The ideal American personality, he argued, stood sufficiently apart from others as to be able to reason independently and choose among alternative courses of action. At the same time, it did not stand alone. American individualism, he wrote, required "a togetherness of several and not the isolation of one, or the absorption of all into a higher unity. . . . Americans do not take naturally to mechanized discipline. They remain an aggregate of spontaneities."[19] Lest the reader misunderstand, Perry hammered home the importance of preserving the diversity of individuals and groups within the American nation. He argued for a nation bound by "collective individualism" and a public consisting of "many nests of distinct individuals, and not their fusion, or their control or replacement by any kind of corporate entity or institution such as race, nation, state or historical or social force."[20]

In popular memory, American culture in the late 1940s has long been a wintry lake, slowly freezing over with racism, anticommunism, and gender conformity. But within some of the most mainstream centers of American intellectual life, these years also saw the promotion of a multiracial, sexually tolerant, egalitarian society. One of the most articulate spokesmen for this more utopian view was philosopher and semiotician Charles Morris, who taught at the University of Chicago and alongside John Cage at Moholy's New Bauhaus as well. Like Moholy and, for that matter, Herbert Bayer, Morris believed that individual psyches had been fractured by the pressures of industrial life and, now, by war. They needed to be reintegrated, but in such a way as to preserve their individuality. Likewise, society itself needed to be unified, but in such a way as to preserve maximum diversity among its members. For Morris, the rebuilding of postwar America, and indeed of the world as a whole, depended on the same promotion of the individual personality that lay behind earlier campaigns for democratic morale. "If an 'implacable opponent' is destroying man, that opponent is man himself," he explained in his 1948 book *The Open Self.* "We sense acutely the dark powers in ourselves. . . . We have new engines, new fabrics, new buildings, new headaches. *We need new selves. And new relationships between selves* [italics original]. . . . We can subordinate impersonal forces to human ends only if we recover the standpoint of the personal."[21]

Like Ralph Barton Perry, or for that matter Margaret Mead, Morris hoped Americans might turn away from the racism and social regimentation of fascism and toward the embrace of other races, other nationalities, and especially "psychological minorities"—which included homosexuals.[22] Morris's views are worth quoting at length, both because they represent the utopian optimism shared by many Americans in the late 1940s and because they so clearly presage the person-centered social movements of later decades. The totalitarian society, he explained, was a closed society of closed selves. It perpetuated itself by the "rationing of food, and the direction of ideas and ideals by the control of the press, the radio, the schools, the arts, the sciences, and the public platform. . . . Belsen, Buchenwald, and Dachau were the fatal fruits of this modern horror."[23] For Morris, as for many others at this moment, fascism and modernity appeared to be dangerously entwined. The solution: a flexible, highly interactive society, united in its heterogeneity. Such a society, he wrote, would "accept and dignify diversity. It will repudiate all attempts to pour its members into a common mold. It will be a society in which all varieties of persons can attain their own unique forms of integrity. It will glory in a multiplicity of arts and philosophies and ways of life. It will recognize that the interactions between persons must be as diversified as interacting persons are diverse. . . . It will be a person-centered society in which no type of person can impose his pattern of selfhood upon other persons."[24]

Though his language prefigured the countercultural idealism of the 1960s, Morris did not envisage a generation of longhairs running wild in the streets. On the contrary, he favored a nation modeled on the well-ordered interactions of the laboratory. "Science," he claimed, "is a miniature example of the open society."[25] Much as scientific communities structured themselves in constant interaction, so should American society structure itself through communication. Morris feared the power of mass media. Like Ralph Barton Perry, he favored a constant conversation among highly individuated, spontaneously acting citizens. Physical and social scientists could guide this exchange by setting the intellectual and social terms on which it could take place, much as they had lately set the terms of weaponry and propaganda for global combat. Within the bounds set by science, Americans would be free to be themselves and to be models for the world their nation was coming to dominate. In that sense, Morris and others in this period sought both to free Americans from totalitarian systems of power and to integrate them into a new system of scientifically managed control.

Perhaps the two most visible proponents of the fusion of liberation and control in the postwar years were the Columbia education professor Lyman Bryson and the MIT mathematician Norbert Wiener. Each gave voice to a widespread hope that social and technological engineering could enable Americans to manage themselves. By the late 1940s, Bryson had established a national reputation as a writer, radio commentator, and popular intellectual. In 1947, his volume *Science and Freedom* launched an extensive promotion of the sort of social engineering imagined by Morris. Bryson called his view "scientific humanism" and explained it thus: "Our humanism is scientific because we believe in control of social change by intelligence and experience, directly and freely applied. . . . we shall use social engineering to solve the problem of setting up the conditions of freedom but not to determine what men shall do with freedom when they get it. Indeed, we are arguing here that the chief uses of freedom are defeated by those who set up the conditions and try also to determine its content."[26] For Bryson, as for Morris, a democratic nation had to use science and technology to build a social arena within which individuals enjoyed a maximum array of choices about how to live their lives.

In the decade to come, the American state would constrain its citizens' political choices far more than Morris or Bryson might have liked. Even so, we need to recognize that in the post–World War II era, liberation and control were not opposites. On the contrary, for many intellectuals at least, the purpose of state control was individual freedom. As Bryson put it, "a Democratic government is one that has for its purpose the creation of such conditions as will best keep and develop the intrinsic powers of man."[27] The nurture of internal powers mattered because for Bryson and his colleagues, the psyche of the individual was a microcosm of society itself. To escape the gravitational pull of authoritarianism, the free individual, like the free society, had to become flexible, generative, and empathetic. Both had to accept diversity. As Bryson put it, "a free society would not be aware that there were many deviants, because in such a society only a great degree of eccentricity in an individual temperament could compel a person to act outside the range of accepted patterns."[28]

In our own time, talk of deviants and accepted patterns of behavior sends a chill through the air. But in the late 1940s, for a generation that had just faced down nations devoted to the mass extermination of those who did not meet their racial, political, or sexual standards, the vision of a government that might set the social stage but leave the action on it unscripted was enormously appealing. Moreover, the major institutions of American life—the state, the military, the corporate sector, and the sciences—enjoyed a level of credibility that few Americans would grant them today. Together they had just liberated Europe and Asia. Who could doubt what they could do at home?

In the late 1940s, no one offered a more compelling account of the power of social and technological systems to free the individual than Norbert Wiener. We remember Wiener today as a theorist of human-machine interaction and as the man who coined the term "cybernetics." But in the late 1940s he was very much a part of the intellectual circle of social and psychological scientists who were focusing their work on questions of culture and personality. As early as 1942, his colleague Arturo Rosenblueth met with Margaret Mead, Gregory Bateson, and Lawrence Frank to discuss, among other things, circular models of causality that he had been developing with Wiener and engineer Julian Bigelow.[29] In 1943 Wiener, Rosenblueth, and Bigelow published a paper that defined these new models of causality for several generations of cyberneticists (under the impossingly abstract title "Behavior, Purpose and Teleology"), and by 1946 these collaborations had spawned the Macy Conferences, within which Wiener and the emerging discipline of cybernetics played central roles.[30] The Macy Conferences too focused on developing new models of individual human agency in terms that were entirely consonant with theories of the democratic personality and with the theories of culture and personality that underlay them. For the members of the Macy Conferences, the individual psyche became a site for rethinking the nature of self-governance and a model for rethinking the nature of the democratic state.[31]

Wiener published his own views on these questions in two very widely read volumes: *Cybernetics, or Control and Communication in the Animal and the Machine* (1948) and *The Human Use of Human Beings* (1950). At one level, both books served as primers for human interaction with then-new information machines. The computer and the human mind both processed information, wrote Wiener; indeed, one could think of biological, mechanical, and electronic systems as mirrors of one another in that each took in information, processed it, and acted upon what it had learned. At another level, though, Wiener's studies of human-machine interaction led him to propose a model of human agency that contrasted sharply with the dominance/submission dynamics of fascism. Wiener's human beings extended their senses outward, and as they did, they received feedback about their actions. They adjusted their movements accordingly, and sought new feedback. In Wiener's model, the human being resembled the machine, but not the human automatons of fascism. Wiener's cybernetic self was collaborative and cooperative—precisely the sort of spontaneity acting among other spontaneities celebrated by writers like Ralph Barton Perry.

It also modeled explicit alternatives to totalitarian psyches and societies. At one level, Wiener's vision had grown out of his scientific practice. In his 1948 *Cybernetics* he explained how he and a group of colleagues had first come across this model in a laboratory as they sought to understand the origins of tremors in the hand.[32] Elsewhere, Wiener ascribed his fascination with systemic models of agency to the work he had done developing an antiaircraft predictor during the war.[33] At another level, however, his vision grew directly out of his concern with fascism. In the first edition of *The Human Use of Human Beings* he argued that the cybernetic mode of agency could form the basis of an antifascist society. "Our view of society differs from the ideal of society which is held by many Fascists, Strong Men in Business, and Government. . . . Such people prefer an organization in which all orders come from above, and none return."[34] Wiener had seen such societies in Europe and he feared that the Red Scares then afoot in the United States might bring them to life there as well. In both cases, he suggested, totalitarian systems resembled ant colonies: "In the ant community, each worker performs its proper functions. There is a separate cast of soldiers. Certain highly specialized individuals perform the functions of king and queen. If man were to adopt this community as a pattern, you would live in a Fascist state, in which ideally each individual is conditioned from birth for his proper occupation . . . this aspiration of the Fascist for a human state based on the model of the ant is due to a profound misapprehension both of the nature of the ants and of the nature of man."[35]

In his account of an individual who found his or her agency in relation to others, Wiener offered a model of the self and the ideal society very much like those proposed by his friend Margaret Mead in *And Keep Your Powder Dry* . . . or, for that matter, by Gordon Allport in his search for democratic morale. Wiener celebrated a world in which individuals had to be whole people rather than specialists; in which collective social order would emerge from the individual actions of independent citizens; and in

FIGURE 5.1.

Participants at the tenth Macy Conference (1953), one of a series of meetings at which members of the culture-and-personality school of anthropology and kindred psychologists met theorists of communication engineering. Despite their suits and ties and their visible adherence to the race and gender norms of the day, this group shared a deep attraction to nonhierarchical modes of communication and social organization. Participants pictured include Margaret Mead, Gregory Bateson, Lawrence Frank, Ralph Gerard, Julian Bigelow, and Warren McCulloch. Norbert Wiener, who had participated in many earlier meetings, did not attend this one. Courtesy of the Josiah Macy Jr. Foundation.

which a benevolent caste of experts would manage the social whole using devices that, after all, were simply models of the human mind in metal: computers. For Wiener as for writers like Lyman Bryson, science led to freedom. And for the cyberneticists who followed him, as for Morris, it was communication that would serve to shape the individual psyche and the collective good. In fact, it was communication that would make possible the proper governance of both.

THE DREAM OF A WORLD WITHOUT TENSIONS

In the years when psychologists and anthropologists were repurposing theories of the democratic self for utopian postwar ends, they were also reimagining international relations in psychological terms. Particularly among social scientists associated with the earlier morale debates, a consensus had emerged: the individual psyche served as the breeding ground for war; small group processes both formed individual psyches and suffered from interpersonal psychological tensions; small groups and their tensions scaled to create tensions within individual nations; and international relations between nations too could be modeled as if they were small-group interpersonal relations taking place on a global scale. This new view, in turn, presented social scientists with an important postwar role on the national stage. At the start of the fighting, the essential question had been a national one: How could the scientific understanding of democratic personalities and societies aid in strengthening the United States? Social scientists had helped answer that question by designing propaganda campaigns, analyzing enemy media, and serving overseas in the precursor to the CIA, the Office of Strategic Services or OSS. With America and its allies victorious, the question shifted to one of international relations: How could understandings of the democratic mind aid in creating a more peaceful postwar world?

To answer this question, social scientists once again gathered in a variety of societies, some brought together for many years, some for only a few meetings. In 1947, for instance, an influential group of social scientists and humanities scholars led by Lyman Bryson met in Philadelphia to discuss "Learning and World Peace."[36] Though we might reasonably expect the group to have dealt with questions of statecraft, economics, and history, they dealt instead primarily with questions of psychology. In their published report, the contributors to the conference repeatedly described individual nations as having minds of their own. The globe too could be thought of as a single psychological system, they suggested. Like the elements of an individual mind, the nations of the world existed in a state of tension with one another. As Herbert Finer, a professor of political science at the University of Chicago, explained, an individual nation might be thought of as sane when it was at peace; the globe as a whole could be thought of as mentally stable when the tensions that ran through it did not lead to armed conflicts.[37] In this context, he argued, social scientists and politicians needed to unite in developing state-based "therapy" for individual nations and the world.[38] If necessary, such work could involve economic intervention or even military action, but ideally, it would proceed through international organizations such as the United Nations and its cultural agency, the United Nations Educational and Scientific Organization, or UNESCO.

The power and ubiquity of the psychological approach to international relations in this period can be seen in the first words of the preamble to the UNESCO Constitution: "Since wars begin in the minds of men, it is in the minds of men that the defenses of peace must be constructed." UNESCO was founded in November 1945, just three months after the dropping of the first atom bombs and only a month after the United Nations itself had begun operations. To American intellectuals and many political leaders, both the United Nations and UNESCO represented opportunities to perpetuate the cooperation of the wartime Allies.[39] In combat, that cooperation had been military; now, in peacetime, it would need to be intercultural. The enemy, however, would remain the same. During the war, the Allies had defeated not only particular political regimes and particular nations; they had defended an entire worldview — one in which perceptions of racial, national, and cultural difference played central roles. If they were to keep the peace, the Allies would now need to promote a universal humanism, a sense that all people were in fact equal no matter their culture or race, and to foster actual cross-cultural collaborations to make that ideal come alive.

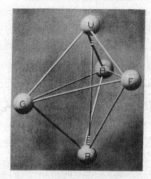

Fig. 1. —Psychic Distances of Major Powers: Measured by Content Analysis

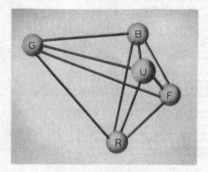

Fig. 2. —Psychic Distances of Major Powers: Klingberg Study

FIGURE 5.2.

By the early 1950s, social scientists such as Ithiel de Sola Pool at the Massachusetts Institute of Technology believed that nations could be thought of as individuals with psyches—psyches whose contents could be divined by analyzing the contents of the nation's mass media. Here Pool models the psychological relationships between Germany, Britain, France, Russia, and the United States. From de Sola Pool, *Symbols of Internationalism*, 18. Used by permission of the Massachusetts Institute of Technology.

When representatives from some forty-three anti-Axis nations as well as a variety of civil society groups gathered in London at UNESCO's founding congress, they agreed that UNESCO would have to ward off the pernicious doctrines of racial inequality and instead promote "the democratic principles of the dignity, equality and mutual respect of men." Over the next decade, American leaders would gradually come to see UNESCO as a tool for the "cultural containment" of communism.[40] But in the heady months that followed the end of the war, UNESCO seemed to offer a way to turn the egalitarian ideals behind the antifascist war effort into the basis of a new world order. As the preamble explained, "Peace must . . . be founded . . . upon the intellectual and moral solidarity of mankind."[41]

For American social scientists, the project of promoting international moral solidarity offered a chance to project techniques they had developed in the study of small groups onto the international stage. For UNESCO's early leaders—and particularly for its first chairman, British biologist and eugenicist Julian Huxley—social scientists were just that, *scientists*, and as such they were experts who might be called upon to solve this pressing postwar problem just as so many other kinds of scientists had lately helped solve the problem of winning the war. At its second general assembly held in Mexico City at the end of 1947, UNESCO authorized an international group of sociologists and psychologists to undertake a multiyear investigation into "tensions affecting international understanding."[42] Over the next three years, social scientists ranging from sociologists Edward Shils and Max Horkheimer to psychologist Gordon Allport and psychiatrist Harry Stack Sullivan sought to analyze "the development and perpetuation of attitudes which make for national aggression" and "to recommend ways . . . of promoting . . . attitudes that would increase international understanding."[43]

In the early days of the Tensions Project, as it was called, its sociologists enjoyed visions of grandeur. Participant Hadley Cantril, for instance, reflected the pride of his profession when he wrote that international support for the project was "of historic significance when viewed in the light of man's long evolutionary development. For this is apparently the first time in world history when the people of many lands have officially turned to the social scientist to seek his aid in man's quest for enduring peace."[44] UNESCO officials hoped that the social scientists would survey the intellectual landscape, gather data from around the globe, and ultimately help develop an international program designed to transform the citizens of various nations into citizens of the world—that is, into people whose global outlook would prevent them from adopting the racist views that had sparked World War II. While UNESCO did ultimately fund a series of educational efforts in this area as well as the construction of an extensive bibliography by psychologist Otto Klineberg, the program never developed into the social scientific equivalent of the wartime work of physicists and engineers.[45]

However, it did stage a conference in Paris in the summer of 1948 that garnered international press coverage and that articulated new and important roles for psychology and communication in the postwar world. The conference brought together eight leading social scientists and psychologists from six nations, including Horkheimer, Allport, and Stack Sullivan from the United States. In the wake of the gathering, the members issued a "common statement" in which they announced: "The problem of peace is the problem of keeping group and national tensions and aggressions within manageable proportions and of directing them to ends that are at the same time personally and socially constructive." The members acknowledged the power of governmental and economic systems to increase the frustrations of various national groups, but ultimately they argued that that it was the psychological susceptibility of various peoples to false images of alien others, to demagoguery, and to the mass media that sparked actual combat.

The Tensions group included no artists, but its precepts echoed ideals common to modernist art worlds and particularly to the Bauhaus. To reduce the tensions that cause wars, these social scientists argued first, that personality and psychology more generally must be recognized as the foundations of social change, and second, that new modes of communication must be developed that could shape personalities that would be open to such change. In 1950, UNESCO published a complete report of the conference edited by Hadley Cantril and entitled *Tensions that Cause Wars*. It featured lengthy individual essays by each member of the conference. Despite the varied professional backgrounds and ideological orientations of their authors, these writings show a remarkable agreement as to the central cause of international conflict: the cultural shaping of the individual personality. Even Max Horkheimer, who at times during the conference protested the psychologization of what he believed were also economic and political conflicts, argued that the Nazis would never have come to power had German parents not turned the personalities of their children in authoritarian directions. "Men . . . who have not been browbeaten in childhood," he wrote, "will not be driven by irrational anxieties . . . [to] aggressive nationalism."[46]

To prevent future eruptions of international aggression, the members agreed that societies must focus renewed attention on the formation of the individual personality and on the communication processes that did that work. In his essay, Gordon Allport distinguished two types of personalities especially prone to fascism: first, the unintegrated, helter-skelter personality of the "many-minded person," a person who lacked confidence in his own values; and second, the rigid, fearful personality that had already "developed a 'totalitarian' character structure." To prevent the development of more such personalities, and so to prevent war itself, Allport recommended the cultivation of an "altruistic and world-minded citizen, who has no difficulty enlarging his circles of loyalty."[47] Harry Stack Sullivan agreed with Allport, though he couched his argument in different terms. Stack Sullivan argued that all human personalities were vulnerable to manipulation. According to Stack Sullivan, the individual psyche and the interpersonal group were each systems of tensions, and the stresses within each influenced the behavior of the other. When confronted with threats, he explained, both systems engaged in psychological "security operations"—such as demonizing those by whom they felt threatened.[48] It was these operations, he implied, that had generated much of the bigotry behind World War II.

How then, asked Stack Sullivan, could psychologists—and, by implication, governments—prevent such operations? Good psychiatrists tried to do two things with their patients, he explained. First, they aimed to "map the areas of disjunctive force [i.e., tensions] that block the efficient collaboration of the patient and others," and second, they worked to "expand the patient's awareness so that this unnecessary blockage can be brought to an end."[49] The conference attendees agreed that this would be a good model for international peacemaking as well. As Norwegian philosopher Arne Naess put, much of the future of "international understanding" hinged on "the removal of obstacles hindering the free flow of sympathy reactions."[50] At the interpersonal and international levels, this required developing new forms of communication. As Horkheimer argued, in words that could have been spoken by Erich Fromm, "the Germans were conditioned for fascist regimentation by the general structure of modern society. They were used to accepting the models submitted to them by radio, motion pictures, and the illustrated weekly long before they heard the Führer himself."[51] Thus, the group's common statement argued that communication between individuals and nations must always be "two-way."[52] Like the citizens and governors of Norbert Wiener's cybernetic ideal, they must learn to interact and to shape one another's destinies through a process of mutual feedback—that is, of communication.

For the members of the Tensions Project, as for many internationalists in the late 1940s, the key to creating sympathy across national boundaries was to create new contexts for interpersonal exchange. Whether undertaken in small groups such as the Tensions meeting or in global bodies such as the United Nations, these conversations would allow individuals and nations to enjoy free individual agency within a community of others who were similarly free. They could choose with whom to associate, they could open their senses to ideas and interaction styles unlike their own, and they could ideally come to appreciate the beauty of peoples and cultures that the more authoritarian members of their own societies might already have marked as alien.

A WORLD OF TWO MINDS

American analysts and policy makers would continue to promote international exchange as a means to reduce international tensions for the next three decades. Yet the one-world optimism behind the Tensions Project vanished almost immediately after its completion. In 1949 the Soviet Union exploded its first atom bomb; that same year, Mao Zedong took power in China. In the summer of 1950, communist North Korea invaded American ally South Korea, and once again American troops found themselves at war with a totalitarian enemy. American policy makers, journalists, and scholars began to assign the Soviet Union and China the villainous role most lately played by Nazi Germany. Communism became the new fascism; Stalin and Mao, new Hitlers. Domestic perceptions shifted apace. A decade earlier, Americans on the left had feared the rise of fascism in the United States and Americans on the right had feared the domestic threat of communism. Now, with fascism defeated and communist nations overseas resurgent, Americans across a much wider political spectrum feared the rise of communism at home. In 1947 an infamous round of witch hunts ensued, led by the House Un-American Activities Committee and culminating in the work of Senator Joseph McCarthy and his Senate Subcommittee on Investigations. The Red Scares of the late 1940s in turn bred a new fear, especially among intellectuals and artists: that in its efforts to crack down on political dissent, the American government itself might become a totalitarian force.

Even as they dissolved the optimism of the immediate postwar years, these events did not corrode the popular faith in psychological approaches to politics, or in communication as a means by which to shape the structures of minds and nations. On the contrary, in 1949 and 1950 the nature of democratic versus authoritarian personality types and of the societies that might sustain them became key objects of debate. On one hand, psychological distinctions offered a means to map the differences between the communist East and the democratic West. Once again, analysts argued that America and its allies possessed democratic personalities and democratic governments, while their enemies suffered under authoritarian psychological and political regimes. On the other hand, however, questions of personality became key elements in a debate about the future of American society. To the extent that sociologists and psychologists feared the encroachment of communism—or of authoritarianism in the effort to contain it—they also feared the spread of the authoritarian personality type.

Social scientists and policy makers who hoped to resist the spread of authoritarianism from the left or the right faced three familiar challenges: they needed to define the democratic and authoritarian personalities, develop a democratic mode of national unity at home and abroad, and deploy a form of media that did not trigger authoritarian impulses in their audiences but instead bolstered democratic personality traits. In each case they tended to frame the tasks ahead in terms set by the war they had just passed through. No single work did more to shape postwar studies of psychological character than *The Authoritarian Personality*. Almost a thousand pages long, written by four authors and three collaborators, and featuring a dazzling array of sociological and psychological instruments, *The Authoritarian Personality* presented a new fusion of social and psychological analysis. Like the members of the Committee for National Morale a decade earlier, authors Theodor Adorno, Else Frenkel-Brunswik, Daniel Levinson, and R. Nevitt Sanford believed that a totalitarian social order could grow only in the presence of personality types predisposed to trust its propaganda. As the authors explained in their introduction, fascist governments required mass support and yet they benefited only small elites. To come to power, they needed to play to "the emotional needs–often to the most primitive and irrational wishes and fears" of citizens.[53] This was the work of propaganda: work "rendered easier to the degree that anti-democratic potentials already exist in the great mass of people."[54]

Working with funding from the American Jewish Committee, the authors of *The Authoritarian Personality* sought to understand not only the roots of recent fascist persecutions, but the potential for America and its allies to turn in a fascist direction. To that end, they transformed the psychological understandings developed around actually existing authoritarians in prewar Germany into frameworks for understanding *potential* developments in the United States. In 1920s Europe, psychologists such as Erich Fromm and Wilhelm Reich had shown that authoritarian family structures, coupled with widespread economic distress and social unrest, helped shape a generation of Germans who desired the sadomasochistic pleasures of membership in the Nazi order. Building on their work, Adorno and his coauthors turned to the study of Americans. In 1945 and 1946, they surveyed students at the University of California and the University of Oregon, prisoners at San Quentin Prison, and members of various northern California civic organizations. In many cases, they performed in-depth individual interviews and the Thematic Apperception Test, in which they presented subjects with various images of people and asked them to invent stories about them. Their results led them to construct an exceptionally influential measure of fascist tendencies: the F scale.

The F scale featured nine axes along which an individual's vulnerability to fascism could be measured. The first three—"conventionalism," "authoritarian submission," and "authoritarian aggression"—assessed a person's faith in established systems of authority and in authority itself. The more conventional the person, the more trusting of those in power, the more open to antidemocratic politics the individual would be. The second set—"anti-intraception" (that is, "opposition to the subjective, the imaginative, the tender-minded"), "superstition and stereotypy," "power and 'toughness,'" and "destructiveness and cynicism"—marked the degree to which a person objectified the world around him. Those with a broadly antidemocratic personality structure were unable to recognize other people as individuals, but saw them only as types. They were unable to recognize the uniqueness of others and could not sympathize with their fellow human beings, and so they found themselves emotionally isolated, angry, and enamored of feelings of toughness that might keep their loneliness at bay. The last axes on the F scale—"projectivity" (that is, "the projection outward of unconscious emotional impulses") and "sex" (an "exaggerated concern with sexual 'goings-on'")—pointed to the protofascist's fear that "wild and dangerous things go on in the world" and that they needed to be contained.[55]

In the F scale, the authoritarian personality structure took on a substantial psychological specificity. The protofascist loved order and authority, feared desire and independence, and above all, could not recognize that other human beings were fundamentally like himself, no matter their racial, political, or economic differences. Potential totalitarians craved order in large part because they could not access their own unconscious. Just as they could not recognize or sympathize with other people, they could not recognize or sympathize with their own unconscious desires. By contrast, the authors argued, the prodemocratic personality drew on its unconscious desires, managed them with the ego, and so engaged in unified, rational action.[56]

But how did these patterns take hold in individual minds? In part because they had built their analysis on the foundation of earlier studies by

Erich Fromm and Wilhelm Reich, Adorno and his coauthors took an essentially Freudian view of self-formation. The family more than any other force shaped the structure of the psyche, they argued. But the family itself operated within a larger social milieu that in turn shaped its internal authority structures and, through them, the personality of the child. Once outside the family, the child's personality did not cease to change. On the contrary, like Gordon Allport, Harry Stack Sullivan, and other American-born theorists at the time, the authors saw the personality as a dynamic system, able to change, albeit not in unlimited ways. It was here that the problem of mass media entered the equation: outside the family, no force spoke as directly to unconscious desires as did mass media. And no forces had shown themselves more capable of manipulating that ability than those of fascism. Here, then, the authors' definition of the authoritarian personality came full circle: rigid, fearful, ethnocentric, it awaited a call to action from mass-mediated propaganda.

The impact of *The Authoritarian Personality* on American psychologists and sociologists of the 1950s and 1960s was profound. It provided what appeared to be a scientific basis for the widely shared view that nations shared and fostered certain personality types and that the psyche itself, as much as any economic or political concerns, could lead to war. It offered a series of new techniques and tools for measuring psychological conditions within large populations. Above all, it modeled an interdisciplinary approach to a critical social problem: an approach that justified the continued engagement of sociologists and psychologists in national affairs. To prevent the reappearance of fascism, Adorno and his colleagues argued, policy makers would have to learn from social and psychological scientists. They would have to refuse the manipulative tactics of totalitarian propagandists and turn instead to the techniques of psychotherapy. Together, scholars and government officials could help Americans do what authoritarian personalities could not: "see themselves and . . . be themselves."[57]

For social scientists at the time, the protofascist figures at the heart of *The Authoritarian Personality* served as lenses: as they gazed into the rigid precincts of the totalitarian psyche, analysts also glimpsed its democratic opposite. In 1951, political scientist Harold Lasswell summed up what they saw in his book-length essay *Democratic Character.* Lasswell had traveled extensively across the social worlds of American psychology and sociology, and his book reflects the consensus then emerging among his colleagues. Building on *The Authoritarian Personality,* as well as on work by Margaret Mead, Ruth Benedict, Harry Stack Sullivan, and Karen Horney, Lasswell argued that personality, culture, and nation were isomorphic and entwined.[58] Societies tended to produce personalities that were in synch with their collective values, and tended to do it within the family and within the larger adult social milieu. Analysts should not think of the boundary between the individual psyche and the larger social system as impermeable, he explained. Rather, character and culture constantly shaped one another within a single "Character-Culture Manifold."[59]

In a democratic society, both personality and social order depended on the recognition of the individual's uniqueness. According to Lasswell, the core of the democratic personality was "an open as against a closed ego." Lasswell's description of this openness is worth quoting at length:

> . . . the democratic attitude toward other human beings is warm rather than frigid, inclusive and expanding rather than exclusive and constricting. We are speaking of an underlying personality structure which is capable of "friendship," as Aristotle put it, and which is unalienated from humanity. Such a person transcends most of the cultural categories that divide human beings from one another, and senses the common humanity across class and even caste lines within the culture, and in the world beyond local culture.[60]

If authoritarians would not tolerate racial, sexual, or cultural differences, democrats would. Lasswell's model of the democratic psyche embraced both the conscious and unconscious elements of the mind and integrated them into a single affective-intellectual unity that would be capable of making informed political choices.

Lasswell also envisioned a democratic sociability that echoed theories of democratic unity proposed both a decade earlier during the morale debates, and more recently in the essays on American character penned by Ralph Baron Perry and others. If potential fascists showed a psychological propensity to give themselves over to the will of another, to dissolve their own desires into those of the throng, the democratic psyche longed for a different kind of intimacy. The democratic personality enjoyed "a degree of detachment which enables the individual to sense the feelings and viewpoints of others in the life of the entire group."[61] Totalitarian order depended on the manipulation of individual unconscious desires and their fusion into a single unreasoning and dependent mass. Lasswell's democratic order grew from mutual recognition, the simultaneous maintenance of empathy for another and independence for oneself. To the extent that such an order represented individual and national health, it should also be the end goal of postwar reconstruction at home and abroad. "When we speak of democratic character . . . we have in mind the development of self and energy systems which withstand adversity on behalf of democratic patterns of value and practice," he explained. "The task [of building democratic character] is nothing less than the drastic and continuing reconstruction of our own civilization, and most of the cultures of which we have any knowledge."[62]

A NEW CENTER?

But what might that civilization look like? And how would it hold together against the threat of communism abroad and totalitarian tendencies at home?

In 1949 and 1950, two volumes answered these questions in ways that would define debates about the nature of American society for a decade to come. The first was Harvard historian Arthur Schlesinger Jr.'s best-selling polemic, *The Vital Center: The Politics of Freedom*, in 1949. Like intellectuals across the political spectrum that year, Schlesinger feared that the war and the bomb had given rise to a tremendous insecurity across the Western Hemisphere. "Western man in the middle of the twentieth century is tense, uncertain, adrift," he wrote. "We look upon our epoch as a time of troubles, an age of anxiety. The grounds of our civilization, of our certitude, are breaking up under our feet, and familiar ideas and institutions vanish as we reach for them, like shadows in the falling dusk."[63] Americans found themselves threatened from without and within: "The rise of totalitarianism . . . signifies more than an internal crisis for democratic society. It signifies an internal crisis for democratic man. There is a Hitler, a Stalin in every breast."[64]

During the war, Schlesinger had served in the Office of War Information and later in the Office of Strategic Services. Like others in both organizations, including many former members of the Committee for National Morale, Schlesinger had come to see Americans as facing two isomorphic enemies: totalitarianism abroad and authoritarianism at home. At one level, these enemies were the products of fascist politics and human psychology. But at another, they were products of modern society more generally and of industrialization in particular. Industrial society, wrote Schlesinger, had lessened individuals' abilities to feel for one another. It had required them to treat one another instrumentally. "Industrialism . . . imposed on the world a sinister new structure of relationships," he wrote. "The result was to give potent weapons to the pride and the greed of man, the sadism and the masochism, the ecstasy in power and the ecstasy in submission . . . ."[65]

Just as psychologists such as Lawrence Frank had seen World War II as a fight for the freedom of the individual personality, so now, argued Schlesinger, Americans needed to challenge the logic of instrumental power and psychological fragmentation manifested in fascism, communism, and industrialization. They needed to fight to create democratic selves and political structures that would sustain them. Much like Charles Morris, Harold Lasswell, and other proponents of a person-centered democracy, Schlesinger argued that Americans must "extirpate the prejudices of bigotry in our environment, and, above all, in ourselves."[66] In place of a society built on a system of social distinction, Americans needed to "tap once again the spontaneous sources of community."[67] Americans needed to pursue their own individuality and the collective good simultaneously, within a social order that was not imposed from above but which emerged from these pursuits. The result should be a balance of "individualism which does not wall man off from community" and "community which sustains but does not suffocate the individual."[68]

Schlesinger called this balance of individual and collective power the "vital center." Though often remembered today as a call for a liberal *po-litical* position, Schlesinger's vital center in fact partook of the individual-nation-globe homologies that had long driven culture and personality anthropology, pro-democratic morale theory, and postwar attempts to ensure global peace. To fight for the center was to fight for psychological freedom at the individual level and, with it, the liberation of individuals at the political level. "Can we win the fight?" asked Schlesinger. "We must commit ourselves to it with all our vigor in all its dimensions: the struggle within the world against communism and fascism; the struggle within our country against oppression and stagnation; the struggle within ourselves against pride and corruption: nor can engagement in one dimension exclude responsibility for another."[69]

For Schlesinger, the personal was already political. Long before the feminists of the early 1970s or even the civil rights marchers of the late 1950s linked their sense of self to the political order around them, Schlesinger and other liberal intellectuals had imagined a society focused precisely on the development of independent, collaborative and unique individuals. In Schlesinger's somewhat hazy analysis, order in such a society would emerge largely out of the benevolent interactions of its members. Voluntary associations, spontaneous collaborations—only such grassroots interactions, he suggested, could ultimately save democracy. The job of government was to create the conditions within which such interactions could occur.

In this respect, Schlesinger's theories of the vital center echoed Norbert Wiener's cybernetics and Lyman Bryson's scientific humanism. All three called for individual autonomy within a collaborative, empathetic society, and a state that would guarantee both. For Schlesinger, this pattern could provide the sort of democratic unity that could sustain the United States in a long conflict with communism.

David Riesman, however, was not so sure. In 1950, Riesman's widely acclaimed *The Lonely Crowd: A Study of the Changing American Character* challenged the confidence of *The Vital Center* even as it echoed its preoccupation with personality. Drawing on earlier analyses by Margaret Mead, Ruth Benedict, and Geoffrey Gorer, and especially on those by his mentors Harry Stack Sullivan and Erich Fromm, Riesman believed that individual personality patterns and social structures shaped one another. Together they helped produce what Riesman, following Fromm, called a "social character."[70] Like the concepts of the authoritarian and democratic personalities in this period, Riesman's social character emerged alongside and also helped determine macrosocial formations. Riesman identified three types of society—traditional, frontier, and industrial—and argued that they had helped generate three types of personality—traditional, inner-directed, and outer-directed. Citizens of traditional societies operated within a firm system of external rules which they tended to follow rigorously. Frontier societies, like the America of the eighteenth and nineteenth centuries, asked their citizens to internalize their rules and norms and to manage their own lives by drawing on their internal resources. Finally, bureaucratic, industrial systems of the kind that dominated the mid-twentieth century, required individuals to constantly measure themselves in terms set by the social group around them. In this sense, they were other-directed: in order to determine a proper course of action, they needed to scan their peers as if they were human radar systems and act primarily on the basis of the signals they received.[71]

The Lonely Crowd painted a portrait of contemporary Americans much in keeping with the ideals of writers like Norbert Wiener and Lyman Bryson. Like cybernetic organisms, Riesman's other-directed individuals reached out for feedback and redirected themselves accordingly. And like the citizens of Bryson's scientifically managed America, Riesman's other-directed individuals were free to do as they liked, thanks to boundaries on their action placed by the leaders of corporate, state, and scientific institutions. In Riesman's account, these new people seemed to pose a clear alternative to the rigidities of the authoritarian personality. After all, they trusted in others, worked collaboratively, and not only tolerated but sought the approval of their fellow citizens. This interactive mode of agency stood in stark contrast to that of the inner-directed people of preceding generations. The American frontiersmen had mastered resources and exploited them. In fact, they had reveled in just the sort of instrumental power that authors like Schlesinger associated with totalitarianism and industrial bureaucracy.

In that sense, the other-directed citizens of *The Lonely Crowd* seemed to model a pro-democratic alternative to the psychologically fractured potential fascists of *The Authoritarian Personality*. But as Riesman pointed out, they also represented the emergence of a new mode of industrial production and a powerful method of social control. The industry of 1949, wrote Riesman, "is concerned with techniques of communication and control, not of tooling or factory layout. It is symbolized by the telephone, the servomechanism, the IBM machine, the electronic calculator, and modern statistical methods of controlling the quality of products; by the Hawthorne counseling experiment and the general preoccupation with industrial morale."[72] In this new system, he explained, "the product now in demand is neither a staple nor a machine: it is a personality."[73] To produce themselves as proper workers, Americans needed not only to listen to their parents but to monitor their friends, their radios, their local movie halls. They needed to put together their personalities not from symbolic resources handed down by their parents so much as from the images and sounds around them. Even as such an orientation freed individual Americans to make their own way in the world, it knit them ever more tightly into the systems of production and consumption within which they worked.

In the decades to come, young Americans would become increasingly aware of the constraints of "the system" on their self-expression. But it took time for Riesman's ambivalence to permeate popular culture. Five years after World War II, many Americans were more than happy to stock their kitchens and their driveways with the products of American industry, and their bookshelves with the writings of American psychologists and sociologists. By the early 1950s, for many intellectuals at least, the pursuit of the democratic character had become a defining feature of American life. The open, tolerant ego and its habit of loose, nonexclusive sociability could be sources of national unity in the face of communist aggression abroad and, depending on your political position, left-wing or right-wing totalitarianism at home.

Given the importance of the democratic personality to the future of the nation and, in a nuclear world, to the future of the globe, analysts and policy makers alike found themselves preoccupied with familiar questions: How could Americans produce and sustain more such personalities? And in particular, how could they develop modes of communication that promoted spontaneous individuality, interpersonal openness, and interracial and international empathy?

For concrete answers to these questions, social theorists and political leaders once again had to look outside their own circles, to the worlds of art and design.

6

The Museum of Modern Art Makes the World a Family

In the early spring of 1955, more than a quarter of a million people streamed through the doors of the Museum of Modern Art in New York. They came to immerse themselves in *The Family of Man.* An exhibition of 503 photographs of men, women and children, made by 273 photographers from around the world and selected by photographer Edward Steichen and his assistant, Wayne Miller, *The Family of Man* filled the entire second floor of the museum. A series of temporary walls channeled visitors through the images, allowing them to move at their own pace, to pause where they liked, and to pool at pictures of particular interest. Visitors gazed at photographs of children dancing, families gathering, and men and women of myriad nations working, walking, marrying, fighting. Some pictures dangled from wires overhead, some hung from poles, and at least one faced downward from the ceiling. Some filled entire walls while others were as small as a handbill. Together, the installation and the images left viewers few places to turn in which they would not encounter a picture of another person doing something they were likely to recognize.

The Family of Man quickly became one of the most popular—and, ultimately, controversial—exhibitions in the museum's history. In the wake of its run at the Museum of Modern Art, five copies of the show traveled around the United States and, thanks to funding from the United States Information Agency, to thirty-seven foreign countries as well. The USIA estimates that more than 7.5 million visitors saw the exhibition abroad in the ten years after it opened in New York.[1] By 1978 the exhibition catalog had sold more than five million copies, and it remains in print today. Yet *The Family of Man* also became a critical whipping boy. Particularly since the late 1960s, writers have attacked the show as a species of American mythology, an attempt to mask domestic and international problems of race and class, and even an act of aesthetic colonialism.[2] Many have implied that the exhibition resembled the postwar American family and postwar American culture, and that all three were systems of psychological and political containment.

Yet, if we return to World War II and the Museum of Modern Art in New York, we can see *The Family of Man* as part of a widespread effort to democratize American families and, through them, American society. By late 1943, the leaders of the museum and the intellectuals who surrounded them agreed: cultures and nations had personalities; those personalities depended on the psyches of individual citizens; and communication, whether through mass media or art or interpersonal interaction, could turn the minds of citizens in authoritarian or democratic directions. Museum officials no longer feared for American morale since it was increasingly likely that the Allies would eventually win the war. As they turned toward the postwar future, though, museum officials joined many analysts in fearing for the psychological health of two specific groups: children and returning veterans.[3] If the individual personality reflected and shaped the personality of the nation, they agreed, then the future of America depended quite literally on the mindsets of its children. Likewise, if veterans who had been forced to sublimate their individuality and join the military mass were to refrain from bringing the authoritarianism of the battlefield home, they too would need to be transformed.

In both cases, the museum drew on Bauhaus pedagogy, and particularly on the work of László Moholy-Nagy, to build communicative environments in which these changes could take place. Since 1937 the museum had employed a former schoolteacher named Victor D'Amico to introduce New York children to the pleasures of modern art. During the war, D'Amico brought the Progressive learning philosophy of John Dewey and the training practices of the Bauhaus together—first to teach children the ways of democratic interaction, and later to rehabilitate combat veterans. In 1944, D'Amico drew on a set of therapeutic and instructional practices outlined by Moholy-Nagy and transformed his classes into a national model for using art to resocialize veterans at the Museum of Modern Art's new War Veterans' Art Center. In 1948, as veteran demand eased, the museum turned the Veterans' Center into a public resource, the People's Art Center. By the early 1950s, with a national baby boom well under way, D'Amico's Bauhaus-infused teaching environments had become places where parents and children created art together, in self-consciously democratic harmony.

In the wake of the McCarthy hearings and the Korean War, these environments and the idea of the family itself took on a deeply political valence. In *The Family of Man*, Steichen brought together the antiauthoritarian, family-centered teaching mission of the People's Art Center and the surround aesthetics of Herbert Bayer that he had first deployed in the *Road to Victory* exhibition. Steichen and his designers presented viewers with an array of images displayed in varied sizes, at different heights, and at all angles. The installation asked viewers to follow their own course among the images, to focus on the pictures that were most meaningful to them, and to knit their subjects into the fabric of their own personalities. *The Family of Man* thus became a three-dimensional arena in which visitors were asked to practice psychological individuation in a social context. They could also engage in acts of mutual recognition, choice and empathy. These were the core perceptual and affective skills on which efforts to boost American morale and democratize children and veterans had depended during and just after the war. Now, as Americans began to divide the world into two psychological and political camps, they became the basis of a Cold War vision of national unity as well.

In that sense, the exhibition also became a fulcrum moment in the development of an increasingly ubiquitous mode of media power. Even as he gave Americans what he and they saw as a democratic degree of freedom in relation to imagery and so to one another, Steichen asked them to pursue their individual experiences within collective terms set by his own aesthetic expertise. Though they moved at their own pace through the galleries, though they could enjoy an enormous variety of visual opportunities for pleasure and engagement with others both like and unlike themselves, visitors also made their choices in terms that had been set for them long before they entered the room. In other words, even as it freed Americans from the massifying effects of totalitarianism and its media, *The Family of Man* invited them to adjust themselves to a softer but equally pervasive system of management—a system pioneered, in part, in Victor D'Amico's classrooms.

DEMOCRATIZING CHILDREN AND VETERANS

Though we may think of the Museum of Modern Art today primarily as a place for exhibiting art, its founders saw it as an educational institution.[4] In the 1930s, this meant teaching Americans to appreciate modern art by exhibiting it but also by teaching children how to make it. Beginning in 1937, Victor D'Amico began teaching children's classes in the fine arts at the museum in the evenings and on weekends; by 1941 he had become a full-time member of the museum's staff and created teaching programs linked to twenty-five New York City high schools. He had also developed a Young People's Gallery which doubled as a studio in which students curated exhibitions of modern art and made objects of their own.[5] D'Amico taught in accord with the ideals of John Dewey: he wanted art to be not just a set of skills, but an experience that might awaken the creativity and individuality of his pupils. To that end, he eschewed such then-common teaching methods as asking groups of students to copy models or draw identical subjects. "Indoctrinary teaching stifles creativeness," he later wrote, and because it did, D'Amico encouraged children to work toward individual expression, collaboratively when it suited them, alone when it didn't.[6] He supplied the materials they worked with, but their artistic directions were their own.

In the years before the war, D'Amico and other Progressive educators saw art as a means of individual psychological growth.[7] With the arrival of World War II, they and art instructors across the country linked their teaching and the psychological growth it promoted to the war effort.[8] In January 1941, President Roosevelt had identified "freedom of speech and expression" as the first of the Four Freedoms for which America would soon have to fight. Museum officials and art teachers nationwide quickly framed their work in his terms. By January 1943, the Museum of Modern Art had mounted an entire exhibition on the theme, called *Art Education in Wartime.* In a draft press release, museum officials argued that art educators were helping to win the war from kindergarten through college by helping children avoid becoming authoritarians. Rigidity, obedience, uniformity—these were the psychological characteristics of fascists, the pamphlet suggested. Art classes encouraged flexibility, creativity, and individuality, the psychological characteristics on which democracy depended.

During the war, Victor D'Amico's educational philosophy achieved its most concise and widely seen form in an annual winter fair ultimately known as the Children's Art Carnival. Started in 1942 and recreated regularly over the next twenty years, the carnival showcased the individual creativity of its visitors. In the winters of 1945 and 1946, for instance, children sat surrounded by stained glass windows created by artists such as Marc Chagall and Alexander Calder. The students made their own windows by pasting cellophane between pieces of black paper. They were not to copy Chagall and Calder, but to see them as inspirations. The environment of the Carnival was to draw out the individuality of each student, while the particular project of the window was to give it a collective form. In this way, the Carnival encouraged the sort of unity-in-diversity then much celebrated as the basis of national morale. Moreover, D'Amico asked the children to create under the most egalitarian conditions. In 1947, a writer for *House and Garden* magazine put it this way: "Parents are not invited to this party; they may only peep at their young after they have pushed through a bright red turnstile. The room itself is carnival-gay and equipped with everything an artist needs. There are no instructors. Mr. D'Amico has learned that you do not *teach* children art [italics original]. You give them the tools, stand by in case of storms, and let them work their own way."[9]

In 1944, D'Amico brought the techniques he used to teach children into a new venture designed to aid combat veterans: the War Veterans' Art Center. In teaching children, D'Amico had introduced comparatively new-formed psyches to the pleasures of individual expression and egalitarian collaboration. With veterans, he confronted individuals who had experienced a totalitarian military environment. In a 1943 article in the museum's *Bulletin,* D'Amico explained how the sort of freedom he promoted in his children's classes might enable veterans to adjust to civilian life. "It has been found that free expressions in art become a mirror of the individual's inner life and personality to the trained eye," he wrote. Works of art, he suggested, mediated between their individual creators and the world of experts who sought to help individuals reenter the social world. The artist needed to be "free" as he or she worked, in part so as to experience a democratic form of independence, and in part so as to render his or her interior life available to expert guidance. Much like the children at the Children's Art Carnival, veterans at the center had to be themselves, but under the watchful eye of more mature guides. As D'Amico put it, "Dictated or academic methods are totally unreliable, for they reveal nothing of the inner life and may aggravate mal-adjustment by increasing frustration and tension."[10]

FIGURE 6.1.
A poster for the War Veterans' Art Center at the Museum of Modern Art, New York. At the end of World War II, many saw art as a way to reindividuate men who had experienced deindividuation in the military. From Victor D'Amico, "Art for War Veterans," 4. Digital Image © The Museum of Modern Art, licensed by SCALA / Art Resource, New York.

For D'Amico and the leaders of the Museum of Modern Art, the art classroom modeled a larger political world. Both the individual mind of the student and the social relations of the classroom suffered from tensions—intrapsychic in the first case and interpersonal in the second. Veterans lived with memories of the obedience required of men who had become accustomed to uniforms and orders and, at the same time, memories of how their acceptance of the military's total authority had led many to experience the madness of combat. Authoritarian teaching threatened to amplify their suffering and release it into the larger American body politic. By contrast, egalitarian methods might prevent such infection. "The war has created new and greater tensions which will cause their share of mental and emotional maladjustments," wrote D'Amico in 1943. "If the therapeutic value of art is employed in a plan for re-education [of veterans], America may be spared a phenomenal rise in mental illness and emotional disturbance."[11]

By 1943 the Museum of Modern Art had in fact become a national center for rethinking the use of art in the healing of wounded and traumatized soldiers. In late 1942, James Thrall Soby, the director of the museum's Armed Forces Program, began reaching out to psychiatrists, psychologists, and rehabilitation specialists to see how the arts were being used in hospitals. At this time, art therapy did not exist as the discipline it is today. Rather, the arts were used largely by occupational therapists to aid the injured in passing the time and recovering lost motor skills. Therapists encouraged soldiers to work with craft kits and to copy established models when they painted or sculpted. Free expression played little role in this work. In the wake of the Freudian revolution of the 1920s and 1930s, however, psychiatrists had turned their patients toward the arts and particularly toward painting and drawing. These doctors believed that when done with the proper degree of independence, such work revealed the inner state of its maker and so could aid in diagnosis. At the same time, they thought it could speed the amateur artist on the way to health by releasing the internal psychological pressure of traumatic memories and so reducing the intrapsychic tensions they caused.

In 1943, Soby organized an exhibition in which the views of the psychiatrists and the occupational therapists collided. Entitled *The Arts in*

Therapy and designed by Herbert Bayer, the exhibition featured two distinct areas. In the first, the museum displayed the work of the winners of a nationwide competition to develop projects designed to provide new and more creative modes of occupational therapy. These projects ranged from the painting of ceramics to the making of paper sculptures, and included, among other things, a series of exercises developed by László Moholy-Nagy and his colleagues at the School of Design in Chicago. In the second area, the exhibition featured paintings and drawings by patients in psychiatric hospitals and by members of the armed forces, some still on active duty. In an essay for the museum's *Bulletin*, Dr. Edward Liss, a practicing psychiatrist and one of James Soby's primary consultants, argued that psychologically therapeutic art did more than simply restore skills for living. It made the personality whole again by fusing "thought and action" in a single "psychosomatic unit." The arts and the sciences, he wrote, worked together, on the shared principle of "creativity," to reunify the fractured psyche.[12]

Such views paralleled those of social scientists concerned with the nature of democratic morale. But they also echoed the teachings of the Bauhaus, and particularly of László Moholy-Nagy. By the middle of World War II, Moholy's School of Design had also turned toward the rehabilitation of veterans and had begun offering courses to train art therapists. In a 1943 article, Moholy argued that the multimodal methods for training artists that he and others had developed at the Bauhaus should now become techniques for restoring veterans to psychological health. According to him, nineteenth-century industry tended to obliterate the individuality of workers. It neglected "the biological, physiological, and psychological requirements of the individual, his need for a balanced program of work, recreation, and leisure." As a result, "the mental health of the people deteriorated."[13] Now, he suggested, military experience had done the same thing to soldiers. To make the injured veteran whole, Moholy recommended the same multisensory training the Bauhaus had developed to build up a new kind of artist. The handicapped veteran "must be trained in the use of all his faculties. In order for his buried energies to be released for contemporary orientation, he has to overcome his old habits, ideas, and judgments not any longer applicable to our age. Creative work and conscious personality development can overcome maladjustment or feelings of inferiority . . . and may open the way for free, efficient, and satisfactory activities."[14]

Moholy went on to propose the development of "a laboratory school and research department for programs of rehabilitation" designed along the lines of the original Bauhaus.[15] Such a school was beyond the means of his own struggling School of Design, but not beyond those of the Museum of Modern Art. In 1944, at the urging of Mrs. John D. Rockefeller, the museum established the War Veterans' Art Center in its own facility at 681 Fifth Avenue, and appointed Victor D'Amico to head it.

The program of the Veterans' Art Center resembled that of the first-year curriculum at the Bauhaus—quite probably because of the museum's many ties to former Bauhaus faculty, including Soby and D'Amico's familiarity with Moholy's recent therapeutic efforts. Between 1944 and 1948, the center taught courses in ten areas ranging from drawing, painting, and typography to woodworking, sculpture, and the principles of design. To incoming students it offered an orientation course: like the first-year program at the Bauhaus, this class introduced students to each of the media on offer and to the ways in which each stimulated the artist's senses. Students then pursued advanced work in the areas to which they were best suited. And much as courses at the Bauhaus sought to produce psychological integration and professional self-sufficiency, so too did the offerings at the center. In his 1948 director's report, Victor D'Amico recalled that "the object was to help veterans find themselves through creative art."[16]

To do so, however, veterans needed to take up art in a way that echoed both Bauhaus ideals of self-formation and the therapeutic agenda of the psychiatrists with whom James Soby had been working. Teachers at the center encouraged students to integrate "form and content" in their work, and to bring together multiple media where appropriate, much as Bauhaus instructors had in years past. And as it had at the Bauhaus, success at the center "had to be both visual and emotional."[17] To make coherent art and to integrate the personality of the artist were one and the same project. As formerly Bauhaus craftsmen had rebelled against the strictures of modern industry, so now veterans cut themselves free from the restraints of military life. The socialist impulse behind the original Bauhaus now became a democratic American impulse. Freedom of individual expression, egalitarian collaboration, creativity itself—in the late 1940s, all remained essential elements of the democratic personality and democratic society. Art too changed: at the War Veterans' Art Center, it was not simply the product and emblem of the artist's own integration. Rather, in keeping with the ideals of men like Edward Liss, it became a mirror of the inner life of the veteran and a window through which he could see and express himself. Bernard Pfriem, who taught advanced drawing and painting at the center, recalled that his own class began "largely as therapy, offering relaxing recreational outlets to men tensed by military experiences." As the class went on, however, it became "mainly . . . an opportunity [for the veteran] to be an integrated individual, to reflect an indigenous personality, to voice graphically an identity and independence which had been lost, shattered or smothered by regimentation."[18]

THROUGH THE ENCHANTED GATE

In the four years of its existence, the center treated nearly 1,500 veterans, most of whom were suffering from psychological distress. Like virtually all of the Museum of Modern Art's educational programs in the 1940s, it received national coverage in the press and one of its classes was featured on the newsreel *The March of Time*.[19] When in 1948 the museum decided to transform the War Veterans' Art Center into a wholly civilian enterprise, the People's Art Center, it repurposed the highly individual, collaborative, and multisensory teaching tactics of the Veterans' Center—this time, to help democratize the American family.

By the late 1940s, the global *political* utopianism of the immediate postwar period had begun to fade, but its psychological analog—the hope for a tolerant, egalitarian, and cosmopolitan American who could also be a world citizen—had not. On the contrary, the sort of open, democratic self described by writers like Charles Morris and Harold Lasswell was, if anything, in more demand. If the democratic personality had been the basis of national morale in the early 1940s, it was now becoming the basis of a liberal self and of a liberal Western polity that could withstand a confrontation with international communism. In this context, the family became a symbolic redoubt for American democracy.[20] As the editors of the maga-zine *American Home* put it in their November 1946 issue, "parents" were to be "architects of peace." This task sometimes meant turning the home into a fortress against a threatening world, complete with a well-stocked bomb shelter in the backyard. But for many in the late 1940s and early 1950s, it also meant working to raise the sort of open-minded, empathetic, emo-tionally flexible children who would not start the kinds of wars they them-selves had just survived.

In a preface to the 1959 reissue of a widely read 1949 collection of es-says entitled *The Family: Its Function and Destiny*, for instance, popular journalist and editor Ruth Nanda Anshen made this point explicitly. The family must be a bulwark against the threat of nuclear war, she argued. But the source of its power would have to be "creative work, nourished by the nexus between parents and children."[21] Creativity could bring about a new sense of global responsibility in child and parent alike. At the same time, it could help create a simultaneously more diverse and more unified Amer-ica. "Even as the cell is the unit of the organic body, so the family is the unit of society," wrote Anshen in her essay for the original volume. "The ultimate harmony is the harmony of enduring individualities joined in the unity of a common frame of reference."[22] The alternative to such a highly American vision was the mechanical unity of fascism. In his essay for the volume, Max Horkheimer described how the authoritarian family could breed future Nazis. "Subjects who may be regarded as highly susceptible to fascist propaganda profess an ideology calling for rigid, uncritical identifi-cation with the family and reveal their absolute submission to familial au-thority in early infancy," he explained. "Fascist-minded subjects show, on a deeper level, no genuine attachments to the parents, whom they accept in a fairly conventionalized and externalized way. It is this configuration of submissiveness and coldness which more than anything else defines the potential fascist of our time."[23]

In the view of Anshen and her collaborators, the American family that could confront the authoritarian regimes of the early 1950s needed to be anything but rigid and conformist. It needed to be an intimate, playful, egalitarian group devoted to the sharing of creativity. Toy makers agreed.[24] As the birth rate exploded in the decade after World War II, toy makers sought to supply the new generation with devices designed to help them become more creative. For instance, the company Creative Playthings, founded in 1947, supplied jungle gyms and wooden swings to schools, building playgrounds that would encourage individualized yet collaborative exploration. A firm called Playskool likewise sold its ubiquitous Tinkertoys, sets of rods and wheels that let children build in whatever way they saw fit. As a 1956 ad for Playskool in *Playthings* magazine made clear, the emphasis on childhood creativity in this period was ubiquitous: "When a toy is designed to make the most of a child's natural creativeness," explained its copywriters, "you gain an unlimited selling market."[25]

In 1948, when the Museum of Modern Art opened its People's Art Center, the national push for creative play was just getting under way. D'Amico and his staff at the center met it with a political and aesthetic sensibility formed by the museum's earlier push against fascism. When D'Amico and his colleagues looked out onto the landscape of American art teaching, they saw "a proliferation of school contests and competitions, paint-by-numbers kits" and the like, all of which taught "art through copying."[26] As D'Amico put it, "these devices . . . are all based on a method of imitation that is slavish and dictatorial. They deny the right of individual choice and freedom and sow the seed for a dictator type of society. They threaten the creative life of our country because they strike at the heart of creative education. How can anyone who believes himself to be creative, whether he be artist or amateur, or anyone who respects individuality, endure these methods or fail to see the inherent menace?"[27]

To counter this protofascist sort of instruction and to bolster the creativity of the American family, D'Amico developed the Parent-Child Class at the People's Art Center. Begun in 1950, the Parent-Child Class extended the circle of egalitarian play formerly drawn by the walls of the Children's Art Carnival to include parents themselves. Parents were to be not instructors, but collaborators for their children. In the classroom, parents and children found themselves surrounded by identical materials and worked on them independently or together as they saw fit, each at his own skill level and each toward his own end. Parents became childlike once again, while their children enjoyed managing themselves within an environment established for the purpose. In short, the classroom became a world without a dictator, unified in its pursuit of individual diversity.

Like workshops of the War Veterans' Art Center, or of the Bauhaus long before that, the Parent-Child Class focused on introducing individuals to an array of materials, allowing them to select those that mattered most to them, and urging them to integrate their engagement with these materials into a new sense of themselves as creative individuals—and of the family as a center for the development of creative and therefore nonauthoritarian citizens. Yet the Parent-Child Class also modeled a new way to structure political authority in a democracy. Even as it leveled the playing field between parent and child in the classroom, the Parent-Child Class shifted the locus of control over children themselves. Within its confines, power now resided in two places: first, in the hands of those who built the room in which the class took place and selected the materials with which the children would work, and second, within the children themselves. In this setting children needed to learn not only how to make art, but how to manage themselves in terms set by largely invisible others. Their parents had been demoted from instructors and role models to artistic equals.

To the extent that social analysts and even the general public recognized art teaching and the family in this period as key settings for personality formation, the Parent-Child Class also became a prototype of an emerging political ideal. Moreover, it did so well beyond the confines of the Museum of Modern Art, through the new medium of television. In 1952, Victor D'Amico and his staff worked with the National Broadcasting Company (NBC) to produce a new program, *Through the Enchanted Gate*, for television station WNBT in New York, as well as an accompanying guide for parents.[28] Together these materials modeled a world of empathetic, racially and sexually diverse individuals, each pursuing their own individuality in the company of others.

The first year's thirteen half-hour episodes borrowed the structure of the Children's Carnival. The show opened with a shot of the wire gate— just big enough to admit a child of twelve or so—that had served to keep parents out of the workspace of the Carnival. "This is an enchanted gate and it's like no other gate you've seen," intoned an invisible narrator. It admitted only children ages three to ten, he explained. Adults could come

FIGURE 6.2.

A father and daughter make hats in the Parent-Child Class at the Museum of Modern Art on the television program *Through the Enchanted Gate*.

in only "if you still believe in fantasy, if you can see with your fingers . . . ."[29] Once inside, the eight children in each episode found themselves surrounded by art materials and accompanied by a teacher as they pursued a particular theme. Victor D'Amico served as an on-camera host, visiting the classroom now and again and summarizing its achievements at the end of the show.

Within the classroom, children made art, but they also made a particular kind of community. In an episode devoted to exploring texture and vision, for example, four boys and four girls closed their eyes and whacked a beach ball. "What did you miss?" their teacher, Maureen Maser, asked. "You need both your fingers to tell you . . . and your eyes to tell you it has stripes."[30] At one level, viewers at home could see a lesson in aesthetic perception. At another, however, they could see a lesson in social collaboration. Of the eight students, six were white, one was Asian American, and one African American. Today we might call such a distribution tokenism; but in 1952, to display a social group in which a quarter of the participants were both people of color and completely equal participants in all activities was, to say the least, unusual. Moreover, these sorts of racial distributions obtained across the show's two seasons. On the show's soundstage, children of many races pursued their own creative expressions, and out of that process, social unity emerged. Such authorities as revealed themselves on screen—Mauren Maser, Victor D'Amico—were hardly authoritarian. Rather, they deployed their expertise in order to promote the psychological, social, and aesthetic growth of their charges.

That growth took place by means of a guided encounter with the senses. In an episode devoted to making "space designs," for instance, children brought objects from home with which to work, such as straws, sticks, and a pinwheel. Their teacher then showed them a potted plant and explained that it, too, possessed elements of design. "Nature has a lot to teach us about space designs!" she exclaimed. Happily inspired, her charges plunged off to assemble a cornucopia of different materials into their own abstract constructions. As they worked, they exercised their senses of sight, touch, hearing, and smell. They interacted with each other and with their teacher. And at the end of their time together, they emerged with objects that served as mirrors of their moods and windows into their minds. "They're all so different!" said Victor D'Amico as he entered the on-air classroom. "Yes, it's always such fun to see what they've done because each child has his own way of doing things," replied the teacher, Miss Wilson.[31]

In the second season, parents accompanied their children through the enchanted gate and onto the screen. "Here are the families!" announced the narrator as they walked hand-in-hand through the gate, the grown-ups ducking. "They're people who live together and play together and work together."[32] Once again, the classroom became a model of an idealized postwar America. An episode focused on helping families express their feelings about cities, for example, featured a Japanese-American family, the Kawachis, whose father spoke limited English. Only a decade after American officials had forced thousands of Japanese-Americans into internment camps, and only eight years after American bombers had leveled Hiroshima and Nagasaki, the Kawachi family worked side-by-side with two American families of European descent, the Zankers and the Halls. Children and parents massaged balls of clay, built windowed towers from sticks, and piled blocks up on a table. Together they built new cities, almost literally out of the ruins of World War II. "I guess in art you can be pretty free," said Mrs. Kawachi. "Yes," replied Victor D'Amico, "that's what art's for."[33]

At the end of each episode, Victor D'Amico asked children at home to send in their own artwork and offered their parents his printed guide to family art making. He also held up pictures and sculptures he had received the week before, and discussed their merits. For D'Amico, the television soundstage was meant to launch the building of similar classrooms—and similarly creative, egalitarian families—in homes everywhere. In 1954, D'Amico published a slim volume entitled *Art for the Family* in which he codified his ambitions. Drawing many of his examples from episodes of *Through the Enchanted Gate*, he encouraged parents to step down from their authoritarian perches in the family and collaborate with their children. He especially recommended the development of "a family art gallery" in every house, where each member of the family could choose examples of his or her own creations to hang. In the family gallery, children would learn from parents and parents from children. No one would copy each other or anyone or anything else. "The camera can do that better,"

FIGURE 6.3.
A family working in its playroom. Victor D'Amico recommended that every family establish a gallery in their home to display artworks made by parents and children. At the height of the Cold War, D'Amico hoped such galleries would foster a culture of egalitarian, even democratic creativity. Photograph by Arthur Rothstein. Courtesy of Dr. Annie Segan.

wrote D'Amico. "The camera cannot think or feel or select or imagine. That is what you can do."[34]

As D'Amico's critique of the camera suggests, art was to help produce an organic and thus democratic solidarity among family members, and not the mechanistic unity of fascism. The basis of that solidarity was psychological. D'Amico urged family members to regularly examine their art for signs of aesthetic and psychological development. "Some signs of growth will show in your work," he explained, "but the most important ones happen inside of you and show in the way you see and feel and work."[35] By 1954, D'Amico's ideal family had become a link in a chain of environments devoted to the reformation of the self through art. The Children's Art Carnival, the War Veterans' Art Center, the People's Art Center, *Through the Enchanted Gate*—each provided an arena in which individuals could practice the perceptual skills that helped develop democratic inclinations. At the same time, these environments modeled a world managed from without by benevolent experts. Even as they pursued what all described as their own unique psychological and artistic development, the students in these environments did so in terms and with materials set for them by others. To put it another way, even as they pursued the freedom of expression associated with art, they practiced precisely the kind of social adjustment called for by contemporary psychiatrists.

FROM THE FAMILY ART GALLERY TO *THE FAMILY OF MAN*

In 1955, the politically prototypical families, immersive artistic environments, and psychotherapeutic understanding of the artwork that animated Victor D'Amico's education projects became central elements in *The Family of Man*. To understand how, though, we need to scrape away several decades of critical disdain. Since the 1970s, critics have based their assaults on two kinds of claims. First, even the most sympathetic analysts of recent years have argued that the show was essentially a *Life* magazine photo essay writ large. In this view, Steichen and his colleagues arrayed their images like words in a sentence so as to deliver a particular message to a relatively passive audience. Second, critics have suggested that the images chosen for the exhibition, coupled with their arrangement at the Museum of Modern Art and elsewhere, sought to contain problems of sexual and racial difference within the symbolic confines of the nuclear family.

These views have been compounded by the museum's promotion of Edward Steichen as a creative genius and by Steichen's own egotism. As told by Steichen and the many journalists and historians who have followed his lead, *The Family of Man* emerged primarily out of Steichen's own heroic impulses. One of the most well known American photographers of the early twentieth century, a chronicler of America's artistic and corporate elites, and from 1947 to 1962 the director of the Museum of Modern Art's photography department, Steichen was in his mid-seventies when he started working on *The Family of Man*. He came to do the show, he later claimed, because of the failure of earlier exhibitions he had organized to spark antiwar activism. During World War II, Steichen served as the head of a Navy photographic team and also staged two large and popular photography exhibitions designed to boost American morale: *Road to Victory* in 1942 and *Power in the Pacific* in 1945, both at the Museum of Modern Art. In February 1951 he mounted a third exhibition at the museum focused on combat, *Korea: The Impact of War in Photographs*. He hoped these shows would help viewers come to hate warfare, but they didn't: "Although I had presented war in all its grimness in three exhibitions, I had failed to accomplish my mission. I had not incited people into taking open and united action against war itself. . . . What was wrong? I came to the conclusion that I had been working from a negative approach, that what was needed was a positive statement on what a wonderful thing life was, how marvelous people were, and, above all, how alike people were in all parts of the world."[36]

According to the now-canonical history of the show, this inspiration led Steichen to begin scouting for images to include in such a project. He and his assistant Wayne Miller scoured the files of the Farm Security Administration (FSA); the National Archives; the Library of Congress; photo agencies such as Black Star, Magnum, and the Soviet Union's SovFoto; and magazines including *Life* and *Seventeen*.[37] Steichen also traveled to Europe seeking images. He reached out to friends such as Dorothea Lange, one of the foremost FSA photographers, who in turn promoted the project among their colleagues. In a 1953 recruiting letter headlined "A Summons to Photographers All Over the World," for instance, Lange told her peers that the exhibition would "show Man to Man across the world. Here we hope to reveal by visual images Man's dreams and aspirations, his strength, his despair under evil. If photography can bring these things to life, this exhibition will be created in a spirit of passionate and devoted faith in Man. Nothing short of that will do."

In one draft of this letter, Lange listed thirty-three terms that she thought might inspire her colleagues. They still serve as a convenient map of the conceptual field within which she and Steichen were working:

Man	Friends	Government
Universal	Work	Competition
Timeless	Home	Invention
Love	Worship	Beauty
Create	Peace	Migration
Birth	Conflict	Fear
Death	Abode	Hope
Family	Hunger	Cooperation
Word	Pestilence	Dream
Father	Communication	Woman
Mother	Ancestors [sic]	Descendents [sic][38]

With the assistance of Lange and many others, Steichen and Miller ultimately reviewed two million images. They winnowed these down to ten thousand, and then, working in a small loft on 52nd Street, to the 503 photographs that ultimately hung in the museum. Steichen all but prohibited abstract images from the exhibition. Instead, he drew primarily on the realistic snapshot aesthetics of contemporary photojournalism. Steichen and Miller's final selection included images by Edward Weston, Ansel Adams, Robert Capa, and Dorothea Lange. It also featured images by photographers who were soon to make names for less mainstream work, such as Robert Frank, Diane Arbus, and Bill Brandt. Steichen also thumbed through literature and journalism, seeking quotations to accompany the images on the museum's walls. He turned to his brother-in-law, poet Carl Sandburg, for help. Sandburg wrote a prologue for the exhibition; its walls ultimately also featured passages from the Bible, Navajo Indian lore, and even the writings of acerbic philosopher Bertrand Russell.

When the exhibition finally opened in 1955, the museum and the press made a great deal of Steichen and Miller's editorial efforts. Most reviewers loved the show. Many lauded Steichen as a sort of author—speaking in what he and reviewers alike called the "universal language" of photography—and the exhibition as a text, an essay even.[39] Over the years, however, critics have come to decry what they saw as Steichen's transposition of the photo essay from magazine page to museum wall. For the last forty years at least, most have agreed with journalist Russell Lynes's 1973 account, in which he wrote that *The Family of Man* "was a vast photo essay, a literary formula basically, with much of the emotional and visual quality provided by sheer bigness of the blow-ups and its rather sententious message sharpened by juxtaposition of opposites—wheat fields and landscapes of boulders, peasants and patricians, a sort of 'look at all these nice folks in all these strange places who belong to this family.'"[40]

In the post-1960s writings of Lynes and others, the notion that the exhibition was an essay and the implication that Steichen was its "author" has worked to support the notion that the exhibition modeled the conformity of 1950s American culture. In these accounts Steichen has become a patriarch, the curatorial equivalent of a Cold War politician, manipulating his audience with bombast. His power resides principally in the images he has selected. The manner of their installation at the Museum of Modern Art goes largely unanalyzed. Their audience, largely absent, can present no explanation for the show's unceasing appeal. Melted down into the anonymity of attendance figures, those who visited the exhibition and bought the book become dupes: unlike the citizens of parti-colored post-countercultural 1973, the museum visitors of 1955 remain trapped in a black-and-white episode of *Leave It to Beaver*. "Look at all these nice folks . . . who belong to this family" indeed.

A NEW GENEALOGY

Yet *The Family of Man* did not emerge solely in response to the cultural politics of the 1950s—nor, for that matter, wholly out of the genius of Edward Steichen. Rather, it grew as much if not more from the promotion of diversity as the basis of national unity in the early 1940s and from the museum's wartime efforts to train its visitors in the ways of the democratic personality.

In November of 1950, as Steichen was still gathering his materials for his Korean War exhibition, the museum's director, René d'Harnoncourt, wrote a letter to Henry Ford II, chairman of the board of trustees of the Ford Foundation. In 1948 the trustees had convened a committee to outline a new funding agenda for the organization; in September 1950 they published its conclusions. D'Harnoncourt set Steichen's new project within a framework outlined in the Ford Foundation's annual report of 1950. Writing in the dominant idiom of the day, the foundation trustees argued that all of humanity faced a choice between two modes of living. "One is democratic, dedicated to the freedom and dignity of the individual," they wrote. "The other is authoritarian, where freedom and justice do not exist, and human rights and truth are subordinated wholly to the state."[41] From a distance of sixty years, it is easy to layer these words onto the global map of the Cold War and so to see them as promoting a new American hegemony. But it is harder to recognize that within that work, there was another, antistatist impulse. The trustees of the Ford Foundation articulated this impulse with characteristic white-collar restraint: "Human welfare requires tolerance and respect for individual social, religious, and cultural differences. . . . Within wide limits, every person has a right to go his own way and to be free from interference or harassment because of nonconformity."[42]

To make such individual freedom a reality, the trustees advocated not hierarchical control, but governmentality. Democracy was not simply a design for state government, they explained. "It is a way of total living, and to choose it means to choose it again and again, today and tomorrow, and continuously to reaffirm it in every act of life."[43] The job of government was not to control the choices of citizens, but rather to set a principled framework within which they might make their own choices. For the trustees, such a system was the opposite of hierarchies of fascism and communism, in which men were slaves or masters. In the more egalitarian democratic system, they wrote, "principles become actions."[44] The job of the Ford Foundation in the coming years would be to promote such principles—and by implication, such a mode of control—worldwide.

In his letter to Henry Ford, d'Harnoncourt noted that the museum's director of photography, Edward Steichen, had been at work for more than a year on an exhibition tentatively called "'the family of man'" that might become a "demonstration of this basic concept of a free society." The word "demonstration" is important here. The exhibition was "not to be a propaganda show," wrote d'Harnoncourt. It would not bend the truth, nor would it try to deliver a message a single, identical message into every viewer's mind. On the contrary, by gathering multiple images the exhibition would avoid replicating the one-to-many, top-down messaging patterns of fascist propaganda. As d'Harnoncourt put it, "Our beliefs will be told by means of the faces, actions and achievements of free people from all over the world."[45]

In other words, while Steichen's show would have a message in the general sense, it would not seek to *impose* its views upon the audience. Rather, it would attempt to build a framework of principles, draw visitors into that framework, and there allow them to see themselves as free individuals among a world of others. The exhibition would employ not the narrative mode traditionally associated with propaganda, but a more psychologically driven visual idiom. In their report, the trustees of the Ford Foundation had stressed that the most important problems facing humanity stemmed from interpersonal and international conflict, and that such problems could only be solved by "whole persons" who could "work together in confidence and mutual respect."[46] René d'Harnoncourt pointed out that the Museum of Modern Art had long been concerned with creating just those psychological and social conditions. The museum's education department, for instance, had developed a series of techniques that had proven especially effective at promoting the "basic democratic objective, the full development and use by each person of his inherent potentialities." During the war years, these techniques had healed returning veterans. Now, he wrote, they had "been incorporated into our general program and are bringing excellent results."[47]

When visitors arrived at the Museum of Modern Art in 1955, they encountered an exhibition that drew extensively on those techniques as well as on the extended field of vision aesthetic and the prodemocratic, Gestaltist psychology of viewing that had characterized Steichen's earlier *Road to Victory*. As they moved toward the stairs that would take them to the second-floor viewing galleries, visitors received a pamphlet with a prologue by Carl Sandburg that set the interpretive stage: "The first cry of a newborn baby in Chicago or Zamboango, in Amsterdam or Rangoon, has the same pitch and key, each saying, 'I am! I have come through! I belong! I am a member of the Family.'" Lest his audience miss the point, Sandburg explained that in the exhibition, "you travel and see what the camera saw. . . . You might catch yourself saying, 'I'm not a stranger here.'"[48]

Pamphlets in their hands, viewers then passed into an entryway and under an arch covered with images of a huge crowd seen from the air. Directly in front of them, they saw a river. To walk under the arch and into the exhibition space was to step into the river of humanity, flowing through time. But it was very definitely *not* to become part of an anonymous mass. On the contrary, when they left the foyer, visitors largely left images of crowds behind. As they entered the exhibition proper, visitors faced a Lucite wall hung with images of individuals and couples—sitting under a tree, chatting on a street corner, kissing, working—as well as a wedding procession. By implication, the entryway reminded visitors that much as America had defeated the fascists of World War II, the Americans of 1955 could defeat the new authoritarian forces of massification at home and abroad, and enter a peaceful, global society of individuals. Moreover, as Sandburg had told them, they would not be strangers; on the contrary, in all of the racial and cultural differences they would see, they would recognize themselves.

That recognition would depend on two aesthetic elements: the welding of the Bauhaus surround to the pattern of the individual life course, and the use of individual images as mirrors and windows into the psyches of visitors. Consider the layout of the exhibition. Its architect, Paul Rudolph, who was trained at Harvard by Walter Gropius, described his design as "telling a story."[49] Over the years, critics have agreed: many have characterized the show as drawing viewers down a thematic tunnel. At the entrance to the exhibition, they note, Steichen placed images of love and marriage; in its central hall, pictures of large, established families; and in its final, narrow passages, images of old age, death, and at the very end, childhood once again. To walk through the exhibition was in some sense to walk through Steichen's vision of the life course—a vision that critics have castigated for its patriarchal, heterosexual conventionality.

At the broadest level, such readings make sense. Steichen did indeed structure the show to take visitors from birth to death and even to rebirth at the end. Yet critics writing in this vein have dramatically underplayed both the flexibility of Rudolph's installation and the range of social, racial and national possibilities represented in the pictures on the walls. Seen from overhead, Rudolph's plan for the exhibition reveals that it did not in fact require visitors to take each life stage in sequence. Nor did it demand they move through the exhibition together in a herd. After entering the museum's second-floor galleries, visitors turned right, into a small circular area which Rudolph had lit with fluorescent lights and hung with thin curtains to suggest hospital wards. On the walls, viewers saw pictures of women in labor, a child being born, mothers nursing. After that, however, visitors were on their own.

As viewers left the birth pavilion, the exhibition space opened out and presented them with an array of choices. To their right, they faced a display of images of children and, visible beyond it, a walkway with images of families playing and celebrating together. If they walked straight ahead or turned left, they found themselves in the open center of the exhibition. There they encountered enormous, wall-sized images of family groups hung from the ceiling at different heights and facing different directions. In a single glance, viewers could take in a Japanese farm family in traditional dress, a polygamous African family outside of their hut, two images of rural Italian farm families, and a multigenerational white American family posed around a wood stove, with portraits of nineteenth-century ancestors on the wall behind. Seen individually, these images could be read as stereotypical depictions of "primitive" Africans, "tradition-bound" Japanese and Italians, and "hillbilly" Americans. But seen together, as they were meant to be, the images *challenged* stereotypes. Far from privileging either whites or Americans, the photographs in fact equate them with two groups suffering extraordinary prejudice in America at that moment—Africans (and, implicitly, African Americans) and America's former enemies,

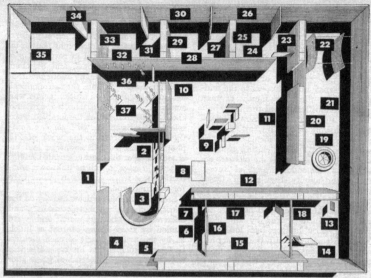

HERE'S A GUIDE TO THE FAMILY OF MAN

Architect: Paul Rudolph

Steichen's photographic tribute to humanity is so huge and covers such a wide scope that it requires new approaches to organization and display. The architect's drawing above shows how some of the problems were solved. Groups of related pictures are indicated by number in approximately the order they are seen by a visitor walking through the exhibition: **1** entrance arch, **2** lovers, **3** childbirth, **4** mothers and children, **5** children playing, **6** disturbed children, **7** fathers and sons, **8** photograph displayed on the floor, **9** "family of man" central theme pictures, **10** agriculture, **11** labor, **12** household and office work, **13** eating, **14** folk-singing, **15** dancing, **16** music, **17** drinking, **18** playing, **19** ring-around-the-rosy stand, **20** learning, thinking, and teaching, **21** human relations, **22** death, **23** loneliness, **24** grief, pity, **25** dreamers, **26** religion, **27** hard times and famine, **28** man's inhumanity to man, **29** rebels, **30** youth, **31** justice, **32** public debate, **33** faces of war, **34** dead soldier, **35** illuminated transparency of H-bomb explosion, **36** UN, and **37** children.

FIGURE 6.4.

Though *The Family of Man* was organized around the individual human life cycle, viewers did not have to follow that order as they moved through the exhibition. Instead, until they reached the final hallway, they were in charge of their own movements. From *Popular Photography* (May 1955), 148. Used by permission of *Popular Photography*, a division of Bonnier Corporation.

the Japanese—and with another former enemy, the Italians. To stand among these images was to stand in a three-dimensional environment built along the lines laid down by theorists like Harold Lasswell in his essay on democratic character: it was to be invited to perceive the Africans and Japanese not as somehow lesser people, but instead, to recognize a *likeness* between them and more dominant groups. Though the images certainly echoed stereotypes, they also solicited empathy—and that at a time when such fellow-feeling was rare in the United States.

From the central area, visitors could turn right and examine the hallway of families playing if they had ignored it at first, or they could walk forward into a long, baffled room with massive landscapes on the walls. These last included Ansel Adam's *Mount Williamson* and fields of waving grain, and set here and there among them, smaller, varied images of European peasant families at the dinner table, and Mongolian horsemen galloping across

FIGURE 6.5.
The central display in *The Family of Man* at the Museum of Modern Art in New York, 1955. Photograph by Ezra Stoller. Digital Image © The Museum of Modern Art, licensed by SCALA / Art Resource, New York.

the steppes. At the opening to this room stood a wheel of images the size of a small merry-go-round on a children's playground. The images mounted there depicted children from around the world playing Ring Around the Rosie. And at the other end, large convex panels hung from the wall, with images of funerals and mourning. In each case, visitors confronted images of individuals from around the world engaged in activities that Steichen saw as both regional and universal. Moreover, they encountered those images at eye level, overhead, and well below the waist. They were in fact surrounded by the families of the globe.

Viewers could linger among all of these images for as long as they liked. They could return to either of the long rooms or to the central family area as well. But when they were finished with these zones, they had to turn into a long hallway, with images jutting from the walls at ninety degrees. About halfway down this hall, they faced a wall with nine close-up portraits of identical size and, set among them, a mirror. Alongside these pictures, Steichen placed the words of Bertrand Russell: "The best authorities are unanimous in saying the war with hydrogen bombs is quite likely to put an end to the human race. There will be universal death—sudden only for a fortunate minority, but for the majority a slow torture of disease and disintegration." The portraits in turn featured the suffering faces of three men, three women, and three children, and among them an American soldier fresh from battle, almost certainly in Korea.

At the center of these pictures, viewers saw their own faces. Steichen and Miller removed the mirror after two weeks, having come to believe that it was "corny and wrong."[50] But the hope behind it remained. As Steichen put it, "When people come out of this show they'll feel that they've looked in a mirror; that we're all alike."[51] Steichen's hope echoes both the goals and the aesthetic psychology that drove the museum's efforts in art therapy for veterans and art education for children. If a painting or a drawing by a traumatized veteran revealed his unique humanity, Steichen suggested that the photographs in *The Family of Man* likewise opened windows onto the interior humanity of their subjects. He hoped that by gazing into images of others who were racially and culturally different from themselves, visitors could see beyond skin color and beyond whatever prejudices they themselves might carry. He hoped they could see through the image until, at a psychological level, its transparency transformed it into a mirror of their own interior individuality. In a sense, Steichen asked his viewers to stare *through* the images on the wall and, thereby, into their own humanity. Much like veterans at D'Amico's War Veterans' Art Center, visitors were to use art to simultaneously engage their own, individualized responses and to rejoin a larger community of human beings. And like parents and children in a home art gallery, they were to see pieces of themselves on the walls and so come to understand themselves as unique members of a creative, egalitarian family.

Even as they saw themselves in the mirror, viewers could glimpse another wall beyond the faces and a soldier, nationality unknown, face down in the dirt, his rifle stuck in the ground to mark his body. When they turned and walked past the soldier, visitors entered a chamber and faced the one color image in the show: an eight-foot-tall transparency of a mushroom cloud. Until this point in the exhibition, they could meander among arrays of images. This picture of a hydrogen bomb exploding was a choke point, a single image every viewer had to confront before moving on. For Steichen, the image clearly represented what might happen to the human race if individuals failed to recognize the qualities they shared. In 1955 America, the image also likely reminded American viewers, first, that theirs was the only nation that had dropped an atomic bomb on civilian populations and, second, that they might be the objects of such attacks themselves. To drive these points home, the exhibition even included the image of a Japanese boy wandering in the ruins of Nagasaki.

Beyond the bomb, viewers continued down a wide hallway and faced a series of portraits of male-and-female couples, each labeled "We two form a multitude." These images hung like street signs at a ninety-degree angle from a wall-sized picture of the United Nations General Assembly. Just beyond the delegates, again at a ninety-degree angle, viewers could see the torso of a woman draped in flowers, walking along the edge of the ocean. Beyond her, they came first to a roomful of pictures of children playing, and finally to one of *Life* photographer W. Eugene Smith's most well-known images, *The Walk in Paradise Garden*. Just as they were preparing to leave the exhibition hall, visitors saw Smith's two toddler subjects, walk-

FIGURE 6.6.

Photographer Wayne Miller's wife and children in front of a wall-sized color transparency of the H-bomb at *The Family of Man*, the Museum of Modern Art, New York, 1955. Photograph by Wayne Miller, Magnum Photos. Used by permission.

ing up out of a darkened, leafy bower. In the exhibition catalog, the caption to this image reminded them of its meaning in an atomic era: there was "A world to be born under your footsteps . . ."[52]

In its final spaces, *The Family of Man* was as heavy-handed in its message as a supermarket greeting card. Yet this does not mean that we should read the exhibition simply as a piece of propaganda. Rather, in the terms of its own time, it was an effort to make visible a new, more diverse, and more tolerant vision of both the United States and the globe. It was also an effort to help produce citizens who might see themselves and racial Others as equals, who might see in the strangeness of African polygamy a mirror of down-home white America. The key to this process was not simply asking viewers to see others like themselves. Instead, it was borrowing the educational ideals of Victor D'Amico and László Moholy-Nagy and the extended field of vision technique developed by Herbert Bayer, and deploying both in a new political context. With images literally all around them, visitors to *The Family of Man* had to make choices about where to look and how to integrate what they saw into their own worldviews. This process, in turn, exercised the psychological muscles on which democracy and perhaps even the future of the world depended.

In 1955 a number of reviewers marveled at the show's installation and its implications for viewers. One, photographer Barbara Morgan, even argued that the combination of architectural and photographic elements in the show constituted a new medium: "Here one is instantly conscious that this is no orthodox show of 'exhibition prints' hung salon-wise. It is something for which we need a new term. . . . Several have been suggested, 'photographic-Mosaic,' 'three-dimensional editorializing,' 'movie of stills,' yet they all fail—too cumbersome—not accurate enough. . . ."[53] Morgan went on to select her own term, the "theme show," and to describe it as a new "photographic genre. . . . which fuses science, photography, architecture, layout and writing into a compelling synthesis." Above all, this new genre forced individuals to develop independent psychological reactions to what they saw: "Juxtaposition of photographs meant to be seen in relation to each other begets new meaning to a thoughtful visitor. . . . Our blind spots and sensitivities being semantically what they are, to every thinking onlooker these cross-connected ways of life will mean vastly different things." Yet they would not lead to an *unlimited* range of interpretation. Rather, they would lead to a diverse but unified condition of interpersonal and international empathy. As Morgan put it,

> In comprehending the show the individual himself is also enlarged, for these photographs are not photographs only—they are also phantom images of our co-citizens; this woman into whose photographic eyes I now look is perhaps today weeding her family rice paddy, or boiling a fish in coconut milk. Can you look at the polygamist family group and imagine the different norms that make them live happily in their society which is so unlike—yet like—our own? Empathy with these hundreds of human beings truly expands our sense of values."[54]

FREEDOM AND SELF-MANAGEMENT

Over the next decade, the United States Information Agency would send the exhibition around the world and transform it into essential tool for the promulgation not only of the psychology of democracy, but of American economic and political expansionism. But even as the state worked to turn it into a piece of propaganda, *The Family of Man* carried with it undercurrents of protest and of utopian globalism that would flow directly into the 1960s. Less than a year before Rosa Parks sat down in the front of a bus, *The Family of Man* modeled the kind of society that she was about to call for. Did that world encompass all human differences? No. Did the exhibition acknowledge any kind of sexuality other than heterosexuality? No, it didn't. But at one of the most gender-conservative, race-sensitive, and hypermilitarized moments in American history, *The Family of Man* presented a three-dimensional environment in which Americans were asked to accept practitioners of alternative sexuality (polygamy) and members of routinely demonized groups (Africans, Japanese, communist Russians and Chinese) as people like themselves. And they were asked to reject warfare as a crime against the species.

At the same time, *The Family of Man* asked visitors to practice the perceptual skills on which the development of democratic personalities—and thus, democratic societies—depended. In keeping with both D'Amico's immersive teaching methods and Bayer's extended field of vision, the makers of *The Family of Man* surrounded their audiences with images. At one level, each image offered viewers a potential moment of identification, a window through the life of another that allowed visitors to reflect on their own lives. At another level, however, the pictures acted as an ensemble, an array of images that visitors needed to rearrange within their own psyches. In the process of aggregating and organizing these images, visitors could, at least in theory, engage in a degree of self-formation not open to citizens of authoritarian regimes. Most important, they could emerge from this process psychologically whole and self-directing. Unlike the citizens of Nazi Germany or of the Soviet Union, China, or North Korea—at least as so many Americans imagined them—visitors to *The Family of Man* would not suffer from psychological fragmentation or interpersonal atomization. As a result, they would not be victimized by despots.

Nor would they run wild, however. Even as they offered viewers the chance to do the democratic psychological work of choosing others with whom to identify, Steichen, Miller, and Rudolph constrained their visitors' choices. *The Family of Man* thus modeled a more diverse and tolerant society, but also a society whose members had adjusted themselves to an array of opportunities chosen on their behalf by those in power. In comparison to fascist alternatives, the world brought to life at the Museum of Modern Art in 1955 must have looked enormously individualistic, varied, and free. But even as it challenged the hierarchies of totalitarianism, the exhibition modeled the emergence of a society whose citizens were to manage themselves in terms set by the systems within which they lived—and by the experts who developed those systems.

7

Therapeutic Nationalism

In a small gray box on a metal shelf deep in the cool recesses of the National Archives, there is a typescript labeled "Communications Research and USIS Operations." Written in 1959, it is one of hundreds of such papers prepared over the years for officers of the United States Information Agency and its overseas operational element, the United States Information Service, by the agency's research wing. Most such documents surveyed public attitudes toward the United States abroad or plotted propaganda tactics to change them. But this one made a different, more comprehensive case: It argued that the USIA should think of each of its communication operations as an act of psychotherapeutic intervention.

The USIA should divide each action into three phases, the report explained: diagnosis, treatment, and the evaluation of effects. The "diagnostic task" consisted of assessing the target nation's attitudes toward the United States, as reflected primarily in the press and in surveys of citizens. Treatment consisted of enlisting target audiences in modes of communication that could provide "*prophylaxis* to avoid an 'unhealthful' condition and *therapy* to bring about recovery from such a condition [emphases original]." After treatment, the report explained, the agency would need to assess the target audience's state of mind by once again analyzing the contents of mass media, by conducting surveys of the populace, or, where that was not possible, by sending American personnel out among the people to report their impressions as best they could. In any case, the report suggested that even as it tried to change international attitudes on specific questions of policy, the USIA should aim to foster deeper "sociopsychological" transformations. When confronted with communists or fascists, for instance, the USIA should not challenge their belief systems individually, but should instead aim to defuse the authoritarian psychology underlying both. As the report put it, they should not "work at the level of symptoms" but "closer to the level of causes."[1]

Today, the notion that psychotherapy could provide a model for propagandists may seem deeply alien. We tend to think of therapy as an interpersonal process and one aimed at empowering rather than controlling the person seeking aid. But by the late 1950s, a substantial number of American intellectuals and government officials understood international relations in essentially interpersonal terms. Individuals and nations each had dominant personality styles, as the relevant experts in the social sciences had shown. And since they did, managing the psychological reactions of individual citizens and of whole nations became two sides of the same coin. In the early 1940s this understanding shaped the promotion of democratic morale at home. In the second half of the 1950s, it helped guide American propaganda tactics abroad.

Not all American propaganda in this period had a psychotherapeutic cast. As a generation of historians has amply demonstrated, the late 1950s saw the American government deploy an incredibly diverse array of propaganda methods.[2] But among them, the psychotherapeutic pattern outlined in the 1959 report did in fact enjoy an important and long forgotten place. So too did the aesthetic form developed to promote personality change in earlier years, the surround. In the late 1950s, *The Family of Man* toured the globe under the aegis of the USIA; Victor D'Amico built creative art classrooms for American pavilions at European trade fairs; and the USIA even commissioned Buckminster Fuller to construct new versions of the geodesic dome he had first tried to build at Black Mountain College. Overseas, the work of Steichen and Bayer, D'Amico, Fuller, and others again asked their visitors to engage in the perceptual practices associated with the formation of democratic personalities: mobility, choice, the constraint of emotion, the elevation of rational thought, and the assertion of individuality within an egalitarian group. As they did, they transformed the universal values they had once invoked to boost American morale in the face of fascism into tools with which to bring together the citizens of the world, as if they were all Americans, to face down communism.

These new uses for the surround evolved alongside a new vision of the democratic personality. In the 1940s, the whole, free person envisioned by, say, Gordon Allport or Erich Fromm enjoyed freedom of choice and expression primarily in the interpersonal and political realms. By the late 1950s, government officials, corporate leaders and a number of well-placed American academics had begun to argue that these life spheres had been ineluctably shaped by the American economy. The democratic person, in turn, became one who enjoyed a freedom to choose not only from an array of expressive styles or a slate of political leaders, but from a range of consumer goods. As the engines of postwar industry thrummed, politics, economics, and the making of American selves became so entwined that to many theorists, choices in one realm often seemed to be choices in the others as well. Designers and architects, in turn, became not only the shapers of consumer goods and of consumers' encounters with them, but of psychological and political choices at home and abroad.

THE CAMPAIGN FOR TRUTH BECOMES
THE PEOPLE'S CAPITALISM

The turn toward fusing consumption and politics paralleled a shift in the American propaganda enterprise. Since the end of World War II, the United States had bombarded the Soviet Union and its allies with a steady barrage of pro-democratic messages. In April 1950, just before North Korea invaded the South, President Truman intensified the assault by launching a "campaign of truth" in a speech to a group of newspaper editors. The Cold War, he said, was "a struggle, above all else, for the minds of men. . . . Unless we get the real story across to people in other countries, we will lose the battle for men's minds by default."[3] By 1952, on any given day the Voice of America could be heard in a hundred nations and forty-six languages; an American government press service fed stories to some ten thousand newspapers; and Americans sponsored US information centers in sixty countries and 190 cities.[4] For the propagandists of the Truman era, and for those of the first years of Eisenhower's administration as well, the primary goal of such programs was, as Eisenhower put it using the dominant metaphor of the day, "to improve our penetration of the Iron Curtain."[5]

By the mid-1950s, however, it had become clear that such methods were not working. The Soviets retained their grip on their satellite states even after Stalin's death in 1953. With a few small-scale exceptions, the peoples of communist nations remained quiescent. In response, American leaders simultaneously redoubled their efforts to undermine communist regimes and turned toward a less ballistic model of communication. In January 1955, a National Security Council memorandum articulated a new international information objective. The United States should "stress evolutionary rather than revolutionary change," it wrote, and should employ "a forceful and direct approach, avoiding a propagandistic or strident tone."[6]

This memo marked a dramatic widening of the cultural portion of America's propaganda offensive, and the opening of a new front in the ideological battle: trade fairs and international expositions. Over the preceding four years, the Soviet Union had sent delegations to more than 130 trade fairs around the globe, while the United States had sent almost none.[7] In 1954, President Eisenhower ignited a new American effort to participate. Over the next six years, the Department of Commerce helped fund American participation in 97 exhibitions in 29 countries. More than five thousand American companies contributed to these events, and according to the Commerce Department, more than sixty million people visited them.[8]

Trade exhibitions thus became premier venues for displaying both American goods and American ideals. At one level, American industries of the late 1950s hoped to secure new markets. At another, though, they hoped to join their government in entwining democratic citizenship, universal humanism, and the consumption of mass-produced goods. A sales manager who traveled to Italy in 1955 recalled that "our objective was selling; selling on many levels. We were selling our government's sincerity and interest in promoting two-way trade; selling our president's over-all interest and sincerity of purpose in bringing a closer rapprochement between countries; selling the American way of life and the democratic philosophy of our government."[9]

As President Eisenhower framed it, the struggle with communism was as much as anything a struggle to direct human desire. On the one hand, when he established the USIA he pointed out that the agency's primary goal was to enlist citizens of foreign countries in following an American agenda. On the other, in a speech to USIA staffers later that year he argued that human beings worldwide longed for the sorts of freedoms of speech, association, and movement enshrined in the American Constitution. The American system had a "greater appeal to the human soul, the human heart, the human mind" than did the communists', precisely because its national values were grounded in universal human values.[10] By pairing the American and the universally human, Eisenhower rhetorically transformed the job of the propagandist: no longer was he the tool of an expanding state, but rather the servant of the species as a whole.

Alongside these lofty ideals, Eisenhower and leaders of American industry worked closely together to establish American goods as intermediaries between the craven, earthly desire for things and more abstract human longings for social justice. In the mid-1950s, Soviet propagandists routinely claimed that communism brought about a higher standard of life for ordinary citizens than did capitalism. Rapacious bankers and landlords preyed on the American working class, miring its members in poverty, while the benevolent Soviet state worked hand in hand with industry to provide for all according to need, they explained. At trade fairs the products of Soviet industry seemed to prove the point as they stood alone, unchallenged by American exhibitions.

To counter the Soviets, the American advertising industry tried to rebrand the American economy.[11] In 1955 the president of the Advertising Council, Theodore Repplier, hit on a phrase that seemed to bottle the essence of American life: "People's Capitalism." The council quickly began to promote it and the editors of *Collier's* magazine heralded its arrival with a full-page editorial. "People's Capitalism" made the perfect counterpunch to the Soviet term "people's democracy," they explained. Under People's Capitalism, individuals competed with one another and made money, and when they did, they bought shares in the companies in which they and their fellow citizens worked. They became owners of the means of production—not through the state but directly, through the stock market.

The wealth they accumulated through their labors and their investments underwrote a flowering of material, political, and intellectual opportunities. As *Collier's* put it, People's Capitalism "means the washing machine, the tractor and the power mower that give us time to take part in civic affairs, to think and dissent. . . . [It] means Social Security, *Porgy and Bess*, hospitalization benefits, *Robert Montgomery Presents* . . . and the *Saturday Review*. It means public education for thought, not some purpose of the state. . . . It means security and challenge in the same breath."[12]

THE CHARACTER OF ABUNDANCE

President Eisenhower agreed and made People's Capitalism the unifying theme of all American exhibitions in 1956. When he did, he also internationalized a vision of the American psyche articulated two years earlier by Yale historian David Potter. In his extraordinarily popular volume *People of Plenty: Economic Abundance and the American Character*, Potter brought together Frederick Jackson Turner's famous "frontier thesis" of American development with work on culture and character published by Margaret Mead, Ruth Benedict, Erich Fromm, Karen Horney, David Riesman, and others. Drawing primarily on the anthropologists, Potter argued that the individual psyche and the society at large structured one another through the medium of culture. For that reason, the character of the individual, his or her social group, and his or her society tended to mirror one another. At the same time, Potter invoked neo-Freudians Horney and Fromm to point out that cultures relied on material goods to transmit their values across generations and to shape patterns of interpersonal interaction. Thus he argued that the material conditions in which children were brought up shaped their personalities as well.

Finally, Potter turned to Turner. Most American historians at the time agreed with Turner that the key characteristics of the democratic individual—a willingness to change oneself, to uproot one's family, to form egalitarian communities—emerged as America expanded westward. Potter pointed out that neither the westward migration nor the democratic character could have come into being had the American landscape not been extraordinarily fertile. Only its abundance had made the democratic personality and the democratic political system possible. That abundance persisted despite the fact that the western frontier had closed long ago. In fact, if anything, mid-20th century American science and industry were bringing the nation to new levels of wealth. This new wealth, Potter argued, had begun to make individuals geographically mobile, psychologically flexible, and interpersonally tolerant, even of racial and class differences, all over again. In the home it had allowed men and women to achieve a new equality, and family structures to become less authoritarian. On the job, it had done the same thing for workers and managers. Equality had not yet spread across the land—African Americans in particular remained disenfranchised—but thanks to America's increasing economic might, it soon would. Moreover, if American leaders would only recognize the importance of abundance to our national character, they might also spread democracy around the globe. Americans had been promoting the overthrow of communist regimes without understanding that principles alone could not sustain democracies, Potter claimed. The democratic character of individuals and nations depended on their collective wealth. For that reason, he implied, Americans should promote not only political democracy, but consumer capitalism. Both helped produce democratic personalities and, through them, democratic and presumably pro-American states.

For Repplier and the Advertising Council, Potter's logic and prestige were unassailable. In November 1956, the council convened a roundtable to discuss the ideas behind the "People's Capitalism" slogan, and asked Potter to chair it. Over two days, in a forum later transcribed and published as a pamphlet, a dozen notables ranging from the editor of *Fortune* magazine and the president of the Bristol-Meyers Company to Yale professor Harold Lasswell sought consensus on the relationship between America's economic system and the psychological and political benefits it conveyed. At a political level, they agreed that People's Capitalism fused the pursuit of abundance and the pursuit of democracy. In the marketplace, people had the opportunity to "vote with their dollars," and thus to decide "for themselves what would be produced."[13] Economic and political life, in turn, relied on individuals psychologically attuned to practices of choice, physical mobility, and adaptability in the face of change. In that sense the group concluded, in Potter's words, that "material and spiritual values" went "hand-in-hand" in American society.[14] Together with the leisure provided by the mechanization of labor, these values helped make People's Capitalism "an extraordinary opportunity for the realization of human potentialities."[15]

A NEW ARCHITECTURE FOR THE SURROUND ABROAD

Few communities were better positioned to help export these values than the loose network of artists and designers associated with the Bauhaus, Black Mountain College, and the Museum of Modern Art in New York. By 1954 Herbert Bayer, Buckminster Fuller and many others had participated in an annual design symposium in Aspen, Colorado, that set the agenda for American design in Bauhaus terms. High in the mountains, Moholy-Nagy's former patron in Chicago, Walter Paepcke, president of the Container Corporation of America, promoted the fusion of good design and mass production and, with them, the old Bauhaus ideal of the psychologically integrated, industrially sustained "New Man."[16] In Washington, DC, the same Nelson Rockefeller who had served as president of the Museum of Modern Art from 1939 to 1948 had become a special assistant to President Eisenhower and formed a committee to advise him on how to bring together economic and psychological elements in American policy abroad.[17] László Moholy-Nagy was dead, but his visual idealism lived on in Edward Steichen's *Family of Man*. Buckminster Fuller continued to champion the design-oriented approach to community building pioneered at the Bauhaus and at Black Mountain College. Individually and together, these artists, designers, and administrators helped set the aesthetic terms for America's international exhibitions across the 1950s and beyond.

It was Buckminster Fuller who supplied the canonical architectural form for American exhibitions. In 1956, at the Kabul International Trade Fair in Afghanistan, Fuller designed the first of at least nine geodesic domes to house American exhibitions.[18] Originally, the United States had planned to skip the Kabul fair. But in the spring of 1956 they learned that China and the Soviet Union were each planning massive pavilions. The Eisenhower administration wanted to meet them in the field, but had to move quickly: the fair was scheduled to open in August. Jack Masey, the

USIA official charged with mounting the show turned to Fuller. Two years earlier, Fuller had shown two large cardboard geodesic domes at the Milan Triennale to great effect.[19] Masey correctly believed that the dome might be one of the few structures that could be built in time for Kabul. Fuller designed a dome one hundred feet in diameter, made of 480 aluminum tubes covered by a nylon skin, and had it shipped to Afghanistan. There a handful of American engineers worked with several dozen Afghan laborers and erected the dome in forty-eight hours.

The propaganda value of this event was substantial. The Soviets and Chinese had built their pavilions using only their own workers—two hundred of them in the Soviet case—and had taken weeks with their work. When the Americans teamed up with locals and produced a pavilion in mere hours, the Afghans marveled. The dome itself seemed to whisper of the power of American engineering. An American press release told visiting journalists that "The American building . . . turned out to be U.S. Exhibit #01. Covered with a translucent plastic-coated nylon which glowed at night, the geodesic dome called dramatic attention to American technological progress."[20] Guides told visitors that the dome was a "demonstration of the degree of industrial progress attained in the U.S. . . . It emphasizes the marriage of aesthetics and technology—two very vital phenomena which are symbolic of a people who believe that only through peace can there be progress."[21]

The geodesic dome would become a symbol of American innovation well into the 1980s. As a close look at the Kabul pavilion suggests however, Cold War domes did not simply *represent* a modern American vision; they transformed it into a three-dimensional, all-encompassing experience. When they entered the dome, visitors found themselves surrounded by black-and-white photographs of Americans hung at every level on a lightweight metal framing system much like the one used to hang *The Family of Man* at the Museum of Modern Art. Around the rim of the dome, the designers arrayed static displays of sewing machines, aircraft models, and life-sized plastic models of farm animals, as well as black-and-white panoramas of the American landscape. Toward the center of the dome, they installed a model of a television studio.

In a sense, the dome served as model of America itself. Its roundness

FIGURE 7.1.
Geodesic dome housing the American exhibition in Kabul, Afghanistan, at the International Trade Fair of 1956. United States Information Agency photograph. Courtesy of Special Collections, Stanford University Libraries.

hinted at the roundness of the globe and the universality of American ideals. The openness of the space it enclosed suggested the wide-open vistas of the American landscape and the American technological future. Visitors' freedom to pick their own direction through the show echoed the claims of Hollywood Westerns that Americans could wander the land in any direction they wished. And like postwar Americans, Afghan visitors found themselves surrounded by abundance. Images, artifacts, and the dome collaborated to invite Afghans into a three-dimensional representation of a world of commercial, perceptual, and ultimately political possibilities: a world in which you could see what you had never seen before and do what you had never done, a world in which you could experience yourself as modern, driven by your own desires, supported by a well designed aesthetic infrastructure and a powerful mass-production economy.

Despite their admiration for the dome, Afghan visitors were not bowled over by the exhibition as a whole. The USIA sponsored a public opinion poll at the fair, which revealed that the Afghans had expected the American pavilion to be much more sophisticated than those of the seven other countries on display. When it wasn't, they were disappointed. The poll showed the American pavilion as the fourth favorite at the fair, behind those of the Soviet Union and China.[22] Yet the fact that Americans sought this information at all marked an important transition in the nature of the surround form. At one level, Masey and his team had commissioned the dome and designed its contents to represent America to the Afghans. The high-tech dome, the cutaway plastic farm animals, even the arrays of multisized photographs—all were built to channel Afghan desires for modernization in a Western direction. In that sense, the Kabul dome resembled *The Family of Man*: both were environments designed to offer visitors a range of choices as to where to place their attention, from a set of objects that had already been selected by invisible experts. This time, though, the environment also rendered visitors available to monitoring. The designers of the Kabul pavilion did not simply want to offer Afghans the opportunity to practice the perceptual skills of independent democratic citizens, nor did they merely want to orient their affections toward America. They wanted to be sure that the environment had caused measurable psychological change.

The techniques by which they assessed this change drew on the mirroring that Edward Steichen had sought to create with *The Family of Man*. Pollsters at the fair solicited viewers' opinions in two ways. First, twelve professors from the University of Kabul recruited to survey the audience simply asked visitors to express their opinion verbally—that is, to answer questions. Second, the professors showed the often illiterate Afghans drawings of turbaned men ostensibly expressing different moods and asked them to pick the one that represented their own mood most effectively. Like the photographs hung in *The Family of Man*, these images were meant to be mirrors into which visitors could gaze and recognize themselves. Much as *The Family of Man* asked viewers to tune their perceptions of themselves to images selected by Steichen, the surveyors' test images required Afghans to orient their own identities toward images supplied by American psychologists. To recognize their feelings and answer the ques-

FIGURE 7.2.

Drawings by Emily Jones used by the USIA in an opinion poll measuring visitor reactions to Western and Soviet bloc pavilions. United States Information Agency photograph. Digital images courtesy of Jack Masey.

tions, they had to match their emotions to images the psychologists had designed to represent universal human feelings and universal human expressions. For a moment, at least, these images asked Afghans to imagine themselves as representatives of a universal human type.

As they interacted with the images, the Afghans also transformed their emotions into data. Collated by researchers and delivered to their American managers, Afghan responses to the exhibition could shape the design of future exhibitions, and perhaps even that of American policy toward Afghanistan and other nations. In this way, visitors became elements in an extended feedback loop. By measuring audience responses to the exhibition, American officials could feed them back into the next round of exhibition design. Each iteration of the cycle would in turn, in theory at least, intensify the psychological impact of the next exhibition.

MAKING CREATIVE CHILDREN FOR A DEMOCRATIC GLOBE

Psychological assessment became a standard element of subsequent fairs. Between 1954 and 1957, the Office of International Trade Fairs at the Commerce Department mounted some forty-five American exhibitions abroad. As a 1957 article in the trade journal *Industrial Design* put it, design at these shows became "a political force."[23] Designers took skills honed in the presentation of commercial goods and brought them to bear on the presentation of the nation. In keeping with the therapeutic paradigm outlined in the 1959 USIA report, they often began their work by assessing the psychological and social conditions of their host countries as reported by anthropologists.[24] The American government measured the success of their designs through public opinion surveys and less formal assessments of public mood made during and after their trade shows. The exhibitions became sites of psychological change, designed and evaluated in terms set in part by commercial architects and display artists, and in part by social scientists.

At Kabul, American officials hoped to win the allegiance of Afghan adults at two psychological levels: prophylaxis and therapy. If any Afghans had already begun to embrace communism, the American pavilion could reorient their senses, heal their ideological misunderstandings, and introduce them to a new, Americanized realm of political and commercial freedom. If Afghans had not yet committed themselves to a psychological allegiance with another nation, a visit to the pavilion might prevent them from doing so. In the wake of the Kabul fair, pavilion builders began to include education through play and artmaking alongside prophylaxis and therapy as means to raise a new generation of democrats abroad.

In Salonika, Greece, in 1956, for example, the Commerce Department laid out twenty-nine thousand square feet of indoor display space under the thematic banner "Fruits of Freedom." Having learned from their failures in Kabul, designers at Salonika focused on what they called "activated exhibits"—that is, live demonstrations and interactive displays.[25] These exhibits stayed close to the household and to professional environments Greeks might encounter in everyday life, such as a surgery and a dentist's office. For women, it offered shows of dressmaking and fashion; for men, woodworking and metal shops and model trains. The Salonika fair also featured a playground equipped with swings, slides, balls, and blocks as well as painting supplies, all meant to bring out the native talents and desires of children, and so to illustrate "a psychological approach to child training."[26] Around the playground, designers built a railing. As the children played under the watchful eyes of their playground managers, their parents and other visitors leaned in and watched them as well. Neither they nor the playground guides instructed the children; rather, both were to watch as the children discovered themselves.

Visitors to the fair could also walk over to a closed-circuit television studio exhibition labeled "See Yourself on TV." Reports at the time described mothers positioning their children in front of television monitors and then waving to them from in front of television cameras; the children routinely waved back, into the monitors.[27] At Salonika, and later at a number of other fairs, closed-circuit television drew visitors into precisely the sorts of feedback loops modeled by the surveyors' pictures in Kabul. Once again, visitors were offered a mediated version of an image of themselves and, through it, access to their own emotions. At the same time, they encountered these images within an environment constructed for the purpose and carefully overseen by American experts. In these environments, television screens facilitated a low-grade version of the sort of self-discovery promoted by *The Family of Man*. Here too, visitors could stand as individuals, examining their likeness to others depicted on the walls around them. Here too they could discover themselves as members of a playful egalitarian social group. They could imagine themselves as individuals with characters made free and creative by the abundance of American capitalism. As they did, they could also absorb the subtle but omnipresent message that a world watched over by Americans was a world devoted to self-discovery for individuals and nations alike.

The immersive architecture of Fuller's Kabul dome and the mix of interactive and static displays of the kind laid out at Salonika quickly became generic. So too did a focus on the nuclear family. In 1955 the American trade fair exhibition in Paris featured a fully stocked American house in which a mother cooked in the kitchen while a father puttered in the garage. It also offered a complete kindergarten, watched over by American wives from a local army base. In 1957 the American pavilion in Poznan, Poland, had become "a geodesic dome packed with things that the average American can buy to eat, wear or use to make work easier and leisure more pleasant," as *Life* magazine put it. The exhibition was a "U.S. wonderland . . . filled with hi-fi sets, dishwashers, automatic ironers, air conditioners, jukeboxes, frogman flippers and power tools for the home handyman."[28]

American designers took pains to show that this consumer cornucopia depended on and helped to produce the creative, individualistic personality types associated with political democracy. In 1957, American officials invited Victor D'Amico of the Museum of Modern Art to bring his Children's Holiday Carnival—rechristened the Children's Carnival of Modern Art—to two exceptionally large and important trade fairs, the Triennale in Milan and the Feria Internacional de Muestras in Barcelona. American exhibitions at both fairs focused on the benefits of consumer capitalism for children. Yet they also revealed the importance of cultivating particular personality traits so as to promote economic productivity. As they had at the Museum of Modern Art, D'Amico's installations celebrated individual creativity, driven from within and practiced in an egalitarian collective, as a basis of psychological, economic, and political security. Once again they offered children a Bauhaus-derived introduction to texture, light, and color. This time, though, D'Amico's classes became a model not only of a new and more tolerant America, but of a new global political order.

In Italy, the Children's Carnival of Modern Art was called "The Children's Paradise;" in Spain, "The Children's Art Festival."[29] In each case it served several functions. First, it provided an actual training space for teaching international children skills with which they might integrate their individual personalities. Second, it modeled the sort of collaborative, egalitarian, but carefully monitored social order promoted by American foreign policy makers at the same moment. And third, it simultaneously excluded adults from the classroom and provided them with opportunities to watch the children learn. In this way, it showed adults the effectiveness of leaving the future in the hands of American leaders—in the classroom and, by implication, in the world.

D'Amico and the staff of the Museum of Modern Art brought the entire Children's Carnival of Modern Art with them to Milan and Barcelona. Once again the Carnival consisted of two rooms: the first designed to inspire creativity, and the second to allow children to exercise it. Children entered the first room through the same wire frame for which *Through the Enchanted Gate* was named. Once inside, they found themselves surrounded by toys. They could pet a furry model cat whose back would arch at their touch, explore patterns made with strings, or step up to a mock spaceship console and pretend to steer themselves through the universe. Colored discs behind a screen changed patterns on a hidden cyclorama as the children pressed pedals to make their imaginary spaceship go. Each of these toys was designed to highlight a particular sense: touch, sight, sound. Others, such as the "color player," facilitated a synthesis of the senses. The color player consisted of a large box with an abstract tree inside, upon which children hung precut shapes. When they were ready, they lowered a glass window over the box, pressed a group of keys and foot pedals, and marveled as patterns of colored light suddenly swirled over the glass and the tree within.

Part piano, part kaleidoscope, the color player operated on principles of synesthesia that were to become commonplace in the light shows of the 1960s counterculture. But in 1957, D'Amico and his team hoped that it would inspire children to build a more egalitarian postwar international order. After letting them play for some time with the toys in the Inspiration Room, guides invited children into the Workshop Gallery. There they found tables littered with paper, scissors, pens, easels equipped with paints, pipe cleaners, and other bits of wire for making mobiles. Teachers, either brought from the Museum of Modern Art or taught by its personnel, gently dissuaded children from using these materials to produce realistic images or copy one another's work. They did point children to projects that had been featured on *Through the Enchanted Gate*, such as making a picture of their feelings. But they were careful to avoid seeming to indoctrinate the students. Indoctrination was the tool of totalitarianism; democracy required self-discovery. They believed, in D'Amico's words, that "each child must work in a way natural to him. The real problem is to free the child of his clichés or imitated mannerisms and to help him discover his own way of seeing and expressing."[30]

In retrospect, it may seem strange that the Department of Commerce should have gone to such lengths to bring a children's art program to trade fairs. But in Milan, the department created a pamphlet in English and Italian, illustrated with pictures from D'Amico's classroom at the Museum of Modern Art, that explained the connection. "This is an exhibit about increased productivity," it said. "Productivity means the more you produce the more there is for everybody to share. Those who benefit most from productivity are the children."[31] In keeping with the tenets of People's Capitalism, the pamphlet argued that the capitalist system freed individuals of all ages to pursue individual psychological satisfaction. By implication, it also suggested that carefully guided creativity was the basis of America's productivity. In the early years of World War II, Margaret Mead had linked American individualism and American national morale. In the wake of World War II, Victor D'Amico argued that the use of Bauhaus-derived art training techniques could reindividuate and so democratize American veterans. Now, the Children's Paradise offered a living example of how the production of a creative, individuated psyche helped drive the production of diverse consumer goods and a more peaceful globe.

The Italian press caught the drift immediately. Italian children had had their heads stuffed with "undue prejudice" by adults, wrote one reporter. But when they played with the toys in the Inspiration Room, they lost their worries and their fears and came face-to-face with what the reporter, in translation, called "their 'I.'" In the Children's Paradise, in other words, Italian youngsters let go of the prejudices they had inherited from their

(presumably once fascist) parents, encountered their individual psychological cores, and, with them, their universal humanity. "What better way
is there to develop a feeling of brotherhood among nations than to stimulate the creativeness of their children?" asked the reporter.[32]

In Spain, organizers tried to put that brotherhood on display by surrounding the Children's Festival with a glass wall. D'Amico's representative at the site objected that the glass would distract the children by letting
them look outside, toward others who would be playing on an outdoor
playground. The organizers backed down and built walls featuring small
windows through which adults could peer, much like those used in Milan. Thus displayed, the children's activities were meant to showcase the
benefits of progressive art teaching. But in the context of an international
trade fair, they also showcased patterns of power within the classroom
as prototypes for the international political scene. As Italian and Spanish
children worked within an artistic training regime loosely inherited from
the Bauhaus, and under the eye of American instructors who would guide
but not indoctrinate them, they made visible the promise of American
international policy in this period: under the watchful, dominant eye of
the United States, individuals and nations the world over would be free
to become ever more themselves and, at the same time, ever more collaborative and interdependent. Victor D'Amico would later argue that "the
Children's Carnival of Modern Art . . . has proved that children can be developed creatively the world over." They simply needed to be placed in "a
stimulating environment" with "ideal teaching."[33] At the global level, the
United States promised to enclose its allies in a "free world," watched over
by a benevolent, all-seeing military and guided by disinterested American experts. At the Children's Carnival the citizens of Milan and Barcelona
caught a glimpse of that world, peopled by their own children.

AMERICA IN THE ROUND:
THE BRUSSELS WORLD'S FAIR OF 1958

In 1958, the techniques developed on the trade fair circuit became the basis
of the American contribution to the Brussels World's Fair, the first such
fair held since World War II. Because of their primarily national rather

than commercial orientations, world's fairs served as a premier ideological battleground across the Cold War. They also provided a set of propaganda opportunities that few other media could supply. Since the early years of the decade, American information officers had sought to reach several types of foreign audiences simultaneously. On the one hand, they wanted to win the affections of ordinary citizens; on the other, they hoped to influence leaders in politics, business, and the arts who might sway the minds of their colleagues. Fairs such as the one at Brussels provided a unique opportunity to do both things at the same time. As a grand international event, the Brussels fair attracted global press coverage. At the same time, as a gathering located in a particular landscape with eye-catching buildings and flags waving overhead, the fair also brought together local and international leaders for speeches, side meetings, and parades. Over the six months it was open, the Brussels exposition drew more than fifty million visitors and hosted more than three hundred international conferences.[34]

Because the fair was so important, American planners undertook extensive research before they began building their pavilion. Representatives from the USIA travelled the United States asking leading public intellectuals what the exhibition should contain. In part, these interviews built support for the fair among leading American opinion makers. Perhaps more important, they also allowed planners to build some kind of consensus about what it meant to be American. By 1958, memories of the national unity of World War II had faded, the Cold War had if anything become chillier, and racial tensions had leapt to the fore. In the fall of 1956, Soviet troops crushed the Hungarian uprising; a year later, the Soviet space program launched Sputnik. And only a month before that, in September 1957, television viewers around the Western world watched as members of the Arkansas National Guard escorted nine black teenagers to their classes at Little Rock Central High School. How, planners wondered, could they project a coherent image of America's strength? And how could they use the fair to transform international perceptions of the United States?

Part of the answer came from the fair's commissioners in Brussels. As planning for the fair got under way, the Belgian hosts circulated a pamphlet outlining a theme for the entire event. In a voice haunted by the memory of World War II and the specter of nuclear annihilation, the general secretary for the fair argued that human beings had become isolated and dehumanized.[35] Though science and technology had rid the globe of the racism that drove World War II, they had also come to threaten the world in their own right. The secretary thus urged each exhibiting nation "to show the methods it advocates for the 're-humanization' of the modern world."[36] He and his colleagues argued that such methods should have two sides: first, they should acknowledge that "man" formed the basis of many different types of civilizations, and second, they should acknowledge that international understanding could only result "from each and every person knowing and understanding themselves better."[37]

By 1958, American designers were well practiced in constructing environments that promoted self-reflection and global humanism. Yet they also struggled to find a way to blend those goals with the more instrumental aim of promoting America's political and economic expansion. In April 1957, exhibition planners convened a two-day conference at MIT's Center for International Studies (CENIS). The center had been founded in 1951 with a grant from the Ford Foundation and received substantial secret funding from the CIA. Its roster blended faculty who had helped imagine international relations in interpersonal terms, such as anthropologist Clyde Kluckhohn and political scientist Ithiel de Sola Pool, with a new generation of political scientists, such as Walt Rostow, who were devoted to promoting international economic development. In the years before the Brussels fair, the leaders of CENIS had developed a simultaneously psychological and economic approach to international influence. "We became convinced," recalled one member some years later, "that our strongest psychological weapon was our potential ability to help the nations of the free world achieve political stability by helping them to expand their productivity and their standards of living."[38] To that extent, the sages of CENIS agreed with the ad men behind People's Capitalism. But for Brussels they added a new element: race. In the wake of Little Rock, the world knew only too well that universal human rights did not apply to all American citizens. The study group recommended that organizers acknowledge this fact and that a section be added to the exhibition that showed what work the nation still had to do for racial integration.

The CENIS meetings left the Brussels planning group with three overlapping challenges: they needed to represent the United States as it was, racial tensions included; they needed to convince international audiences of the power and benevolence of their nation; and they needed to draw audience members into a psychological version of what Walt Rostow would later call a "partnership for growth."[39] In response, designers developed a multi-building site that drew on multiple modes of persuasion. By far the most commanding of these was the official United States pavilion. Designed by Edward Durrell Stone, the architect who had designed the Museum of Modern Art's home in Manhattan, the pavilion was a massive golden circle, 340 feet in diameter and 95 feet high. Stone ringed the outside of the building with golden mesh, as well as golden pillars. With its supports externalized, the pavilion presented a wide-open interior. On the ground, eleven willows native to the site stood near a reflecting pool. Overhead, the center of the roof opened to the sky. A second-floor balcony rimmed the interior as well. And from it, a single, wide, modern staircase descended to an island in the pool.

At the time, Stone compared his design to the Roman Colosseum.[40] And in the years since, scholars have described the pavilion primarily as an imperial edifice, designed to project American might. Yet, for all its links to empire, the circular pavilion also represented an expansion of the ideals behind Buckminster Fuller's Kabul dome. Like Fuller's dome, Stone's circular arena modeled an American landscape open to roaming. Stone even built some forty entrances and exits, so that visitors could come and go as they pleased.[41] The interior of the pavilion had no clear beginning and no clear end. It was a landscape that welcomed all comers and granted them their freedom—a kind of freedom that American leaders had suggested was simultaneously American and universal. Moreover, in keeping with the therapeutic modernism of the Bauhaus refugees, the pavilion aimed to give visitors an experience of wholeness. In a feature article on the pavilion, the editors of *Industrial Design* noted that in contrast to other exhibition structures, Stone's circular design "gives a total impression of America rather than a series of compartmentalized views."[42]

The State Department hired Peter Harnden, an experienced display designer, to furnish the interior of Stone's edifice. Harnden transformed the building's two tiers into a kaleidoscope of opportunities for visitors to step

FIGURE 7.3.

The American pavilion in Brussels: a circular golden structure surrounded by state flags. Visitors could enter and exit from any direction. United States Information Agency photograph.

into America. In one room they could sit in the latest modern chairs while an attendant played one of hundreds of stereo LPs. In another, they could watch a man work electromechanical hands to pick up objects behind a windowed wall. They could travel down an American street, complete with street signs and shop fronts, and stop at a dime-store lunch counter for a Coca-Cola. And on the ground floor, they could peruse scale models of everything from the skyscrapers of Manhattan to American nuclear reactors.

Like American pavilions at earlier trade fairs, the Brussels display paid particular attention to the domestic sphere, to the body and to the child. If science and technology had dehumanized the world, the American pavilion promised to rehumanize it in terms set by the People's Capitalism campaign and its associated theories of the democratic personality. On the second floor of the pavilion, Harnden installed Victor D'Amico's Carnival of Modern Art—now called the Children's Creative Center. Brought from Barcelona, the center featured the same two rooms, sense-stimulating toys, and teaching methodology. Once again, as the American guidebook put it, "the imagination and spontaneous inventiveness of [children of all nations] are given free play."[43] Around the walls of the pavilion, visitors could also stop to see what designers called "islands for living." These installations featured washing machines, patios, living rooms, and kitchens, all of which could be explored. Alongside these displays, designers also installed television-sized boxes projecting film loops of everyday life in America.

On the second floor, visitors could see a display of American fashions culled from the pages of *Vogue*. At least once a day, models changed into the latest designs, stepped out of this section, and walked down the pavilion's grand stairway onto the platform at the center of the pool. There, ringed by admiring audiences bundled in coarse wool jackets and Homburg hats, women twirled their skirts with a distinctly American ease. Their clothes were meant to mirror the stages of a typical woman's day. As a reporter for *Vogue* explained, "There's the super-wife dress, for instance, that might walk the children to school or cruise the local A&P or Grand Union supermarket. There are dresses for parties, blue jeans for the country, a dress for golf, suits for swimming, pants for being at home, and the famous American split-personality dresses—they go on from where you are to where you're going: Red Cross meeting to luncheon, P.T.A. to dinner, office to cocktail party to theater. They're the American look."[44]

Together these displays solicited the modes of attention and interaction that theorists had long associated with the democratic personality. The fashion models, for example, oriented viewers' desires not only toward coats and skirts, but toward a vision of individuality, of a self that could stand at the center of a wide-open, abundant world. The islands of living, in turn, provided an array of images and tools from which visitors could imaginatively select and so knit together a new picture of themselves in their homes, at their jobs, and in the street. The Children's Creative Center reminded them that such self-integration grew out of and reflected the exercise of individual creativity. It also demonstrated that the pursuits of individuality and of egalitarian multiracial community could enhance

FIGURE 7.4.

The interior of the American pavilion at the 1958 Brussels World's Fair during a fashion show. The model is standing on a platform in the middle of a reflecting pool, surrounded by viewers. Photograph from Commissariat général du Gouvernement près l'Exposition universelle et internationale de Bruxelles.

one another and, in the context of the pavilion's abundance of consumer goods, economic productivity as well.

From an aesthetic point of view, what made this fusion of American idealism, economic expansionism, and universal humanism possible was the surround. The circular architectural form, the freedom of movement it allowed, the nonhierarchical social structure it embodied—all echoed the logic of Buckminster Fuller's Kabul dome, and before it, *The Family of Man*. The multi-mediated displays, in turn, recalled Herbert Bayer's designs for displays in which images would meet viewers from overhead and down by their feet, as well as at eye level. If mass media attempted to inflict a single point of view on a mass audience, the aesthetics of the American pavilion at Brussels offered a crowd of Europeans the chance to literally feel their way into the American ideological system. They could not only see and hear American ideals but sense them in their bodies, as they lifted the lids on laundry machines and imagined themselves dressed like the models on the stage.

ENVIRONMENTS FOR INSTRUMENTAL CONTROL

To see how much the American pavilion owed to earlier forms of the surround, we need only compare it to two other media environments at the Brussels fair. The first is the Circarama, a movie theater that stood behind the pavilion and a bit off to the side. Designed by Walt Disney and deployed first at Disneyland, Circarama was a technique through which eleven film projectors created a moving film image that could be displayed around the entire interior of a circular wall (in later years, often the wall of a geodesic dome). For the Brussels fair, Disney and his team developed a nineteen-minute movie travelogue called *The USA in Circarama*.[45] Shot from the windows of automobiles and from the wings of a B-52 bomber, the film raced and swooped across the American landscape. Wheat fields in Montana melted into Yellowstone Park; Pittsburgh steel mills led to the Santa Fe Railroad. The film culminated in an airborne swing through the Grand Canyon and a sunset over the Golden Gate Bridge.[46] A reporter for the *Atlantic Monthly* described the impact of these scenes: "The 19-minute movie, a masterpiece by Disney, sweeps its audience through the United States with one dramatic gesture. Americans walk out, heads high, tears in their eyes, still hearing the strains of *America the Beautiful*. Visitors from abroad burst out with their favorite superlatives, fantastique, magnifique, formidable."[47]

Circarama was indeed tremendously popular. And like Stone's pavilion, it surrounded viewers with walls and images. But far from offering visitors an experience of individual agency, the Circarama controlled their senses with an iron grip. The film shown at Brussels grew out of an earlier

FIGURE 7.5.

Disney's Circarama at the Brussels World's Fair. Circarama was designed to immerse viewers in a single image. Viewers often reported that watching it felt like taking a carnival ride. Photograph from Commissariat général du Gouvernement près l'Exposition universelle et internationale de Bruxelles.

travelogue, *The Tour of the West*, that Disney had developed for his theme park. Though it was a film, *The Tour of the West* offered the experience of a carnival ride. So too did the Brussels Circarama. A reporter for the *New York Times* described "the sense of motion, or moving with the picture" as "overwhelming."[48] A writer for *Variety* who visited the Circarama in Brussels described the viewing experience thus: "The auditors stand in the center and thus have the sense of complete audience-participation in the degree that one roller-coaster number had to be excised because of the equilibrium impact. The viewers would lean back so far, because of the overly realistic effect, as to fall on their backs."[49]

To the intellectuals and artists who sought to boost American morale in the 1940s, Circarama might well have looked like an excellent tool for cultivating authoritarian personalities. Like the jazz music that drove Adorno's jitterbugs—or, for that matter, like Hitler himself railing from a podium out over the sea of a Nazi party rally—Circarama took charge of its audience's senses, undermined its viewers' ability to reason, and set their bodies in motion in a single, swaying, overawed mass. Where Stone's American pavilion celebrated the broad American landscape as a space for the exploration and expression of individuality, Circarama offered it as a mechanism with which to melt individuals into an irrational crowd. Where Stone's pavilion presented viewers with an endless array of images and experiences from which to select, Circarama disabled the faculty of selection entirely. There was no choosing in Disney's world; there was only going along for the ride.

A third element of the American site, called *The Unfinished Work*, borrowed from both the tradition of the democratic surround and the more instrumental propaganda mode of Circarama. Set to the side of the American pavilion, *The Unfinished Work* consisted of three multisided, multicolored structures, each about twenty feet long and twelve feet high, laid end to end. When visitors entered the first structure, they found themselves surrounded by a collage of newspapers mounted to the wall and jutting out at all angles, their headlines reporting racist mayhem in the United States. This first section focused on the unfinished business of integration, as well as on problems with urban crowding and the challenges of self-governance. The second structure, built to illustrate the theme "the people take action," posted statistical charts mapping Americans' reduction of prejudice and class distinctions alongside portraits of figures such as Martin Luther King Jr., and labor leader Walter Reuther.[50] When they left this section, visitors stepped into a final room in which they found large murals, at least one of which—an image of children playing Ring Around the Rosie—echoed the specific theme as well as the visual humanism of *The Family of Man*.

Thematically, *The Unfinished Work* offered a deliberately noncommercial alternative to the product-centered displays of the main pavilion.[51] Its multicolored exterior offered a visual analogue for an integrated America and an integrated globe. Its pro-integration message was in fact so strong that Southern congressmen and other government officials ultimately had the display shut down. But despite its humanistic and even utopian ambitions, as well as its aesthetic debt to Bayer's *360 Degrees of Vision*, *The Unfinished Work* dramatically constrained its visitors' freedom. The track through the exhibition allowed only forward motion; the images and text on the wall bore down on a narrow set of themes; together, the three structures told a story that visitors imbibed step by step. If the pavilion aimed to give visitors a total impression of America, *The Unfinished Work* aimed to deliver a message, even to penetrate the iron curtain in visitors' minds. In that sense, it had far more in common with the instrumental propaganda techniques of the early 1950s than with the more open-ended style of the pavilion.

The pavilion also stood in stark contrast to its Soviet competition. The Soviet pavilion, next door to the American site, featured a long rectangular hangar. At one end, visitors walked between two statues, each about forty feet tall: one a male ironworker clasping a steel poker, the other a female peasant, her hands filled with a sheaf of wheat. At the far end of the pavilion, with a mosaic of the Kremlin behind him, stood an even larger statue of Lenin, with a model of the Sputnik satellite at his feet. Side walls featured massive murals of Soviet crowds marching under streaming banners, each figure twice the size of the pavilion visitors below. Like the American pavilion, the Soviet Hall featured a main floor with a balcony above. As a rectangle, though, the pavilion featured a single linear walkway, a sort of avenue that led visitors down the center of the building to the feet of Lenin. Where the circular form of the American pavilion emphasized equality—

FIGURE 7.6.
Interior view of the rectangular, monumental Soviet Hall at the Brussels World's Fair. Photograph from Commissariat général du Gouvernement près l'Exposition universelle et internationale de Bruxelles.

in point of view, in mobility, in access to its parts—the Soviet pavilion presented what must have looked to visitors who remembered World War II like an homage to fascism. Once again, a leader towered over his people. Once again, individuals were asked to meld together into a muscular mass and to follow him into a highly idealized future.

Yet for all its apparent openness, the American pavilion was in fact suffused with an essentially managerial mode of state power. In the Circarama and even in the tunnel of *The Unfinished Work*, American designers sought to manipulate the minds of visitors directly and to turn them in a uniform direction. But at the pavilion, designers deployed the more subtle techniques of interactivity. The *Vogue* fashion show asked viewers to encircle, observe, and ultimately identify with models on a platform. The Children's Creative Center allowed visitors who peered through its windows to practice monitoring—not instructing or indoctrinating, but watching, encouraging, and so helping to set the boundary conditions for their children's performances. Elsewhere in the exhibition, visitors toyed with voting machines and a stock market demonstration and saw themselves on closed-circuit television. In each case, visitors were enjoined to express themselves—imaginatively, through identification, or mechanically *and* imaginatively, by voting or picking stocks. As they did, they simultaneously produced themselves as new, creative citizens of a massively abundant world and practiced engaging with democratic politics, market capitalism, and the progressive child-rearing techniques that were thought to produce people who would thrive in those systems. They both imagined themselves as and, for an instant at least, *became* highly individuated members of a seemingly egalitarian society—an Americanized global community whose stability was guaranteed by military forces arrayed invisibly far beyond the circle of the pavilion's walls.

THE FAMILY OF MAN ON THE ROAD

During the same years in which American exhibitions were introducing the world to the People's Capitalism, the USIA was promoting a noncommercial vision of universal brotherhood. No sooner had *The Family of Man* closed at the Museum of Modern Art in 1955 than the museum sent six copies of the show on tour around the United States and, with the USIA's help, around the globe. By the spring of 1959, the USIA had sponsored forty-six exhibitions in twenty-eight countries, and nearly four million people had seen the show.[52] At particularly important locations, the USIA flew in Edward Steichen to introduce the exhibition. Visitors swooned wherever *The Family of Man* appeared. Some wrote to Steichen at the Museum of Modern Art, recounting how the show had changed their lives. Others wrote to the editorial pages of their local newspapers. Reporters tripped over themselves to celebrate the show when it came to their cities. "I am writing this under the spell of an exhibit that could change the face of South Africa if it were seen and felt and understood by the right people," exclaimed a reviewer for *The Johannesburg Sunday Times*, entirely typically. "No human being seeing it and understanding its message could ever hold race hate in his heart again."[53]

For the staff of the USIA, the exhibition was a godsend. With its emphasis on global humanism, the racial diversity in its imagery, and its utter absence of pro-American bluster, the exhibition seemed to have little if anything to do with propaganda. Visitors might even forget that the United States was sponsoring the show (an occurrence that American embassy officials routinely took steps to prevent). When they did notice American sponsorship, USIA officials hoped that visitors would associate their own desires for peace, familial intimacy, and egalitarian community with the guiding international hand of the United States. In this sense *The Family of Man* became a species of propaganda especially well suited to tuning the emotional lives of target populations toward the ambitions of the American state. In countries under threat of communist seduction, such as Laos, the exhibition could perform a prophylactic function; in allied nations such as West Germany, Holland, and Japan, it could do the therapeutic work of aiding formerly fascist populations and their victims in putting the war behind them. In each case, USIA officials followed the therapeutic intervention procedures outlined in the 1959 research report. First, with the aid of local diplomats, they assessed the political and cultural situation. Next, with Steichen's permission, they adjusted the contents of the exhibition to fit that situation and installed the show. Finally, during and after the show, researchers assessed viewer responses to see if in fact the exhibition had sparked psychological changes.

Two of the first places to receive *The Family of Man* were the former German capital, Berlin, and the birthplace of the Nazi Party, Munich. In the fall of 1955 the threats to Germany's psychological and political health were apparent to all. Only ten years after Hitler had shot himself in a bunker near the center of Berlin, memories of fascism remained unavoidable. Once the inhabitants of Berlin and Munich had cheered as troops hauled their Jewish neighbors from their houses. Now those houses stood in ruins. Bullet holes pockmarked whole blocks in both cities, and in Berlin, residents still recalled the violence inflicted by Soviet troops at the end of the war. Soviet-sponsored communists governed the eastern half of the city and all of the land surrounding the metropolis. Though it had not yet been walled in, the western sector of Berlin had already become an island. And Germany itself was now a divided nation: a living object lesson on the struggle between democracy and communism.

For all of these reasons, Germany provided an ideal site at which to deploy a culturally psychotherapeutic intervention. In the fall of 1955 the USIA brought the show first to Berlin and then to Munich. In Berlin, USIA officials hoped to draw multiple audiences, including political and cultural leaders from both sides of the city as well as ordinary citizens. They engineered a massive publicity effort before the show arrived, with advertisements in the press, coordinated letters to editors, posters, a sneak preview for dignitaries, outreach to German camera clubs, and the mailing of three hundred exhibition catalogs to influential citizens.[54] They even brought in Steichen himself. At speeches and press conferences, the State Department presented the photographer as a model creative American, and the Germans responded. "He was treated not only as dean of American photographers, but as dean of world photographers," reported one American official.[55]

By the time the show opened, USIA officials noted that it had become a "must" for Berliners to see.[56] But the show that opened in Berlin differed from the one that opened in Manhattan. USIA officials had removed sixteen images from the original collection.[57] They included pictures of a naked child lying face down in the woods, a group of Japanese men surrounding a ceremonial gong, and an exhausted, obviously impoverished African American climbing a staircase. Other images featured couples embracing, the wheat harvest on the Great Plains, and Native Americans dancing. The woman in charge of installing the show told USIA officers in Washington that the pictures had been pulled for "mainly aesthetical" reasons.[58] She also pointed out that after some heated discussion, officials had carefully left in an infamous image of German troops chasing Jewish residents out of the Warsaw ghetto. Yet it also seems likely that in 1955, organizers were trying to accommodate German squeamishness about public displays of affection, downplay its former alliance with Japan, and ease suspicions that America itself remained a racist nation.

To judge from press accounts at the time, many Germans read the exhibition as an invitation to put away the racism and the shame of the Nazi era. Surrounded by images of Africans, Asians, and Mediterranean peoples, German critics told their readers, "Look, this is man. Wherever he lives, whatever he does, whichever language he speaks—basically, he is subject to the same kinds of joys, sorrows, needs and hopes. Look around, here is proof."[59] As the title of one review put it, the people in the pictures were "Like You and Me."[60] After the show opened in Munich, one of Germany's leading newspapers, the *Süddeutsche Zeitung*, explained that "above all, these photos teach brotherhood . . . . Not only the world is indivisible, man is indivisible . . . . When we see this exhibit, we look into a mirror. We recognize ourselves, we are not alone and everyone of us is responsible for everyone else."[61] In the international political context of the 1950s, to recognize oneself in this way was also to undergo a psychosocial transformation. To acknowledge one's German self as fundamentally identical to peoples so recently derided as less than human was not only to undo the intellectual legacy of Nazism. It was also to imaginatively enter into a new international political realm. Just as the individual German could be a member of the "family of man," so now too the German nation could be one among many countries gathered together to defend humanity against communism.

USIA officials at the time were fascinated by this transformation. "The impact of *The Family of Man* was . . . a thrilling spectacle to witness," exclaimed one USIA official. "The Germans gave way to open emotion be-

FIGURE 7.7.

Edward Steichen and officials of the United States Information Agency hoped that post–World War II Germans would see themselves as similar to other peoples once again, even across racial lines. Here a young couple in Munich peers at a polygamous African family. United States Information Agency photograph.

fore many of the photographs."[62] Joseph Phillips, a public affairs officer, even requested that a photographer be sent to Munich from Bonn to record German interactions with individual images. Phillips himself hovered among the visitors to the Munich showing, angling to overhear responses to the images. In a report home, he described watching a university professor introduce his students to the now-infamous image of German soldiers holding a Jewish boy at gunpoint in the Warsaw ghetto, his hands in the air. "I don't know how much more I can impress upon you . . . that this is something we should never forget," Phillips heard the professor say. "Some of you perhaps will soon be in uniform [with the West German army] and I want you to remember this: Always keep in mind that the army that points guns at little children . . . has lost the fight before it ever began."[63]

The recollections of American observers and the German press both suggest that the encounter with *The Family of Man* could be something close to a conversion experience. Surrounded by images of the peoples of the world, the hardened Nazi trooper of American myth could feel, could identify with others unlike himself, and in so doing, could join a new German army dedicated to the principles of universal humanism and arrayed against totalitarianism. For the USIA, both elements of this conversion process mattered a great deal. To see whether they had in fact occurred, officials monitored the exhibitions closely from start to finish, tracking the number of attendees, interviewing them inside and outside the shows, listening in at parties and public events, and collecting every piece of press published about the show.

Their observations revealed that the show had reached a wide swath of German society. Though no East German papers covered the exhibition, USIA officials in Berlin noted that perhaps a third of the visitors had come from the eastern sector of the city.[64] In Munich, officials reported that visitors had come from across southern Germany and had included university students, factory workers, and a wide variety of notables. In both cases, officials were jubilant. The public affairs officer charged with summing up the impact of the Berlin exhibition put it this way: *The Family of Man* "was as effective a vehicle as an exhibit of this nature can be for demonstrating, convincingly, American interest in furthering peace and international understanding, and America's belief in the dignity of man." It also demonstrated America's particular commitment to supporting Berlin. For both reasons, the official argued, the exhibition "did not fail . . . to make many a visitor review his opinion of the United States."[65]

Over the next three years, *The Family of Man* traveled across Europe and India to Southeast Asia and the southern tip of Africa. At each showing, USIA officials repeated the steps they used in Germany: analyzing the character of the target audience, adjusting the contents of the exhibition to maximize its psychological impact on that group, and analyzing visitor reactions to confirm that their minds had been changed. Though it lacked the explicit pro-Americanism of the People's Capitalism campaign, and though—or perhaps, because—Steichen and the USIA routinely denied that the show had any propagandistic intent, *The Family of Man* became one of the most widely used propaganda weapons in the American arsenal of the late 1950s.

THERAPEUTIC NATIONALISM: MOSCOW, 1959

In 1959, the United States State Department brought Edward Steichen and *The Family of Man* to the single most important American exhibition of the Cold War: the American National Exhibition in Moscow's Sokolniki Park. Two years earlier, Soviet Premier Nikita Khrushchev was giving a live interview to the CBS television news show *Face the Nation* when he suddenly proposed that Americans and Soviets build a series of cultural and scientific exchanges. The State Department had hoped for several years to stage an American exhibition in Moscow. Now, after much haggling, the United States and the Soviet Union agreed: in the summer of 1959, the Soviet Union would host an American cultural, scientific, and industrial exhibition in Moscow, and the United States would host a similar Soviet show in New York.[66]

Publicly, American and Soviet officials agreed that the exhibitions should promote "mutual understanding." Internally, however, the Americans had different ambitions. Planners drafted three versions of their "basic policy guidance" for the exhibition: one public, one confidential, and one secret. All of three of these documents agreed that the exhibition should give Soviet viewers a broad understanding of everyday life in the United States. The "confidential" version added that the exhibition "should create in the minds of the Soviet peoples a desire for a wider choice of quality goods and services than are presently available to them," and thus put pressure on the Soviet economy and the nation's ability to wage war.[67] It also argued that the show should demonstrate the fundamentally peaceful, consumer-oriented nature of American industry. The "secret" version of the document went one important step further. The exhibition's goal, it argued, was "to increase understanding by the peoples of the Soviet Union of the American people and American life, with particular emphasis on American products, practices and concepts which might contribute to existing pressures tending in the long run toward a reorientation of the Soviet system in the direction of greater freedom."[68] Publicly, the exhibition aimed to inform the Soviet public about the nature of America. But internally, American planners understood that the exhibition was to reorient Soviet citizens' individual desires in a direction that would corrode their state. More specifically, it was to turn Soviet citizens toward the creative self-expression and self-development that characterized the democratic personality—in this case, through consumption—and at the same time toward an egalitarian mode of unity based on individualism, that ostensibly characterized the United States.

By 1959 their experience at trade fairs had given designers a substantial toolkit with which to work. The USIA appointed Jack Masey, veteran of the Kabul fair, to direct design and construction in Moscow. Masey in turn recruited George Nelson, a famed industrial designer much influenced by Herbert Bayer, and through Nelson he also recruited Buckminster Fuller and the designers Ray and Charles Eames.[69] As soon as the Soviets and Americans agreed that the Americans could build their exhibition in Moscow's Sokolniki Park, American architects began laying out a complex campus. Like the Brussels World's Fair, the central American pavilion would be an enormous, glittering, circular building: in this case, a geodesic dome built by the Kaiser Aluminum Corporation. Behind the dome, under a glass pavilion, in a warren of crisscrossing metal pipes that workers called "the jungle gym," designers installed displays of furniture and books, kitchenware and fashion, and abstract modern art. Beyond the glass pavilion stood a complete Circarama just like the one at Brussels. And a bit to the side of the glass pavilion, George Nelson installed a pavilion of linked plastic umbrellas. Under these, visitors would explore the *Family of Man* exhibition and a set of large-scale photographs of American buildings. They could also attend continuous shows of men's and women's fashions. Around these buildings the designers arrayed modern sculptures, the latest automobiles, a Pepsi-Cola drink stand, and a playground. In the park's pond, they even placed American dinghies.

In the variety of its persuasion structures, the American National Exhibition in Moscow resembled the world's fair of the year before. Once again, designers deployed a mix of highly controlling media environments (the Circarama) and wide-open display spaces (the dome, the *Family of Man* pavilion, the park itself). Once again, a shining circular building stood at the center of the exhibition, offering visitors the freedom to wander among its representations of the United States as if they were in fact American citizens, wandering the open land. This time, though, designers dramatically amplified the degrees to which they immersed their visitors in American media and to which they monitored their psychological responses to what they saw.

Some of these techniques aped the methods of amusement parks. Across the outdoor areas of the American Exhibition, for instance, programmers installed speakers and played carefully selected mixes of American jazz and classical music. Designers also introduced an array of opportunities for Soviets to interact with American information systems—computational, cinematic, and human. Even as these systems offered to improve Soviet understanding of American life, most generated records of visitors' opinions about America, the exhibition, and the Soviet Union. From their earliest meetings, the design team assembled by Masey had identified the Kaiser Dome as an "information center." At one level, as a "fact sheet" developed for the press in April, 1959, explained, the dome would inform visitors in the traditional sense by housing "exhibits on science and research, education, labor, productivity, health and social services, agriculture and other subjects."[70] At another level, the dome would serve as a model of the United States, and so instruct viewers by offering them a chance to imagine they were inside America. As it presented "the immense variety, the great freedom of choice, enjoyed by the American family," the dome would be a "corner of America" in Moscow.[71]

At a third level, however, the dome would become a model of a world managed by American information technology and information technologists. In January 1959, George Nelson and the deputy director of the USIA met with a team of journalists with Soviet experience to discuss their plans for the exhibition. Nelson explained that the dome would be the first building visitors entered, and would be designed to overwhelm them with highly credible facts and images from the United States. These would help persuade the Soviets that Americans could be trusted to tell the truth. At the same time, Nelson pointed out, the dome would be "a mechanized information center, with [IBM's] RAMAC [computer] at the heart of it."[72] When visitors entered the hall, they would be able to walk up to the computer and ask the person running it questions about the United States. The computer, preprogrammed with replies to more than four thousand questions, would supply the answers. It would also record the visitors' questions.

Even before they came to the computer, visitors would walk under an enormous seven-screen documentary film created by the Eameses and titled *Glimpses of the U.S.A.* As Nelson explained, the seven screens would stretch across almost a hundred feet. Each screen would show a different image of life in America. They would show supermarkets, automobiles, playgrounds, and people from many places in the nation simultaneously. "It isn't the thing: it's dozens, hundreds or thousands of things like supermarkets," Nelson told the journalists. "The film won't be in the sense of a movie film but *a projection of data* so that Russians can't possibly be convinced that these were movie sets built for this purpose [italics added]."[73] Throughout the exhibition, visitors could ask questions of some seventy-five Russian-speaking American guides, most of whom were college students and four of whom were African-American.[74] The visitors could also see themselves on television thanks to a closed-circuit TV system built by RCA. They could use a polling machine to "vote" for their favorite displays. They could pen comments in books scattered around the

FIGURE 7.8.
Soviet visitors entering the main pavilion of the American National Exhibition in Moscow, 1959, under the Eameses' *Glimpses of the U.S.A.* United States Information Agency photograph.

grounds for that purpose. And if they attended a fashion show, they might have their picture taken with a Polaroid instant camera and take it home as a souvenir.

Together these interactions allowed Soviets to express themselves and, at the same time, rendered their psyches available to surveillance. In the trade fairs of the mid-1950s, designers had asked visitors to move among displays, to practice the freedom of mobility, choice, and association that they claimed defined American society. American officials, in turn, commissioned surveys to confirm that these experiences had changed visitors' beliefs about the United States. In Moscow, designers drew on emerging computer technology and a model of subjectivity drawn from cybernetics and information theory to fuse the work of persuasion and monitoring. Even as they exercised an independent, even democratic mode of agency in asking questions of RAMAC and the guides and in expressing opinions via the voting machines, Soviet visitors submitted themselves to two forms of control. First, for all their variety, the facts, images, and displays with which they interacted had been selected for them by American organizers. Visitors were free—but within an environment whose boundaries had been carefully set and were now, like the borders of the United States, being monitored by information technologies. Second, each time a Soviet visitor made a choice or otherwise expressed a desire or an opinion, American interaction systems transformed that action into a data point through which to understand the broader "mood" of the Soviet Union.

Throughout the exhibition, USIA officials combined surveys of the Soviet press with data from RAMAC, the polling machine, and informal conversations with visitors and guides. The weekly reports they filed record an obsession with understanding Soviet responses to the exhibition and to American life more generally. They listed the questions asked of RAMAC. (Number one in the first week: "How much do cigarettes cost?" Number two: "What is meant by the American dream?")[75] They noted that Circarama was the most popular display, according to the polling machine. They counted the books visitors stole from the book display, and tracked their titles. They listed the patterns of visitors' conversations with guides, and summarized the notes complaining about life in the Soviet Union that visitors sometimes slipped to the guides. And officials paid special attention

FIGURE 7.9.
Visitors to the American National Exhibition in Moscow put questions about America to the IBM RAMAC computer through a Russian-speaking computer operator. The USIA monitored their questions in order to learn more about Soviet opinions of the United States. United States Information Agency photograph.

to recording evidence of consumer desire. One American embassy official, for instance, stationed himself near the outdoor display of American cars, where he heard a visitor exclaim, "If the devil could supply me with one of those, I would sell him my bicycle in a minute."[76]

After the exhibition ended, the USIA's Office of Research and Analysis attempted to synthesize these reports in a single document titled "Soviet

Curiosity About America." While they were able to construct a rough index of Soviet interests in American daily life, the document actually revealed very little about the psychology of Soviet visitors. The fact of its existence, however, says a great deal about how American officials sought to wield power in the era. The stridently anticommunist propaganda of the early 1950s had disappeared. In its place, Americans deployed an all-encompassing system of information provision and information extraction. At the exhibition, Soviet visitors practiced the skills on which the development of the democratic personality was once thought to depend, and at the very moment that they did, their performance was transformed into data which American officials could then use to build new media and information systems—systems that could shape their views even more effectively. In essence, the sort of feedback loop pioneered with the surveys at the Kabul fair had been diffused throughout the entire exhibition.

Underlying that diffusion was a deeper shift. In the 1930s and early 1940s, anthropologists and sociologists had conceived of the democratic person essentially as a monad, created through interaction with others but, once created, able to move independently among a sea of similarly independent beings. By the late 1950s, however, the arrival of computers and the broad acceptance of cybernetics and information theory among American intellectuals had given rise to a vision of a kind of self that enjoyed both the agency of the democratic personality and the systems orientation of the computer. Theorists of the democratic and authoritarian personalities had long agreed: the individual psyche took form as individuals interacted with their families and with the wider society. Now analysts began to imagine the communications that were part of those discreet interactions as the foundation of all social and biological activity. The democratic person and the democratic society resembled healthy natural organisms, in this line of thinking. All three processed information and acted on it; when they did, their actions in turn became information for others. In this view, information was the basis of both individual freedom and social order.

Nowhere was this new kind of democratic person more visible than in the work of Ray and Charles Eames, who had become entranced with the information theories of mathematicians Claude Shannon and Norbert Wiener. In 1953 they made a film to introduce the general public to these ideas, entitled *A Communications Primer*. The film argued that the process of communication, especially digitized communication, promoted individual independence and social cohesion. Though the film did not depict this process in political terms, it would have been hard for an audience in 1953 America not to hear its political overtones. A society linked by the intercommunications of independent individuals was a far cry from one organized by the top-down dictates of a totalitarian regime.

A Communications Primer grew out of an experimental class that the Eameses, George Nelson, and designer Alexander Girard had created for the Department of Fine Arts at the University of Georgia in 1952.[77] Together they designed what was ostensibly a lecture on the nature of communication, but was in fact a full-blown multimedia extravaganza. Working with a film projector, three slide projectors, several screens, ambient music, and even smells piped in through the air ducts, the designers had attempted to bombard and thus awaken the senses of their audience.[78] As *A Communications Primer* points out, the Eameses envisioned their audiences for both lecture and film as information processors in two distinct senses. The first was built on Claude Shannon's theory of information. Shannon had boiled communication down to messaging, as the film explained: a sender encoded a message which was in turn transmitted through a channel to a receiver who decoded it. Along the way, external forces of various kinds introduced "noise" into the message, making it potentially difficult to decode. The Eameses noted that to reduce the effects of noise, senders could take two steps: first, they could amplify the signal; and second, they could simply repeat the message so often that it would get through despite the noise.

In Shannon's vision, humans and machines both encoded and decoded messages and so could be considered similar sorts of operators. But the Eameses also drew on the more encompassing vision of Norbert Wiener. In Wiener's view, communication was not simply a matter of exchange; it was the essence of social and natural order. Computers, human brains, natural organisms, and society itself—all were held together by exchanges of information. Electrical circuits, neurons, the telephone and telegraph and newspaper—all, as Wiener had written in *The Human Use of Human Beings*, were systems of communication that linked otherwise free-standing individual machines, people, and social groups. In this vision, the individual was not only an information processor in Shannon's sense, but a person whose ability to be a unique individual and at the same time a member of a well-ordered society derived from the same process: the communication of information.

The Eameses thus spoke in terms that linked new modes of information processing to the agency and choice associated with predigital versions of the democratic personality. By 1953, as many Americans began to fear that information machines might someday automate them out of their jobs, the Eameses depicted computers as tools that would enhance individual independence and social cohesion. Each bit in a complex information system was the result of an individual decision, they explained. As a result, computers could hardly undermine the creativity of individuals. On the contrary, they enhanced it—first, by providing new information on which creative individuals could act, and second, by enabling even those lowest down on the information food chain, the people who did little more than feed a single yes/no data point into the system, to make a decision and have it registered as data. Information systems ranging from computers to societies were held together by individuals in interaction with each other—that is, by individuals seeking and acting on feedback. Thanks to the comprehensiveness of digital data sets, no one in a highly computerized society would or even could be excluded from this process. At the same time, individuals remained responsible for seeking out patterns of information, knitting them together, and so becoming agents in their own right. "No matter where it occurs," intoned the film's narrator, "communication means the responsibility of decision all the way down the line."[79]

In Moscow, the Eameses' understanding of information theory filtered through much of the American exhibition. As it did, it linked an emerging aesthetics of information to the earlier aesthetics of the democratic surround. *Glimpses of the U.S.A.*, for instance, clearly put Claude Shannon's principles of amplification and repetition to work. With their sheer size and prominent placement just inside the entrance to the American dome, the screens of *Glimpses* represented a kaleidoscopic vision of American messages. Their multiplicity, in turn, allowed for a persuasive repetition of key points. The Eameses knew full well that no viewer could focus on the seven screens simultaneously. Yet they hoped that the sheer variety of the images on the screens would convey the message that the United States was a land of abundance. As George Nelson explained, they repeated images of supermarkets to make sure that Soviet visitors would believe, despite the "noise" of Soviet propaganda, that Americans shopped in them.

At the same time, the Eameses mimicked the multiscreen designs and Gestalt psychology of Herbert Bayer's 1930s exhibitions.[80] Along with Shannon and Wiener, the Eameses counted photographer and painter Gyorgy Kepes, a pupil of László Moholy-Nagy, among their most prominent influences. In 1944, Kepes had published a volume of images and essays entitled *The Language of Vision*. Like his teacher, Kepes believed that the industrial world and the combat of World War II tended to fracture the individual psyche. Only by surrounding the eye with new images and offering the individual the chance to link them together—that is, by asking both artists and viewers to speak a new language of vision—could designers begin to help individuals become psychologically whole. Like Moholy and Bayer, Kepes embraced Gestalt psychology. But he also celebrated the integration of the individual as a way to achieve a new and more integrated society. "To perceive a visual image implies the beholder's participation in a process of organization," he wrote. "The experience of an image is thus a creative act of integration. . . . Here is a basic discipline of forming . . . a discipline of utmost importance in the chaos of our formless world. Plastic arts, the optimum forms of the language of vision, are, therefore, an invaluable educational medium."[81]

With *Glimpses*, the Eameses not only built a multiscreen display in terms set by Kepes and Bayer. They also took the fusion of Bauhaus aesthetics, Gestalt psychology, and pro-American psychological training born during World War II and turned it to a new purpose: integrating the psyches of our potential enemies, the citizens of the Soviet Union. First, they asked individual viewers to select among a variety of images on display and integrate their selections into a single, individualized internal picture. In this way, according to Gestalt theory at least, viewers could experience true individuation—an experience that the USIA saw as central to undermining the massified psychology of Soviet communism. Second, they asked viewers to encounter images in a particularly egalitarian way. If traditional films asked viewers to submit to the will of a single image onscreen, and so aped the dynamics of totalitarian political power, *Glimpses* asked viewers to interact with a multiscreen information system, to sort and reassemble the data it provided, and so to become information processors. That is, it asked them to participate in a society whose order was maintained by free association (in both the political and psychological senses), by communication, and by information technology.

Here then was a new kind of democratic personality, fit for the age of information. Like the democratic individuals theorized by Gordon Allport in the 1930s or by Harold Lasswell in the early 1950s, visitors to the American National Exhibition were to experience themselves as simultaneously independent and collaborative. Within the American zone, so to speak, they would be surrounded by choices—commercial, political, artistic— and their choices would be recorded and evaluated for further action by the American state. Like the individuals in Norbert Wiener's cybernetics, though, they would advance by participating in feedback loops. They would seek, find, and adjust their seeking in turn. In Wiener's vision, as in that of the designers of the American exhibition, the pursuit of individuation and happiness would naturally lead visitors ever deeper into a web of communicative relationships—with each other, with American corporations, and ultimately with the American nation.

Judging by reports of the USIA officers on the scene, as well as by American and Soviet press reports, Soviet visitors found this vision utterly compelling. More than fifty thousand swarmed into Solkolniki Park on the average day; by the end of the exhibition, approximately 2,700,000 had attended. The automobiles, kitchen equipment, magazines, and books on display had fascinated many; the modern paintings and sculptures largely disturbed and confused an equal number. By all accounts, what Russians of all social strata found most compelling was the chance to interact with Russian-speaking American guides. To their astonishment, the guides were allowed to think on their feet and to acknowledge economic and racial problems in the United States. Some visitors were put off by the show's emphasis on consumer goods. "I expected more and I am disappointed," wrote one in a comment book. "Is it possible you think our mental outlook is restricted to everyday living only? There is too little technology. Where is your industry?"[82] But the great majority of comments were highly positive.

This was especially true for visitors to *The Family of Man*. Early on, the State Department and the USIA had very nearly declined to include the show in the exhibition. This was to be a pro-American affair; leaders in both institutions feared that *The Family of Man* was far too humanistic an undertaking to put the American message across. But when Steichen and others pointed out the extraordinary popularity of the show, officials relented. *The Family of Man* then became one of the most popular events in Sokolniki Park. In a report for the USIA's Office of Research and Analysis that summarized responses to the entire American effort in Moscow, Ralph K. White, an assistant to the exhibition's director, wrote that he believed *The Family of Man* was the most popular display in the exhibition. "Unlike automobiles and TV, which moved people only to a kind of impersonal admiration, the Family of Man seemed to move them emotionally as human beings, and move them toward a changed image of America and Americans," he wrote. "Indirectly, and without any 'propaganda'—in fact, partly because of the complete absence of propaganda in the usual sense of the word—they were pulled out of their normal nationalistic Soviet frame of reference and given, at least momentarily, a feeling of kinship with the whole human race. At the same time they must have realized that it was America, their alleged enemy, that moved them in this way."[83]

By the time the Moscow exhibition closed, the transformation of *The Family of Man* and of the universal humanism that underlay it was complete: together, they had become tools of the American state. The USIA had adapted the aesthetics and the ideals of the surround to the work of reorienting the desires of foreign nationals away from the temptations of communism and toward the carefully managed consumer society of America. Steichen's own hope to end war melted almost imperceptibly into the Cold War ambitions of the United States. So too did earlier longings for making a more democratic, egalitarian America and a more psychologically and socially stable Weimar Germany.

Yet even as the American press proclaimed the exhibition a national triumph, a small group of artists was already decoupling its multimedia aesthetics and surround-based architecture from the work of the state. Within a few short years, their efforts would provide the aesthetic foundations of the 1960s American counterculture.

8

The Coming of the Counterculture

In 1957 and 1958, John Cage taught a course in experimental composition at the New School for Social Research in New York. Photographs of the class published a few years later show Cage at the front of the room in a rumpled white suit and black tie.[1] Half a dozen lanky young men and one woman sit around the classroom, shirts tucked in, shoes polished. One holds a baby rattle, another a plastic machine gun. Here and there a student sports a beard or a pair of dark glasses or a denim jacket, but most look as earnest as junior executives in a slightly offbeat manufacturing firm.

The students in the pictures were the cream of the downtown New York art scene at the time, including Jackson Mac Low, a poet and playwright; Al Hansen, a performance artist; Dick Higgins, a composer; and Allan Kaprow, a painter who had begun creating mixed-media assemblages. Some had come to Cage in the hope that he could teach them new techniques for making sounds; others had come to absorb his orientation toward performance and maybe even life itself. In the years since he first staged his silent composition *4'33"*, Cage had dramatically extended his earlier work, developing new ways to reduce the agency of sound producers and democratize relations among musicians, sounds, and audiences. By the late 1950s he had developed an international reputation for turning the concert hall into an arena in which listeners could be equal participants in knitting together the sounds they heard into individually meaningful wholes. In his class, Cage transmitted that legacy to a group of artists who were seeking to escape the confines of the genres in which they worked.

His students, in turn, transformed it into a foundational framework for the quintessential mode of 1960s performance and protest: the Happening.

When they did, they helped infuse an emerging counterculture with elements of the person-centered collectivity called for by promoters of democratic morale twenty years before. In Happenings and later, be-ins, organizers asked individuals to come together of their own volition, to work collectively, to unite across previously impermeable social boundaries, and, in the process, to become newly sensitized and more psychologically whole human beings. At the same time, almost imperceptibly, they turned away from the antiracist and antisexist ambitions of the World War II generation. Even as they embraced the utopian humanism of earlier decades, many young Americans turned inward, away from campaigns for racial and sexual equality and toward a new psychological politics: the politics of consciousness.

This new ideology embraced the core assumption behind earlier efforts to promote the democratic personality. As Theodore Roszak explained in his 1968 bestseller *The Making of a Counter Culture*, the young communards of the 1960s, like their parents, assumed that the individual psyche was the ultimate basis of social order and that to change or preserve society, one must engage in "the reformulation of the personality."[2] Yet, unlike their parents, young adults who had come of age in the shadow of the atomic bomb distrusted the state, its experts, and even reason itself. For many young Americans in the early 1940s, to lose oneself in irrational, ecstatic gatherings was to enjoy the forbidden fruits of fascism. For their children in the 1960s counterculture, it was to reject the ostensibly fascist tendencies of their own government. Within the politics of consciousness, the individual reason and the governing institutions of the state mirrored one another: each sought to constrain the otherwise natural, organic, and pleasurable growth of the regions under its control. In order to subvert that control, individuals turned toward media, and especially music, multiscreen images, and light shows, to shut down the analytical mind, awaken the unconscious, and allow individuals to come together in communities organized around a shared state of awareness.

Like the ideal democratic polities of the 1940s and early 1950s, such communities aimed to empower their members to seek psychological satisfaction. Unlike those communities, they also encouraged their members to turn away from the state and, in many cases, from traditional politics altogether. In that sense, even as it celebrated the psychologically liberated individual and the egalitarian polity called for by social scientists and artists two decades earlier, the emerging counterculture also traded away the vision of a racially and sexually diverse American nation for a glimpse of a mystical transnational human whole.

JOHN CAGE AND THE RISE OF HAPPENINGS

Though many remember him today as an almost underground figure, in the late 1950s John Cage was a leading member of the New York art world and, in Europe at least, an emblem of American ideals. On May 15, 1958, the painters Jasper Johns and Robert Rauschenberg and filmmaker Emile de Antonio arranged for Cage to give a three-hour retrospective concert of his work at New York's Town Hall.[3] More than a thousand people attended, confirming Cage's place at the forefront of the downtown New York art scene. A few months later, Cage traveled to West Germany to give a series of concerts and lectures at the Darmstadt International Summer Courses for New Music, a program first mounted in 1946 with an eye to introducing Germany to high modern composition, and later, to Brussels, where he lectured at the World's Fair. At both sites, Cage's efforts to break down musical hierarchies modeled the egalitarian impulses that in the same years the United States Information Agency was saying defined the American character. In Darmstadt, Cage spoke to and performed before about three hundred guests, including half a dozen avant-garde composers. While at least one critic thought Cage resembled Buster Keaton, others agreed with a young German musicologist who argued that Cage had granted performers "the dignity of autonomous musical subjects . . . just as in an emancipated society everyone will be permitted to realize his work without enforcement."[4]

At the Brussels World's Fair, Cage delivered his essay "Indeterminacy." A decade earlier he had attacked German Romanticism in his "Defense of Satie" at Black Mountain College. He repeated the performance here, arguing that European music retained a linear melodic structure, punctuated by climaxes. In essence he accused European music of embodying and perpet-uating tensions—the very psychological forces underlying the antagonisms of the Cold War. As an antidote to this condition he proposed his own American example of indeterminate composition. Not only did he recom-mend the creation of soundscapes without linearity or structured climax, but he urged the physical separation of performers. Pulling them apart, he explained, facilitated their independence and allowed individual sounds to emerge "from their own centers." Lest a recently de-Nazified German audi-ence underestimate the political implications of this auditory model, Cage not so subtly reminded them that "There is the possibility when people are crowded together that they'll act like sheep rather than nobly."[5]

In his class at the New School, Cage taught techniques for composi-tion and collaboration that were designed to preserve the individuality of sounds and performers and to prevent the creation of anything like a sonic herd. "To a great extent, and probably to John Cage's disgust, the class became a little version of Black Mountain," recalled Al Hansen.[6] Each week, Cage asked students to explore chance operations at home and to bring their works to class for performance. Students brought band saws, toys, and glasses half-filled with water and played them alongside drums and other instruments pulled from the classroom's closet.[7] Some brought whole scores for their classmates to perform.

Allan Kaprow recalled that the class was "very small, choice, and John was at his finest energy, and he knew he had people that were eating up everything he suggested and giving it back in ways you could hardly even expect. And that's where I did my first Happening, and he encouraged it. I wasn't a musician, I just wanted to make noise."[8] Like several of his class-mates, Kaprow had been a painter. Inspired by Jackson Pollock and Robert Rauschenberg, he had begun to attach objects to his canvases, and gradu-ally to imagine leaving the picture plane behind for the three-dimensional world of performance. In Cage's class, he found rules for how to organize such work, a community of artists with whom to do it, and two key prac-tices around which to build his performances: the use of chance operations in composition and the promotion of noise as music.[9] "It was apparent to everyone," said Kaprow, "that these two moves . . . could be systematically carried over to any of the other arts."[10]

In April 1958, Kaprow staged his first Happening outside Cage's class. He had been invited to give a midday lecture at Douglass College in New Brunswick, New Jersey, as part of a series focused on the theme of "communications" that also featured talks by Cage, Rauschenberg, and pianist David Tudor.[11] Instead of giving a speech, Kaprow simply sat on the stage. From a balcony behind the audience, a tape recorder began to play a recording of Kaprow giving a speech and soon two other tape recorders began playing the same speech, out of synch with the first. Suddenly someone dropped long banners from the balcony, a woman started bouncing a ball in the aisle, and a red light began flashing on the lectern, near an array of painted and mirrored panels. Kaprow later recalled the event's ending thus: "After twenty seconds I arose, walked to the mirrored panel, turned my back to the audience, looked closely into the mirror, examined my eyes in a formal way, and carefully lit dozens of matches, blowing them out one after the other. Following this I returned to my red seat and . . . sat there for the remaining time."[12]

The audience must not have known what hit them. Kaprow called the event "Communication," but it had no obvious message to convey and the word "Happening" had not yet entered the public lexicon. From a distance, though, we can see that his performance marked an extension of two techniques Cage had emphasized in class: the orchestration of human actions so as to produce a diverse array of events, and the notion that any and all sights and sounds could be beautiful. At the same time, it marked an important move away from Cage's efforts to democratize the production of performances. In his lecture at the Brussels World's Fair, Cage noted that in his early work he had used chance methods to compose his pieces, but that once composed, the pieces themselves often demanded particular actions on the part of performers. In that sense, Cage feared that the pieces wielded an almost dictatorial kind of power over the minds and bodies of musicians. In his more recent indeterminate pieces, Cage believed he had found a way to relinquish this power and to free both sounds and musicians from external control.

Kaprow was almost a generation younger than Cage. He shared little of his teacher's World War II exposure to fascism or the fears of irrational, centralized authority that it provoked. On the contrary, he came of professional age in the wake of the abstract expressionists, apparently heroic painters and sculptors who seemed to dominate their canvases with the sheer force of their inner lives. In the 1958 essay in which he coined the term "Happening," entitled "The Legacy of Jackson Pollock," Kaprow explained that the painter had inspired him to imagine extending the space in which one might express oneself from two dimensions into three. Pollock's drip paintings were so huge as to constitute "environments," wrote Kaprow, and so they represented a first step in expanding the signifying gestures of painting to fill actual three-dimensional spaces. These spaces would not be governed by a Gestaltist urge for the rational integration of sights and sounds into the personality, however. Something else was afoot. "Pollock gives us an all-over unity [in his paintings] and at the same time a means to respond continuously to a freshness of personal choice," wrote Kaprow. "But this form allows us equal pleasure in participating in a delirium, a deadening of the reasoning faculties, a loss of 'self' in the Western sense of the term. This strange combination of extreme individuality and selflessness makes the work remarkably potent but also indicates a probably larger frame of psychological reference."[13]

On the one hand, Pollock seemed to surround Kaprow-the-viewer with a field of images in which, as Kaprow put it, "Anywhere is everywhere, and we dip in and out when and where we can."[14] In that sense, it solicited a mode of interaction common to the American pavilion at Brussels or *The Family of Man*, environments in which spectators were invited to wander at will and to remake their sense of themselves as they moved among the images. On the other hand, Kaprow thought it invited him to give up his reason and to submerge himself in the sea of Pollock's unconscious. To Americans of Cage's generation, submitting control over one's identity to a powerful individual—even temporarily—smacked of fascism, not freedom. But for Kaprow, the reverse was true. Long conversant with surrealism and Dada and their desire to help audiences break free from the chains of routine consciousness, Kaprow believed that giving up one's reason could in fact liberate the individual psyche. He thus went on to marry the aesthetics of the antifascist surround—originally designed to *enhance* viewers' analytical and choice-making faculties—to efforts to *disable* the reason. Twenty years earlier, such efforts would have conjured up fears of fascism. Now they pointed the way to artistic independence and distinction.

They also led Kaprow to carefully script his early Happenings and to structure the actions of his performers with a degree of control that offended Cage.[15] If Cage hoped to remove the artist from the situation so that the audience could appreciate the universe of sounds as it was, Kaprow wanted to build a universe of signs and sounds and events that performers and audiences could inhabit together. Their roles might blur, but they would remain citizens within a country whose borders Kaprow had constructed and still policed with his performance score.

Consider the Happening that, perhaps more than any other, introduced the form to the world at large. Called *Eighteen Happenings in Six Parts* and staged in October 1959 at the Reuben Gallery in New York, the event featured six sets of occurrences separated by the ringing of a bell, each set consisting of movements, sounds, and silences occurring simultaneously in three adjoining rooms. In part, *Eighteen Happenings* resembled a concert by John Cage that had exploded into pure theater. Kaprow invited a heavily art-world audience into the gallery, assigned them seats in different rooms, and surrounded them with activities borrowed from everyday life. Much as Cage encouraged his listeners to hear noise as music, Kaprow encouraged his viewers to see the lifting of a leg or to hear a snatch of conversation as art. And like Cage, he scripted his performance using a grid system that seemed to separate his agency from events in the gallery. Kaprow's Cagean grid seemed designed to create just enough order in the performance system to allow the audience to experience and enjoy random actions.

But *Eighteen Happenings* was not *4'33"*. Kaprow did not simply create an environment and encourage visitors to move within it as they liked, knitting its parts together in a way that was meaningful to them. Rather, he gave them marching orders. When the audience arrived, he handed them index cards that told them to get up and move to other rooms at certain points during the event. For his performers, he drew diagrams of the movements they were to make and set precise time limits on how long they were to make them. Neither performers nor viewers could act from their own individual centers, as Cage might have put it. No performer

FIGURE 8.1.
Allan Kaprow (with flute) rehearsing *18 Happenings in 6 Parts*, 1959. Photograph by Fred W. McDarrah. Courtesy of Getty Images.

could see or be part of the entire event, nor could any audience member. Only Kaprow himself, in his mind's eye, could see the whole.

Since its first staging, critics have regarded *Eighteen Happenings* as an act of artistic liberation.[16] The lines between audience and performer, between art and everyday life, between the ordinary object and the beautiful thing—Kaprow seemed to have blurred them all. Critics at the time did note the Happening's debt to earlier artistic movements and particularly to Dada, Futurism, surrealism, and the Total Theater of the Bauhaus. But in the wake of the formal precision of much abstract expressionism, the

Happening still felt new. Not long before Kaprow staged *Eighteen Happenings*, he and his New School classmates George Brecht and Robert Watts tried to describe the groundswell they felt beneath their feet:

> In all the arts, we are struck by a general loosening of forms which in the past were relatively closed, strict, and objective, to ones which are more personal, free, random, and open, often suggesting in their seemingly casual formats an endless changefulness and boundlessness. In music, it has led to the use of what was once considered noise; in painting and sculpture, to materials that belong to industry and the wastebasket; in dance, to movements that are not "graceful" but which come from human action nevertheless. There is taking place a gradual widening of the scope of the imagination, and creative people are encompassing in their work what has never before been considered art. And to the new viewpoint a direct, almost crude freshness has arisen, which we feel is particularly characteristic of our country.[17]

In the late 1950s and early 1960s, the Happening became the modal form of this new kind of art, thanks largely to veterans of Cage's class. Very few Americans actually saw a Happening in person. Yet, by the early 1960s, thanks to nearly constant hype in the press, the word "Happening" had become both an adjective and a noun for all things forward-looking. By 1967, Allan Kaprow was amazed at the ubiquity of a word that he had first chosen precisely for its blandness: "hippie groups, discotheques, PTA meetings, Rotary club outings, a popular rock 'n roll band, a hit record by the Supremes, a party game kit, and at least two regular run movies—all are called Happenings," he marveled.[18]

As the term "Happening" migrated out of the art world, it carried with it several of the ambitions built into the surrounds of the 1940s. In a 1961 essay, Kaprow pointed out that "Happenings are not just another new style. Instead, like American art of the late 1940s, they are a moral act, a human stand of great urgency, whose professional status as art is less a criterion than their certainty as an ultimate existential commitment." He went on to contrast European and American art. Europeans, he suggested, remained wedded to a model of artistic production that featured a single overpowering artist inflicting his or her will on some material and ultimately creating a commodity such as a painting or sculpture that could be bought and sold. Happenings, by contrast, required collaborative action by performers and viewers who were, if not peers, at least significantly more equal in the production process than painters and their patrons. Happenings could not be bought or sold, but only supported and enjoyed, and briefly at that. As such, Kaprow argued, the Happenings embodied "the special character of our mores in America." As they challenged American myths of success, they reached deeper into "what is characteristically American . . . America's special strength." Happenings were made by people who were "free," he explained, and they were "in no small part an expression of this [individual] liberty."[19]

Despite their anticonsumerist bent, Kaprow's Happenings shared in the national pride modeled almost simultaneously in the pro-consumerist multimedia environment of the American National Exhibition in Moscow. They also featured a softer version of the Moscow show's therapeutic ambitions. They promoted what Kaprow called "moral intelligence," a mindset that deflected the certainties of "moralism or sermonizing" and that came alive "in a field of pressing alternatives."[20] Like the promoters of the democratic personality of the 1940s and early 1950s, Kaprow aimed to have his viewers find themselves surrounded by sounds and sights and so enjoy the chance to tune their senses to their ebb and flow. He believed that Happenings could help snap people out of the perceptual routines foisted on them by mass media and everyday life in a bureaucratized society. At a Happening, Kaprow told critic Richard Kostelanetz, with Cagean understatement, "One becomes more attentive."[21]

Nor was Kaprow alone in this view. In the 1940s, Steichen and Bayer's exhibitions at the Museum of Modern Art aimed to help Americans resist the temptations of mass propaganda. In the early 1960s, writers hoped that the Happening might help Americans resist the pressures of mass culture in the same way. In 1962, Susan Sontag hoped Happenings might "stir the modern audience from its cozy emotional anesthesia."[22] A few years later, performance theorist Richard Schechner argued that "just as pop art has made us somewhat immune to certain kinds of advertising, so, perhaps, we become somewhat immune to other forms of mass persuasion after participating in a Happening."[23] And in 1970, Canadian English professor Darko Suvin summarized what he saw as something of a critical consensus: "Happenings at their best may prefigure possible new modes of human relations and living. . . . Happenings use special devices to overcome communication barriers in a manipulated consumer society, in an age of TV addiction, public relations credibility gap, mass propaganda techniques marketing everything from pollutants to genocidal imperialist wars such as in Vietnam. In such a context, a re-education of audience perceptions, a depollution of senses, is most urgent."[24]

Such a mission echoed the perceptual politics of John Cage and, before him, László Moholy-Nagy, Herbert Bayer, and many of their Bauhaus colleagues. At the same time, Kaprow and his fellow makers of Happenings turned away from the explicitly antidiscriminatory politics promoted by others who had adopted the surround in the 1950s, such as Edward Steichen, and advocates of democratic morale in the 1940s, such as Ruth Benedict and Margaret Mead. Happenings offered their audiences the chance to integrate a variety of sights and sounds; but unlike, say, *The Family of Man,* they did not ask viewers to imaginatively integrate themselves into a racially diverse society. Virtually all the performers in the New York Happenings of the late 1950s and early 1960s were white, as were their audiences. For many of these artists the transformation of consciousness had become primarily a personal, aesthetic project. Racial diversity was simply not an issue in their work. This seems extraordinary given that by the time Kaprow mounted *Eighteen Happenings,* the civil rights movement had been staging theatrical protests across the American south for several years. At lunch counters and in bus stations it had turned three-dimensional arenas into semiotic spaces that could and did transform the mindsets of onlookers. But Kaprow and his colleagues showed no interest in this sort of work, as Kaprow told Richard Kostelanetz at the time: "There are no new great ideologies today, as far as I can see. Surely you have local causes, such as civil rights and peace movements and things like that; but these are not essential philosophical problems, it seems to me. I will support, in whatever way I can, local causes. I once considered doing a 'sit-in' as a Happening; but I decided not to, because I thought it would be bad politics, if it were good art. I believe educational and economic reforms—sometimes even guns—to be a lot more effective."[25]

On questions of gender, with rare exceptions, Kaprow and his colleagues tended toward misogyny. The naked young woman became a cliché in early Happenings. She might be draped with a sheet and then have it soaked with water and so stand shivering with her breasts silhouetted by bright white lights. She might stuff her mouth full of broccoli plants until they seemed grow from her face. Or she might sit still on stage while men covered her in whipped cream and then licked it off.[26] With the prominent exception of Carolee Schneeman, virtually all of the leading Happening-makers were men. And while men sometimes doffed their clothes too, Happenings that featured nudity more often than not presented a woman to be gazed upon in ways that celebrated male control.

It was here, along the fault lines of power and discrimination, that the Happening diverged most strongly from the surrounds of the preceding decades. In *Road to Victory* and *The Family of Man*, Edward Steichen exerted what control he had over his spectators by selecting and arranging images. Within the environment he built, viewers could move at will and respond as they liked. As they did, they encountered images of men and women of all races, presented in such a way as to assert their equality and likeness to the viewer. In his performances, John Cage likewise used the containing structures of the concert and the concert hall to free an array of sounds. Listeners too could respond to those sounds as they pleased. In Cage's compositions all sounds could be part of the music, just as in *The Family of Man*, people of all races could be members of the human family. Like Cage and Steichen, Kaprow and his colleagues built environments that surrounded viewers. Yet they controlled both the boundaries of those environments and the actions of performers and viewers within them. Like Cage and Steichen, they hoped to awaken their audience's senses. But they showed little interest in working toward a diverse and tolerant polity. Rather, they hoped to temporarily stop their audience from reasoning, and so to shock their senses into fully apprehending the sensual world these artists had made for them and, through it, the world outside the theater too.

RETRIBALIZATION

By the early 1960s, the effort to awaken the senses promoted by the makers of Happenings was beginning to stand in contrast to calls for direct political action emerging from what would soon be called the New Left. In 1962, a group of college students calling themselves Students for a Democratic Society (SDS) gathered in Port Huron, Michigan, and drafted a statement that put the political case succinctly. An American government that had permitted racism, poverty, and the development of the atom bomb could not be trusted, they suggested, but it could be changed. Drawing inspiration from the "old" left of the 1930s, the students of the SDS aimed to organize around issues, to rally, to march, and so to shift control of the state and of American culture into more benevolent hands. In 1964, their ambitions shaped the Free Speech Movement at the University of California in Berkeley; in the middle of the decade, they helped drive mass protests of the Vietnam War.

The perceptual politics animating Happenings, on the other hand, led away from the collective political action of the New Left and toward the individual psyche as the source of social change. According to Theodore Roszak, who remains the movement's foremost chronicler, the politics of consciousness emerged as a mirror to the dark statecraft that produced the atom bomb. "Orthodox [American] culture . . . is fatally and contagiously diseased," he wrote. "The prime symptom of that disease is the shadow of thermonuclear annihilation. . . . an evil which is not defined by the sheer *fact* of the bomb, but by the total *ethos* of the bomb. . . . We are a civilization sunk in an unshakeable commitment to genocide. . . . [a civilization that] insists, in the name of progress, in the name of reason, that the unthinkable become thinkable and the intolerable become tolerable."[27]

To older Americans, these accusations had a familiar and disturbing ring. The youth of the early 1940s had taken up arms precisely to defeat a genocidal, intolerant Nazi Germany. Now at least some of their children seemed to be arguing that a hyper-rationalized, bureaucratic American state had taken on a fascist mien. According to Roszak, such a society needed to be healed, one personality at a time. Mainstream society and its attendant mindset were "mechanistic," he wrote. To change both, one needed to turn inward, to embrace the organic, the unconscious, and the irrational, and to bring them to bear in a new kind of polity. "What is of supreme importance is that each of us should become a person," he wrote, "a whole and integrated person in whom there is manifested a sense of the human variety genuinely experienced, a sense of having come to terms with a reality that is awesomely vast."[28] Only then could Americans take apart the war machine their state had become.

According to Roszak, two tools had proven especially useful in changing people's mindsets: LSD and the poetry of the Beats. Both expanded the individual consciousness and enabled it to glimpse the organic interconnections that people shared with one another and the natural world, he argued. From a distance of several decades, though, we can see that two other forces also played an important role in shaping the politics of consciousness at the time: the sudden efflorescence of new media technologies and the arrival of a Canadian English professor who seemed to be able to explain them, Marshall McLuhan. By the early 1960s, young adults whose parents had grown up with the living room radio, the daily newspaper, and maybe a weekly trip to the movies found themselves able to buy portable stereos, inexpensive printing presses, amplified keyboards and guitars, and massive speakers that could transform the plucking of a string into something that felt like an earthquake. What's more, almost every house in America featured a new and fascinating device: the television set. To Marshall McLuhan, these technologies promised global integration and international harmony.

Today we tend to remember McLuhan for his aphorisms and for the ways in which his theories borrowed from those of his colleague at the University of Toronto, political economist Harold Innis. In fact, key elements of McLuhan's thought grew out of his engagement with the theories of self and communication that had animated debates about the psychology of democracy and fascism years earlier. In 1951, McLuhan conceived his first book, *The Mechanical Bride*, as an attempt to train readers' senses to resist commercial propaganda. "Today the tyrant rules not by club or fist, but . . . disguised as a market researcher," he wrote.[29] Commercial mass media sought "to get inside the public mind . . . in order to manipulate, exploit, control . . . [and] to keep everybody in the helpless state engendered by mental rutting."[30] McLuhan believed that the best way to armor citizens against these assaults was to help them see that the assaults were underway. In *The Mechanical Bride* he plucked more than fifty advertisements from magazines and printed them next to a similar number of brief essays of his own. Between image and text, he popped a set of satirical questions — "Moral: You, too, can be a harem cutie in a gas-station?" or "Modern business is a game, just like philosophy or art, only more creative?" — to puncture the pleasures offered by the ads.[31]

Throughout the book, McLuhan leaned on Margaret Mead and especially her books *And Keep Your Powder Dry . . .* and *Male and Female*, as well as Siegfried Gideon's study of the social impact of technology, *Mechanization Takes Command.* Together they helped McLuhan make a case much like the one made by members of the Committee for National Morale in 1941: mass media shaped the individual personality; they did so on behalf of an ever more mechanized, even inhuman set of institutions; they appealed to unconscious desires and thus shut down the reason; and in that way they rendered individuals helpless before the onslaught of tyrannical forces. Never mind that the new tyrant was commerce rather than fascism — the role mass media played in rendering individuals vulnerable to being taken over psychologically and socially remained the same.

If media shaped the personality, McLuhan explained, then it was his job to surround his reader with images, to hold those images still, and to guide the reader in their interpretation. It was, as he put it, to stop the "whirling phantasmagoria" of the media from spinning and to allow the reader to analyze it.[32] To that end, he created a book that had little in the way of a beginning, middle, or end. Rather, like the American pavilion in Brussels or the paintings of Jackson Pollock, it could be entered at any point. Viewers could select which images seemed most important to them. They could engage them with their analytical minds. And thus sensitized to the threat these media posed, they could return to the hurly-burly of the everyday and make sense of it on the fly.

The McLuhan of 1951 shared the modernist orientation of László Moholy-Nagy and Herbert Bayer. Like them, he brought together multiple images and multiple texts in the hope that he could train the senses of his audience. And like them, he hoped to help his fellow citizens become more psychologically whole and independent within mass industrial society. In 1954, McLuhan extended the environmental orientation to persuasion he displayed in *The Mechanical Bride*. In an essay for the journal he edited with anthropologist Humphrey Carpenter, *Explorations*, McLuhan articulated an assumption that had become a commonplace in North American social science at the time: "Communication is the common ground for the study of individual and society." Then McLuhan took a conceptual leap that would soon make him famous. Communication was not simply the exchange of messages, he explained. Rather, it consisted of "participation in a common situation." The *"form* of communication"—that is, its genre and medium—determined the boundaries of the situation and so was "more significant than the information or idea 'transmitted'" in shaping both individual and society.[33] In short, the medium was the message.

In the mid-1950s, McLuhan still retained the suspicions of mass media that animated *The Mechanical Bride*. But in 1962 he divided print from electronic media in his analyses, and so opened the door to a far more utopian view. In his book *The Gutenberg Galaxy*, McLuhan assigned to the technology of print the rationalizing, dehumanizing effects that artists and analysts had earlier ascribed to industrialization and fascism. Before the advent of writing, he argued, human beings had lived in relatively egalitarian and intimate societies built on oral communication. When writing and especially printing appeared, a "fragmented and homogenous lineality" emerged within individual psyches and whole societies.[34] Where before a person might confound myth and analysis in his view of the world, printing separated the two, privileging the analytical and giving the lie to the sort of fictions that organized tribal life. Likewise, the printing press brought with it bureaucracy and, ultimately, industrialization.

In McLuhan's account, print was responsible for fragmenting the individual psyche and the polity and, by implication, for rendering both vulnerable to rule by anyone who could climb to the top of a literate society's pyramidal hierarchy. How might such hierarchies be dissolved? According to McLuhan, by electronic media such as television. If print segregated all things, television, radio, and telephony reunited them. Electronic media constituted extensions of our abilities to see and hear and feel, he argued. Amplified by media institutions and then-new media technologies, images and sounds circled the globe, allowing individuals to sense the unity of the whole world and the nature of their place in it. "The electro-magnetic discoveries have recreated the simultaneous 'field' in all human affairs so that the human family now exists under conditions of a 'global village,'" exclaimed McLuhan. "We live in a single constricted space resonant with tribal drums."[35]

By splitting print and electronic media, McLuhan made it possible to retrieve mass media's power to stir ecstatic experiences from the memory of fascism and transform it into a tool for remaking democracy. In his view, electronic media could fulfill the ambitions of László Moholy-Nagy, Herbert Bayer, UNESCO, Victor D'Amico, and Edward Steichen all at once. By turning the globe back into a single village, electronic media would simultaneously reintegrate the fragmented psyches of individuals and reintegrate a globe threatened by political conflict. Interpersonal and international tensions would disappear. Psychological and political harmony would be one, brought about by the daily drumbeat of television.

To those who promoted democratic morale at the start of World War II, such a retribalization of society through media would have been anathema. After all, that was precisely what they thought Nazi propaganda had been designed to do. With its pseudo-Roman banners, anachronistic salutes, and mass rallies, hadn't fascist stagecraft tried to convince Germans that they were members of a single race, a mythical tribe born to rule all of Europe? And hadn't radio and film and the German press so amplified that Teutonic breast-beating as to turn the citizens of one of the most sophisticated nations in Europe into a seething, racist mass?

To Americans of the early 1940s, the fascist effort to reinsert myth into everyday life had helped spark an international conflagration. To the makers of Happenings, though, McLuhan's call for retribalization through electronic media provided a logic by which they could turn the media technologies of mass culture toward the mission of mass individuation. John Cage in particular embraced McLuhan's vision. In 1960 he struck up a mutually admiring correspondence with McLuhan that continued for two decades, and he was an early reader of a report that McLuhan had written for the National Association of Educational Broadcasters. In 1964 that report became the book that made McLuhan a household name, *Understanding Me-*

dia. The "mechanical age," it declared, was "now receding."[36] In its place, a new, globalized order was emerging—organic, flexible, cosmopolitan, and above all, borne on the seas of the media themselves. The lockstep era of fascism was over. So too, at least among the young, was the fear of mass media technology, the unconscious, and the swaying crowd. Married to the perceptual politics of the Happenings, media technologies could now produce a simultaneously tribal and egalitarian society.

TOTAL ENVIRONMENTS

Over the next two years, especially in New York and San Francisco, media forms collided and cross-pollinated with abandon. Critics tried to keep up, coining terms like "intermedia," "expanded cinema," and "the theatre of mixed means," but their taxonomies could never quite capture the sheer variety of projects under way. Underground filmmakers abandoned storytelling, and strung together streams of flickering images. Dance hall owners paired slide shows and strobe lights with live rock and roll bands. At the 1964 World's Fair in Queens, New York, Ray and Charles Eames built a huge multiscreen presentation for IBM called the "Information Machine," whose displays mirrored Herbert Bayer's designs for an expanded field of vision. And in the woods a little north of Manhattan, a former Black Mountain College student named Stan VanDerBeek turned the top of a former grain silo into a dome and then filled its interior surfaces with collaged projections of still and moving images.

As diverse as these productions were, their makers shared an understanding that media should be used to create environments, that such spaces could produce individual psychological changes, and that altered audiences could ultimately change the world. They differed, though, in the degree to which they hoped to engage their audience's reasoning faculties, engage them in making choices, and encourage them to turn from their experience of media to some form of social action. At one pole, Stan VanDerBeek's Movie-Drome conjured up the international utopianism of the late 1940s and the media aesthetics of *The Family of Man*. VanDerBeek studied photography at Black Mountain College in 1949, and he was there in 1952 when Cage and his colleagues staged *Theater Piece No. 1*. For VanDerBeek, this first Happening was a formative experience. "The fact that everything happened at once was very inspirational," he later recalled. It "triggered off a lot of ideas about how you can make things grow and collage together."[37] So too did getting to know John Cage. In 1963, after living in Manhattan and filming a number of downtown Happenings, VanDerBeek moved himself and his family to the Gate Hill Cooperative in Stony Point, New York, where John Cage and Merce Cunningham lived along with other Black Mountain veterans, including M. C. Richards and David Tudor.

VanDerBeek built his Movie-Drome at Gate Hill between 1962 and 1966 by mounting the domed top portion of a grain silo on a wooden platform. Audience members entered through a trapdoor in the floor. Once they were inside, VanDerBeek asked them to lie on the floor, side by side. They pulled the trapdoor up and watched as more than a dozen film and slide projectors sent images to the ceiling and fragments of sound and conversation flicked through the air.[38] The images largely reflected popular Ameri-

FIGURE 8.2.
Interior of VanDerBeek's Movie-Drome, Gate Hill Cooperative, Stony Point New York, ca. 1963–65. Photograph by Stan VanDerBeek. Courtesy of the Estate of Stan VanDerBeek.

can life. Celebrities, politicians, and athletes jostled with fashion models and advertising slogans, all culled from magazines and newspapers. In between these very American pictures, VanDerBeek inserted images of artistic monuments from around the world. Together they presented something like a collage of the globe as a whole, dominated by American commercial culture.

To many in the art world, VanDerBeek's projection techniques seemed to represent a multi-image future for single-screen cinema. In September 1966, the New York Film Festival featured VanDerBeek on a panel on "expanded cinema" that garnered a great deal of attention. Festival organizers were so intrigued by his Movie-Drome that they gathered a group of forty or so reporters and artists and bused them to Stony Point, where they lay on the floor as VanDerBeek's images flashed and overlapped overhead.[39] The reporters were variously baffled and impressed, and responded with somewhat tentative applause. Few felt able to take in the whole of the experience. Andy Warhol was reported to have "gazed imperturbably at the ribbed, cylindrical ceiling" for the entire performance.[40]

VanDerBeek, however, was not trying to overwhelm his audience so much as empower them. Critic Robert Christgau reported that VanDerBeek hoped his Movie-Drome would be the first of many "electronic Grange Halls, where images might be received by satellite from far-flung storage centers, orchestrated by a core of artists and presented so that each member of the local audience could arrive at his own sense of the world, picking and choosing from the bombardment of images as he reclines in the dark."[41] Like Edward Steichen, VanDerBeek believed that atomic weapons imperiled the entire human race and that artists had a duty to help Americans imagine themselves so thoroughly integrated into the world community that they would not destroy it. And like Herbert Bayer and John Cage, he believed that individual spectators could take in images and sounds from many directions at once and knit them into their own unique gestalts. In a widely circulated 1966 manifesto entitled "Culture: Intercom and Expanded Cinema," VanDerBeek argued that Movie-Dromes could be built around the world as nodes on an international network. The role of film had to be expanded far beyond mere entertainment, he suggested; it had to be devoted to producing intercultural understanding.[42] "We must hold the world through this next period, which is an extremely delicately balanced nuclear-judgment time period," he told an interviewer in 1967. "We must somehow find a way to talk to each other, to talk to ourselves and understand ourselves."[43]

In many ways, VanDerBeek's Culture Intercom project echoed the goals of the UNESCO Tensions Project two decades earlier. It also shared that project's guiding psychology. VanDerBeek aimed to simultaneously enhance each individual's ability to make first aesthetic and then political choices, and to integrate both into his or her own unique, freestanding personality. These were just the personality attributes that psychologists such as Gordon Allport most closely associated with democratic character. At the same time, VanDerBeek's aesthetics and ambitions mirrored those of Ray and Charles Eames. For the IBM Pavilion at the New York World's Fair of 1964, the Eameses likewise invited visitors into a dome of images.[44] The IBM Pavilion consisted of a giant egg-shaped building mounted on a set of treelike metal supports. As in VanDerBeek's backyard silo, viewers entered its ovoid interior through a door in the bottom. Once inside, they took their seats in traditional auditorium rows. After a few remarks from a tuxedoed emcee, they found themselves lifted, five hundred of them together, seats and all, fifty-three feet up into the air. From there, surrounded by bits of narration and music beamed toward them from eight different speakers, they watched as fifteen screens, arrayed in the pattern first described by Herbert Bayer, projected a mix of moving images and stills.

The title of the show they saw was "Think." As the Eameses explained, it aimed to demystify the workings of computers for a lay audience. By way of demonstrating the computer's problem-solving abilities, for example, it depicted a hostess trying to arrange a seating chart so as to maximize the happiness of her guests. On a series of screens she drew a diagram, moved markers for her guests from seat to seat, and finally settled on an arrangement that generated a warm buzz of conversation. At one level, the Eameses aimed to use such analogies to teach viewers about the ways in which computers worked. But at another, they aimed to immerse their viewers in a world in which everything—pictures, sounds, and even such everyday tasks as arranging a dinner party—could be transformed into information. Like VanDerBeek's Movie-Drome, the Eameses' projections

FIGURE 8.3.
Screens from Ray and Charles Eames's *Think* at the IBM Pavilion, New York World's Fair, 1964, arranged in a pattern first mapped by Herbert Bayer. © 2012 Eames Office, LLC. Used by permission.

at the IBM Pavilion literally lifted people out of their ordinary lives and placed them within a network of images. This network included pictures of people like themselves with whom they could identify, and so offered them a chance to imagine themselves as signifiers floating through computational space. At the same time, the show's overwhelming multiscreen, multi-sourced-sound array asked viewers to do the perceptual work prescribed by Herbert Bayer of selecting and integrating sounds and images into their own individual psyches. In that sense, it asked viewers to become information processors in terms set by the industrial-therapeutic aesthetics of the Bauhaus and of pro-democratic Cold War surrounds such as *The Family of Man*.

Both VanDerBeek and the Eameses knew their audiences might be unable to make sense of all the images they saw, but they did not actually *try* to overwhelm them. Instead, they provided arrays of images from which the audience members might choose, in the process increasing both their knowledge of the world and their ability to acquire it rapidly under conditions of ubiquitous mediation. In the early 1960s, however, other artists were beginning to use multiscreen imagery and multisource sound in ways that likely prevented their audiences from reasoning altogether.

At the time, the most infamous of these was Andy Warhol. On the evening of January 13, 1966, Warhol brought a pack of artists and musicians from his downtown Factory to the Delmonico Hotel in Manhattan, where they had been hired to perform for the annual dinner of the New York Society for Clinical Psychiatry.[45] As the psychiatrists arrived in the hotel lobby, the men in tuxedos and their wives in evening gowns, Warhol shook their hands. Before dinner, Warhol showed several of his films. Then, as waiters served roast beef, string beans, and baby potatoes, the Velvet Underground took the stage. A reporter for the *New York Times* described their music as "a combination of rock 'n' roll and Egyptian belly-dance music."[46] While they played, filmmakers Barbara Rubin and Jonas Mekas roamed the floor, stalking individual psychiatrists and their wives with cameras and floodlights and attacking them with questions such as, "Does he eat you out?" and "Is his penis big enough?"[47]

The psychiatrists tried to keep a stiff upper lip. "Creativity and the artist have always held a fascination for the serious student of human behavior," said the doctor who booked Warhol and the Velvets. "And we're fascinated by the mass communications activities of Warhol and his group."[48] But the formality of the psychiatrists' dinner, their clothing, their rational, careful demeanor—these were the things that Warhol and the Factory crew had set out to undermine. They called their show *Up-Tight* because it was designed to break through the protective psychological barriers individuals and social groups had built around themselves and to show them just how uptight they actually were.[49] At the same time, the words came to stand for a particular aesthetic. Ingrid Superstar of Warhol's Factory explained, "Uptight means to have so many different confusing things going on at one time, to attract or detract the audience's attention in order to confuse them and make them nervous. Sometimes it even makes us nervous."[50]

Warhol soon took *Up-Tight* to the Film-Makers' Cinematheque, a small theater on West 41st Street.[51] There he showed an hour of his film homage to Lupe Velez, a Hollywood star who planned the perfect suicide, starring Edie Sedgwick. Then he brought out the Velvets, black sunglasses making blanks of their eyes, and as they tuned their instruments, he began projecting images from his films onto their bodies and the wall beyond. As they slid into their eerie dirge "Venus in Furs"—the first words of which are, "Shiny, shiny, shiny boots of leather / Whiplash girl-child in the dark"—Edie Sedgwick and poet Gerard Malanga moved to the front of the stage, their bodies bathed in images, and began a free-form dance. After a while, a spotlight beamed out into the audience and Barbara Rubin ran down, bombarding members with questions and filming them while they answered. The Velvets then picked up the pace and launched into "Run Run Run." Malanga and one of the band's most ardent fans, Victor Bockris, later recalled, "For the most part the audience sat there too stunned to think or react. The music was supersonic and very loud. The Velvets turned their amps up as high as they could go. The effect vibrated all through the audience. To some it seemed like a whole prison ward had escaped. Others speak of it today as hypnotic and timeless."[52]

Like Stan VanDerBeek and many other artists on both coasts at that moment, Warhol and his crew had created an all-encompassing media environment. Images, sounds, and movements swirled over the stage, and later, when *Up-Tight* became the traveling multimedia extravaganza known as *Andy Warhol's Exploding Plastic Inevitable*, they swirled over the bodies of the audience too. Like VanDerBeek, Warhol offered audiences a psychic awakening of sorts, if only to their own uptightness. But there the similarity ended. At the *Exploding Plastic Inevitable*, sensitizing audience members to the world around them meant turning off their internal censors, shutting down their reason, and so perhaps freeing them to recognize and make visible long-hidden desires. While VanDerBeek tried to turn his audience's attention outward to the public arenas of celebrity and art and international affairs, Warhol turned them inward and underground, toward the taboo regions of gay sex, heroin, and sadomasochism. Not surprisingly, critics responded with fear and trepidation. Reviewer Michaela

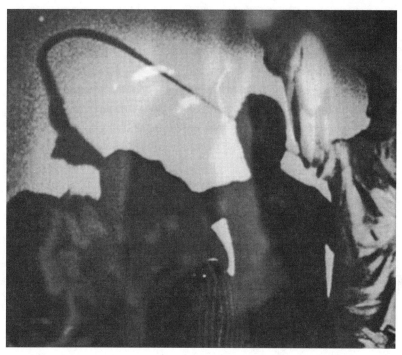

FIGURE 8.4.
Andy Warhol's Exploding Plastic Inevitable in action, ca. 1966, featuring Gerard Malanga dancing with a whip and Ingrid Superstar dancing with herself. From the film *Andy Warhol's Exploding Plastic Inevitable*, directed by Ronald Nameth, 1967.

Williams spoke for many when she described her responses to the *Exploding Plastic Inevitable*:

> [Warhol] has indeed put together a total environment, but it is an assemblage that actually vibrates with menace, cynicism and perversion. To experience it is to be brutalized, helpless. . . . The strobe lights blaze, spots dart, flickering pistol lights start in on [the audience] and their humanness is destroyed; they are fragments, cutouts waiving [sic] Reynolds Wrap reflectors to ward off their total disintegration. . . . Eventually, the reverberations in your ears stop. But what you do with what you still hear in your brain? The Flowers of Evil are in full bloom with the Exploding Plastic Inevitable; let's hope it's killed before it spreads.[53]

PSYCHEDELIA

Warhol's aesthetic would spread, of course, especially into the punk and glam of the 1970s. But in the early 1960s, the *Exploding Plastic Inevitable* represented the dark extreme of environmental media. Between Warhol's S&M stylings and the classic Cold War individualism of VanDerBeek's Movie-Drome, a wide variety of artists were beginning to explore a way of making media that borrowed from both traditions: psychedelia. Like the *Exploding Plastic Inevitable*, psychedelic media environments sought to break through the rational shell of the individual mind and help audience members travel down through the layers of their psyche into regions of which they had formerly been unconscious. They did not seek to bring individuals to awareness of their own neuroses, though. Instead, as a guide to psychedelic art put it at the time, the psychedelic artist "rejects the now all-too-familiar motifs of madness, aberration, degeneration. He feels he has something better to communicate. Essentially, this is life—a life moving forward, dancing and ecstatic, one with the cosmic process, not a maimed, defeated, or alienated life slipping shudderingly back into death."[54]

Like VanDerBeek's Movie-Drome, psychedelic art aimed to make its viewers aware that they shared the planet with millions of other people who, in their humanness at least, fundamentally resembled themselves. At the same time, it transposed the universal humanism of the Cold War into raw mysticism. One of the earliest and most influential groups to undertake this transposition was the Us Company, or USCO. Sometime in 1962, Gerd Stern, who had studied poetry at Black Mountain College in 1950, met a young bohemian painter named Steve Durkee at the San Francisco Tape Music Center. Both Stern and Durkee traveled back and forth between Manhattan and San Francisco, and both were regulars in the downtown New York art scene. Around the time Stern met Durkee, Stern's friend and former teacher M. C. Richards loaned him a copy of the report for the National Association of Educational Broadcasters that would become McLuhan's *Understanding Media*. Stern was blown away. Much as Allan Kaprow had begun to play with three dimensions in his paintings, Stern had long played with space and time as he arranged the lines of his verse on the page. McLuhan now offered him a way not only to extend his linguistic experiments into three-dimensional space, but to electrify them.

In November 1963, the San Francisco Museum of Art invited Stern to give a reading. Instead, he, Durkee, and a young sound engineer named Michael Callahan, together with more than sixty of their friends, presented a multimedia performance called *Verbal American Landscape*. For months they had taken pictures of words they saw on signs along the street. Now, using a bank of slide projectors, they flashed these images on the walls. Performers on telephones received calls from other performers and heard their conversations broadcast into the hall. Closed-circuit televisions showed the audience and the performers to themselves and one another. And throughout the event, music and fragments of spoken language circled through the air.[55]

As the audience arrived, a child handed out a program inscribed with a passage by Marshall McLuhan that gives a clue as to how Stern and Durkee hoped their work would be interpreted: "All [media specialization] ends in the electronic age whose media substitute all-at-onceness for one-thing-at-a-timeness. The movement of human information at approximately the speed of light has become by far the largest industry in the world. . . . Patterns of association based on slower media have become overnight not only irrelevant and obsolete, but a threat to continued existence and sanity."[56] With *Verbal American Landscape*, Stern and Durkee built an environment in which they hoped electronic media would replace not only print media but the entire array of linear, hierarchical, psychological, and social arrangements that McLuhan claimed print had brought into being. Like Allan Kaprow and the makers of Happenings in New York, they surrounded their audiences with sights and sounds that threatened to overwhelm their ability to reason. But having taken on board McLuhan's theories of communication, they hoped to do much more than simply awaken their audience's senses.

"Most of our work was involved in two things: Changing consciousness . . . and changing the world," Stern's then-wife Judi later recalled. "I don't believe that there was any separation between what was going on in the world and our lives and what we were doing."[57] Over the next several years, *Verbal American Landscape* morphed into a series of multimedia

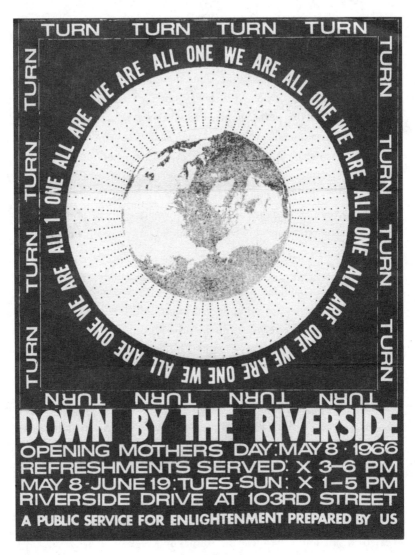

FIGURE 8.5.
Poster advertising USCO's multimedia be-in at the Riverside Museum in New York City,
1966. Courtesy of Gerd Stern.

events with titles like *Who R U? And Where R U Going?* Stern, Durkee, and Callahan gathered together with friends and spouses and began to live communally at a decommissioned church they bought in Garnerville, New York. They began performing as USCO at museums and colleges across the country—twice alongside McLuhan himself. In their earliest performances, the members of USCO sought to swamp audiences with sound and light, and so to engender in them a mystical sense of their own oneness with other human beings. "There were babies crying and angels and flowers, the insides of flowers and there were skies with clouds coming through and airplanes and country shots," recalled Barbara Durkee (now Asha Greer) of USCO's traveling shows. "There were usually two to five screens going all the time, with these images fading in and out as we got more sophisticated. . . . There was enough of that kind of thing that goes deep in, those kind of key places where new people can be touched in their hearts, you know, opened. . . . After about an hour and a half then it would slowly slow down, and then at the end of it there would be this long 'OM' and the oscilloscope would be down to one place. I just loved it because I thought it was true."[58]

Audiences varied in their responses. One San Francisco critic called the *Verbal American Landscape* a "landmark of a flop."[59] Those who were more in tune with the emerging psychedelic scene thought they recognized a multimedia equivalent to LSD. An USCO show, wrote Richard Kostelanetz, was "somewhat similar to the psychedelic experience, for in both an awareness of sensory overload disrupts all attempts at concentrated focus—and also initiates a gamut of emotional and psychological changes. An intrinsic purpose of such an environment is the challenging of linear habits of organization."[60] Jonas Mekas, filmmaker, critic, and sometime collaborator of Andy Warhol, went so far as to say that he thought he was "witnessing the beginnings of a new religion" as he watched USCO perform.[61]

In their early performances, USCO showed little reluctance to shut down the reasoning capacities of their audiences and dominate their other senses. But unlike Warhol's *Exploding Plastic Inevitable*, with which they sometimes competed for commissions, USCO never sought only to make audiences aware of their hidden desires. Rather, the members of USCO became increasingly committed to using electronic media as McLuhan intended, to reveal the universal connections among all human beings.

In the spring of 1966, USCO built a multimedia environment at the Riverside Museum in Manhattan called *Down by the Riverside*. Visitors entered beneath a sign labeled "N / TRANCE" and soon walked into a room in which an aluminum tube, pierced at the top, projected colored lights toward the ceiling. On one wall they saw a nine-foot-high painting of the Hindu god Shiva overlaid with an image of the Buddha. Around the painting, red lights pulsated in heartbeat rhythm. On another wall a massive three-dimensional eye, lit from within, stared out unceasingly. Visitors were free to move through the room at their own pace. When they were done, they could settle on the floor around the aluminum tube or move to another room, in which they could turn on flowers made of lights by walking on switches embedded in the floor. Finally they entered a third space, a so-called cave entirely covered in tie-dyed fabrics, in which they were encouraged to lie down on a slowly rotating parti-colored couch.[62]

To the editors of *Life* magazine, who featured USCO's *Shrine* in a September 9, 1966, cover story on psychedelic art, their work was the epitome of a "drugless trip."[63] Far from the overwhelming blasts of Warhol's *Plastic Inevitable* or even the chaos of USCO's own *Verbal American Landscape*, visitors to the environment at the Riverside Museum found it calming and contemplative. Electronic media seemed to externalize internal body processes, much as Marshall McLuhan had said they would. "In this electric age we see ourselves being translated more and more into the form of information, moving toward the technological extension of consciousness," he wrote in *Understanding Media*.[64] Now, within the rooms of USCO's Riverside environment, visitors could experience this fact for themselves. At the same time, though, they could enjoy their own agency. Like visitors to VanDerBeek's Movie-Drome, audiences at the Riverside would be surrounded by images not in such a way that they would lose their ability to reason altogether, but in such a way that they would appreciate the oneness of all living things with *both* their sensual and analytical faculties. Like visitors to *The Family of Man* or students in Victor D'Amico's art classes, audiences at the Riverside Museum were invited to be themselves and to experience their individuality in relation to others—from strangers who were there in the room with them to people they had never met who lived around the world. They were to participate in a new kind of gathering, simultaneously social and mystical, embodied, and transpersonal. They were to be completely themselves, and they were to dissolve into the universal human pool.

THE NEW MAN AT THE HUMAN BE-IN

The members of USCO called this kind of gathering a "be-in." The headline writers at *Life* picked up the phrase, and in January 1967 so did the editors of San Francisco's leading underground newspaper, the *Oracle*. The Californians had become frustrated as they watched a chasm appear between the politically driven New Left, centered in Berkeley, and the consciousness-centered hippie community that had grown up in San Francisco's Haight-Ashbury neighborhood. They proposed to stage what they called "A Gathering of the Tribes" and a "Human Be-In" at the Polo Field in Golden Gate Park that would bring the two groups together "ecstatically" in a "union of love and activism."[65] They invited notables from each side of the ideological fence, including Allen Ginsberg and Timothy Leary from the psychedelic community and future Yippie Jerry Rubin and Free Speech Movement veteran Jack Weinberg from the New Left. They constructed a stage at the east end of the field from which these notables could speak, and where a host of local bands including the Grateful Dead, Big Brother and the Holding Company, and Quicksilver Messenger Service would play.

When they announced the event, the editors of the *Oracle* explained that more than a hipster rapprochement was at stake. "Now in the evolving generation of America's young the humanization of the American man and woman can begin in joy and embrace without fear, dogma, suspicion, or dialectical righteousness," they explained. "A new concert of human relations being developed within the youthful underground must emerge, become conscious, and be shared so that a revolution of form can be filled with a Renaissance of compassion, awareness, and love in the Revelation of the unity of all mankind. The Human Be-In is the joyful, face-to-face

289

beginning of the new epoch."[66] The *Oracle's* East Bay counterpart, the *Berkeley Barb,* joined in. At the Human Be-In, they wrote, "the spiritual revolution will be manifest and proven. In unity we shall shower the country with waves of ecstasy and purification. Fear will be washed away; ignorance will be exposed to sunlight; profits and empire will lie drying on deserted beaches; violence will be submerged and transmuted in rhythm and dancing."[67]

On the bright, clear morning of January 14, more than twenty thousand people began streaming toward Golden Gate Park. Journalist and doctor Helen Zwick Perry was among them and described what she saw:

> The gathering was scheduled as an all-day affair . . . so we began our trek at about noon from Stanyan Street on the edge of Golden Gate Park and walked into the Polo Field . . . some thirty blocks from the center of the [Haight-Ashbury] neighborhood. By that time, there was a steady stream of people walking in, winding over the hillocks and through the glades as far as the eye could see. And facing us as we moved along with this human stream of communicants was a stream of people who had been there and were winding their way home; they all seemed enchanted, happy, and smiled like a welcoming committee upon us, as they trundled along with baby carriages and picnic hampers. It would seem almost as if they had been to early morning mass, which had turned out to be a huge picnic. Their costumes were varied and imaginative, or again they wore ordinary street clothes; but each person had his sign of participation somewhere upon him—a young boy with a nasturtium stuck behind his year, a gray-haired woman with a flower tied on her cane with a ribbon.
>
> But it was the Polo Field itself that presented a new world. It was a medieval scene, with banners flying, bright and uncommitted; the day was miraculous, as days can be in San Francisco at their best, and the world was new and clean and pastoral. Children wandered around in the nude. People sat on the grass with nothing to do, sometimes moving up near to the small platform where a poetry-reading might be going on, or where a band might be playing. There was no program; it was a happening. Sounds and sights turned me on, so that I had the sensation of dreaming. The air seemed heady and mystical. Dogs and children pranced around in blissful

abandon, and I became aware of a phenomenon that still piques my curiosity: the dogs did not get into fights, and the children did not cry.[68]

For those who were there and for those who have written about it over the years, the Human Be-In marked the beginning of the headiest phase of the 1960s. Within months, teenagers would be hopping buses to San Francisco for the Summer of Love, and the neighborhood's early homesteaders would be lighting out for rural regions to build domes and yurts and cabins in which to house the community of consciousness they had glimpsed in San Francisco.

But the Human Be-In also marked an ending, a culmination even, of a way of imagining the relationship between media, polity, and self that had its beginnings thirty years earlier. At the start of World War II, a generation of social scientists and artists had imagined an American mode of unity that paradoxically drew its strength from the individuality of its members. They imagined an environmental mode of media making that would promote the development of that individuality, and which would offer Americans opportunities to practice it together. In museum exhibitions and classrooms, in stuffy meeting halls and grandly airy national pavilions, Americans built media surrounds in which the democratic character theorized by psychologists and anthropologists could become the basis of a more egalitarian, more tolerant, more open society. In the early 1940s that society was meant to embrace the kinds of diversity attacked by totalitarian societies—diversity of race, sexual preference, and religion foremost among them. At the same time, it was meant to stimulate the human senses, to call forth and celebrate the full range of human expression, and to make both the sensual centers of an antiauthoritarian political consensus.

As they lay in the grass of Golden Gate Park, feathers and banners and ribbons expressing pieces of their individuality, turning away from the events on stage and toward the pleasures of watching one another, those who attended the Human Be-In brought to life something very much like democratic morale. True, it would still take decades before the civil rights movement could bring Americans an African-American president or the gay rights movement could succeed in normalizing the diversity of sexual

preference in mainstream American society. But at the same time, the sorts of personality that were on display in the park that day owed a great deal to the World War II fight against fascism, to the Cold War push against communism, and to the vision of a free, expressive individual that underlay the work of influential communities in each movement.

In the wake of the 1960s that debt has become hard to recognize, in part for reasons that Margaret Mead articulated in 1942: "Were the world we dream of attained, members of that new world would be so different from ourselves that they would no longer value it in the same terms in which we now desire it. . . . We would no longer be at home in such a world . . . We who have dreamed it could not live in it."[69] As Mead seemed to foresee, the crowds at the Human Be-In looked little like her buttoned-down friends on the Committee for National Morale. To themselves, and still to many of us, the long hair, loud music, and self-centered search for satisfaction that characterized the 1960s counterculture marked a new and permanent opening in American society, a cultural revolution even.

But, as I hope this book has shown, the children of the 1960s did not only overthrow their parents' expectations. They also fulfilled them.

Acknowledgments

Some people say writing is a solitary process. They're wrong. From start to finish, this book has depended on the generosity of colleagues and friends, and a few strangers too. I'd like to thank them here.

The book got under way with a great flurry of reading at the Center for Advanced Study in the Behavioral Sciences at Stanford University. When I arrived there for a fellowship year in the fall of 2007, I was wondering what to do next. I had just finished writing a book in which I'd been surprised to find that members of the 1960s counterculture were steeped in the cybernetics of the 1940s. I had an inkling that the connections between the decades ran deeper, but I didn't know how. Thanks to the year at the center, and especially to the efforts of its librarian, Tricia Soto, I was able to roam the intellectual landscape of the Cold War with abandon and find my way to the story told here. I would like to thank my center colleagues Gail Hershatter, Katie Trumpener, Eric Klinenberg, and Don Brenneis for their early faith that all my reading was leading somewhere. I'm also grateful to Jay Hamilton, Tanya Luhrmann, Rogers Hall, Kate Zaloom, Paula Findlen, Sarah Maza, and the master of our wonderful menagerie that year, Claude Steele, for their conversations and, even more, for the examples of rigorous, public-spirited scholarship they set in their own work. Finally, I'd like to thank Howard Becker for his early kindness and persistent encouragement.

As my research developed over the next several years, I was exceptionally lucky to find my way into three new intellectual communities: the

University of California Humanities Research Institute's working group "The Material World in Social Life"; the Media Places Project, a joint effort of researchers at Stanford University and Umeå University, Sweden, funded by the Knut and Alice Wallenberg Foundation; and Culture Digitally, a research network supported by the National Science Foundation. I'm grateful to the organizers of all three groups—Marian Feldman and Chandra Mukerji at the University of California, Patrik Svensson at Umeå University, and Culture Digitally co-founders Tarleton Gillespie at Cornell University and Hector Postigo at Temple University—and to our colleagues for the many ways they have encouraged and improved my work. I'm especially grateful to the Wallenberg Foundation for funding portions of the research presented here.

As any historian knows, the true keepers of a culture's memories are its archivists and curators. In this project I've worked with some of the best, including Michelle Elligott, Michelle Harvey, and MacKenzie Stevens at the Museum of Modern Art in New York; Catherine Bruck of the IIT Archives at the Illinois Institute of Technology; Roberto Trujillo of Stanford University Library's Special Collections; Laura Kuhn of the John Cage Trust; Elizabeth Siegel of the Art Institute of Chicago; Martha Rawls of the Forsythe County Public Library in Winston-Salem, North Carolina; Heather South of the North Carolina State Archives; Catherine Wallack at the University of Arkansas Libraries; Bruce Kirby of the Library of Congress; Holly Reed of the National Archives and Records Administration Still Picture Team; Larry Hughes of the National Archives and Records Administration Motion Picture, Sound, and Video Branch; Rachel Stuhlman, librarian at the George Eastman House International Museum of Photography and Film, in Rochester, New York; and Greg MacAyeal and D. J. Hoek of the Northwestern University Music Library.

I would also like to thank the many audiences who patiently listened to me try to explain what I was writing about and who then taught me, with their questions and suggestions, what I was *in fact* writing about. These groups included students and faculty in the Comparative Media Studies Program at the Massachusetts Institute of Technology; at the Annenberg School for Communication at the University of Pennsylvania; at the Center for the Study of the United States at the University of Toronto; in the

Departments of Communication, Information Science, and Science and Technology Studies at Cornell University; at the Medium to Medium Conference at Northwestern University; at the Rob Kling Center for Social Informatics and the Department of Communication and Culture at Indiana University; and in the Frontiers of New Media Symposium at the University of Utah. They also included generous colleagues at the National Air and Space Museum, Smithsonian Institution; the Hamburger Institut für Sozialforschung, in Hamburg, Germany; the Consejo Superior de Investigaciones Cientificas, in Madrid, Spain; the John Cage Centenary Symposium, in Lublin, Poland; and at the annual meetings of the International Communication Association, the National Communication Association, and the Society for Cinema and Media Studies.

My colleagues and students at Stanford have been unflagging in their encouragement, and I appreciate it. I owe a special thanks to Professor Pamela Lee of Stanford's Department of Art and Art History and the students in our biannual PhD seminar, "Media Cultures of the Cold War." In our classroom, the history of art and the history of electronic mass media have entwined and overlapped in ways I would never have expected; I hope I've captured some of the flavor of our conversations in this book. I'd also like to thank my colleagues in the Department of Communication, Professors Jeremy Bailenson, Jim Fishkin, Ted Glasser, Shanto Iyengar, Jon Krosnick, Cliff Nass, and Byron Reeves, and our incomparable staff, including Joyce Ichinose, Susie Ementon, Lisa Suruki, Mark Sauer, Katrin Wheeler, Mark DeZutti, and the recently retired Barbara Kataoka. Both groups have provided steady, welcome support for my work. Finally, I'd like to commend and thank my graduate research assistant, Amy DaPonte, and my three undergraduate research assistants, Colleen Sauer, Brandon Garcia, and Ben Cortes, for their able labors.

This book owes a special debt to a small group of readers and friends. One is Moira Roth. From the very beginning she has hovered like a benevolent spirit over this project, nudging, kibitzing, celebrating. The others have read and often reread everything I've written here with an eye to making it better. They are Erica Robles-Anderson, Daniel Kreiss, Lynn Spigel, and Jonathan Sterne. Together with John Durham Peters, Scott Bukatman, and Sharon Ghamari, who worked through several early iterations of the project, they've pushed me very hard and in the nicest possible ways to reach farther with this book, to sharpen its arguments, and to make them more explicitly relevant to the media cultures of today. I'm deeply grateful to every one of them.

I'm also grateful to the anonymous readers for the University of Chicago Press and to my one-of-a-kind editor, Douglas Mitchell, his eagle-eyed co-conspirator Tim McGovern, and my ever-patient agent, Geri Thoma. I would especially like to thank Allison Carruth and Barron Bixler for their uncommon design sense and their generosity. I would also like to thank Duke University Press for permission to reprint portions of my essay "*The Family of Man* and the Politics of Attention in Cold War America," which appeared in *Public Culture* 24, no. 1 (May, 2012): 55–84.

Finally, there are two people who deserve a kind of thanks for which words won't ever be enough: my wife Annie Fischer and my daughter Althea Turner. Suffice it to say that they have lived with this book as long as I have, and with a better sense of humor. I adore them both.

Notes

INTRODUCTION

1. McLuhan, *Understanding Media*, 48.
2. Adorno et al., *The Authoritarian Personality.*
3. As starting points into this literature, see Belgrad, *The Culture of Spontaneity;* Classen, *Watching Jim Crow,* Joselit, *Feedback;* Kuznick and Gilbert, *Rethinking Cold War Culture;* Monson, *Freedom Sounds;* Spigel, *TV by Design.*
4. See Doherty, *Projections of War* and *Cold War, Cool Medium;* McCarthy, *The Citizen Machine;* Spigel, *Welcome to the Dreamhouse.*
5. This book thus builds on the growing body of literature on the politics of attention. See, for instance, Crary, *Suspensions of Perception;* Mirzoeff, *The Right to Look;* Rancière, *The Politics of Aesthetics.*

CHAPTER ONE

1. Stone, "Hitler's Showmen Weave a Magic Spell." *New York Times,* December 3, 1933, SM8–9, 8.
2. Ibid., 9.
3. Some Americans saw Hitler as the latest iteration of a totalitarianism that had emerged earlier in Stalin's Soviet Union and Mussolini's Italy. Especially in the early 1930s, analysts often considered Soviet Communism, Italian Fascism, and German National Socialism as three variations of the same phenomenon. As the decade wore on, however, the German case began to exert a primary hold on the American intellectual imagination. For an astute and comprehensive analysis of American attitudes toward totalitarianism in this period, see Alpers, *Dictators, Democracy, and American*

Public Culture, 1–156. See also Thomas R. Maddux, "Red Fascism, Brown Bolshevism."

4. Thompson, *I Saw Hitler!,* quoted in Alpers, *Dictators, Democracy, and American Public Culture,* 40.

5. McGovern and Sait, *From Luther to Hitler,* 624.

6. Gary, *Nervous Liberals,* 392.

7. Scott Beekman, "Pelley, William Dudley," *American National Biography Online* Dec. 2009. http://www.anb.org/articles/15/15-01310 .html?a=1&n=pelley%2C%20william%20dudley&d=10&ss=0&q=1. Accessed May 1, 2012.

8. Diamond, *The Nazi Movement in the United States,* 217–22.

9. Ibid., 222.

10. "22,000 Rally in Garden; Police Check Foes," *New York Times,* February 21, 1939; 1,5; 5.

11. Ibid.

12. "The 'American Nazis' Claim 200,000 Members." *Life,* March 27 1937, 20–21. For an analysis of *Life*'s coverage of American fascists in the years leading up to the war, see Gary, "The Pitiless Spotlight of Publicity" in Doss, *Looking at Life Magazine,* 77–102.

13. "Fascism in America." *Life,* March 6,1939, 57–63. The *Life* story was only one of many of this kind. See also Johan J. Smertenko, "Hitlerism Comes to America," *Harper's Magazine,* November 1933, 660–70; Ludwig Lore, "Nazi Politics in America," *Nation,* November 29 1933, 615–17; Raymond Gram Swing, "Patriotism Dons the Black Shirt," *Nation,* April 10, 1935, 409–11; Charles Angoff, "Nazi Jew-Baiting in America, Part 1," *Nation,* May 1, 1935, 501–3; Charles Angoff, "Nazi Jew-Baiting in America, Part 2," *Nation,* May 8, 1935, 531–35; Stanley High, "Star-Spangled Fascists," *Saturday Evening Post,* May 27, 1939, 5–7, 70–73; Dale Kramer, "The American Fascists," *Harper's Magazine,* September 1940, 380–93.

14. Leo Ribuffo, "Review: Fascists, Nazis and American Minds: Perceptions and Preconceptions"; Gary, *Nervous Liberals,* 9, 79–80; Alpers, *Dictators, Democracy, and American Public Culture,* 77–80.

15. Kramer, "The American Fascists," 391.

16. "These Are Signs of Nazi Fifth Columns Everywhere." *Life,* June 17, 1940, 10–13.

17. Gary, *Nervous Liberals,* 79–80.

18. Marks, "The Idea of Propaganda in America," 232.

19. Sproule, *Propaganda and Democracy,* 132.

20. Marks, "The Idea of Propaganda in America," 235–36.

21. Chase, *The Tyranny of Words,* 351–52.

22. Hayakawa, introduction to *Language in Action,* xii.

23. Hayakawa, *Language in Action,* 37.

24. Carter, *Historical Statistics of the United States,* online edition: http://
    searchworks.stanford.edu/view/6313765. Accessed May 5, 2012.
25. Sproule, *Propaganda and Democracy,* 35.
26. "3 million" from Sproule, *Propaganda and Democracy,* 33; "nearer to 30
    million" from Cantril, "Propaganda and Radio," 87. In 1937, Cantril noted
    that approximately 26,869,000 homes had radios, allowing 75 percent of
    the population to listen at the same time (ibid.).
27. Bernays, *Crystallizing Public Opinion,* 1961 preface, xxxvi.
28. Lerner, *It's Later Than You Think,* 35.
29. Le Bon, *The Crowd,* 2.
30. Ibid.
31. Ibid.,7.
32. Ibid.,74.
33. Ibid., 78.
34. Ibid., 99.
35. Müller-Dohm, *Adorno,* 98.
36. Adorno, "On the Social Situation of Music," 391.
37. This is true of other essays he wrote on music and mass culture in these
    years as well, essays such as "Kitsch" (1932), "Farewell to Jazz" (1933), and
    "Music in the Background" (1934), all reprinted in Adorno et al., *Essays on
    Music.*
38. Adorno, "On Jazz" in Adorno et al., *Essays on Music,* 470–495; 487.
39. Ibid., 483.
40. It is tempting to read the outrage in Adorno's essays in this period as
    evidence of his resistance to the pro-industrial orientation of the project.
    But the situation was undoubtedly more complicated. He and Lazarsfeld
    shared many friends at the institute, most notably Horkheimer, and many
    of whom also shared Adorno's Marxist-Freudian orientation. Moreover,
    the sorts of questions he asked of media, if not the leftist idiom in which
    he asked them, would have been congenial to Hadley Cantril, a social psy-
    chologist trained by one of the foremost American theorists of personality
    in that era, Gordon Allport. Adorno has often and rightly been depicted
    as an outsider to the project's core mission, and his status there has been
    offered up as evidence of the fundamental contradictions between critical
    and administrative research. Yet the focus on Adorno's differences with his
    colleagues has also made it harder to see how he fused the character theory
    first explored by Erich Fromm in his 1920s research into authoritarianism
    in the German family with the analysis of mass media, and how he brought
    that fusion into American intellectual life. See Fromm, "Sozopsycholo-
    gischer Teil" (English abstract), in Institut für Sozialforschung, *Studien
    über Autoritat und Familie,* 916, and Fromm, *The Working Class in Weimar
    Germany,* 208–10, for more on Fromm's work in this area.

41. Adorno, "On the Fetish-Character in Music," 276.
42. Ibid., 271.
43. Ibid., 273.
44. Ibid., 286.
45. Ibid., 287.
46. Adorno, "On Popular Music," in Adorno et al., *Essays on Music*, 445.
47. Ibid., 450.
48. Ibid., 460.
49. Ibid.
50. Cantril, *The Invasion from Mars*, 56. See also Sconce, *Haunted Media*, 110–18.
51. Ibid., 44.
52. "Radio Listeners in Panic, Taking War Drama as Fact," *New York Times*, October 31, 1938, 1.
53. Holmes, quoted in Cantril, *Invasion from Mars*, 53–54.
54. "Terror by Radio," unsigned editorial, *New York Times*, November 1, 1938, 22.
55. Thompson, "On the Record," November 2, 1938, New York Tribune Inc.; rpt. Koch, Howard, *The Panic Broadcast*, 92–93; 92. All subsequent quotations are from this column.

CHAPTER TWO

1. Taylor, *Strategy of Terror*, 2–3.
2. Ibid., 41–42.
3. Ibid., 63.
4. Ibid., 168.
5. Laurie, *Propaganda Warriors*, 15–28.
6. For a list, see Angell, "The Civilian Morale Agency."
7. The William Allen White Committee to Defend America by Aiding the Allies, for instance, sought to counter the efforts of the America First Committee to keep the United States out of the war; the Federal Union, founded by *New York Times* journalist Clarence Streit, advocated linking the Western democracies into a single antifascist front.
8. Pope, "The Importance of Morale," 203.
9. Ibid., 205.
10. Steele, *Propaganda in an Open Society*, 88–93.
11. Arthur Upham Pope, letter to Kenneth W. Hechler, July 7, 1942, "CNM 'H' Misc." folder, carton 3, Committee on the Cause and Cure of War. Records, 1923–1948, call no.: 87-M111. Repository: Schlesinger Library, Radcliffe Institute.
12. Arthur Upham Pope, letter to C. J. Friedrich, February 27, 1941. Arthur

Upham Pope papers, "Committee for National Morale, 1940–1941" folder, carton 3, Committee on the Cause and Cure of War. Records, 1923–1948, call no. 87-M111. Repository: Schlesinger Library, Radcliffe Institute.

13. Allport, "Morale, American Style," 2, 5, HUG 4118.50, box 1, folder 2, Gordon Allport papers; quoted in Herman, *Romance of American Psychology*, 52.

14. Farago et al., *German Psychological Warfare*, 51.

15. Ibid., 86.

16. Allport, "The Nature of Democratic Morale," in Watson, ed., *Civilian Morale*, 18; quoted in Herman, *Romance of American Psychology*, 48.

17. Frank, "Freedom for the Personality," quoted in Herman, *Romance of American Psychology*, 121.

18. Brennecke et al., *Nazi Primer*, 5.

19. Ibid., 31.

20. Ibid., 28.

21. Ibid., 33.

22. Ibid., 20.

23. See Meyerowitz, "How Common Culture Shapes the Separate Lives: Sexuality, Race, and Mid-Twentieth-Century Social Constructionist Thought," 1057–84.

24. Brennecke et al., *Nazi Primer*, 59.

25. See Norwood, *The Third Reich in the Ivory Tower*.

26. Emerson, quoted in Nicholson, *Inventing Personality*, 5.

27. For a history of this shift, see Lears, *No Place of Grace*.

28. Ian A. M. Nicholson, *Inventing Personality*, 5–6.

29. Ibid., 13; see also Pandora, *Rebels within the Ranks*, 25.

30. Allport, "Gordon W. Allport," in Lindzey et al., *A History of Psychology in Autobiography*, 10.

31. Allport, *Personality*, 48; quoted in Hall and Lindzey, *Theories of Personality*, 262.

32. Lewin, "Krieglandschaft (War Landscape)."

33. Marrow, *The Practical Theorist*, 11; Heider, "On Lewin's Methods and Theory," 7.

34. Lewin et al., "Patterns of Aggressive Behavior in Experimentally Created 'Social Climates,'" 271.

35. Reported ibid., 271–99.

36. McLaughlin, "How to Become a Forgotten Intellectual," 116.

37. These were "Politics and Psychoanalysis" (1931), "Psychoanalytic Characterology and Its Relevance for Social Psychology" (1932), and "The Method and Function of an Analytic Social Psychology" (1932).

38. Fromm, "Analytic Social Psychology," 160, fn. 32 (fn. written in 1970).

39. Fromm, "Analytic Social Psychology," 160.

40. Ibid., 149.
41. Fromm, *The Working Class in Weimar Germany*, 207.
42. Fromm, "Soziopsychologischer Teil" (English abstract), in Institut für Sozialforschung, *Studien über Autorität und Familie*, 916; Bonss, "Critical Theory and Empirical Social Research," 1.
43. Fromm, *The Working Class in Weimar Germany*, 61.
44. Fromm, "Soziopsychologischer Teil" (English abstract), in Institut für Sozialforschung, *Studien über Autorität und Familie*, 916. See also Fromm, *The Working Class in Weimar Germany*, 208–10. As Rolf Wiggershaus points out, Fromm borrowed the term "character" from Wilhelm Reich (Wiggershaus, *The Frankfurt School*, 153).
45. Baars and Scheepers, "Authoritarian Personality," 349–50.
46. Evans, *Harry Stack Sullivan*, 45; McGloughlin, "How to Become a Forgotten Intellectual," 121–23.
47. Paris, *Karen Horney*, 55.
48. Horney, *Neurotic Personality of Our Time*, 285.
49. Paris, *Karen Horney*, 95.
50. Chapman, *Harry Stack Sullivan*, 34–49.
51. Stack Sullivan, quoted ibid., 45.
52. Ibid., 62.
53. Evans, *Harry Stack Sullivan*, 41–43.
54. Rubins, *Karen Horney*, 193–95; Quinn, *A Mind of Her Own*, 286–87; Evans, *Harry Stack Sullivan*, 15.
55. See Stocking, ed., *Malinowski, Rivers, Benedict, and Others*.
56. As Mead would note in her 1959 introduction to the book, it had sold more than eight hundred thousand copies in its first twenty-five years. Mead, "A New Preface," in Benedict, *Patterns of Culture*, vii. For an in-depth account of Mead and Benedict's relationship, see Banner, *Intertwined Lives*.
57. Benedict, *Patterns of Culture*, 237.
58. Benedict, "Configurations of Culture in North America," quoted in Singer, "A Survey of Culture and Personality Research," 23.
59. Singer, "A Survey of Culture and Personality Research," 88.
60. As one psychologist put it, "They have no discriminative understanding of tolerance born out of strength, humor, and an ultimate belief in all human beings' potential goodness, and they consider tolerance a weakness." Bühler, "Why Do Germans So Easily Forfeit Their Freedom?," 157.
61. Maslow, "The Authoritarian Character Structure," 404.
62. Fromm, *Escape from Freedom*, 284.
63. Ibid., 287.
64. Ibid., 299.
65. Ibid., 301.
66. Ibid., 297.

67. Mead, *And Keep Your Powder Dry . . .* , 24.
68. Ibid., 18–19.
69. Ibid., 25.
70. Taylor, *Awakening from History*, 306–8; quoted in Laurie, *The Propaganda Warriors*, 34.
71. Strecker and Appel, "Morale," 162–63.
72. Gary, *Nervous Liberals*, 86–109.
73. John Marshall, "Introduction" (draft), June 1940, in Rockefeller Archive Center, record group I.I, series 200, 200R, box 224, folder 2677; quoted in Gary, *Nervous Liberals*, 87.
74. Gary, *Nervous Liberals*, 100–101.
75. Donald Slesinger, Communications Seminar document no.5, September 29, 1939, Rockefeller Archive Center, record group I.I, series 200, 200R, box 224, folder 2677; quoted in Gary, *Nervous Liberals*, 98.
76. Bryson, letter to John Marshall, September 23, 1940, Rockefeller Archive Center, record group I.I, series 200, 200R, box 24, folder 2674; quoted in Gary, *Nervous Liberals*, 104.
77. Willits, letter to John Marshall, September 30, 1940, Rockefeller Archive Center, record group I.I, series 200, 200R, box 24, folder 2674; quoted in Gary, *Nervous Liberals*, 104.
78. Mead, *And Keep Your Powder Dry . . .* , 26.
79. Howard, *Margaret Mead*, 143–56.
80. Mead and Metraux, *The Study of Culture at a Distance*.
81. Bateson and Mead, "Principles of Morale Building," 213.
82. Ibid., 215.
83. Ibid., 219.
84. Mead, "Comparative Study of Culture and the Purposive Cultivation of Democratic Values," in Bryson and Finkelstein, eds., *Science, Philosophy and Religion, Second Symposium*, 66.
85. Ibid., 68.
86. Ibid., 67
87. Gregory Bateson, "Comment on 'The Study of Culture and the Purposive Cultivation of Democratic Values.'" In Bryson and Finkelstein, eds., *Science, Philosophy and Religion*, 86.
88. Ibid., 92.
89. Howard, *Margaret Mead*, 183.
90. Bateson and Mead, *Balinese Character*, 49.
91. Ibid.
92. Mead, "Balinese Character," in Bateson and Mead, *Balinese Character*, 14.
93. Ibid., 15.
94. Ibid.
95. Bateson and Mead, *Balinese Character*, 49.

96. For more on Kracauer's work and Bateson's connections to it, see Schütt-pelz, "Von der Kommunikation zu den Medien: In Krieg und Frieden (1943–1960)," in Fohrmann, ed., *Gelehrte Kommunikation*; and Gary, *Nervous Liberals*, 115–20.

97. Bateson, "Suggested Materials for Regional Training," typescript, Museum of Modern Art archives, EMH I.3.e, 4; see also Bateson, "The Use of Moving Picture Material to Illustrate Differences in National Culture, September 3, 1942," in EMH I.3.c., Museum of Modern Art archives, New York.

98. Bateson, "Introductory Label to Learning and Skill," in box O-4, folder 5, Margaret Mead papers, Library of Congress.

99. Margaret Mead, "Museums in the Emergency," 67.

100. n.d., unpaginated, no author listed, but reference in text to "subcommittee [of the Committee for National Morale]" as author; box O-5, folder 1, "Exhibits Democracy," Margaret Mead papers.

CHAPTER THREE

1. "Preliminary Course, Weimar, April/May, 1922," in Bayer, Gropius, and Gropius, eds. *Bauhaus, 1919–1928*, 34.

2. Walter Gropius, "My Conception of the Bauhaus Idea" (orig. 1937) in Gropius, *Scope of Total Architecture*, 19–29, 20; quoted in Forgács, *The Bauhaus Idea and Bauhaus Politics*, 143; Moholy-Nagy and Hoffmann, *The New Vision*, 11. As Rheinhold Martin has pointed out, the "New Man" was a ubiquitous figure for early-twentieth-century modernists (Martin, *Organizational Complex*, 21).

3. Gropius, *Scope of Total Architecture*, 20; quoted in Forgacs, *The Bauhaus Idea*, 143.

4. Gropius, introduction to Schlemmer, Moholy-Nagy, Molnár, and Gropius, *The Theater of the Bauhaus*, 7–14; 7.

5. "First Proclamation of the Weimar Bauhaus," in Bayer, Gropius, and Gropius, eds., *Bauhaus, 1919–1928*, 16.

6. Gropius, *Scope of Total Architecture*, 20; quoted in Forgacs, *The Bauhaus Idea*, 143.

7. Theo van Doesburg, *Grundbegriffe der neuen gestaltenden Kunst*, Bauhaus-bücher/Albert Langen, Munich, 1925; quoted in Bayer, Gropius, and Gropius, eds., *Bauhaus, 1919–1928*, 34.

8. Margolin, *The Struggle for Utopia*, 5.

9. Caton, *The Utopian Vision of Moholy-Nagy*, 7.

10. Moholy, "Constructivism and the Proletariat," rpt. Kostelanetz and Moholy-Nagy, *Moholy-Nagy*, 185–86; 185.

11. Theo van Doesburg, "Toward a Newly Shaped World"; quoted in Margolin, *The Struggle for Utopia*, 49.

12. Itten and Bauhaus, *Design and Form,* 11.

13. Moholy, "Education and the Bauhaus," from *Focus* II (London, winter 1938), rpt. Kostelanetz and Moholy-Nagy, *Moholy-Nagy,* 163–70; 166.

14. Ibid., 164.

15. László Moholy-Nagy, "Applied Photography," selection from *Malerei, Photographie, Film,* Bauhausbücher / Albert Langen, Munich, 1925; quoted in Bayer, Gropius, and Gropius, *Bauhaus, 1919–1928,* 152.

16. Moholy-Nagy, *Painting, Photography, Film,* 38.

17. Moholy-Nagy,1934 letter to Fra. Kalivoda, rpt. in Kostelanetz and Moholy-Nagy, *Moholy-Nagy,* 37–42; 40.

18. Moholy-Nagy, *The New Vision,* 38.

19. "Space-time is now the new basis on which the edifice of future thoughts and work should be built," wrote Moholy in 1942. "Contemporary arts, rapid changes in our surroundings through inventions, motorization, radio, and television, electronic action, records of light phenomena, and speed, are helping us to sense its existence and significance." Moholy, "Space-Time and the Photographer," 62–3.

20. Quoted in Moholy-Nagy, *Moholy-Nagy, Experiment in Totality,* 12, and Allen, *The Romance of Commerce and Culture,* 52.

21. Moholy, *The New Vision,* 10.

22. Cohen, *Herbert Bayer,* 1984, 7.

23. Chanzit and Libeskind, *From Bauhaus to Aspen,* 9–18.

24. Cohen, *Herbert Bayer,* 191.

25. Ibid., 14–15.

26. Overy, "Visions of the Future and the Immediate Past"; Staniszewski and Museum of Modern Art, *The Power of Display,* 25–27.

27. Staniszewski, *Power of Display,* 25.

28. The exhibition that Bayer, Moholy, and Gropius ultimately installed pulled back somewhat from Bayer's diagram. While it did feature blown-up photographs, photomontages, and various visual arrays through which the viewer could walk, by and large it kept most of the show's imagery to the exhibition hall's walls rather than its ceilings and floors. Even so, Bayer's drawing, like Bayer himself, would ultimately become a key force in the designing of environmental modes of communication to boost American morale during World War II.

29. Staniszewski, *Power of Display,* 48.

30. Bayer, quoted in Staniszewski, *Power of Display,* 48.

31. Bayer, "Aspects of Design of Exhibitions and Museums" (1961), rpt. Cohen, *Herbert Bayer,* 363–67; 366.

32. Ibid.

33. Staniszewski, *Power of Display,* 50–57.

34. Cohen, *Herbert Bayer,* 41.

35. Ibid.

36. For accounts of this migration and its impact, see Fermi, *Illustrious Immigrants*; Fleming and Bailyn, *The Intellectual Migration*; Coser, *Refugee Scholars in America*; Jay, *Permanent Exiles*.

37. Allen, *Romance of Commerce and Culture*, 35–48.

38. Moholy, August 18, 1937 letter to Sybil Moholy-Nagy, quoted in Sibyl Moholy-Nagy, *Moholy-Nagy: Experiment in Totality*, New York: Harper, 1950, 145.

39. Allen, *Romance of Commerce and Culture*, 48.

40. Moholy-Nagy, foreword to the 1938 edition of *The New Vision*, 5.

41. Ibid.

42. Moholy-Nagy, "Relating the Parts to the Whole," 6.

43. Ibid., 7.

44. Chanzit and Libeskind, *From Bauhaus to Aspen*, 83.

45. Staniszewski, *Power of Display*, 144.

46. Untitled and undated handwritten notes, probably prepared for Alfred Barr's post-exhibition report to the Museum trustees, records of the Registrar Department, *Bauhaus 1919–1928*, Museum of Modern Aart exhibition #82.

47. Ibid.

48. Lewis Mumford, "The Skyline: Bauhaus—Two Restaurants and a Theater," 38; for a summary of reviews of the exhibition, see Staniszewski, *Power of Display*, 151.

49. Alfred H. Barr, Jr., "Notes on the Reception of the Bauhaus Exhibition," records of the Registrar Department, *Bauhaus 1919–1928*, Museum of Modern Art exhibition #82.

50. Jewell, Edward Alden. "Decade of the Bauhaus." *New York Times*, December 11, 1938; quoted in Staniszewski, *Power of Display*, 145.

51. Franklin Roosevelt, dedication of the Museum of Modern Art, May 10, 1939, quoted in Lynes, *Good Old Modern*, 205; recording of full speech available at http://www.history.com/audio/franklin-roosevelt-dedicates -museum-of-modern-art#franklin-roosevelt-dedicates-museum-of-modern -art. Downloaded September 24, 2010.

52. Michelle Elligott, introduction to "Modern Artifacts: Tentative and Confidential." *Esopus* 9 (2007), no pagination.

53. Leslie Cheek, untitled notes on scenario No. 3, in Leslie Cheek, Jr. papers, 12, Museum of Modern Art archives, 1.

54. "Scenario (No. 3) for Proposed Exhibition" (1940), in Alfred H. Barr, Jr. papers, 6.B.13.d. Museum of Modern Art archives, 41.

55. Ibid., 4.

56. Ibid., 5.

57. Ibid., 10.
58. Ibid., 15.
59. Ibid., 16.
60. Minutes of the Museum's Coordinating Committee, July 10, 1940; quoted in Elligott, introduction to "Modern Artifacts: Tentative and Confidential," *Esopus* 9 (2007): no pagination.
61. Cheek, untitled notes on scenario 3, in the Leslie Cheek Jr. papers, 12, Museum of Modern Art archives, 2.
62. Abby Aldrich Rockefeller to Leslie Cheek, October 7, 1940; reprinted "Modern Artifacts: Tentative and Confidential," *Esopus* 9 (2007), no pagination.
63. "The Minutes of the Sixteenth Annual Meeting of the Board of Trustees and Members of the Corporation of the Museum of Modern Art held on Thursday, November 15, 1945," 5–9.
64. Ibid., 5.
65. Phillips, "Steichen's 'Road to Victory,'" 38–39.
66. Ibid., 40.
67. Stange, *Symbols of Ideal Life*, 135.
68. McCausland, "Photographs Illustrate Our 'Road to Victory,'" 4.
69. Staniszewski, *Power of Display*, 215; Stange, *Symbols of Ideal Life*, 137.
70. Phillips, "Steichen's 'Road to Victory,'" 38.
71. Jewell, "Portrait of the Spirit of a Nation," X5.
72. Ibid.
73. McCausland, "Photographs Illustrate Our 'Road to Victory,'" 3. For a parallel argument and similarly positive comments on the show, see Burke, "War and Cultural Life."
74. Kiesler, "Press Release Pertaining to the Architectural Aspects of the Gallery," rpt. Kiesler et al., *Friedrich Kiesler: Art of this Century*, 36–37; 36.
75. Kiesler, "Brief Note on Designing the Gallery," rpt. Kiesler et al., *Friedrich Kiesler: Art of This Century*, 34–35; 34.
76. "Art That's Mysterious and Modern," date and place unknown, quoted in Valentina Sonzogni, "Notes on the Press Clippings 1942–46," in Kiesler et al., *Friedrich Kiesler: Art of This Century*, 26–31; 29.
77. Henry McBride, "New Gallery Ideas," *New York Sun*, October 23, 1942, 27; quoted ibid., 28.
78. Copyright page in Willkie, *One World*, 1943.
79. Willkie, introduction to *One World*.
80. Willkie, *One World*, 173.
81. Ibid., 166, 163.
82. Willkie, opening text from *Airways to Peace,*; rpt. Willkie, Museum of Modern Art and Arno Press. "Airways to Peace," 3.

83. Staniszewski, *Power of Display*, 230–35.

84. Willkie et al., "Airways to Peace," 7.

CHAPTER FOUR

1. Patterson, "Appraising the Catchwords," 63.

2. Ross, *The Rest is Noise*, 122.

3. Saul, *Freedom Is, Freedom Ain't*, 1–6.

4. Ibid., 17; Baraka, *Blues People*, 181.

5. Hicks, "John Cage's Studies with Schoenberg," 125–40; Kahn, *Noise, Water, Meat*, 24; Nicholls, *John Cage*, 23; Joseph, "A Therapeutic Value for City Dwellers," in Patterson, ed., *John Cage*, 136–40.

6. Russolo, "The Art of Noises," available online at http://120years.net/machines/futurist/art_of_noise.html. Accessed December 6, 2010.

7. Cage, "The Future of Music: Credo" (1937), in Cage, *Silence*, 3.

8. For a typology and chronology of Cage's work in this period, see his "Notes on Compositions 1 (1933–1948)," in Cage and Kostelanetz, *John Cage, Writer*, 5–13.

9. Pritchett, *Music of John Cage*, 22–24.

10. Cage, "Goal: New Music, New Dance," originally published *Dance Observer*, 1937; rpt. Cage and NetLibrary Inc., *Silence*, 87.

11. Nicholls, *John Cage*, 11–12.

12. Ibid., 12.

13. John Cage, "Counterpoint," *Dune Forum* 1, no.2 (February 14, 1934); rpt. Kostelanetz, ed., *Writings about John Cage*, 15–17, 17; quoted in Joseph, "A Therapeutic Value for City Dwellers," 137.

14. Catalog, "Summer Session for Men and Women Mills College, June 23–August 3, 1940," 5, Findeli papers 2007.15, box 4 (no folder number), Illinois Institute of Technology.

15. Ibid., 10, 47.

16. Ibid., 10.

17. John Cage, "PROJECT: A Center of Experimental Music," Northwestern University archives; quoted in Silverman, *Begin Again*, 44.

18. Silverman, *Begin Again*, 44–45.

19. Joseph, "A Therapeutic Value for City Dwellers," 136.

20. Silverman, *Begin Again*, 49.

21. Cage, quoted in "Music: Percussionist," *Time*, 70; quoted in Joseph, "A Therapeutic Value for City Dwellers," 144.

22. Moholy-Nagy and Norma K. Stahle, letter to Charles W. Morris, October 28, 1937, in Findeli papers, 2007.15, box 8 (no folder number), Illinois Institute of Design. See also Findeli, "Moholy-Nagy's Design Pedagogy

in Chicago (1937–1946)," 32, and Martin, *Organizational Complex*, 55, 62–63.

23. School of Design, "Day and Evening Classes" (pamphlet), 1940–41, in Findeli papers, 2007.15, Illinois Institute of Technology, box 8 (no folder number).

24. Morris, "The Mechanism of Freedom," 588–89.

25. Ibid., 585.

26. Silverman, *Begin Again*, 54.

27. Cage, "A Composer's Confessions," 39–40.

28. Tomkins, *The Bride and the Bachelors*, 97.

29. "Percussionist," *Time*, 70.

30. Cage, quoted in Revill, *The Roaring Silence*, 88–89.

31. Roth, "The Aesthetic of Indifference," 46–53.

32. For analyses of the relationship of Cage's sexuality to his music, see Jones, "Finishing School," and Katz, "John Cage's Queer Silence."

33. Cage, "Afternote to Lecture on Nothing," in Cage, *Silence*, 127; quoted in Nicholls, *John Cage*, 35.

34. Cage, "An Autobiographical Statement," in Cage and Kostelanetz, *John Cage, Writer*, 237–47, 239; quoted in Nicholls, *John Cage*, 36.

35. Nicholls, *John Cage*, 35–36.

36. Cage, "Notes on Compositions I (1933–1948)," 5–13, 11.

37. Cage, "A Composer's Confessions," quoted in Nicholls, *John Cage*, 36.

38. Cage, "A Composer's Confessions," quoted in Pritchett, *The Music of John Cage*, 37.

39. Cage, "The East in the West," in Cage and Kostelanetz, *John Cage: Writer*, 21–26; 25, quoted in Joseph, "A Therapeutic Value for City Dwellers," in Patterson, ed., *John Cage*, 153.

40. Nicholls, *John Cage*, 39–42.

41. Cage, "Notes on Compositions I (1933–48)," 11, quoted in Nicholls, *John Cage*, 39–40.

42. Nicholls, *John Cage*, 40.

43. Cage, "Notes on Compositions 1, 1933–48," 11.

44. Cage, "Forerunners of Modern Music," in Cage, *Silence*, 66.

45. Ibid., 64.

46. John Cage and Daniel Charles, *For the Birds* (Boston: M. Boyars, 1981), 105; quoted in Kahn, *Noise, Water, Meat*, 171.

47. Cage, "Lecture On Nothing," 117.

48. Cage, "A Composer's Confessions," 41.

49. Ibid., 42.

50. Harris, *The Arts at Black Mountain College*, 8–9.

51. Adamic, "Education on a Mountain," 518.

52. Rice, *I Came Out of the Eighteenth Century*, 328.

53. Duberman, *Black Mountain*, 139–52.

54. Perrow, "Drinking Deep at Black Mountain College," 2.

55. Ibid., 7.

56. Ibid., 14.

57. In June, 1945, for example, Black Mountain College professor Robert Wunsch was arrested for committing "crimes against nature" after being found in his car with a US Marine. His colleagues at Black Mountain did not encourage him to stay after his arrest, and he left the college for good within days (Duberman, *Black Mountain*, 230–31).

58. Harris, *The Arts at Black Mountain College*, 111.

59. Ibid., 108.

60. Herman, *The Romance of American Psychology*, 61.

61. Duberman, *Black Mountain*, 240–41.

62. Ibid., 239.

63. Perrow, "Drinking Deep at Black Mountain College," 12.

64. Ibid.

65. Duberman, *Black Mountain*, 288–90.

66. Quoted in Duberman, *Black Mountain*, 289.

67. Cage's remarks were summarized in the Black Mountain College *Bulletin*, vol. 6, no. 4 (May 1948); rpt. Patterson, "Appraising the Catchwords," 193.

68. Duberman, *Black Mountain*, 290.

69. For a schedule of classes that summer, see Patterson, "Appraising the Catchwords," 197–98.

70. Harris, *The Arts at Black Mountain College*, 154–56.

71. Perrow, "Drinking Deep at Black Mountain College," 16.

72. Patterson, "Appraising the Catchwords," 204.

73. Cage, "Defense of Satie," 81.

74. Ibid., 83.

75. Ibid., 84.

76. Cage, "Composition (1952)," 59.

77. Ibid.

78. Cage, "Composition as Process: II. Indeterminacy," 36.

79. Ibid., 37.

80. Ibid., 39.

81. Joseph, *Random Order*, 54.

82. Ibid., 258.

83. Artaud, letter, February 24, 1948; quoted in Finter and Griffin. "Antonin Artaud and the Impossible Theatre," 16.

84. Brown, *Chance and Circumstance*, 19–21.

85. Cage, *4'33"*, 1960.

CHAPTER FIVE

1. The success of television anchorman Tom Brokaw's 1998 book *The Greatest Generation* has spawned a minor industry around the term. See, for instance, the following: Brokaw, *The Greatest Generation Speaks* (New York: Random House, 1999); United States Congress, Senate Special Committee on Aging, "Our Greatest Generation Continuing a Lifetime of Service: Hearing before the Special Committee on Aging, United States Senate, One Hundred Seventh Congress, First Session, Indianapolis, IN, August 9, 2001"; Lindenmeyer, *The Greatest Generation Grows Up*; Childers, *Soldier from the War Returning*.

2. Jezer, *The Dark Ages*, 78; US Department of Labor, *Handbook of Labor Statistics, 1974, Bulletin 1825* (Washington, 1974), 367; cited in Lichtenstein, *Labor's War at Home*, 46.

3. Diggins, *The Proud Decades*, 23–29.

4. Quoted in Boyer, *By the Bomb's Early Light*, 197.

5. MacDonald, quoted ibid., 234.

6. E. B. White, in *The New Yorker*, August 18, 1945; quoted ibid., 133.

7. Mary McCarthy, "America the Beautiful: Humanist in the Bathtub." *Commentary* 4 (1947): 205; quoted ibid., 251–52.

8. Dwight D. Eisenhower, "Address at the Columbia University National Bicentennial Dinner," Waldorf-Astoria Hotel, New York; quoted in Herman, *The Romance of American Psychology*, 135.

9. Herman, *Romance of American Psychology*, 87–121.

10. Ibid., 108.

11. National Research Council et al., *Psychology for the Returning Serviceman*, 181–94.

12. Herman, *Romance of American Psychology*, 89.

13. Ibid.

14. Quoted in Leja, *Reframing Abstract Expressionism*, 110.

15. Roy R. Grinker and John P. Spiegel, *Men under Stress* (Philadelphia: Blakiston, 1945); quoted in Herman, *Romance of American Psychology*, 99.

16. Quoted in Herman, *Romance of American Psychology*, 245.

17. See Gorer, *The American People*; Bryson, *The Next America*. For a discussion of other volumes in this tradition, see Sammond, *Babes in Tomorrowland*, 210–13.

18. Perry, Ralph Barton. *Characteristically American*, 3.

19. Ibid., 13.

20. Ibid., 37.

21. Morris, *The Open Self*, 6.

22. Ibid., 10.

23. Ibid., 148.

24. Ibid., 149.
25. Ibid., 152.
26. Bryson, *Science and Freedom*, x.
27. Ibid., 15.
28. Ibid., 7.
29. Heims, *The Cybernetics Group*, 14.
30. Rosenblueth and Bigelow, "Behavior, Purpose and Teleology."
31. For a comprehensive account of the Macy Conferences, see Heims, *The Cybernetics Group*.
32. Wiener, *Cybernetics*, 12.
33. Galison, "The Ontology of the Enemy," 232. See also Masani and Phillips, "Antiaircraft Fire-Control and the Emergence of Cybernetics."
34. Wiener, *The Human Use of Human Beings*, 15–16.
35. Ibid., 60.
36. This was the eighth symposium of the Conference on Science, Philosophy, and Religion and Their Relation to the Democratic Way of Life. The conference was founded by seventy-nine well-known American intellectuals in 1940 in response to the rise of fascism. It met almost annually until 1968, and brought together scholars ranging from anthropologist Franz Boas to physicist Enrico Fermi and sociologist Daniel Lerner. With the exception of Boas, the group tended not to overlap with the networks of anthropologists, psychologists, and engineers at the heart of the cybernetics meetings and, before that, the Committee for National Morale.
37. Finer, "How Can Scholarship Contribute to the Relief of International Tensions?" 2–3.
38. Ibid., 18.
39. Ninkovich, *The Diplomacy of Ideas*, 86–94.
40. Ibid., 139.
41. Preamble to the UNESCO Constitution, quoted in Martínez, *A History of UNESCO*, 45.
42. Cantril and UNESCO, *Tensions That Cause Wars*, 7.
43. Ibid.
44. Ibid.
45. Klineberg, *Tensions Affecting International Understanding*.
46. Horkheimer, "The Lessons of Fascism," 214.
47. Allport, "The Role of Expectancy," 66–67.
48. Stack Sullivan, "Tensions Personal and International," 90.
49. Ibid., 116.
50. Naess, "The Function of Ideological Convictions," 288.
51. Horkheimer, "The Lessons of Fascism," 228.
52. Cantril, UNESCO, et al. "Common Statement," 19.
53. Adorno et al., *The Authoritarian Personality*, 10.

54. Ibid.
55. Ibid., 255–57.
56. Ibid., 11.
57. Ibid.
58. Lasswell, *Democratic Character*, 487–91.
59. Ibid., 487.
60. Ibid., 495–96.
61. Ibid., 496.
62. Ibid., 513.
63. Schlesinger, *The Vital Center*, 1.
64. Ibid., 250.
65. Ibid., 5–6.
66. Ibid., 252.
67. Ibid.
68. Ibid., 249.
69. Ibid., 256.
70. Riesman et al., *The Lonely Crowd*, 4.
71. Ibid., 25.
72. Ibid., 128.
73. Ibid., 46.

CHAPTER SIX

1. Szarkowski, John, "The Family of Man," 13.
2. Barthes, "'La Grande Famille des Hommes'"; Phillips, "The Judgment Seat of Photography"; Berger, *About Looking*; Solomon-Godeau, "'The Family of Man': Den Humanismus für ein Postmodernes Zeitalter Aufpolieren/'The Family of Man.' Refurbishing Humanism for a Postmodern Age"; Sekula, "The Traffic in Photographs." See also Kaplan, *American Exposures*. For a summary and analysis of critical responses to the show to 1999, see Berlier, "The Family of Man: Readings of an Exhibition." For a recent collection of essays on related themes, see Back and Schmidt-Linsenhoff, eds., *The Family of Man 1955–2001*. There have been two particularly important exceptions to the string of highly critical responses to the exhibition. See Sandeen, *Picturing an Exhibition*, for a nuanced discussion of the political and cultural context in which the show appeared. See Stimson, *The Pivot of the World*, for a persuasive reading of the exhibition's images in relation to one another and of the show's efforts to foster a new globalist subjectivity.
3. For more on concerns about children in this period, see Dixon, *Keep Them Human*, and Sammond, *Babes in Tomorrowland*.
4. Lynes, *Good Old Modern*, 167.

5. "Modern Art for Children," *Bulletin of the Museum of Modern Art*.

6. Museum of Modern Art, New York Department of Education, and Victor D'Amico, *Experiments in Creative Art Teaching*, 15.

7. Morgan, "From Modernist Utopia to Cold War Reality," 156.

8. Guilbaut, *How New York Stole the Idea of Modern Art*, 57.

9. "Portrait of the Artist as a Child," *House and Garden*, 65.

10. D'Amico, "Art Therapy in Education," 9.

11. Ibid., 10.

12. Liss, "Creative Therapy," 13.

13. Moholy-Nagy, "Better Than Before," 3.

14. Ibid., 5.

15. Ibid., 6.

16. Victor D'Amico, untitled typescript report on the War Veterans' Art Center (June, 1948), 6–14, 6. In Victor D'Amico papers III.A.13, Museum of Modern Art Archives.

17. Ibid., 15.

18. Bernard Pfriem, "Advanced Drawing and Painting," in Victor D'Amico, untitled typescript report on the War Veterans' Art Center (June, 1948), 18–20, 18. In Victor D'Amico papers III.A.13, Museum of Modern Art Archives, New York.

19. Victor D'Amico, untitled typescript report, 6–14, 10.

20. See May, *Homeward Bound*, especially chapter 1.

21. Anshen, "Preface," in Anshen, Ruth Nanda, ed., *The Family* (rev. ed. New York: Harper, 1959), xv–xix, xvi.

22. Anshen, "The Family in Transition," 3.

23. Horkheimer, "Authoritarianism and the Family," 368.

24. Ogata, "Creative Playthings." On the role of creativity as an idea in this period more generally, see Cohen-Cole, "The Creative American."

25. Quoted in Ogata, "Creative Playthings," 142.

26. Morgan, "From Modernist Utopia to Cold War Reality," 162–63.

27. Victor D'Amico, "Point of View: An Occasional Supplement to the Newsletter of the Committee on Art Education" (April 1954), 2; quoted ibid., 163.

28. As Lynn Spigel has shown, the museum had extensive connections to the television industry in this period. See Spigel, *TV by Design*. On the role of television in shaping cold war citizenship, see McCarthy, *The Citizen Machine*, and Doherty, *Cold War, Cool Medium*.

29. *Through the Enchanted Gate*, 1952 (first season), "Feeling Pictures" episode. For more on *Through the Enchanted Gate*, see Harvey, "Through the Enchanted Gate."

30. Ibid.

31. *Through the Enchanted Gate*, 1952 (first season), "Space Designs" episode.

32. *Through the Enchanted Gate*, 1953 (second season), "The City" episode.

33. Ibid.
34. D'Amico, *Art for the Family*, 101. The family gallery echoed a widely shared concern with creating creative spaces for children in the home. See Ogata, "Building Imagination in Postwar American Children's Rooms."
35. Ibid., 105.
36. Edward Steichen, "The Museum of Modern Art and 'The Family of Man,'" in Steichen, *A Life in Photography*, not paginated.
37. Sandeen, *Picturing an Exhibition*, 41.
38. Dorothea Lange, letter, January 16, 1953; quoted in Szarkowski, "The Family of Man," 24.
39. Photography, said Steichen, "communicates equally to everybody throughout the world. It is the only universal language we have, the only one requiring no translation." Steichen, "Photography: Witness and Recorder of History," 160.
40. Lynes, *Good Old Modern*, 325.
41. Ford Foundation, "Report of the Trustees of the Ford Foundation," September 27, 1950, 16.
42. Ibid., 7.
43. Ibid., 17.
44. Ibid., 9.
45. All quotations from René d'Harnoncourt, draft of "Letter to Henry Ford II," n.d., 2–5, in René d'Harnoncourt papers, VII.85, Museum of Modern Art archives.
46. Ibid., 14, 4.
47. Ibid., 5.
48. Carl Sandburg, prologue to Steichen and Museum of Modern Art, *The Family of Man*, 3.
49. Paul Rudolph, interview with Mary Anne Staniszewski, December 27, 1993; quoted in Staniszewski, *The Power of Display*, 240.
50. Wayne Miller, interview with Mary Anne Staniszewski, July 18, 1996, quoted in Staniszewski, *The Power of Display*, 244.
51. Edward Steichen, "'The Family of Man,'" *Vogue*, February 1, 1955, 168; quoted in Staniszewski, *The Power of Display*, 244.
52. St.-John Perse, quoted in Steichen and Museum of Modern Art, *The Family of Man*, 192.
53. Morgan, "The Theme Show," 24.
54. Ibid., 26.

CHAPTER SEVEN

1. US Information Agency, "Communications Research and USIS Operations," USIA special report S–65–59, National Archives and Records

Administration, RG 306, records of the US Information Agency Office of Research, entry P160, special reports (S): 1953–1997 S–51–59 through S–5–60, container 15, folder S–65–59, pp. 1–3, 10.

2. The literature on American propaganda in this period is voluminous. Good places to start include Hixson, *Parting the Curtain*; Cull, *The Cold War and the United States Information Agency*; Saunders, *Who Paid the Piper?*; Osgood, *Total Cold War*; Belmonte, *Selling the American Way*.

3. Harry S. Truman, "Address on Foreign Policy at a Luncheon of the American Society of Newspaper Editors," April 20, 1950; quoted in Hixson, *Parting the Curtain*, 14.

4. Hixson, *Parting the Curtain*, 21.

5. Eisenhower to C. D. Jackson, May 8, 1952, box 69, Jackson papers, Dwight D. Eisenhower Presidential Library; quoted in Hixson, *Parting the Curtain*, 23.

6. NSC 5505/1, January 31, 1955; quoted in Hixson, *Parting the Curtain*, 101.

7. Mitarachi, "Design as a Political Force," 38.

8. Department of Commerce, "What's OITF?" *Fair Facts* 2 (December 1960); quoted in Haddow, *Pavilions of Plenty*, 15.

9. Fred Wittner, "What Should Trade Missions Mean to You?" *Industrial Marketing* 44 (July 1957), 47–48; quoted in Haddow, *Pavilions of Plenty*, 41.

10. Eisenhower, speech to staff of the US Information Agency, November 1953; quoted in Bogart, *Premises for Propaganda*, xiv.

11. Haddow, *Pavilions of Plenty*, 40.

12. "People's Capitalism'—This IS America," *Collier's*, 74.

13. Potter, "The American Round Table Discussions on People's Capitalism," 10.

14. Ibid., 54.

15. Ibid., 25–26.

16. Allen, *Romance of Commerce and Culture*, 269–78.

17. Haddow, *Pavilions of Plenty*, 8.

18. Pang, "Dome Days," 187.

19. Ibid., 179.

20. Untitled press release, United States Office of International Trade Fairs, quoted ibid., 187.

21. Speech by guides at American National Exhibition, quoted in Pang, "Dome Days," 187.

22. US Information Agency, "An Analysis of Visitor Reaction to the US Trade Fair, Kabul, Afghanistan, August 24 to September 7, 1956," RG 306, records of the US Information Agency Office of Research, entry P160, special reports (S): 1953–1997 S–15–56 through S–20–57, Container 11, Folder S-18–56, 1.

23. Mitarachi, "Design as a Political Force," 37.

24. Ibid., 52.
25. Ibid., 40.
26. Ibid.
27. Radio Corporation of America, "Off to the Fair," 18.
28. "The US Exhibit of Freedom a Hit in Poland," *Life*, July 1, 1957, 19–24, 19; quoted in Pang, "Dome Days," 188.
29. Museum of Modern Art and D'Amico, *Experiments in Creative Art Teaching*, 40.
30. Ibid., 15.
31. US Office of International Trade Fairs, "Our Children and Productivity" (unpaginated pamphlet), in Victor D'Amico papers IV.A.ii, Museum of Modern Art Archives.
32. Anonymous, "The Idealist and the Children," typescript translation of Italian news story, print source unknown, in Victor D'Amico papers IV.A.ii, Museum of Modern Art Archives.
33. Museum of Modern Art and D'Amico, *Experiments in Creative Art Teaching*, 34.
34. Exposition internationale: Exposition universelle et internationale de Bruxelles, 1958. Algemene Wereldtentoonstelling Te Brussel, 1958. T. 2., 377–430.
35. Charles Everarts de Velp, "The Theme," in "The Theme Of Brussels 1958," ed. Brussels Universal and International Exhibition 1958, Commissariat General of the Government Brussels, 1958, 5–15, 10. Max Millikan papers, MC 188, box 4, folder 120, Institute archives, Massachusetts Institute of Technology, Cambridge, MA.
36. Ibid., 11.
37. Ibid., 14; Baron Moens de Firneig, untitled preface, "The Theme Of Brussels 1958," ed. Brussels Universal and International Exhibition 1958 Commissariat General of the Government Brussels, 1958, 3, 3. Max Millikan papers, MC 188, box 4, folder 120, Institute archives, Massachusetts Institute of Technology, Cambridge, MA.
38. "Origins and Objectives of the Center for International Studies," April 1952; quoted in Blackmer, *MIT Center for International Studies*, 41. For more on CENIS and modernization theory in this period, see Gilman, *Mandarins of the Future*, 155–240.
39. Walt Whitman Rostow and Max Millikan, "A Proposal for a New United States Foreign Economic Policy," July 1954, quoted in Blackmer, *MIT Center for International Studies*, 97.
40. Edward Durell Stone, "Memorandum on the Design of the United States Pavilion Brussels Exposition," undated typescript, Edward Durell Stone papers, MC 340, box 2, file 866/18, Special Collections, University of Arkansas Libraries, Fayetteville, AR.

41. Haddow, *Pavilions of Plenty*, 110.
42. "USA at Brussels' Fair, 1958," *Industrial Design*, 47.
43. *This Is America: Official United States Guide Book, Brussels World's Fair*, 1958, 30.
44. "Vogue's Eye View of Going to the Brussels World's Fair," *Vogue*, April 15, 1958, 60; quoted in Haddow, *Pavilions*, 145–46.
45. Nilsen, "America's Salesman," 246–49.
46. Ibid., 247.
47. Madeleine May, "Overheard at the Fair," *Atlantic Monthly*, August 1958, 70; quoted ibid., 249.
48. Quoted in Nilsen, "America's Salesman," 244–45.
49. Quoted ibid., 249–50.
50. Haddow, *Pavilions of Plenty*, 175.
51. Ibid., 179.
52. US Information Agency, "Family of Man," unsigned memo marked "ICS/ED:EWaldman:mpw 1/21/59," January 21, 1959, papers and ephemera of Edward Steichen (1879–1973), Richard and Ronay Menschel Library, George Eastman House International Museum of Photography and Film, box 5, folder 2, 1.
53. Ibid.
54. US Information Service Berlin to USIA, Foreign Service Despatch, September 23, 1955, National Archives, RG 306-FM, records of the USIA prints and textual, photos and clippings relating to *The Family of Man* exhibition Amsterdam-Berlin, folders 1–4; folder 4, Berlin, 1.
55. Untitled and undated typescript, National Archives, RG 306-FM, records of the USIA, prints and textual, photographs and clippings relating to *The Family of Man* exhibition, Amsterdam-Berlin, folders 1–4; folder 4, Berlin.
56. Sandeen, "'The Show You See with Your Heart,'" 105.
57. "Omitted from Berlin Showing," unsigned set of photographs, National Archives, RG 306-FM, records of the USIA prints and textual, photographs and clippings relating to *The Family of Man* exhibition, Amsterdam-Berlin, folders 1–4, folder 4 Berlin. The Berlin exhibition was only the first at which the show's contents would be negotiated. In Tokyo, for instance, local organizers inserted pictures of Japanese victims of the Nagasaki bomb, which Steichen ordered removed. In 1959, when the exhibition travelled to Moscow, Steichen himself suggested that images of Berliners throwing rocks at Russian tanks be removed (Yoichi Okamato to Abbot Washburn, Tom Cannon, and Marvin Sorkin, January 22, 1959, papers and ephemera of Edward Steichen (1879–1973), Richard and Ronay Menschel Library, George Eastman House International Museum of Photography and Film, box 5, folder 2, 1). Steichen seems to have insisted that these images be removed on the grounds that they detracted from the humanistic vision

of the whole. Steichen wrote to the Japanese: "The treatment of specific events in a topical manner . . . has been consistently avoided in order to make sure that the presentation of universal human problems would not be overshadowed by the impact of an event and its associations." Steichen quoted by René d'Harnoncourt, letter to Streibert from d'Harnoncourt, March 26, 1956, box 1, folder 4, #147, papers and ephemera of Edward Steichen, Menschel Library, George Eastman House, Rochester, NY.

58. Dorothea V. Stetten to Jackie Martin, September 29, 1955, National Archives, RG 306-FM, records of the USIA, prints and textual, photographs and clippings relating to *The Family of Man* exhibition, Amsterdam-Berlin folders 1–4, folder 4 Berlin, 2.

59. Translation of untitled article in *Der Tag* September 17, 1955, quoted USIS Berlin, "Excerpts, Berlin Press Reviews, The Family of Man," in USIS Berlin to USIA Washington, October 20, 1955, National Archives, RG 306-FM, records of the USIA, prints and textual, photographs and clippings relating to *The Family of Man* exhibition, Amsterdam-Berlin folders 1–4, folder 4 Berlin, 2.

60. "Wie du und ich," *Der Abend*, September 16, 1955, 6.

61. *Süddeutsche Zeitung*, quoted in Joseph B. Phillips, Public Affairs Officer, USIS Munich, "Family of Man Exhibit in Munich," typescript, February 6, 1956, National Archives, RG 306-FM, records of the USIA, prints and textual, photographs and clippings relating to *The Family of Man* exhibition, box 3, Munich-Paris folders 8–12, folder 8, 4.

62. Milton Leavitt to Jackie Martin, February 15, 1956, National Archives, RG 306-FM, records of the USIA, prints and textual, photographs and clippings relating to *The Family of Man* exhibition, box 3, Munich-Paris folders 8–12, folder 8, 1.

63. Joseph B. Phillips, Public Affairs Officer, USIS Munich, "Family of Man Exhibit in Munich," typescript, February 6, 1956, National Archives, RG 306-FM, records of the USIA, prints and textual, photographs and clippings relating to *The Family of Man* exhibition, box 3, Munich-Paris folders 8–12, folder 8, 6.

64. Sandeen, "The Show You See With Your Heart,"105.

65. John E. McGowan, quoted untitled typescript report, RG 306-FM, records of the USIA, prints and textual, photographs and clippings relating to *The Family of Man* exhibition, 1955–1956, box 1, Amsterdam–Berlin folders 1–4, folder 1.

66. Masey and Morgan, *Cold War Confrontations*, 152–58; Hixson, *Parting the Curtain*, 151–76.

67. "Confidential US National Exhibit, Gorky Park, Moscow 1959," National Archives and Records Administration, NND 968156 RG 306 entry A154 box 2, folder: "Basic Policy Guidance Moscow Exhibition," 1.

68. W.W. Littell to McLellan, "Memo (Secret)," November 5, 1958, NND 968156 RG 306 entry A154 box 2, folder: Basic Policy Guidance Moscow Exhibition Memo (Secret) from W.W. Littell to McLellan, Nov 5, 1958; attachment includes all three versions of "Basic Policy Guidelines": secret, confidential, and "Draft General Plan."

69. Sandeen, *Picturing an Exhibition*, 133.

70. "Facts About the American National Exhibition in Moscow 1959, revised as of April 1, 1959," National Archives and Record Administration, RG 306 records of the USIA, Office of Research, entry #P 160, special reports (S), 1953–97, S-15-56 through S-20-57, container 11, folder S-18-56, 3.

71. Ibid., 3 and 1.

72. "Excerpts of Roundtable Discussion on Plans for Moscow Exhibition Held with Newspaper Correspondents in New York City, January 8, 1959," unpaginated, National Archives and Records Administration, NND 968139, RG 306 records of the USIA, entry A154, box 1, folder: Information Center Service Exhibits: 1959, January.

73. Ibid.

74. Hixson, *Parting the Curtain*, 171.

75. "Electronic Memory Keeps Track of Every Question Asked of It by Thousands of Russian Fairgoers," IBM press release, August 4, 1959, National Archives and Record Administration, NN3-306-88-12, RG 306 records of the USIA, box 6, records relating to the American National Exhibition, Moscow, 1957–59, Moscow exhibition through expenditures, current, folder: "Information for Forwarding Weekly."

76. American Embassy, Moscow. "Three Weeks of Sokolniki (Confidential)," August 20, 1959, National Archives and Records Administration, NND 923578 NN3-306-88-12, RG 306 records of the USIA, box 7, folder: Exhibits, American National Exhibition, 10.

77. Colomina, *Domesticity at War*, 257–58. See also Nelson, "Art X: The Georgia Experiment."

78. Neuhart, Neuhart, and Eames, *Eames Design*, 177; quoted in Colomina, *Domesticity at War*, 257.

79. Eames, *A Communications Primer*.

80. Colomina, *Domesticity at War*, 265.

81. Kepes, *Language of Vision*, 13.

82. "Unfavorable Comments on the Exhibition," typescript, n.d., National Archives and Records Administration, NND 968156, RG 306 records of the USIA, entry 154, box 4, folder: Moscow Exhibition, 3.

83. Ralph K. White, "Report on American Exhibition in Moscow; Visitors' Reactions to the American Exhibit in Moscow, A Preliminary Report," National Archives and Records Administration, NND 923578 NN3-306-88-12,

RG 306 box 7, folder: Exhibits-American National Exhibition, 10. See also White, "Soviet Reactions to Our Moscow Exhibit."

CHAPTER EIGHT

1. All images referred to here are available in Hansen, *A Primer of Happenings and Time/Space Art*, 97–101. Cage taught at the New School from 1956 to 1960.
2. Roszak, *The Making of a Counter Culture*, 156.
3. Silverman, *Begin Again*, 152–53.
4. Heinz-Klaus Metzger, "John Cage, or Liberated Music," quoted in Silverman, *Begin Again*, 159–60. For a summary and analysis of the response to Cage's visit to Darmstadt, see Shultis, "Cage and Europe," 38–39.
5. Cage, "Indeterminacy," 39.
6. Hansen, *Primer of Happenings*, 95.
7. Kelley, *Childsplay*, 18.
8. Roth and Kaprow, "Oral History Interview with Allan Kaprow, February 15 and 19, 1981," 29.
9. Kelley, *Childsplay*, 17.
10. Kaprow, quoted ibid.
11. Kelley, *Childsplay*, 24.
12. Kaprow, notes on *Communication*, Allan Kaprow papers, 1940–97, Getty Research Institute, Research Library, accession no. 980063; quoted in Kelley, *Childsplay*, 24.
13. Kaprow, "The Legacy of Jackson Pollock," 5.
14. Ibid., 1.
15. Kelley, *Childsplay*, 22.
16. Rodenbeck, *Radical Prototypes*, ix.
17. Kaprow, Watts and Brecht, "Project in Multiple Dimensions," 155.
18. Kaprow, "Pinpointing Happenings (1967)," 84.
19. Kaprow, "Happenings in the New York Scene," 21, 24, 22, 23.
20. Kaprow, "Pinpointing Happenings (1967)," 88–89.
21. Kaprow, quoted Kostelanetz, *Theatre of Mixed Means*, 132.
22. Sontag, "Happenings," 273.
23. Schechner, "Happenings," 33.
24. Suvin, "Reflections on Happenings," 300.
25. Kaprow, quoted Kostelanetz, *Theatre of Mixed Means*, 130–31.
26. These examples come from Robert Whitman's *Mouth* (1961), Allan Kaprow's *Coca Cola, Shirley Cannonball?* (1960), and Benjamin Patterson's *Licking Piece* (1964) respectively.
27. Roszak, *Making of a Counter Culture*, 47.

28. Ibid., 235.
29. McLuhan, *The Mechanical Bride*, vi.
30. Ibid., v.
31. Ibid., 113 and 135.
32. Ibid., v.
33. McLuhan, "Notes on Media as Art Forms," 9, 6.
34. McLuhan, *Gutenberg Galaxy*, 248 and 266.
35. Ibid., 31.
36. McLuhan, *Understanding Media*, 4.
37. VanDerBeek, interview with Ed Emshwiller, December 15, 1973; quoted in Sutton, "Stan VanDerBeek: Collage Experience," 84.
38. Sutton, "The Experience Machine," 223.
39. Ibid., 41–42.
40. Christgau, Robert. "When VanDerBeek a Movie Drome Decreed," *New York World Journal Tribune*, March 5, 1967, 21–22; quoted in Sutton, "The Experience Machine," 42.
41. Ibid.
42. VanDerBeek, "Culture: Intercom and Expanded Cinema."
43. VanDerBeek quoted in Adrienne Mancia and Willard Van Dyke, "Four Artists as Film-Makers," *Art in America* 55, no. 1 (1967), 73; quoted in Proctor, "From the Ivory Tower to the Control Room," 104.
44. Ben Highmore, "Machinic Magic,"133–41; Colomina, *Domesticity at War*, 265–68.
45. Joseph, "My Mind Split Open," 87.
46. Glueck, "Syndromes Pop at Delmonico's," 36.
47. Quoted Joseph, "My Mind Split Open," 88.
48. Dr. Robert Campbell, quoted Glueck, "Syndromes Pop at Delmonico's," 36.
49. Joseph, "My Mind Split Open," 88.
50. Ingrid Superstar, "Movie Party at the Factory: A Trip and a Half," one-page typed manuscript, dated March 26, 1966, time capsule -7, Warhol archives; quoted ibid., 89.
51. Bockris and Malanga, *Up-Tight*, 7.
52. Ibid.
53. Michaela Williams, "Andy Warhol and his Marvelous Fun Machine," unattributed clipping [preview of first Chicago show at Poor Richard's, 1966], scrapbook vol. 10 large, p. 62, Warhol archives; quoted in Joseph, "My Mind Split Open," 91–92.
54. Masters and Houston, *Psychedelic Art*, 97.
55. Oren, "USCO," 85; Gerd Stern, correspondence with the author, March 25, 2004.
56. Program for *Verbal American Landscape*, quoted in Frankenstein, "A Landmark of a Flop," 6.

57. Judi Stern, quoted in Oren, "USCO," 91.

58. Asha Greer (née Barbara Durkee), quoted in Oren, "USCO," 78.

59. Frankenstein, "A Landmark of a Flop," 6.

60. Kostelanetz, "Scene and Not Herd: USCO," 71.

61. Jonas Mekas, "Movie Journal," May 26, 1966, in Mekas, *Movie Journal,* 242–44, 244; quoted Scott, "Acid Visions," 28.

62. "Psychedelic Art," *Life,* 61.

63. Ibid.

64. McLuhan, *Understanding Media,* 57.

65. "The Gathering of the Tribes," *San Francisco Oracle,* 2.

66. Ibid.

67. *The Berkeley Barb,* quoted in Perry, *Haight-Ashbury,* 122.

68. Perry, *The Human Be-In,* 86.

69. Mead, "The Comparative Study of Culture and the Purposive Cultivation of Democratic Values," 67.

Bibliography

ARCHIVAL SOURCES

Gordon W. Allport papers, 1907–ca. 1974 (inclusive). Accession no. HUG 4118.xx. Harvard University archives. Harvard University Depository. Cambridge, MA.

Black Mountain College Research Project papers, North Carolina State Archives, Raleigh, NC.

Leslie Cheek Jr. papers in the Museum of Modern Art archives. Museum of Modern Art, New York.

Committee on the Cause and Cure of War: Records, 1923–48. Accession no. 87-M111. Arthur and Elizabeth Schlesinger Library on the History of Women in America. Radcliffe Institute, Cambridge, MA.

Victor D'Amico papers in the Museum of Modern Art archives. Museum of Modern Art, New York.

Department of circulating exhibitions records in the Museum of Modern Art archives. Museum of Modern Art, New York.

René d'Harnoncourt papers in the Museum of Modern Art archives. Museum of Modern Art, New York.

Early museum history administrative records in the Museum of Modern Art archives. Museum of Modern Art, New York.

Film Study Center in the Museum of Modern Art archives. Museum of Modern Art, New York.

Alain Findeli papers, Illinois Institute of Technology archives. Paul V. Galvin Library, Illinois Institute of Technology, Chicago.

R. Buckminster Fuller papers, Special Collections, collection M1090, Stanford University Libraries, Stanford University, Stanford, CA.

Margaret Mead papers and the South Pacific ethnographic archives. Library of Congress, Washington.

Max Millikan papers. Accession no. MC 188. Institute archives, Massachusetts Institute of Technology, Cambridge, MA.

Oral history interviews, research collections, Archives of American Art, Smithsonian Institution, Washington.

Registrar exhibition files #82 (*The Bauhaus, 1919–1928*) in the Museum of Modern Art archives. Museum of Modern Art, New York.

Papers and ephemera of Edward Steichen (1879–1973), Richard and Ronay Menschel Library, George Eastman House International Museum of Photography and Film, Rochester, NY.

Edward Durell Stone papers. Accession no. MC 340. Special Collections, University of Arkansas Libraries, Fayetteville, AR.

Records of the United States Information Agency. Record group 306 1900–94 (bulk 1947–86). National Archives and Records Administration, College Park, MD.

TEXTUAL SOURCES

Abraham, Karl, and Johannes Cremerius. *Psychoanalytische Studien Zur Charakterbildung und Andere Schriften. Hrsg. und Eingeleitet von Johannes Cremerius*, Conditio Humana. Frankfurt am Main: Fischer, 1969.

Adamic, Louis. "Education on a Mountain." *Harper's*, April 1936, 516–30.

Adorno, Theodor W. "On the Fetish-Character in Music and the Regression of Listening." In *The Essential Frankfurt School Reader*, edited by Andrew Arato and Eike Gebhardt, 270–99. New York: Urizen Books, 1978.

———. "On Jazz." In *Essays on Music*, edited by Theodor W. Adorno, Richard D. Leppert, and Susan H. Gillespie, 470–95. Berkeley: University of California Press, 2002.

———. "On Popular Music [With the Assistance of George Simpson] (1941)." In *Essays on Music*, edited by Theodor W. Adorno, Richard D. Leppert and Susan H. Gillespie, 437–69. Berkeley, CA: University of California Press, 2002.

———. "On the Social Situation of Music (1932)." In *Essays on Music*, edited by Theodor W. Adorno, Richard D. Leppert, and Susan H. Gillespie, 391–436. Berkeley: University of California Press, 2002.

———. "Radio Physiognomics." In *Current of Music: Elements of a Radio Theory*, edited by Theodor W. Adorno and Robert Hullot-Kentor, 73–200. 1. Aufl. ed. Frankfurt am Main: Suhrkamp, 2006.

Adorno, Theodor W., with Else Frenkel-Brunswik, Daniel J. Levinson, and R. Nevitt Sanford. *The Authoritarian Personality*. Studies in Prejudice. New York: Harper, 1950.

Adorno, Theodor W., Richard D. Leppert, and Susan H. Gillespie. *Essays on Music / Theodor W. Adorno*. Selected, with introduction, commentary, and notes by Richard Leppert; new translations by Susan H. Gillespie. Berkeley: University of California Press, 2002.

Allen, James Sloan. *The Romance of Commerce and Culture: Capitalism, Modernism, and the Chicago-Aspen Crusade for Cultural Reform.* Chicago: University of Chicago Press, 1983.

Allport, Gordon W. "Autobiography." In *A History of Psychology in Autobiography. Vol. V,* edited by Gardner Lindzey, Edwin G. Boring, and the American Psychological Association, 3–25. New York: Appleton-Century-Crofts, 1967.

———. "The Nature of Democratic Morale." In *Civilian Morale,* edited by the Society for the Psychological Study of Social Issues and Goodwin Barbour Watson, 3–18. Boston and New York: Published for Reynal and Hitchcock by Houghton Mifflin, 1942.

———. *Personality: A Psychological Interpretation.* New York: H. Holt and Company, 1937.

———. "The Role of Expectancy." In *Tensions That Cause Wars,* edited by Hadley Cantril and UNESCO, 43–78. Urbana: University of Illinois Press, 1950.

Almond, Gabriel A. "Harold Dwight Lasswell: A Biographical Memoir." Washington: National Academy of Sciences, 1987.

Alpers, Benjamin Leontief. *Dictators, Democracy, and American Public Culture: Envisioning the Totalitarian Enemy, 1920s–1950s.* Chapel Hill: University of North Carolina Press, 2003.

Angell, Ernest. "The Civilian Morale Agency." *Annals of the American Academy of Political and Social Science* 220 (1942): 160–67.

Angoff, Charles. "Nazi Jew-Baiting in America, Part 1." *Nation,* May 1, 1935, 501–3.

———. "Nazi Jew-Baiting in America, Part 2." *Nation,* May 8, 1935, 531–35.

Anonymous. "The 'American Nazis' Claim 200,000 Members." *Life,* March 27, 1937: 20–21.

———. "The Attack on Democracy." *Propaganda Analysis* 2, no. 4 (January 1, 1939): 13–21.

———. "Fascism in America." *Life,* March 6, 1939: 57–63.

———. "The Gathering of the Tribes." *San Francisco Oracle* 1, no. 5 (January 1967): 2.

———. "Music: Percussionist." *Time,* February 22, 1943: 70.

———. "People's Capitalism'—This IS America." *Collier's,* January 1956: 74.

———. "Portrait of the Artist as a Child." *House and Garden,* February 1947: 64–65, 128–29.

———. "Psychedelic Art." *Life,* September 9, 1966: 60–69.

———. "Radio Listeners in Panic, Taking War Drama as Fact." *New York Times,* October 31, 1938: 1.

———. "Terror by Radio" (unsigned editorial). *New York Times,* November 1, 1938: 22.

———. "These Are Signs of Nazi Fifth Columns Everywhere." *Life*, June 17, 1940: 10–13.

———. "22,000 Rally in Garden; Police Check Foes," *New York Times,* February 21, 1939: 1, 5.

———. "USA at Brussels' Fair, 1958." *Industrial Design* 4, no. 9 (1957): 44–55.

———. "Wie du und ich." *Der Abend*, September 16, 1955: 6.

Anshen, Ruth Nanda. "The Family in Transition." In *The Family: Its Function and Destiny*, edited by Ruth Nanda Anshen, 3–17. New York: Harper, 1949.

———. *The Family: Its Function and Destiny*. Revised edition. New York: Harper, 1959.

Arato, Andrew, and Eike Gebhardt. *The Essential Frankfurt School Reader*. New York: Urizen Books, 1978.

Baars, Jan, and Peer Scheepers. "Theoretical and Methodological Foundations of the Authoritarian Personality." *Journal of the History of the Behavioral Sciences* 29, no. 4 (1993): 345–53.

Back, Jean, and Viktoria Schmidt-Linsenhoff (Hg.). *The Family of Man 1955–2001: Humanismus und Postmoderne: Eine Revision von Edward Steichens Fotoausstellung = Humanism and Postmodernism: A Reappraisal of the Photo Exhibition by Edward Steichen*. Marburg: Jonas Verlag, 2004.

Banner, Lois W. *Intertwined Lives: Margaret Mead, Ruth Benedict, and Their Circle*. New York: Knopf, 2003.

Baraka, Imamu Amiri. *Blues People: Negro Music in White America*. New York: W. Morrow, 1963.

Barthes, Roland. "'La Grande Famille des Hommes.'" In Roland Barthes, *Mythologies*, 173–76. Paris: Éditions du Seuil, 1957.

Bateson, Gregory. "Comment on 'The Study of Culture and the Purposive Cultivation of Democratic Values.'" In *Science, Philosophy and Religion, Second Symposium*, edited by Lyman Bryson and Louis Finkelstein, 81–97. New York: Conference on Science, Philosophy and Religion in Their Relation to The Democratic Way of Life, Inc.

Bateson, Gregory, and Margaret Mead. *Balinese Character: A Photographic Analysis*. New York Academy of Sciences Special Publication; 2. New York: New York Academy of Sciences, 1942.

———. "Principles of Morale Building." *Journal of Educational Sociology* 15, no. 4 (1941): 206–20.

Bayer, Herbert, Walter Gropius, and Ise Gropius. *Bauhaus, 1919–1928*. Boston: C. T. Branford Co., 1959.

Belgrad, Daniel. *The Culture of Spontaneity: Improvisation and the Arts in Postwar America*. Chicago: University of Chicago Press, 1998.

Bell, Daniel. "America as a Mass Society: A Critique." In *The End of Ideology: On the Exhaustion of Political Ideas in the Fifties*, edited by Daniel Bell, 21–38. New York: Free Press, 1960.

Belmonte, Laura A. *Selling the American Way: U.S. Propaganda and the Cold War*. Philadelphia: University of Pennsylvania Press, 2008.

Benedict, Ruth. "Configurations of Culture in North America." *American Anthropologist* 34, (1932): 1–27.

———. *Patterns of Culture*. Boston: Houghton Mifflin, 1989.

———. *Race: Science and Politics*. New York: Modern Age Books, 1940.

Bennett, Tony. "Theories of the Media, Theories of Society." In *Culture, Society and the Media*, edited by Michael Gurevitch, Tony Bennett, James Curran, and Janet Woollacott, 30–55. New York: Routledge, 1990.

Berger, John. *About Looking*. New York: Pantheon Books, 1980.

Berlier, Monique. "The Family of Man: Readings of an Exhibition." In *Picturing the Past: Media, History and Photography*, edited by Bonnie Brennan and Hanno Hardt, 206–41. Urbana: University of Illinois Press, 1999.

Bernays, Edward L. *Crystallizing Public Opinion*. New York: Liveright, 1961.

———. "The Engineering of Consent." *The Annals of the American Academy of Political and Social Science* no. 250 (1947).

———. *Propaganda*. Brooklyn, New York: Ig Publishing, 2008 (1928).

Blackmer, Donald L. M. *The MIT Center for International Studies: The Founding Years, 1951–1969*. Cambridge, MA: MIT Center for International Studies, 2002.

Blumer, Herbert. *Movies and Conduct*. New York: Macmillan, 1933.

Bockris, Victor, and Gerard Malanga. *Up-Tight: The Velvet Underground Story*. New York: Quill, 1983.

Bogart, Leo, and Agnes Bogart. *Premises for Propaganda: The United States Information Agency's Operating Assumptions in the Cold War*. New York: Free Press, 1976.

Bonss, Wolfgang. "Critical Theory and Empirical Social Research: Some Observations." In *The Working Class in Weimar Germany: A Psychological and Sociological Study,* edited by Erich Fromm, 1–38. Cambridge, MA: Harvard University Press, 1984.

Boyer, Paul S. *By the Bomb's Early Light: American Thought and Culture at the Dawn of the Atomic Age*. New York: Pantheon, 1985.

Bramson, Leon. *The Political Context of Sociology*. Princeton, NJ: Princeton University Press, 1961.

Brennecke, Fritz, Paul Gierlichs, William Edward Dodd, Harwood Lawrence Childs, and Hitler-Jugend. *The Nazi Primer; Official Handbook for Schooling the Hitler Youth*. New York: Harper, 1938.

Brokaw, Tom. *The Greatest Generation*. New York: Random House, 1998.

Brown, Carolyn. *Chance and Circumstance: Twenty Years with Cage and Cunningham*. New York: Alfred A. Knopf, 2007.

Bryson, Lyman. *The Next America: Prophecy and Faith*. New York: Harper & Brothers, 1952.

———. *Learning and World Peace: Eighth Symposium.* New York: Conference on Science, Philosophy, and Religion in Their Relation to the Democratic Way of Life, 1948.

———. *Science and Freedom.* New York: Columbia University Press, 1947.

Bryson, Lyman, and Louis Finkelstein. *Science, Philosophy, and Religion: Second Symposium.* New York: Conference on Science, Philosophy, and Religion in Their Relation to the Democratic Way of Life, 1942.

Bühler, Charlotte. "Why Do Germans So Easily Forfeit Their Freedom?" *Journal of Abnormal Social Psychology* 38, no. 2 (1943): 149–57.

Burke, Kenneth. "War and Cultural Life." *American Journal of Sociology* 48, no. 3 (1942): 404–10.

Butsch, Richard. *The Citizen Audience: Crowds, Publics, and Individuals.* New York: Routledge, 2008.

Cage, John. "A Composer's Confessions." In *John Cage, Writer: Selected Texts*, edited by John Cage and Richard Kostelanetz, 27–44. New York: Cooper Square Press, 2000.

———. "Composition (1952)." In *Silence: Lectures and Writings*, edited by John Cage, 57–59. Middletown, CT: Wesleyan University Press, 1973.

———. "Composition as Process: II. Indeterminacy" In *Silence: Lectures and Writings*, edited by John Cage, 35–40. Middletown, CT: Wesleyan University Press, 1973.

———. "Counterpoint." In *Writings about John Cage*, edited by Richard Kostelanetz, 15–17. Ann Arbor: University of Michigan Press, 1993.

———. "Defense of Satie." In *John Cage*, edited by Richard Kostelanetz and John Cage. New York: Praeger, 1970.

———. "Forerunners of Modern Music." In *Silence: Lectures and Writings*, edited by John Cage, 62–67. Middletown, CT: Wesleyan University Press, 1973.

———. *4'33".* New York: Henmar Press, 1960.

———. "The Future of Music: Credo (1937)." In *Silence: Lectures and Writings*, edited by John Cage, 3–6. Middletown, CT: Wesleyan University Press, 1973.

———. "Goal: New Music, New Dance." In *Silence: Lectures and Writings*, edited by John Cage, 87–88. Middletown, CT: Wesleyan University Press, 1961.

———. "Indeterminacy." In *Silence: Lectures and Writings*, edited by John Cage, 35–40. Middletown, CT: Wesleyan University Press, 1961.

———. "Lecture on Nothing." In *Silence: Lectures and Writings*, edited by John Cage, 108–27. Middletown, CT: Wesleyan University Press, 1973.

———. "Notes on Compositions 1 (1933–1948)." In *John Cage, Writer: Selected Texts*, edited by John Cage and Richard Kostelanetz, 5–13. New York: Cooper Square Press, 2000.

———. *Silence: Lectures and Writings.* Middletown, CT: Wesleyan University Press, 1973.

Cage, John, and Richard Kostelanetz. *John Cage, Writer: Selected Texts.* New York: Cooper Square Press, 2000.

Cantril, Hadley. "Propaganda and Radio: The National Council for Social Studies Seventh Yearbook." In *Education against Propaganda,* edited by Elmer Ellis, 87–99: National Council for Social Studies, 1937.

Cantril, Hadley, Hazel Gaudet, and Herta Herzog. *The Invasion from Mars: A Study in the Psychology of Panic.* New Brunswick, NJ: Transaction Publishers, 2005 (1940).

Cantril, Hadley, UNESCO, et al. "Common Statement." In *Tensions That Cause Wars,* edited by Hadley Cantril, UNESCO, et al., 17–22. Urbana: University of Illinois Press, 1950.

———. *Tensions That Cause Wars: Common Statement and Individual Papers by a Group of Social Scientists Brought Together by UNESCO.* Urbana: University of Illinois Press, 1950.

Carter, Susan B. *Historical Statistics of the United States: Earliest Times to the Present.* Millennial edition, 5 vols. New York: Cambridge University Press, 2006. Online edition available at http://searchworks.stanford .edu/view/6313765. Accessed May 5, 2012.

Caton, Joseph Harris. *The Utopian Vision of Moholy-Nagy.* Studies in Photography, no. 5. Ann Arbor: UMI Research Press, 1984.

Chanzit, Gwen Finkel, and Daniel Libeskind. *From Bauhaus to Aspen: Herbert Bayer and Modernist Design in America.* Boulder, CO: Johnson Books, 2005.

Chapman, A. H. *Harry Stack Sullivan: His Life and His Work.* New York: Putnam, 1976.

Chase, Stuart. *The Tyranny of Words.* New York: Harcourt, 1938.

Childers, Thomas. *Soldier from the War Returning: The Greatest Generation's Troubled Homecoming from World War II.* Boston: Houghton Mifflin Harcourt, 2009.

Classen, Steven D. *Watching Jim Crow: The Struggles over Mississippi TV, 1955–1969.* Durham, NC: Duke University Press, 2004.

Cohen, Arthur Allen. *Herbert Bayer: The Complete Work.* Cambridge, MA: MIT Press, 1984.

Cohen-Cole, Jamie. "The Creative American: Cold War Salons, Social Science, and the Cure for Modern Society." *Isis,* no. 100 (2009): 219–62.

Colomina, Beatriz. *Domesticity at War.* Cambridge, MA: MIT Press, 2007.

———. "Enclosed by Images: The Eameses' Multimedia Architecture." *Grey Room* 2, Winter (2001): 6–29.

Coser, Lewis A. *Refugee Scholars in America: Their Impact and Their Experiences.* New Haven: Yale University Press, 1984.

Crary, Jonathan. *Suspensions of Perception: Attention, Spectacle, and Modern Culture.* Cambridge, MA: MIT Press, 1999.

Creel, George. *How We Advertised America: The First Telling of the Amazing*

Story of the Committee on Public Information That Carried the Gospel of Americanism to Every Corner of the Globe. New York and London: Harper & Brothers, 1920.

———. "Public Opinion in War Time." *Annals of the American Academy of Political and Social Science* 68 (July 1918): 185–93.

Cull, Nicholas John. *The Cold War and the United States Information Agency: American Propaganda and Public Diplomacy, 1945–1989*. Cambridge and New York: Cambridge University Press, 2008.

D'Amico, Victor. *Art for the Family*. New York: Museum of Modern Art, 1954.

———. "Art for War Veterans." *Bulletin of the Museum of Modern Art* 13, no. 1 (September 1945): 3–15.

———. "Art Therapy in Education." *Bulletin of the Museum of Modern Art* 10, no. 3 (February 1943): 9–10.

D'Amico, Victor, Museum of Modern Art Department of Education, WNET-TV. *Through The Enchanted Gate*. Kinescope. Film Study Center in the Museum of Modern Art archives. Museum of Modern Art, New York.

Diamond, Sander A. *The Nazi Movement in the United States, 1924–1941*. Ithaca, NY: Cornell University Press, 1974.

Dies, Martin. *The Trojan Horse in America*. New York: Dodd, Mead & Company, 1940.

Diggins, John P. *The Proud Decades: America in War and in Peace, 1941–1960*. New York: Norton, 1989.

Dixon, C. Madeleine. *Keep Them Human: The Young Child at Home*. New York: John Day Company, 1942.

Doherty, Thomas Patrick. *Cold War, Cool Medium: Television, McCarthyism, and American Culture*. New York: Columbia University Press, 2003.

———. *Projections of War : Hollywood, American Culture, and World War II*. New York: Columbia University Press, 1999.

Doob, Leonard William. *Propaganda: Its Psychology and Technique*. New York: H. Holt and Company, 1935.

Duberman, Martin B. *Black Mountain: An Exploration in Community*. New York: Dutton, 1972.

Eames, Ray, and Charles Eames. *A Communications Primer, 1953*. Available online at *http://vimeo.com/19906179*. Accessed November 25, 2011.

Edwards, Paul N. *The Closed World: Computers and the Politics of Discourse in Cold War America*. Cambridge, MA: MIT Press, 1996.

Elligott, Michelle. "Modern Artifacts: Tentative and Confidential." *Esopus* 9 (2007), n.p.

Evans, F. Barton. *Harry Stack Sullivan: Interpersonal Theory and Psychotherapy*, Makers of Modern Psychotherapy. London and New York: Routledge, 1996.

Ewen, Stuart. *PR!: A Social History of Spin*. New York: Basic Books, 1996.

Exposition Internationale. *Exposition Universelle et Internationale de Bruxelles, 1958. Algemene Wereldtentoonstelling Te Brussel, 1958.* 8 vols. Brussels: Commissariat général du Gouvernement près l'Exposition universelle et internationale de Bruxelles, 1960.

Farago, Ladislas, Lewis Frederick Gittler, Kimball Young, and Committee for National Morale. *German Psychological Warfare.* New York: Committee for National Morale, 1941.

Fermi, Laura. *Illustrious Immigrants: The Intellectual Migration from Europe, 1930–41.* Chicago: University of Chicago Press, 1968.

Findeli, Alain. "Moholy-Nagy's Design Pedagogy in Chicago (1937–1946)." In *The Idea of Design: A Design Issues Reader,* edited by Victor Margolin and Richard Buchanan, 29–43. Cambridge, MA: MIT Press, 1995.

Finer, Herman. "How Can Scholarship Contribute to the Relief of International Tensions?" In *Learning and World Peace: Eighth Symposium,* edited by Lyman Bryson, 1–19. New York: Conference on Science, Philosophy and Religion in their Relation to the Democratic Way of Life, 1948.

Finter, Helga, and Matthew Griffin. "Antonin Artaud and the Impossible Theatre: The Legacy of the Theatre of Cruelty." *TDR* 41, no. 4 (1997): 15–40.

Fleming, Donald, and Bernard Bailyn. *The Intellectual Migration; Europe and America, 1930–1960.* Cambridge, MA: Belknap Press of Harvard University Press, 1969.

Ford Foundation. "Report of the Trustees of the Ford Foundation." September 27, 1950.

Forgács, Éva. *The Bauhaus Idea and Bauhaus Politics.* Budapest, London, and New York: Central European University Press, 1995.

Frank, Lawrence K. "Freedom for the Personality." *Psychiatry* 3 (1940): 341–49.

———. *Society as the Patient; Essays on Culture and Personality.* New Brunswick, NJ: Rutgers University Press, 1948.

Alfred Frankenstein. "A Landmark of a Flop," *San Francisco Chronicle,* November 13, 1963: 6.

Freud, Sigmund, and Peter Gay. *Group Psychology and the Analysis of the Ego.* New York: Norton, 1989.

Fromm, Erich. *Escape from Freedom.* New York: Avon Books, 1969 (1941).

———. "The Method and Function of an Analytic Social Psychology" (1932). In *The Crisis of Psychoanalysis,* edited by Erich Fromm, 137–62. New York: Fawcett Premier, 1970.

———. "Politics and Psychoanalysis." In *Critical Theory and Society: A Reader,* edited by Stephen Eric Bronner and Douglas MacKay Kellner, 213–18. New York and London: Routledge, 1989.

———. "Psychoanalytic Characterology and Its Relevance for Social Psychology (1932)." In *The Crisis of Psychoanalysis,* edited by Erich Fromm, 163–88. New York: Fawcett Premier, 1970.

———. *The Working Class in Weimar Germany: A Psychological and Sociological Study*. Cambridge, MA: Harvard University Press, 1984.

Funk, Rainer. "Life and Work of Erich Fromm." *Logos* 6, no. 3 (2007).

Galison, Peter. "The Ontology of the Enemy: Norbert Wiener and the Cybernetic Vision." *Critical Inquiry* 21 (Autumn 1994): 228–66.

Gary, Brett. *The Nervous Liberals: Propaganda Anxieties from World War I to the Cold War*. Columbia Studies in Contemporary American History. New York: Columbia University Press, 1999.

———. "The Pitiless Spotlight of Publicity: Life and the World War II–Era Exposure of American Extremists." In *Looking at Life Magazine*, edited by Erika Lee Doss, 77–102. Washington: Smithsonian Institution Press, 2001.

Gilman, Nils. *Mandarins of the Future: Modernization Theory in Cold War America*. Baltimore: Johns Hopkins University Press, 2003.

Glueck, Grace. "Syndromes Pop at Delmonico's," *New York Times*, January 14, 1966: 36.

Gorer, Geoffrey. *The American People: A Study in National Character*. New York: Norton, 1948.

Gropius, Walter. *Scope of Total Architecture*. New York: Collier Books, 1966.

Guilbaut, Serge. *How New York Stole the Idea of Modern Art: Abstract Expressionism, Freedom, and the Cold War*. Chicago: University of Chicago Press, 1983.

Haddow, Robert H. *Pavilions of Plenty: Exhibiting American Culture Abroad in the 1950s*. Washington: Smithsonian Institution Press, 1997.

Hall, Calvin S., and Gardner Lindzey. *Theories of Personality*. New York: Wiley, 1957.

Hansen, Al. *A Primer of Happenings and Time/Space Art*. New York: Something Else Press, 1965.

Harris, Mary Emma. *The Arts at Black Mountain College*. Cambridge, MA: MIT Press, 1987.

Harvey, Michelle. "Through the Enchanted Gate: The Modern on TV." *MoMA Magazine*, September 2001: 27–29.

Hayakawa, S. I. *Language in Action: A Guide to Accurate Thinking, Reading and Writing*. New York: Harcourt, Brace, and Company, 1941.

Heider, Fritz. "On Lewin's Methods and Theory." *Journal of Social Issues*, Supplement Series no. 13 (1959): 1–13.

Heims, Steve J. *The Cybernetics Group*. Cambridge, MA: MIT Press, 1991.

Herman, Ellen. *The Romance of American Psychology: Political Culture in the Age of Experts*. Berkeley: University of California Press, 1995.

Hicks, Michael. "John Cage's Studies with Schoenberg." *American Music* 8, no. 2 (1990): 125–40.

High, Stanley. "Star-Spangled Fascists." *Saturday Evening Post*, May 27, 1939, 5–7, 70–73.

Highmore, Ben. "Machinic Magic: IBM at the 1964–1965 New York World's Fair." *New Formations* 51, no. 1 (Winter, 2003): 128–48.

Hixson, Walter L. *Parting the Curtain: Propaganda, Culture, and the Cold War, 1945–1961*. New York: St. Martin's Press, 1997.

Horkheimer, Max. "Authoritarianism and the Family." In *The Family: Its Function and Destiny*, edited by Ruth Nanda Anshen, 359–74. New York: Harper, 1949.

————. "The Lessons of Fascism." In *Tensions That Cause Wars*, edited by Hadley Cantril and UNESCO, 209–42. Urbana: University of Illinois Press, 1950.

————. Letter to Madame Favez, December 6, 1938. In Rolf Wiggershaus, *The Frankfurt School: Its History, Theories, and Political Significance*, 259–60. Cambridge, MA: MIT Press, 1994.

Horney, Karen. *The Neurotic Personality of Our Time*. New York: W. W. Norton, 1937.

Howard, Jane. *Margaret Mead: A Life*. New York: Simon and Schuster, 1984.

Institute for Propaganda Analysis and Violet Edwards. "Group Leader's Guide to Propaganda Analysis: Revised Edition of Experimental Study Materials for Use in Junior and Senior High Schools, in College and University Classes, and in Adult Study Groups." New York: Institute for Propaganda Analysis, Inc., 1938.

Institut für Sozialforschung (Frankfurt am Main, Germany). *Studien über Autorität und Familie: Forschungsberichte aus dem Institut für Sozialforschung*. 2. Aufl, Schriften Des Instituts für Sozialforschung. Lüneburg: Dietrich zu Klampen, 1987.

Itten, Johannes, and Bauhaus. *Design and Form: The Basic Course at the Bauhaus*. New York: Reinhold, 1964.

Jay, Martin. *Adorno*. Cambridge, MA: Harvard University Press, 1984.

————. *Permanent Exiles: Essays on the Intellectual Migration from Germany to America*. New York: Columbia University Press, 1985.

Jewell, Edward Alden. "Portrait of the Spirit of a Nation," *New York Times*, May 24, 1942: X5.

Jezer, Marty. *The Dark Ages: Life in the United States, 1945–1960*. Boston: South End Press, 1982.

Jones, Caroline A. "Finishing School: John Cage and the Abstract Expressionist Ego." *Critical Inquiry* 19 (Summer 1993): 628–65.

Joselit, David. *Feedback: Television against Democracy*. Cambridge, MA: MIT Press, 2007.

Joseph, Branden Wayne. "'My Mind Split Open': Andy Warhol's Exploding Plastic Inevitable." *Grey Room* no. 8 (2002): 80–107.

————. "'A Therapeutic Value For City Dwellers': The Development of John Cage's Early Avant-Garde Aesthetic Position." In *John Cage: Music, Philosophy, and Intention, 1933–1950*, edited by David Wayne Patterson, 135–75. New York: Routledge, 2002.

Joseph, Branden Wayne, and Robert Rauschenberg. *Random Order: Robert Rauschenberg and the Neo-Avant-Garde*. Cambridge, MA: MIT Press, 2003.

Kahn, Douglas. *Noise, Water, Meat: A History of Sound in the Arts*. Cambridge, MA: MIT Press, 1999.

Kaplan, Louis. *American Exposures: Photography and Community in the Twentieth Century*. Minneapolis: University of Minnesota Press, 2005.

Kaprow, Allan. "Happenings in the New York Scene." In *Essays on the Blurring of Art and Life*, edited by Allan Kaprow and Jeff Kelley, 15–26. Berkeley: University of California Press, 1993.

———. "The Legacy of Jackson Pollock." In *Essays on the Blurring of Art and Life*, edited by Allan Kaprow and Jeff Kelley, 1–9. Berkeley: University of California Press, 1993.

———. "Pinpointing Happenings (1967)." In *Essays on the Blurring of Art and Life*, edited by Allan Kaprow and Jeff Kelley, 84–89. Berkeley: University of California Press, 1993.

Kaprow, Allan, and Jeff Kelley. *Essays on the Blurring of Art and Life*. Berkeley: University of California Press, 1993.

Kaprow, Allan, Robert Watts, and George Brecht. "Project in Multiple Dimensions." In *Off Limits: Rutgers University and the Avant-Garde, 1957–1963*, edited by Joan M. Marter, Simon Anderson, and the Newark Museum, 153–59. Newark and New Brunswick, NJ: Newark Museum and Rutgers University Press, 1999.

Katz, Jonathan D. "John Cage's Queer Silence; or, How to Avoid Making Matters Worse." *GLQ* 5, April (1999): 231–52.

Kelley, Jeff, and Allan Kaprow. *Childsplay: The Art of Allan Kaprow*. Berkeley and London: University of California Press, 2004.

Kellner, Douglas. "Erich Fromm, Feminism, and the Frankfurt School." In *Symposium on Erich Fromm and the Frankfurt School*. Stuttgart-Hohenheim, 1991. Available online at http://www.uta.edu/huma/illuminations/kell8.htm.

Kepes, Gyorgy. *Language of Vision*. Chicago: P. Theobald, 1944.

Kiesler, Frederich, Friedrich Kiesler-Zentrum Wien, and Museum für Moderne Kunst (Frankfurt am Main). *Friedrich Kiesler: Art of This Century*. Ostfildern and New York: Hatje Cantz, 2002.

Kittredge, Eleanor. "Freedom and Fright." *New York Times*, January 4, 1942: BR12.

Klineberg, Otto. *Tensions Affecting International Understanding; A Survey of Research*. New York: Social Science Research Council, 1950.

Koch, Howard. *The Panic Broadcast: Portrait of an Event*. Boston: Little, Brown, 1970.

Kornhauser, Arthur William, and Paul Felix Lazarsfeld. *The Techniques of Market Research from the Standpoint of a Psychologist*. New York: American Management Association, 1935.

Kostelanetz, Richard. "Scene and Not Herd: USCO." *Harper's Bazaar*, December 1967: 52, 71, 75, 84.

———. *The Theatre of Mixed Means: An Introduction to Happenings, Kinetic Environments, and Other Mixed-Means Performances*. New York: Dial Press, 1968.

———. *Writings about John Cage*. Ann Arbor: University of Michigan Press, 1993.

Kostelanetz, Richard, and László Moholy-Nagy. *Moholy-Nagy*. New York: Praeger, 1970.

Kramer, Dale. "The American Fascists." *Harper's Magazine*, September 1940: 380–93.

Kuznick, Peter J., and James Burkhart Gilbert. *Rethinking Cold War Culture*. Washington: Smithsonian Institution Press, 2001.

Lasswell, Harold Dwight. "Democratic Character." In *Political Writings*, 465–525. Glencoe, IL: Free Press, 1951.

———. "Person, Personality, Group, Culture." *Psychiatry* (1939): 533–61.

———. "Psychopathology and Politics." In *Political Writings*, 1–294. Glencoe, IL: Free Press, 1951.

———. "The Structure and Function of Communication in Society." In *Processes and Effects of Mass Communication* (2nd revised edition), edited by Wilbur Schramm and Donald F. Roberts, 84–99. Urbana, Chicago, and London: University of Illinois Press, 1971.

———. *World Politics and Personal Insecurity*. London and New York: Whittlesey House and McGraw-Hill, 1935.

Laurie, Clayton D. *The Propaganda Warriors: America's Crusade against Nazi Germany*. Lawrence: University Press of Kansas, 1996.

Leach, Eugene E. "'Just Human Atoms Massed Together': The Evolution of Mass Society Theory from Ortega y Gasset to Riesman and Mills." *Mid-America* 71, no. 1 (1989): 31–49.

———. "'Mental Epidemics': Crowd Psychology and American Culture, 1890–1940." *American Studies* 33 (1992): 5–29.

Lears, T. J. Jackson. *No Place of Grace: Antimoderism and the Transformation of American Culture, 1880–1920*. New York: Pantheon Books, 1981.

Le Bon, Gustave. *The Crowd: A Study of the Popular Mind*. Mineola, NY: Dover Publications, 2002.

Leja, Michael. *Reframing Abstract Expressionism: Subjectivity and Painting in the 1940s*. New Haven, CT: Yale University Press, 1993.

Lerner, Max. *It Is Later Than You Think: The Need for a Militant Democracy*. New York: Viking Press, 1939.

Levin, Thomas Y., and Michael von der Linn. "Elements of a Radio Theory: Adorno and the Princeton Radio Research Project." *The Musical Quarterly* 78, no. 2 (1994): 316–24.

Lewin, Kurt. "Krieglandschaft (War Landscape)." *Zeitschrift Angewandter Psychologie* 12 (1917): 440–47.

Lewin, Kurt, Ronald Lippitt, and Ralph K. White. "Patterns of Aggressive Behavior in Experimentally Created 'Social Climates.'" *Journal of Social Psychology* 10 (1939): 271–99.

Lichtenstein, Nelson. *Labor's War at Home: The CIO in World War II*. Cambridge and New York: Cambridge University Press, 1982.

Lindenmeyer, Kriste. *The Greatest Generation Grows Up: American Childhood in the 1930s*. Chicago: Ivan R. Dee, 2005.

Lippmann, Walter. *Public Opinion*. New York: Free Press, 1965.

Liss, Edward. "Creative Therapy." *Bulletin of the Museum of Modern Art* 10, no. 3 (February, 1943): 13–15.

Lore, Ludwig. "Nazi Politics in America." *Nation*, November 29, 1933: 615–17.

Lynes, Russell. *Good Old Modern: An Intimate Portrait of the Museum of Modern Art*. New York: Atheneum, 1973.

Maddux, Thomas R. "Red Fascism, Brown Bolshevism: The American Image of Totalitarianism in the 1930s." *The Historian* 40, no. 1 (1977): 85–103.

Margolin, Victor. *The Struggle for Utopia: Rodchenko, Lissitzky, Moholy-Nagy, 1917–1946*. Chicago: University of Chicago Press, 1997.

Marks, Barry Alan. "The Idea of Propaganda in America." PhD dissertation, University of Minnesota, 1957.

Marrow, Alfred Jay. *The Practical Theorist: The Life and Work of Kurt Lewin*. New York: Basic Books, 1969.

Marter, Joan M., Simon Anderson, and Newark Museum. *Off Limits: Rutgers University and the Avant-Garde, 1957–1963*. Newark and New Brunswick, NJ: Newark Museum and Rutgers University Press, 1999.

Martin, Everett Dean. *The Behavior of Crowds: A Psychological Study*. New York: W. W. Norton, 1920.

Martin, Reinhold. *The Organizational Complex: Architecture, Media, and Corporate Space*. Cambridge, MA: MIT Press, 2003.

Martínez, Fernando Valderrama. *A History of UNESCO*. Paris: UNESCO, 1995.

Masani, P., and R. S. Phillips. "Antiaircraft Fire-Control and the Emergence of Cybernetics." In Norbert Wiener, *Collected Works with Commentaries Vol. 4*, 141–79. Cambridge, MA: MIT Press, 1976.

Masey, Jack, and Conway Lloyd Morgan. *Cold War Confrontations: US Exhibitions and Their Role in the Cultural Cold War*. Baden: Lars Müller, 2008.

Maslow, Abraham. "The Authoritarian Character Structure." *Journal of Social Psychology* 18, (1943): 401–11.

Masters, Robert E. L., and Jean Houston. *Psychedelic Art*. New York: Grove Press, 1968.

May, Elaine Tyler. *Homeward Bound: American Families in the Cold War Era*. New York: Basic Books, 1988.

McCarthy, Anna. *The Citizen Machine: Governing by Television in 1950s America.* New York: New Press, 2010.

McCausland, Elizabeth. "Photographs Illustrate Our 'Road to Victory.'" *Springfield Sunday Union and Republican*, May 31, 1942. Reprinted in *Photo Notes,* June 1942: 3–5.

McGovern, William Montgomery, and Edward McChesney Sait. *From Luther to Hitler: The History of Fascist-Nazi Political Philosophy.* Boston and New York: Houghton Mifflin, 1941.

McLaughlin, Neil. "How to Become a Forgotten Intellectual: Intellectual Movements and the Case of Erich Fromm." *Sociological Forum* 13, no. 2 (1998): 215–46.

———. "Nazism, Nationalism and the Sociology of Emotions: *Escape from Freedom* Revisited." *Sociological Theory* 14, no. 3 (1996): 421–41.

McLuhan, Marshall. *The Gutenberg Galaxy: The Making of Typographic Man.* London: Routledge & Kegan Paul, 1962.

———. *The Mechanical Bride: Folklore of Industrial Man.* New York: Vanguard Press, 1951.

———. "Notes on Media as Art Forms." *Explorations.* April (1954): 6–13.

———. *Understanding Media: The Extensions of Man.* Cambridge, MA: MIT Press, 1998.

Mead, Margaret. *And Keep Your Powder Dry: An Anthropologist Looks at America.* New York: W. Morrow, 1942.

———. "Balinese Character." In *Balinese Character: A Photographic Analysis,* edited by Gregory Bateson and Margaret Mead, 1–48. New York: New York Academy of Sciences, 1942.

———. "The Comparative Study of Culture and the Purposive Cultivation of Democratic Values." In *Science, Philosophy and Religion, Second Symposium,* edited by Lyman Bryson and Louis Finkelstein, 56–69. New York: Conference on Science, Philosophy and Religion in Their Relation to The Democratic Way of Life, Inc., 1942.

———. "Museums in the Emergency." *Natural History* 48, no. 2 (1941): 67.

Mead, Margaret, and Rhoda Bubendey Métraux. *The Study of Culture at a Distance.* Chicago: University of Chicago Press, 1953.

Mekas, Jonas. *Movie Journal; The Rise of the New American Cinema, 1959–1971.* New York: Macmillan, 1972.

Meyerowitz, Joanne J. "'How Common Culture Shapes the Separate Lives': Sexuality, Race, and Mid-Twentieth-Century Social Constructionist Thought." *Journal of American History* 96, no. 4 (2010): 1057–84.

Mirzoeff, Nicholas. *The Right to Look: A Counterhistory of Visuality.* Durham, NC: Duke University Press, 2011.

Mitarachi, Jane Fiske. "Design as a Political Force." *Industrial Design* 4, no. 2 (1957): 37–55.

Mock, James R., and Cedric Larson. *Words That Won the War: The Story of the Committee on Public Information, 1917–1919.* Princeton, NJ: Princeton University Press, 1939.

Moholy-Nagy, László. "Better Than Before." *Technology Review* 46, no. 1 (1943): 3–8.

———. "Constructivism and the Proletariat." In *Moholy-Nagy*, edited by Richard Kostelanetz and László Moholy-Nagy, 185–86. New York: Praeger, 1970.

———. "Education and the Bauhaus," from *Focus* 2 (London, winter 1938). In *Moholy-Nagy*, edited by Richard Kostelanetz and László Moholy-Nagy, 185–86. New York: Praeger, 1970.

———. *Painting, Photography, Film.* Cambridge, MA: MIT Press, 1969.

———. "Relating the Parts to the Whole." *Millar's Chicago Letter* 2, no. 23 (1940): 6–7.

———. "Space-Time and the Photographer." *American Annual of Photography* (1942): 57–66.

Moholy-Nagy, László, and Daphne M. Hoffmann. *The New Vision: Fundamentals of Design, Painting, Sculpture, Architecture.* Revised and enlarged edition. New York: W.W. Norton, 1938.

Moholy-Nagy, Sibyl. *Moholy-Nagy, Experiment in Totality.* New York: Harper, 1950.

Monson, Ingrid T. *Freedom Sounds: Civil Rights Call Out to Jazz and Africa.* Oxford and New York: Oxford University Press, 2007.

Morgan, Barbara. "The Theme Show: A Contemporary Exhibition Technique." *Aperture* 3, no. 2 (1955): 8–27.

Morgan, Carol. "From Modernist Utopia to Cold War Reality: A Critical Moment in Museum Education." In *The Museum of Modern Art at Mid-Century: Continuity and Change*, edited by John Elderfield and the Museum of Modern Art, 150–73. New York: Museum of Modern Art, 1995.

Morris, Charles. "The Mechanism of Freedom." In *Freedom, Its Meaning*, edited by Ruth Nanda Anshen, 579–89. New York: Harcourt, 1940.

———. *The Open Self.* New York: Prentice-Hall, 1948.

Müller-Doohm, Stefan. *Adorno: A Biography.* Cambridge: Polity Press, 2005.

Mumford, Lewis. "The Skyline: Bauhaus—Two Restaurants and a Theater." *New Yorker*, December 31, 1938: 38.

Museum of Modern Art. "The Minutes of the Sixteenth Annual Meeting of the Board of Trustees and Members of the Corporation of the Museum of Modern Art held on Thursday, November 15, 1945." *Bulletin of the Museum of Modern Art* 10 (February 1946): 5–9.

———. "Modern Art for Children: The Educational Project." *Bulletin of the Museum of Modern Art* 9, no.1 (October, 1941): 3–12.

Museum of Modern Art, New York Department of Education, and Victor D'Amico. *Experiments in Creative Art Teaching: A Progress Report on the*

Department of Education, 1937–1960. New York: Museum of Modern Art, 1960.

Muth, Rodney, Mary M. Finley, and Marcia F. Muth. *Harold D. Lasswell: An Annotated Bibliography*. New Haven, CT, and Dordrecht, Netherlands: New Haven Press and Kluwer Academic Publishers, 1990.

Naess, Arne. "The Function of Ideological Convictions." In *Tensions That Cause Wars*, edited by Hadley Cantril and UNESCO, 257–98. Urbana: University of Illinois Press, 1950.

National Research Council (United States), Irvin Long Child, and Marjorie Van de Water. *Psychology for the Returning Serviceman*. Washington and New York: Infantry Journal and Penguin Books, 1945.

Nelson, George. "Art X: The Georgia Experiment." In *Problems of Design*, 14–26. New York: Whitney Publications, 1965.

Neuhart, John, Charles Eames, Ray Eames, and Marilyn Neuhart. *Eames Design: The Work of the Office of Charles and Ray Eames*. New York: H. N. Abrams, 1989.

Nicholls, David. *The Cambridge Companion to John Cage*. Cambridge Companions to Music. Cambridge and New York: Cambridge University Press, 2002.

———. *John Cage*. American Composers. Urbana: University of Illinois Press, 2007.

Nicholson, Ian A. M. *Inventing Personality: Gordon Allport and the Science of Selfhood*. Washington: American Psychological Association, 2003.

Nilsen, Sarah. "America's Salesman: *The USA in Circarama*." In *Learning from Mickey, Donald and Walt: Essays on Disney's Edutainment Films*, edited by A. Bowdoin Van Riper, 237–53. Jefferson, NC: McFarland and Company, 2011.

Ninkovich, Frank A. *The Diplomacy of Ideas: U.S. Foreign Policy and Cultural Relations, 1938–1950*. Cambridge and New York: Cambridge University Press, 1981.

Norwood, Stephen H. *The Third Reich in the Ivory Tower: Complicity and Conflict on American Campuses*. Cambridge and New York: Cambridge University Press, 2009.

Ogata, Amy F. "Building Imagination in Postwar American Children's Rooms." *Studies in the Decorative Arts* 16, no. 1 (2008–2009): 126–42.

———. "Creative Playthings: Educational Toys and Postwar American Culture." *Winterthur Portfolio* 39, no. 2/3 (2004): 129–56.

Oren, Michel. "USCO: 'Getting Out of Your Mind to Use Your Head.'" *Art Journal* 69, no. 4 (2010): 76–95.

Osgood, Kenneth Alan. *Total Cold War: Eisenhower's Secret Propaganda Battle at Home and Abroad*. Lawrence: University of Kansas, 2006.

Overy, Paul. "Visions of the Future and the Immediate Past: The Werkbund Exhibition, Paris 1930." *Journal of Design History* 17, no. 4 (2004): 337–57.

Pandora, Katherine. *Rebels within the Ranks: Psychologists' Critique of Scientific*

Authority and Democratic Realities in New Deal America, Cambridge Studies in the History of Psychology. Cambridge and New York: Cambridge University Press, 1997.

Pang, Alex Soojung-Kim. "Dome Days: Buckminster Fuller in the Cold War." In *Cultural Babbage: Technology, Time and Invention*, edited by Francis Spufford and Jenny Uglow, 167–92. Boston and London: Faber and Faber, 1996.

Paris, Bernard J. *Karen Horney: A Psychoanalyst's Search for Self-Understanding.* New Haven, CT: Yale University Press, 1994.

Park, Robert Ezra. *The Crowd and the Public, and Other Essays.* Chicago: University of Chicago Press, 1972.

Patterson, David Wayne. "Appraising the Catchwords, c. 1942–1959: John Cage's Asian-Derived Rhetoric and the Historical Reference of Black Mountain College." PhD dissertation, Columbia University, 1996.

Perrow, Charles. "Drinking Deep at Black Mountain College." Typescript, 2002. Gift to the author.

Perry, Charles. *The Haight-Ashbury: A History.* New York: Random House, 1984.

Perry, Helen Swick. *The Human Be-In.* New York: Basic Books, 1970.

Perry, Ralph Barton. *Characteristically American: Five Lectures Delivered at the University of Michigan, November-December, 1948.* William W. Cook Foundation Lectures, Volume 5. New York: A. A. Knopf, 1949.

Phillips, Christopher. "The Judgment Seat of Photography." *October* 22 (fall 1982): 27–63.

———. "Steichen's 'Road to Victory.'" *Exposure* no. 18 (1980): 38–48.

Pope, Arthur Upham. "The Importance of Morale." *Journal of Educational Sociology* 15, no. 4 (1941): 195–205.

Potter, David Morris. "The American Round Table Discussions on People's Capitalism." Edited by the Advertising Council, Inc., 1957.

———. *People of Plenty: Economic Abundance and the American Character.* Chicago: University of Chicago Press, 1954.

Pritchett, James. *The Music of John Cage.* Cambridge and New York: Cambridge University Press, 1993.

Proctor, Jacob. "From the Ivory Tower to the Control Room." In *Stan VanDerBeek: The Culture Intercom*, edited by Stan VanDerBeek, Bill Arning, and João Ribas, 99–107. Cambridge, MA: MIT List Visual Arts Center, 2011.

Quinn, Susan. *A Mind of Her Own: The Life of Karen Horney.* New York: Summit Books, 1987.

Radio Corporation of America. "Off to the Fair." *Electronics for Living* 16, no. 1 (January 1957): 18–19. Available online at http://www.archive.org/stream/radioageresearch195557newyrich/radioageresearch195557newyrich_djvu.txt. Accessed November 23, 2011.

Rancière, Jacques. *The Politics of Aesthetics: The Distribution of the Sensible.* London and New York: Continuum, 2004.

Revill, David. *The Roaring Silence: John Cage, A Life*. New York: Arcade, 1992.

Ribuffo, Leo. "Review: Fascists, Nazis and American Minds: Perceptions and Preconceptions." *American Quarterly* 26, no. 4 (1974): 417–32.

Rice, John Andrew. *I Came Out of the Eighteenth Century*. New York: Harper & Brothers, 1942.

Riesman, David, Nathan Glazer, Reuel Denney, and Todd Gitlin. *The Lonely Crowd: A Study of the Changing American Character*. Abridged and revised edition. New Haven, CT, and London: Yale Nota Bene, 2001.

Rodenbeck, Judith F. *Radical Prototypes: Allan Kaprow and the Invention of Happenings*. Cambridge, MA: MIT Press.

Rosenblueth, Arturo, Norbert Wiener, and Julian Bigelow. "Behavior, Purpose and Teleology." *Philosophy of Science* no. 10 (1943): 18–24.

Ross, Alex. *The Rest Is Noise: Listening to the Twentieth Century*. New York: Farrar, Straus, and Giroux, 2007.

Roszak, Theodore. *The Making of a Counter Culture: Reflections on the Technocratic Society and Its Youthful Opposition*. Garden City, NY: Doubleday, 1969.

Roth, Moira. "The Aesthetic of Indifference." *Artforum* 16, no. 3 (1977): 46–53.

Roth, Moira, and Allan Kaprow. "Oral History Interview with Allan Kaprow, February 15 and 19, 1981." Washington: Archives of American Art, Smithsonian Institution, 1968.

Rubins, Jack L. *Karen Horney: Gentle Rebel of Psychoanalysis*. New York: Dial Press, 1978.

Sammond, Nicholas. *Babes in Tomorrowland: Walt Disney and the Making of the American Child, 1930–1960*. Durham, NC: Duke University Press, 2005.

Sandburg, Carl. "Prologue." In *The Family of Man: The Greatest Photographic Exhibition of All Time—503 Pictures from 68 Countries*, edited by Edward Steichen and the Museum of Modern Art, 3–4. New York: Museum of Modern Art, 1955.

Sandeen, Eric J. *Picturing an Exhibition: The Family of Man and 1950s America*. Albuquerque: University of New Mexico Press, 1995.

———. "'The Show You See with Your Heart': *The Family of Man* on Tour in the Cold War World." In *The Family of Man 1955–2001*, edited by Jean Back and Viktoria Schmidt-Linsenhoff (Hg.), 100–121. Marburg: Jonas Verlag, 2004.

Sandford, Mariellen R. *Happenings and Other Acts*. London and New York: Routledge, 1995.

Saul, Scott. *Freedom Is, Freedom Ain't: Jazz and the Making of the Sixties*. Cambridge, MA: Harvard University Press, 2003.

Saunders, Frances Stonor. *Who Paid the Piper? The CIA and the Cultural Cold War*. London: Granta Books, 1999.

Schechner, Richard. "Happenings." In *Happenings and Other Acts*, edited by Mariellen R. Sandford, 216–18. London and New York: Routledge, 1995.

Schlemmer, Oskar, László Moholy-Nagy, Farkas Molnár, and Walter Gropius. *The Theater of the Bauhaus*. Middletown, CT: Wesleyan University Press, 1961.

Schlesinger, Arthur Meier. *The Vital Center: The Politics of Freedom*. Boston: Houghton Mifflin, 1949.

Schüttpelz, Ehhard. "Von der Kommunikation zu den Medien: In Krieg und Frieden (1943–1960)." In *Gelehrte Kommunikation: Wissenschaft und Medium Zwischen dem 16. und 20. Jahrhundert*, edited by Jürgen Fohrmann, 483–551. Vienna: Böhlau, 2005.

Sconce, Jeffrey. *Haunted Media: Electronic Presence from Telegraphy to Television*. Durham, NC: Duke University Press, 2000.

Scott, Felicity D. "Acid Visions." *Grey Room* no. 23 (2006): 22–39.

Sekula, Allan. "The Traffic in Photographs." *Art Journal* (Spring 1981): 15–21.

Shils, Edward. "The Theory of Mass Society: Prefatory Remarks." *Diogenes* 10 (1962): 45–66.

Shultis, Christopher. "Cage and Europe." In *The Cambridge Companion to John Cage*, edited by David Nicholls, 20–40. Cambridge and New York: Cambridge University Press, 2002.

Silverman, Kenneth. *Begin Again: A Biography of John Cage*. New York: Alfred A. Knopf, 2010.

Singer, M. "A Survey of Culture and Personality Theory and Research." In *Studying Personality Cross-Culturally*, edited by B. Kaplan, 9–90. New York: Harper and Row, 1961.

Smertenko, Johan J. "Hitlerism Comes to America." *Harper's Magazine*, November 1933: 660–70.

Society for the Psychological Study of Social Issues and Goodwin Barbour Watson. *Civilian Morale*. Boston and New York: Houghton Mifflin, 1942.

Solomon-Godeau, Abigail. "'The Family of Man.' Den Humanismus für ein Ostmodernes Zeitalter Aufpolieren/'The Family of Man.' Refurbishing Humanism for a Postmodern Age." In *The Family of Man 1955–2001*, edited by Jean Back and Viktoria Schmidt-Linsenhoff (Hg.), 28–55. Marburg, Germany: Jonas Verlag, 2004.

Sontag, "Happenings: An Art of Radical Juxtaposition." In Susan Sontag, *Against Interpretation and Other Essays*, 263–74. New York: Delta Books, 1981.

Spigel, Lynn. *TV by Design: Modern Art and the Rise of Network Television*. Chicago: University of Chicago Press, 2008.

———. *Welcome to the Dreamhouse: Popular Media and Postwar Suburbs*. Durham, NC: Duke University Press, 2001.

Sproule, J. Michael. *Propaganda and Democracy: The American Experience of Media and Mass Persuasion*. Cambridge and New York: Cambridge University Press, 1997.

Stack Sullivan, Harry. "Tensions Personal and International: A Psychiatrist's

View." In *Tensions That Cause Wars*, edited by Hadley Cantril and UNESCO, 79–138. Urbana: University of Illinois Press, 1950.

Stange, Maren. *Symbols of Ideal Life: Social Documentary Photography in America, 1890–1950*. Cambridge and New York: Cambridge University Press, 1989.

Staniszewski, Mary Anne. *The Power of Display: A History of Exhibition Installations at the Museum of Modern Art*. Cambridge, MA: MIT Press, 1998.

Steele, Richard W. *Propaganda in an Open Society: The Roosevelt Administration and the Media, 1933–1941*. Westport, CT: Greenwood Press, 1985.

Steichen, Edward. *A Life in Photography*. Garden City, NY: Doubleday, 1963.

———. "Photography: Witness and Recorder of History." *Wisconsin Magazine of History* 41, no. 3 (1958): 159–67.

Steichen, Edward, and the Museum of Modern Art. *The Family of Man: The Greatest Photographic Exhibition of All Time—503 Pictures from 68 Countries*. New York: Museum of Modern Art, 1955.

Stimson, Blake. *The Pivot of the World: Photography and Its Nation*. Cambridge, MA: MIT Press, 2006.

Stocking, George W. *Malinowski, Rivers, Benedict, and Others: Essays on Culture and Personality*. History of Anthropology. Volume 4. Madison: University of Wisconsin Press, 1986.

Stone, Shepard. "Hitler's Showmen Weave a Magic Spell." *New York Times*, December 3, 1933: SM8.

Strecker, Edward A., and Kenneth E. Appel. "Morale." *American Journal of Psychiatry* 99 (1942): 159–63.

Sutton, Gloria. "The Experience Machine: Stan VanDerBeek's Movie-Drome and Expanded Cinema Practices of the 1960s." PhD dissertation, University of California, Los Angeles, 2009.

———. "Stan VanDerBeek: Collage Experience." In *Stan Vanderbeek: The Culture Intercom*, edited by Stan VanDerBeek, Bill Arning, and João Ribas, 78–89. Cambridge, MA: MIT List Visual Arts Center, 2011.

Suvin, Darko. "Reflections on Happenings," *The Drama Review* 14, no. 3 (T47) (1970). In *Happenings and Other Acts*, edited by Mariellen R. Sandford, 285–309. London and New York: Routledge, 1995.

Swing, Raymond Gram. "Patriotism Dons the Black Shirt." *Nation*, April 10, 1935: 409–11.

Szarkowski, John. "The Family of Man." In *The Museum of Modern Art at Mid-Century at Home and Abroad*, edited by John Szarkowski and the Museum of Modern Art, 12–37. New York: Museum of Modern Art, 1994.

Taylor, Edmond. *Awakening from History*. Boston: Gambit, 1969.

———. *The Strategy of Terror: Europe's Inner Front*. Boston: Houghton Mifflin, 1940.

This Is America: Official United States Guide Book, Brussels World's Fair. Office of US Commissioner General, Brussels World's Fair, 1958.

Thompson, Dorothy. *"I Saw Hitler!"* New York: Farrar and Rinehart, 1932.

Tomkins, Calvin. *The Bride and the Bachelors: The Heretical Courtship in Modern Art.* New York: Viking Press, 1965.

Tribot, Pierre-Jean. *Bruxelles 58, Année-Lumière.* Collecion Lieux De Mémoire. Bruxelles: CFC-éditions, 2008.

Truman, Harry S. "Address on Foreign Policy at a Luncheon of the American Society of Newspaper Editors," April 20, 1950. Harry S. Truman Library. Available online at http://www.trumanlibrary.org/publicpapers/index.php?pid=715&st=Campaign&st1=Truth. Accessed October 19, 2011.

United States Congress, Senate Special Committee on Aging. "Our Greatest Generation Continuing a Lifetime of Service: Hearing before the Special Committee on Aging, United States Senate, One Hundred Seventh Congress, First Session, Indianapolis, IN, August 9, 2001." Washington: US Government Printing Office, 2001.

United States Department of Labor, *Handbook of Labor Statistics, 1974, Bulletin 1825.* Washington: US GPO, 1974.

VanDerBeek, Stan. "Culture: Intercom and Expanded Cinema." *Tulane Drama Review* 11, no. 1 (1966): 38–48.

Vaughn, Stephen. *Holding Fast the Inner Lines: Democracy, Nationalism, and the Committee on Public Information.* Supplementary Volumes to the Papers of Woodrow Wilson. Chapel Hill: University of North Carolina Press, 1980.

Weitz, Eric D. *Weimar Germany: Promise and Tragedy.* Princeton, NJ: Princeton University Press, 2007.

White, Ralph K. "Soviet Reactions to Our Moscow Exhibit: Voting Machines and Comment Books." *Public Opinion Quarterly* 23, no. 4 (1959–1960): 461–70.

Wiener, Norbert. *Cybernetics; or, Control and Communication in the Animal and the Machine.* New York: MIT Press, 1961.

———. *The Human Use of Human Beings: Cybernetics and Society.* Boston: Houghton Mifflin, 1950.

Wiggershaus, Rolf. *The Frankfurt School: Its History, Theories, and Political Significance,* Studies in Contemporary German Social Thought. Cambridge, MA: MIT Press, 1994.

Wilde, Lawrence. *Erich Fromm and the Quest for Solidarity.* New York: Palgrave Macmillan, 2004.

Willkie, Wendell L. *One World.* New York: Simon and Schuster, 1943.

Willkie, Wendell L., Museum of Modern Art, and Arno Press. "Airways to Peace: An Exhibition of Geography for the Future." *Bulletin of the Museum of Modern Art* 11, no. 1 (1943): 3–21.

Young, Kimball. "A Recent Contribution of Psychoanalysis to Political Science: Notes on Lasswell's Psychopathology and Politics." *Journal of Abnormal Psychology* 25, no. 4 (1931): 465–73.

Index

of, 32; "rhythmically obedient" type of,
33. *See also* jazz
Port Huron (Michigan), 271
Postman, Leo, 135
Potter, David, 218–19
Powdermaker, Hortense, 54
Power in the Pacific (exhibition), 198
Poznan (Poland), 227
Princeton Radio Research Project, 28
propaganda, 4, 40, 61, 65, 73–74, 101–2,
115–16; analysis of, 22; democratic
modes of, 82; and fascism, 171; General
Semantics movement, 22–23; and
Hitler, 15; and museums, 75; and
Nazism, 61; and psychotherapy, 213–14;
and repetition, 27; and totalitarianism,
44, 171; and U.S., 42, 78, 214, 216–18,
220–23, 225
Protocols of the Elders of Zion, The (pamphlet), 18
Providence Journal (newspaper), 35
psychedelia: LSD, as equivalent to, 287;
mysticism of, 284; and psychedelic art,
284, 288
Psychiatry (journal), 53
psychoanalysis, 47–48, 51
Psychology for the Fighting Man: (Boring
and Allport), 154
Psychology for the Returning Serviceman
(Boring), 154
psychotherapy: propaganda, as model
for, 213–14; state-based therapy, for
individual nations, 164
Pueblo Indians, 56
punk, 284

Quicksilver Messenger Service, 289

racism, 157–58, 232, 244; and race riots,
151; racial superiority, Nazi theories of,
46; in U.S., 46, 57, 110, 239, 244
Radcliffe College, 135
Rauschenberg, Robert, 133, 146–47, 261–63
RCA, 250
Red Scares, 161, 170
Reich, Wilhelm, 51, 171, 173

Repplier, Theodore, 217, 219
Reuben Gallery, 265
Reuther, Walter, 239
Rhode Island, 35
Rice, John, 133–34
Richards, M. C., 7, 140, 146–47, 277, 284
Riesman, David, 177, 218; industrial
production, new mode of, 179; other-
directed citizens, as pro-democratic
alternative, 178–79; social character,
emergence of, 178
Rio de Janeiro (Brazil), 102
Riverside Museum, 288
Road to Victory (exhibition), 5–6, 102–5,
107–8, 110, 112, 115–16, 124, 154, 183, 198,
203, 270; attendance of, 106; popular-
ity of, 109
rock concerts, 1
Rockefeller, Abby Aldrich, 95–96, 99,
101–2, 107, 189
Rockefeller, John D., 95
Rockefeller, Nelson, 95, 99, 102, 220
Rockefeller Center, 96–97
Rogers, Carl, 156
Rollins College, 133
Roman Colosseum, 233
Rome (Italy), 90
Rosenblueth, Arturo, 160
Roosevelt, Franklin D., 2, 17–18, 35, 41–42,
99, 111; and Four Freedoms, 184
Rostow, Walt, 232–33
Roszak, Theodore, 260, 271–72
Roth, Moira, 127
Rubin, Barbara, 281–82
Rubin, Jerry, 289
Rudolph, Paul, 203–4, 212
"Run Run Run" (Velvet Underground),
282
Russell, Bertrand, 200, 207
Russia, 110. *See also* Soviet Union
Russian Constructivism, 82–83
Russolo, Luigi, 117–18

Salonika (Greece), 226–27
Sandburg, Carl, 104–7, 199–200, 203
Sanford, R. Nevitt, 171